The Welfare State
in Canada
A Selected Bibliography, 1840 to 1978

Allan Moscovitch
with the assistance of Theresa Jennissen and Peter Findlay

The first major reference work of its kind in the social welfare field in Canada, this volume is a selected bibliography of works on Canadian social welfare policy. The entries in Part One treat general aspects of the origins, development, organization, and administration of the welfare state in Canada; included is a section covering basic statistical sources. The entries in Part Two treat particular areas of policy such as unemployment, disabled persons, prisons, child and family welfare, health care, and day care. Also included are an introductory essay reviewing the literature on social welfare policy in Canada, a "User's Guide," several appendices on archival materials, and an extensive chronology of Canadian social welfare legislation both federal and provincial. The volume will increase the accessibility of literature on the welfare state and stimulate increased awareness and further research. It should be of wide interest to students, researchers, librarians, social welfare policy analysts and administrators, and social work practitioners.

Allan Moscovitch, School of Social Work, Carleton University, Ottawa, is co-editor (with Glenn Drover) of Inequality: Essays on the Political Economy of Social Welfare. *His current work includes the preparation of a history of Canadian housing policy.*

Peter Findlay, a member of the same faculty, has written on critical theory and social welfare and on the nature and role of the state in relation to social welfare policies and programmes.

Theresa Jennissen is a doctoral student in the School of Social Work at McGill University. Her research is on the inception and evolution of workers' compensation in Canada.

The Welfare State in Canada

A Selected Bibliography, 1840 to 1978

Allan Moscovitch
with the assistance of Theresa Jennissen and Peter Findlay

Wilfrid Laurier University Press

Canadian Cataloguing in Publication Data

Moscovitch, Allan, 1946-
  The welfare state in Canada : a selected bibliography, 1840 to 1978

Bibliography: p.
Includes index.
ISBN 0-88920-114-5

1. Public welfare — Canada — Bibliography. 2. Charities —
Canada — Bibliography. 3. Canada — Social policy —
Bibliography. I. Jennissen, Theresa, 1950-
II. Findlay, Peter, 1936-   III. Title.

Z7164.C4M6   016.3616'5'0971   C83-098517-4

Copyright © 1983

WILFRID LAURIER UNIVERSITY PRESS
Waterloo, Ontario, Canada   N2L 3C5

83 84 85 86 4 3 2 1

Cover Design: Polygon Design Limited

Table of Contents

Appendices

Indexes

Detailed Table of Contents for Parts One and Two

Part One

Part Two

Detailed Table of Contents—*Continued* (3)

Detailed Table of Contents—*Continued* (5)

Preface

The impetus for the development of this *Bibliography* was the result of efforts at the School of Social Work, Carleton University, to develop a course program in social policy and administration since 1973. It was the immediate need for access to source materials that gave rise to the *Bibliography* project.

The original conception and framing of an approach was undertaken by Allan Moscovitch, with consultative contributions by Peter C.Findlay. Subsequently, a proposal, jointly sponsored by the Centre for Social Welfare Studies at Carleton University and by the Canadian Association of Schools of Social Work (C.A.S.S.W.), was submitted to the Welfare Grants Division of Health and Welfare Canada. The joint submission has been given generous funding by Welfare Grants and we are grateful for the assistance given to us by the C.A.S.S.W., by Welfare Grants, and in particular by Allan Douglas and Robert Hart, project officers of Welfare Grants. The organization and content of the *Bibliography*, of course, are the responsibility of the authors, and not of the funding or sponsoring bodies.

The major share of the organization of the work was directed by Allan Moscovitch, with assistance from Peter Findlay; the general management and administrative work was handled cooperatively. Funding enabled us to hire a team of workers which included a librarian, Ingrid Draayer, and two researchers, Lisa Hamlet and Theresa Jennissen, the former to prepare the bibliography of archival papers in Appendix I, and the latter to undertake the bulk of the work of reviewing periodicals and of collecting and verifying citations. Debbie Hughes and Doreen Hallam were the project secretaries, and Penny Williams did the major part of the copy editing. Additional editorial assistance was provided by Paula LaPierre. Without the individual and collective efforts of this team, this *Bibliography* would not now be available.

In addition, we had the assistance of several graduate students of the School of Social Work and the Institute of Canadian Studies at Carleton University, including Bruce Stewart, Patrick Storey, Joseph Bolger, Shirley Yumansky, Harold Davidson, Murray Angus, and Lesley Silver. We also received the help of many librarians and researchers across the country in libraries, archives, and special collections. Special mention should also be made of the archivists at the Public Archives of Canada, and, in particular, of Peter Gillis and John Smart, who generously provided assistance. Several colleagues in the School of Social Work were also of particular assistance. James Albert as Director

i

during the reorientation of the School gave valuable encouragement to those of us engaged in the preparation of courses and research in the field of social policy formation. Roy Parker, a visiting professor at the School in 1976, was influential in encouraging us to undertake the task. We have also been aided in our work by the thoughtful reading given the manuscript by two reviewers and by detailed and cogent editorial guidance from Harold Remus, the Director of Wilfrid Laurier University Press. In preparing the manuscript for publication we had the benefit of assistance provided by Gaynor Hitchcock, Chris M. Girard, Bente Logan, and Malcolm MacMillan of Apcom who handled word processing, typesetting and layout.

Publication of this volume has been made possible by a further grant from Welfare Grants, Health and Welfare Canada, which we gratefully acknowledge.

A work of this kind is fertile ground for errors because of the very large number of individual items, the variety and range of topics surveyed, the immense diversity of sources, and the long time period covered. Intensive efforts were made to ensure that the references are accurate and complete, to provide users with sure access to the items listed. The final arduous task of bringing the work to completion was sufficiently harrowing to allow us to accept contentedly full responsibility for any errors that remain.

Allan Moscovitch
Peter C. Findlay
Theresa Jennissen

Carleton University
January 1982

Social Welfare and Social Policy in Canada: Historical Background and Sources

The growth and proliferation of state-funded and state-administered social welfare policies during the nineteenth and twentieth centuries have resulted in a major structural change in the basic nature and organization of Western capitalist nations. In this change, Canada is no exception.

If we date the early development of capitalism in Canada from the 1840's, then the years from that decade until the 1890's represent a period in which we observe the establishment of the legislative and institutional precursors of modern welfare state policy in Canada. Gradually, charitable institutions began to obtain state funding, prisons were built, judicial systems were established, and education for the young became both state-funded and enforced. Hospitals, houses of industry and refuge, asylums, and other types of institutions, which all made their appearance in the late seventeenth and the eighteenth centuries, were extended in numbers and importance in nineteenth-century Upper Canada, Lower Canada, Nova Scotia, and New Brunswick. The spread of contagious disease occasioned first temporary and then permanent provincial public health laws and municipal bylaws. In the latter years of the nineteenth century provincial laws setting limits on the employment of women and children, and providing a form of state-authorized protection for children, were also passed.

The period from the 1890's until the end of the decade of the depression constitutes the transition phase towards a welfare state. As industrial accidents increased with the expansion of manufacture and industry, liability laws were passed leading to the establishment of provincial worker's compensation legislation immediately before and during the First World War. Other forms of state-aided social welfare did not arise until the period after the First World War. As pensions, health, town planning, and housing schemes appeared variously in Europe and in the Dominions, their coming in the years preceding the War was noted in Canada, but Canadian state-aided schemes in these fields did not appear until later.

It was in the interwar period, particularly in the context of the economic and political turmoil after the First World War and of the Great Depression of the 1930's, that a considerable number of programmes were initiated that we now know as constituting integral parts of the modern Canadian welfare state. Policies such as federally funded relief, unemployment insurance, pensions, grants-in-aid of private and public housing construction, and provincially based mothers' allowances, minimum wages, and limitations of hours of work, all have their origins in this period.

The turmoil of the Second World War and the years of postwar adjustment provided the context in which already existing legislation was expanded and some new legislation was introduced. During the period from the beginning of the war until the 1970's, the building blocks for a welfare state were slowly put into place. Unemployment Insurance and Old Age Pensions were revised in scope and coverage and legislation was passed guaranteeing federal support for hospital construction. In the housing field the Central Mortgage and Housing Corporation was created as an independent vehicle for the administration of housing policy. The Beveridge Report in England, and in Canada, the Marsh Report (1943), more particularly provided a widely publicized plea for a change of direction in public welfare policy, a shift that would lead to the development of an actual welfare state in Canada. Despite the considerable political and social pressures for reform the only tangible result was the federally initiated Family Allowances (1945), the first welfare scheme of more universal application. The Dominion-Provincial Conference of 1945 held the promise of further social reforms but ended without agreement. In the aftermath of war came a series of debates and struggles which led to the establishment of Dominion hospital grants, the expansion of provisions for the support of the aged, and the passage of the first permanent program of funding of relief in the mid 1950's. Federal schemes for the support of higher education and vocational rehabilitation also appeared before the period of high reform in the 1960's.

The relative economic prosperity, the existence of successive Conservative and Liberal minority governments and the "rediscovery" of poverty common to many Western countries at the time provided the context of the last major wave of social reforms. In 1965 the Canada Assistance Plan formalized the federal funding of welfare, while the Canadian and Quebec Pension Plans (1966) introduced a pension scheme of considerable significance. The 1960's also witnessed the establishment of a national scheme of health insurance, an idea which had been a subject of political debate and conflict for more than forty years. In 1964, amendments to the National Housing Act opened up the development of a large-scale public housing program. Four major studies of poverty, studies of taxation, the status of women, bilingualism, low income housing, urban renewal, and unemployment insurance preceded changes in the late 1960's and early 1970's in divorce and abortion legislation, unemployment insurance, income and corporate taxation, family allowances and housing policy. This is the legislation which is now the basis of a complex system of subsidy, regulation, and control that comprises the Canadian welfare state.

Social Welfare and Social Policy in Canada

The history of social welfare in Canada is the history of first private and then public welfare, the expansion of both, and the absorption of the private by the public. Throughout the nineteenth century Canada remained largely an agrarian society, with an economy based on the exploitation of resources for export to European markets. Fur, timber, and wheat trade were the staples of the Canadian economy, underpinning a rural society which was based largely on individual labour and in which there was a strong philosophical commitment to self-reliance. Despite the individualized nature of much of economic production and the commitment to self-reliance, individual and social problems necessitated the establishment of public institutions such as schools and gaols, and private charitable institutions such as homes for children and hospitals. The development of welfare institutions was influenced in form and approach by French, English, and American ideas, institutions, and policies, but the determining factors were the ideas of the ruling elites and the conditions they confronted in the various parts of British North America. Private and state practices varied considerably; yet by the early twentieth century, as mining and manufacturing gained in importance, the social conditions of industry and neighbourhood in the cities were resulting in demands for a greatly increased role for the state throughout the country.

The resultant social welfare policies have developed not so much gradually and continuously, as sporadically and discontinuously. Depressions and wars, the major economic and political disruptions of the twentieth century, have led to the state's assuming greater responsibility for what were previously private matters, both individual and institutional. Periodic economic difficulties, especially the Great Depression of the 1930's, necessitated state interventions to offset the conditions experienced by many segments of the population, and some of the policies and programs thus originated were either retained without change or continued to evolve. The requirements of a country at war, of both the home population and the military, prompted the establishment of a range of wartime public welfare policies not all of which were dismantled after each war ended. In this way, the Canadian welfare state came into existence disjointedly, piece by piece.

A theme particular to the history of social welfare policy in Canada has been the "constitutional question." Matters that are now accepted as the responsibility of the federal government were, as a result of the nineteenth-century confederation debate, assigned largely to the provinces and to their creatures, the municipalities. When, with the advance of industry, there arose demands for reforms, often from businessmen, reformers, farmers, and workers alike, these demands were directed at the Dominion (federal) level of government. Yet this level of government was interpreted by the courts and the British Privy Council to be lacking the powers to enact such reforms. To a great extent, the constitutional question has been concerned with which level of government has responsibility for and jurisdiction over all aspects of welfare policy, social, industrial, and fiscal. It has also been interwoven with attempts, particularly by successive Quebec governments, to protect provincial autonomy as a means of preserving a particular idea of culture and society, and with a struggle among businessmen, social reformers, farmers, and workers, men and women over the appropriate form of state intervention.

These struggles have been particularly manifest during several periods in Canadian history. During the 1930's, the Depression prompted a wide-ranging assessment of Canadian capitalism and of federalism. In the latter years of the Second World War and in its aftermath there was considerable political and ideological conflict over the role of the state in the provision of family allowances, medical care, and a range of other services. In the 1960's, there was a conflict over the consolidation and extension of state welfare as well as over subsequent rationalization and reduction of the range of welfare policies in the 1970's.

While dramatic economic and political conditions have occasioned change, the roots of change are in most cases deep in the past. State intervention after World War I did not occur in an historical vacuum but as the culmination of changes in the forces of production, the relations of social classes, of women and men and in the ideas that were influential during the preceding thirty years. The development of a significant industrial sector, of an unskilled and skilled urban workforce, and of industrial and trade union organizations were significant factors. The response to rapid economic and demographic changes was in the form of movements of social concern and social protest. Organizations or groups concerned with the social gospel, votes for women, temperance, municipal reform, public health, mental hygiene, social and community services, child protection, industrial welfare, progressive management, all played a part in the development of a climate of reform. Businessmen, professionals, farmers, workers and women, all had particular interests in reform. At the formal political level since 1919, it has been the Liberal Party which was able to mold a coalition of classes, races, and sexes out of this reform impetus in maintaining a strong grip on the central government for all but eleven of the subsequent sixty-three years.

In a fundamental way, the welfare state is bound up with the history of women, children and the family. Social welfare has been concerned with regulating the biological and social reproduction of the family. The importance of legal limitations on sexuality such as laws relating to consent, marriage, divorce, contraception and abortion can too easily be overlooked when social welfare is only considered to be expressed in state expenditures. Such regulations are relatively costless but of key importance to understanding the nature of the welfare state. Legal limits on where and at what times women and children could perform paid work were also a part of the extension of state control of the family. Similarly debates and struggles over minimum wages, mothers' allowances, workers' compensation, relief and unemployment insurance were in no small way related to the financial means which would be available for family support.

The history of social welfare policy is, finally, also the history of the improvement of the conditions of life for the mass of Canadians. Provisions for unemployment insurance, welfare, health insurance, workers' compensation, family and mothers' allowances, child welfare, public, non-profit and private housing have served to increase the standards of living for the many. However, this history of improvement is not without limitation or paradox. As studies have begun to show, social welfare policies have not meant a redistribution of income and/or wealth, nor consequently a narrowing of the range of inequality in society. A relatively small number of Canadians owns a great portion of wealth and garners a very large share of income; a relatively large number owns little wealth and garners a small share of income. More significantly, these proportions have changed hardly at all with the development of welfare state policies. And the expenditure to support the wide range of social welfare programmes is derived from the taxation of individual income and corporate profits but in such a way as to take relatively more from those with relatively less income.

Sources for the History of the Welfare State

The Social Research Tradition

One important source of writing on social welfare and social policy is the tradition of social research, a form of research which has been inextricably bound to the advocacy of reform and to the promotion of particular social welfare policies. However, the social research which assisted in exposing the conditions of life and work of the working class and the poor of other countries was slow to develop in Canada. One can point to such early works as those by Ames in Montreal, Kelso, Hodgetts, Hastings and the Bureau of Municipal Research in Toronto, Woodsworth in Winnipeg, Thomas Adams for the Commission of Conservation, and Edmund Bradwin on work in the lumber camps, all produced in the period up to and during the First World War.[1] Yet, these works constitute a limited record of inquiry. More is contained in the reports of Royal Commissions, House of Commons Committees, and Task Forces, such as those undertaken by the Royal Commission on the Relations of Labour and Capital (1889), the Ontario Royal Commission on the Prisons (1890), the Ontario Commission on Unemployment (1913), and the (Dominion) Board of Inquiry into the Cost of Living (1915). Several surveys were undertaken by Helen MacMurchy for the Ontario Government which detail the numbers of the "feeble-minded" and their treatment.[2]

Most social researchers were either amateurs or civil servants. There were as yet few academics or trained researchers concerned even with historical questions; there were even fewer whose teaching and research were concerned with social and political questions or with social reform.

In the interwar years a substantial number of studies of social conditions was produced with varying political motivations, but all aimed at influencing social reform. Charlotte Whitton at the Canadian Council on Child Welfare devoted her efforts to research and reform in three major areas: child and family law reform, child immigration, and the development of provincial departments of public welfare administration.[3] Thomas Dalzell, formerly an associate of Thomas Adams, was invited by the Social Service Council of Canada to write several studies of the housing of the Canadian working class (1928).[4] Pioneering social surveys were conducted by the Canadian National Committee for Mental Hygiene in the 1920's.[5] Town planning schemes were developed in several cities and towns by Adams, first while working for the Dominion government and subsequently on contract while employed by New York City.[6]

The social conditions of the Depression were the subject of research and the promotion of social reform by a group of Canadian intellectuals associated in the League for Social Reconstruction (LSR) whose motivations and approach were similar to the British Fabian Society. Frank H. Underhill, an historian at the University of Toronto, had been a prewar student of G.D.H. Cole at Balliol College, Oxford, where he had been attracted by the Fabian Society. Underhill brought to the LSR considerable experience in social research and criticism from his work for J.S. Woodsworth and his writing for the *Canadian Forum*, a leading left-wing magazine of the 1920's and 1930's. F.R. Scott, a lawyer at McGill, King Gordon and Eugene Forsey, also at McGill, were other leading members. The LSR's *Social Planning for Canada* (1935), edited first by Harry Cassidy, then by Leonard Marsh, stands as a major summation of social research and ideas for social reform in the midst of the Depression.[7]

Leonard Marsh had been a research assistant to Wiliam Beveridge at the London School of Economics, and then was invited to become the Director of a Social Research Project at McGill University in 1931. Marsh and his associates at McGill produced a major series of social studies on working conditions and unemployment in Canada during the Depression.[8] Harry Cassidy had produced an early study of unemployment in Ontario, promoted unemployment insurance, and was secretary to the Bruce Commission on slum conditions in Toronto, before becoming Director of Social Welfare in the Liberal government of T. Dufferin Pattullo in the province of British Columbia.[9]

Government inquiries such as the Royal Commission on Technical Education (1915), the Special Committee on the Cost of Living (1919), the Mather Commission (1919), the Manitoba Unemployment Commission (1928), the Quebec Social Insurance Commission (1930-34), the Ontario Royal Commission on Toronto (1934), the (Dominion) Royal Commission on Price Spreads (1934), the Special Committee on Housing (1935), the Purvis Report (1937), and the monumental Royal Commission on Dominion-Provincial Relations (1939) elicited reports and submissions which contributed in no small way to the recording and analysis of conditions of farmers, workers, and the poor, including the recording of a considerable amount of personal testimony. It was also in the interwar period that Canadian charities and charitable institutions increasingly formed into city-wide councils. Those in Halifax, Montreal, Toronto, and Winnipeg were particularly active in the commissioning of reports and the promotion of social legislation. Often background reports for submissions to government commissions, as well as reports issued by social welfare institutions, were written by one or several of the relatively small band of social researchers.[10]

In Quebec, the Ecole Sociale Populaire and the Semaines Sociales provided a major focal point for (conservative) social research and criticism. In this period their publications were often at odds with the English-language publications, fighting to protect the central role of the church in charitable activities against the encroachment of the provincial and Dominion governments. Independent writers such as Esdras Minville played leading public roles both within Quebec and more broadly in Canada.[11] Father Léon Lebel became an early advocate of family allowances, publishing a book on the subject in 1927.[12]

During the war a considerable number of social research studies were undertaken for state committees and commissions. Marsh took up a position as Research Director for the Advisory Committee on Reconstruction where he drafted the *Report on Social Security for Canada*, and assisted in the drafting of the *Report on Housing and Community Planning*.[13] These are two of the most prominent wartime documents on social reform. George Davidson, who succeeded Charlotte Whitton at the Canadian Welfare Council, wrote studies for the 1944 Nova Scotia enquiry into social welfare.[14] Others were more independent of the state. Charlotte Whitton, Harry Cassidy, and Humphrey Carver wrote major studies of social welfare policy in the areas of family allowances, public health, and housing respectively. In Quebec, family allowances was a major issue taken up by such writers as Angers, Bouvier, and Lébel among others.[15]

The postwar "White Paper on Employment" (1945), written by W.A. MacIntosh, the liberal economic historian and a prominent wartime economic advisor, promised the binding of the state to the protection of public welfare as well as the binding of Fabian social research advocacy to Keynesian liberalism. In hindsight this document marks the beginning of the end of an important period of social research and reform. Some of the most active reformers joined the civil service, others retired to the university. The volume of social research in the fifteen years following the war declined; among the publications were Marsh's study of urban rehabilitation in Vancouver (1950), and Rose's study of the genesis of Toronto's Regent Park public housing project (1957).[16]

Government commissions and reports remained, however, a source of some further research during the period. Parliamentary enquiries on the Old Age Pension (1950), the Federal Royal Commission on Economic Prospects (1957), the Quebec Royal Commission on the Constitution (1955), and several provincial commissions on education provide a fertile source of additional research and advocacy for the design of social welfare policy.[17]

The years from 1963 to 1973 were a period of reform and of consolidation of social legislation unparalleled in Canadian history. Reforming impulses in the federal and provincial governments prompted a series of state-sponsored enquiries. Federal commissions and committees on pensions, health insurance, poverty and social security, taxation, bilingualism and biculturalism, women, unemployment insurance, immigration, delinquency, urban renewal, and public housing were part of an unprecedented outpouring of social research.[18] Provincial commissions and committees were also active. The Quebec Boucher, Parent, and Castonguay-Nepveu Reports were important examples.[19] The same period also saw the re-emergence of social research in social welfare institutions and reform groups such as the Social Planning Councils of Toronto and Vancouver, and the Canadian Council of Social Development (the Canadian Welfare Council).

Histories of Social Welfare Policy

A second source of writing on social welfare and social policy is found in historical analyses of the development of the Canadian social welfare state in particular periods, analyses of particular policies, and analyses of organizations which have influenced the development of policy. In the first category are articles by such writers as Herman (1961), Govan (1950), Morgan (1961), Wallace (1952), and Goffman (1968), covering varying periods. The first such survey, by Margaret K. Strong, was published in 1930. It contains a descriptive review of legislation and administration from the seventeenth century through to 1930. The second is by Richard Splane and is a similarly descriptive record of social welfare institutions, legislation, and administration in nineteenth-century Ontario.[20] The single most important unpublished work is the doctoral dissertation prepared by Elizabeth Wallace entitled "The Changing Canadian State" (1950), which emphasizes the history of ideas of social welfare and social policy from 1867 to 1948.[21] Alvin Finkel's recently published study (1979) of social reform in the 1930's is a strongly analytic work which contains much that is revealing of that period. Examples of other studies of particular periods are those by Margaret Ormsby on the Liberal government of Pattulo in British Columbia and by J.L. Granatstein on Mackenzie King's government during World War II.[22]

In the second category are studies of particular social welfare policies. There has been a recent revival of interest in the history of social welfare policy. Published books and articles include those by Michael Piva on workers' compensation, Kenneth Bryden on pensions, B.L. Vigod on the Quebec Charities Act, M. Taylor on hospital insurance, Houston, Prentice, Stamp, Morrison, Sutherland, and Jones and Rutman on education and child welfare, Strong-Boag on Mothers' Allowances, Cuneo on unemployment insurance, Guest on income security, and Rose and Bettison on housing.[23] Edited collections by Stelter and Artibise contain several articles of relevance to social welfare history and indicate that the work of a growing group of urban historians may prove to be a fertile source of new material, particularly on the way in which social welfare policies have been administered locally.[24] Recent books by Copp on Montreal, Piva on Toronto, and Artibise on Winnipeg are all examples of the growing interest in urban history.[25] Several studies have also appeared which provide much needed detail on the early administration of the poor laws in New Brunswick and Nova Scotia. Articles by Finguard, Whalen, and Greenhaus illustrate the conditions of the poor and the institutions and practices of the poor law in the eighteenth and nineteenth centuries. Allana Reid writes of the emergence of the Bureau des Pauvres in seventeenth- and eighteenth-century Quebec.[26]

There are important early works on social welfare policies which, like Strong's book, have been largely forgotten. J.L. Cohen's books on Mothers' Allowances (1927) and on Unemployment Insurance (1935), C.W. Topping on Canadian prisons (1929), and Duncan Scott on native policy, are but a few examples.[27] Histories, usually disappointingly descriptive, are often among the background papers for Royal Commissions. Among background studies for the Rowell-Sirois Commission are those by A.E. Grauer on housing, public welfare, and health, and by Esdras Minville on labour legislation and social welfare in Quebec.[28] The few histories of Quebec social welfare policies are contained in the Tremblay, Boucher, and Castonguary Reports, prepared in the first case by F.-A. Angers and by Gonzalve Poulin, and in the latter two by Poulin alone.[29]

Increasingly, newer journals such as *Urban History Review, Histoire Sociale, Archivaria,* the *Journal of Canadian Studies, Studies in Political Economy,* and *Canadian Journal of Social Work Education* are providing a forum for historians of Canadian social welfare policy. The work is of varying quality and approach but it is appearing more regularly.

A third category of source material comprises the writings on organizations and individuals having had a close involvement in the development of social welfare policy. The church has been of particular importance in the provision of social services, and of lesser importance in the distribution of information on social conditions and the campaigns for reform. The attempt by progressive church members to involve the various churches in improving the conditions of life of working people through political, trade union, and social welfare organizations was known as the social gospel movement. Richard Allen has provided the most extensive examination of this movement, but there are others. Books such as those by Innis on the YWCA, and Strong-Boag on the National Council of Women provide insight into the connection between national voluntary institutions and the development of social welfare policy.[30] Unfortunately we are lacking in histories of several important social welfare institutions such as the Canadian Welfare Council, the Dominion Health Council, and the Social Service Council of Canada. Works by Granatstein on Mackenzie King and the Liberal Party and by Trofimenkoff and Levitt on Henri Bourassa are examples of works relating to political parties and social reform.[31]

Biographies of individual reformers are a limited though fruitful source of description and some analysis. There are published biographies of Goldwin Smith, J.S. Woodsworth and now J.J. Kelso, and unpublished work on Adams and Charlotte Whitton, as well as work in progress on Whitton, Marsh and Cassidy.[32] Brief biographical notes appear in the earlier pages of *Canadian Welfare* on Cassidy, Winona Armitage, and Bishop Bourget, among many others.[33] Humphrey Carver has written one of the few autobiographies of Canadian social reformers.[34]

Unpublished work is a potentially rich source from which the history of the welfare state, social welfare policies and practices, and social institutions will be written. Graduate theses on particular social welfare policies abound. The passage of legislation has precipitated the preparation of many theses on the social reforms of the 1930's, 1940's, 1950's, and 1960's. The doctoral dissertation by Elizabeth Wallace has already been cited. Others by Morrison, Jolliffe, Dawe, and Ramsay on child welfare, Kitchen on family allowances, Cane, Schweitzer, and Duncan on unemployment and relief, Allen, Royce, and Palker on the church and social welfare are also of note.[35]

Conclusion

Social research, published and unpublished studies of the welfare state and of particular policies, and unpublished personal and governmental papers represent a considerable volume of material reflected in the large number of citations in this *Bibliography*. As yet, however, there is insufficient work of an analytic and more general nature which would link the development of social institutions and social welfare policy to the transformation of economic and political relations which has been wrought in Canada. Neither are there the studies which treat individual social welfare policies with sufficient analytic, and in many cases sufficient descriptive, scrutiny. It is the major purpose of this *Bibliography* to encourage and facilitate the examination of the development of the social welfare state.

Notes

1. H.B. Ames "*The City Below the Hill*. Toronto: University Press, 1975; J.J. Kelso, 1766, 2014; C.A. Hodgetts, 2494, 2495, 3131, 3251; C.J. Hastings, 2184; Bureau of Municipal Research 2443, 2618; J.S. Woodsworth, 332; Thomas Adams, 2145-2164; Edmund Bradwin. *The Bunkhouse Man*. Toronto: University of Toronto Press, 1972.
2. Ontario. *Census of Feeble-Minded*. Toronto, 1908.
3. Elizabeth Hamlet, 1763.
4. A.G. Dalzell. *Housing in Canada*. Toronto: Social Service Council of Canada, 1928; A.G. Dalzell. *The Housing of the Working Classes*. Toronto: The Social Service Council of Canada, 1928.
5. National Committee for Mental Hygiene. *Study of the Distribution of Medical Care and Public Health Services in Canada*. Toronto: The Committee, 1939.
6. A.H. Armstrong, 2119; L. Corea, 2127.
7. Carl Berger, *The Writing of Canadian History*. Toronto: University of Toronto Press, 1976. pp. 54-84; Leonard Marsh, 404; Allan Irving "Canadian Fabians: the Work and Thought of Harry Cassidy and Leonard Marsh." *Canadian Journal of Social Work Education*. 7:1 (1981), pp. 7-28.
8. See for example, L.C. Marsh, 703; Fred Stone, 713.

9.   The study by Cassidy is *Unemployment and Relief in Ontario 1929-1932*, 692. For details of Cassidy's career see Alan Irving. "Canadian Fabians," and Margaret Ormsby, 64.

10.   For example Harry Cassidy was active in the League for Social Reconstruction (LSR) and the joint editor with Marsh of the LSR's Social Planning for Canada. He was also the author of the report of the Unemployment Research Committee of Ontario (cf. 9), and the secretary to the Bruce Commission which examined slum housing in Toronto in 1934, 2265.

11.   Robin Neill, "Pensée economique au Québec: the economics of survival." *Journal of Canadian Studies*. 4 (August 1969), pp. 7-21.

12.   Léon Lebel, 2062, 2063. For more detail on family allowances see Brigitte Kitchen, 1767.

13.   Leonard Marsh, 386, 2202.

14.   George F. Davidson, 21.

15.   Charlotte Whitton, 413, 414, 415; Harry Cassidy 391, 392, 393, 525, 526; Humphrey Carver, 2175, 2291, 2485, 2510; F.-A. Angers, 2036, 2037; Emile Bouvier, 2040, 2041; Léon Lebel, 2061, 2062, 2063, 2064, 2065, 2066.

16.   Leonard Marsh, 2396; Albert Rose, 2316.

17.   Canada. Parliament. Joint Committee on Old Age Security, 934. The Royal Commissions produced such works as: Yves Dubé, J.E. Howes, and D.L. McQueen. *Housing and Social Capital*, 2224; Gonzalve Poulin. "L'assistance sociale dans la province de Québec," 65. The commissions on education included those in Manitoba, 2809, New Brunswick, 2813, Ontario, 2827, Prince Edward Island, 2829.

18.   Senate. Special Committee on Aging, 937; Royal Commission on Health Services, 3171; Senate. Special Committee on Poverty, 346; Department of Health and Welfare, 337, 338, 342; Royal Commission on Bilinguilism, 1625-1629; Royal Commission on the Status of Women, 1833; Committee of Inquiry into The Unemployment Insurance Act, 772; Department of Employment and Immigration, 1453-1465; Department of The Solicitor General, 1194; Federal Task Force on Housing and Urban Development, 2209. The report on public housing was privately published as Michael Dennis and Susan Fish. *Programs in Search of a Policy*, 2293.

19.   Boucher Report, 1881; Parent Report, 2832; Castonguay — Nepveu Report, 561-563.

20.   Kathleen Herman, 40; E.S.L. Govan, 291; J.S. Morgan, 61; Elizabeth Wallace, 83; I.J. Goffman, 528; Margaret Strong, 532; Richard Splane, 77.

21.   Elizabeth Wallace, 82.

22.   Alvin Finkel, 27; Margaret Ormsby, 64; J.L. Granatstein. *Canada's War: The Politics of the MacKenzie King Government 1939-45*. Toronto: Oxford University Press, 1975.

23.   M. Piva, 824; K. Bryden, 915; M. Taylor, 3145, 3237, 3272, 3280; S. Houston, 2681; A. Prentice, 2706, 2707; R.M. Stamp, 2897, 2726; T.R. Morrison, 1770, 1772; Neil Sutherland, 1788; Dennis Guest, 36; Albert Rose, 2137; David Bettison, 2122.

The following have appeared subsequent to the compiling of the citations here: A. Jones and L. Rutman. *In the Children's Aid: J.J. Kelso and Child Welfare in Ontario*. Toronto: University of Toronto Press, 1981; V.

Strong-Boag "'Wages for Housework': Mothers' Allowances and the Beginnings of Social Security in Canada." *Journal of Canadian Studies.* 14:1 (Spring 1979), pp. 24-34; Carl Cuneo. "State Mediation and Class Contradictions in Canadian Unemployment Insurance 1930-35". *Studies in Policital Economy.* 3 (Spring 1980), pp. 37-66; B.L. Vigod, "Ideology and Institutions in Quebec: The Public Charities Controversy 1921-1926." *Histoire sociale/Social History.* 21 (May 1978), pp. 167-182.

24. G.A. Stetter and A.F.J. Artibise, 5, 79.

25. Terry Copp. *The Anatomy of Poverty.* Toronto: McClelland and Stewart, 1974; Michael Piva. *The Condition of the Working Class in Toronto 1900-1921.* Ottawa: University of Ottawa Press, 1979; A.F.J. Artibise, 4.

26. J. Finguard, 103, 104; B. Greenhaus, 107; J.M. Whalen, 85, 115, 116; Allana Reid, 99.

27. J.L. Cohen, 2029, 731; C.W. Topping, 1178; D.C. Scott, 1747; also see Appendix I, MG 19. F26, pp. 175.

28. A.E. Grauer, 373, 2226, 3128; Esdras Minville, 59.

29. F.-A. Angers, 592; Gonzalve Poulin, 65, 69, 561, 1881.

30. M.Q. Innis, 261; V. Strong-Boag, 267.

31. J. Levitt. *Henry Bourassa and the Golden Calf: The Social Programme of the Nationalists of Quebec.* Ottawa: University of Ottawa Press, 1969; S.M. Trofimenkoff. "Henri Bourassa and the Woman Question." In *The Neglected Majority.* edited by S.M. Trofimenkoff and A. Prentice. Toronto: McClelland and Stewart, 1977; J.L. Granatstein, cf. 22.

32. Elizabeth Wallace. *Goldwin Smith: Victorian Liberal.* Toronto: University of Toronto Press, 1957. K. McNaught, 55; Olive Ziegler, 88; A. Jones and L. Rutman. *In the Children's Aid: J.J. Kelso and Child Welfare in Ontario.* Toronto: University of Toronto Press, 1981. Unpublished work on Whitton by E. Hamlet, 1763; on Kelso by I. Bain, 1763.
Since preparation of this bibliography several articles on Whitton have appeared. See for example Patricia Rooke and R.L. Schnell. "Child Welfare in English Canada, 1920-1948." *Social Service Review,* 55 (Sept. 1981) pp. 484-506. Work in progress includes a monograph on Whitton by Rooke and Schnell and a doctoral thesis on Marsh and Cassidy by Alan Irving, University of Toronto, Faculty of Social Work. A recently completed work is by J. Keck. "Social Reform in Periods of Crisis. The Work of Leonard Marsh as Social Reformer, 1930-1945." M.S.W. Carleton University, 1981.

33. A. Peebles, 65; Anne Margeret Angus, 1749; Léon Pouliot, 215.

34. Humphrey Carver, 2123.

35. T. Morrison, 1772; R. Joliffe, 1765; J.-A. Dawe, 1759; D. Ramsay, 1782; B. Kitchen, 1767; T. Cane, 728; P.R. Schweitzer, 753; A.S. Duncan, 695; Richard Allen, 192; M. Royce, 216; E. Palker, 212.

Introduction and Guide to the Use of the Bibliography

Although we have tried to be rigorous and clear in the development and conceptualization of the categories that appear in the *Bibliography*, nonetheless a number of thorny problems arose regarding whether to include and where to place particular types of materials. In this Guide we have tried to outline the principles and rationale that have guided us in making our decisions on which materials to cite, how to cite them, and in which section to cite them. We have made a concerted effort to be consistent in the application of the principles we developed.

The Range of Source Materials in the Bibliography

To facilitate access to the considerable array of primary and secondary source material which has been uncovered we have constructed the *Bibliography* in two parts. Part One is concerned with major themes in the development of the welfare state. The origins of the welfare state, the development of an ideology of state welfare, the organizations that have influenced the conception, passage, and practice of social welfare policy, the influences from other countries, and the methods of administration of policy are the subjects of the five sections of Part One.

Part Two of the *Bibliography* contains five sections, each devoted to an area of social welfare policy. We distinguish social welfare policy from two other types of categories of welfare policies. Industrial welfare policies are those concerned with the conditions of work, more particularly minimum wages, hours of work, benefits, health, and safety. Fiscal welfare policies are those that determine the terms and administration of the system of taxation. Lastly, social welfare policies are those that affect the social conditions of people in society. It is this third category, namely social welfare policies, which is the primary subject of this *Bibliography*. The five sections on social welfare policy in Part Two bring together source material on policies for people (1) out of work, (2) who cannot work, (3) who are outsiders and (4) for women, children and the family. The fifth section groups material on policies (5) for maintaining the labour force. Since the range of policies and material which has been included in each section is not self evident, some explanation of the categories employed in Part Two is necessary.

The Categorization of Social Welfare Policy

The most important social welfare policies are those which have developed historically for people who are *out of work* (Sec. 6 of the *Bibliography*). Since the basic position in society for people in the workforce is determined according to whether they are working or not, the first set of social welfare policies are those which are intended to ensure that those among the unemployed who can work do so. Such policies have been directed at providing a reduced income to the unemployed while they are unemployed, and at attempting to get them back into the labour force when jobs are available. At the same time, these policies function to maintain a labour force on call in times of recession ready for the next round of economic expansion in which there will be demands by capital for more labour. Such policies also function to socialize the cost to the employer of maintaining the labour force at the ready. In effect, working people pay to maintain other working people so that profits can be sustained. Historically these policies tend to insulate working people from the full brunt of the pressure to find a job, from the so-called "discipline of the market-place." This section covers unemployment insurance and relief.

A second set of social welfare policies has arisen for people *who cannot work* (Sec. 7). This group includes those people who become the casualties of the search for profit in our society: those who have been injured through work; those whose best years have been given to the production of profit and are now considered too old to make an economic contribution; those who have mental and physical handicaps and who, for ideological as well as material reasons, are commonly excluded from the labour market. Policies for people who cannot work socialize the cost of their maintenance. They also deflect workers towards accepting compensation for being society's victims, while drawing attention away from the conditions of work which are the source of the workers' problems. Included in this category of policies are long-term welfare, workers' compensation and pensions, and specific welfare programmes for the assistance of the mentally and physically disabled.

The third group of social welfare policies has arisen for the containment of the outsiders in our society, those who as a consequence of structures and ideology are forced to be "*marginal*" (Sec. 8). Marginal people are those who have been colonized, brutalized, and beaten, those who have been held apart from the mainstream of activity, those against whom discrimination has been directed, those who have not been seen as whole or wholly capable, those whose actions have been considered rebellious, those who have violated, in one way or another, the laws that protect property. It also includes immigrants who, as immigrants and recent arrivals, are outsiders until assimilated. Included in this category of social welfare policies are the laws of property and debts, the operation of the judicial system, which shapes and enforces these laws, the courts, and the prisons. The activities of native peoples, particular ethnic and racial groups, and immigrants are regulated by a particular set of policies which are included in this category.

In our capitalist society, the family is not simply the group of people with whom individuals have their closest relationships. The family also has a contradictory side as an institution of social control. This dual nature of the family has its most crippling effect on women. In most families it is women who raise the children, do the housework, and prepare the meals. More recently, in a growing number of cases, women work not only in the home but they also perform work for a salary or wage in the labour market. There has arisen a separate category of social welfare policies directed at ensuring that the family continues to function as the unit that provides the workers to run offices, shops, and factories. The family not only provides workers from day to day, but since it is the institution in which children are raised, it also provides workers for the future. Included in this category are such social welfare policies as family allowances, the operation of family courts and family law, including laws relating to juvenile delinquency, and a variety of social services operating to keep the family together, often serving to counsel members of the family to accept their problems rather than to fight against them. Entries in this category are grouped under *women, children, and the family* (Sec. 9).

Lastly, there are a number of more general policies, all of which have developed to ensure the continued existence of a well-trained, quiescent, and relatively healthy labour force. Included in this category are health care, education, and housing.* In fact, these policies benefit not just those who do work for a wage or salary, but also those who do not. The key characteristics of these policies is that they socialize the cost of maintaining the labour force necessary for production and profits. Entries in this category are grouped under *maintaining the labour force* (Sec. 10).

Section Subheadings

Each of sections one through five in Part One and sections six through ten in Part Two contains subheadings, and in some cases further subdivision of the citations. While we began with a larger list of standard subheadings for each of the sections, those which appear in

---

* It was decided to provide only limited coverage of public health in the subsection on health care where related to social welfare.

each section are those which are supported by the literature. In Section 1 of Part One subheadings appear relating to early social welfare institutions and policies. Section 2 contains references to five types of organizations, namely, those for which we were able to discover a literature relating organizations to social welfare policy. In Section 3, we have listed materials relating to the historical debate on the appropriate role of the state in the social welfare field. In three instances we have singled out particular debates, grouping the literature on the constitutional questions in the 1930's, on social security in the 1940's, and on social security, poverty, and the guaranteed annual income in the 1960's. Subheadings in Section 4 are self explanatory. The lack of comparative literature forced us to list these citations without grouping them either by policy area or by country or region.

Our original intention in Part Two was to use a standardized list of subheadings and further subdivisions. Again the literature required some alterations in our format. Subsections entitled *General*, *Historical Development*, *Government Policy and Documentation*, *Financing*, *Administration*, and *Special Issues* have been used as the first level of subdivision. Where these headings do not appear, we have simply not found a body of literature which would justify their use. In certain instances additional subheadings appear where they were found to reflect the specificities of the particular area of social welfare policy. For example, under *Housing Policy* (10.1) we have added the subheading *Market Relations* (10.1.6)

Manner of Citation

In the course of collecting references, we discovered a variety of styles of citation. In establishing the style for the *Bibliography* we have been guided by K.L. Turabian in *A Manual for Writers of Term Papers, Theses, and Dissertations*, Chicago: University of Chicago Press, 1973, and *Student's Guide for Writing College Papers*, University of Chicago Press, 1976, as well as the advice of many researchers and librarians and the examples provided by other bibliographies.

Citation of Publications in the French Language

French language articles, journals, and books are cited in that language and not in translation, but the bibliographical information such as place of publication appears in English. Over the years, the style of publication of federal government publications in the French language has altered considerably. Three styles are apparent; we have taken care to list these government publications according to their style. Earlier

publications were printed only in the French language. Later ones uti-
lize either the French and English together in alternate columns on
the same page or facing pages, or provide a separate French text which
is published in the same volume as the English but inverted. Many
government documents cited in English are not cited in French. While
it has been our policy to cite French language documents where they
exist, we have likely introduced some inconsistencies. However, it
should be noted that often government documents are simply not
available in French.

Citation of Materials on Social Welfare Policy for Veterans

Rather than establishing a separate section grouping references to
policies for veterans we have listed this literature in the relevant sections in Part One or Part Two. For example, references to veterans
pensions may be found under 7.2, to veterans rehabilitation under 7.3,
and veterans housing under 10.1.

Citation of Materials on Private and Voluntary Social Welfare Institutions

While the purpose of the *Bibliography* is to provide a guide to the literature on social welfare policy, exceptions have been made to include
literature which refers to private and voluntary institutions and practices which are the historical antecedents of social welfare policy and
administration, and to private and voluntary organizations which influenced the formulation and development of policy.

Cross-referencing of Citations

Because of the volume of available materials, we have employed a
system of cross-referencing. Each citation appears only once in the *Bibliography*. This decision posed problems in the allocation of particular
citations. Consequently, we have referred the reader to other salient
sections of the *Bibliography* where related materials may be found.
Cross-references appear under the heading of each section or major
sub-section in Part Two.

Annotations

The annotating of citations was considered but not undertaken.
Such a step would be both expensive and time-consuming. The result

would likely be the production of a more detailed research handbook in a field which in our view now needs a basic research guide. Further, annotating the number of citations which appear here would necessitate the production of a much larger, more expensive, and therefore less accessible bibliography. A much reduced number of annotated citations would equally not serve the purpose of encouraging more research in a field with as yet relatively few published interpretive works.

Period Covered

Our concern in the *Bibliography* is to cite materials relevant to the history of modern state social welfare which we take to begin with the appearance of capitalist forms of economic, social and political organization in Canada. Consequently, we have dated the *Bibliography* from 1840. Some materials relevant to earlier developments have been grouped primarily in section 1.0 under particular subheadings. We completed the collection of materials in the autumn of 1978 when the first draft of the manuscript was prepared. For these reasons, the dates 1840 to 1978 appear in the subtitle.

Primary Sources: Appendix I

A special effort was made to perform a detailed and extensive search of papers at the Public Archives of Canada, the results of which appear in Appendix I. We were not able to do such a systematic search of papers held in provincial, university or private archives.

Annual Reports

Many hundreds of government and private institutions, commissions, departments, committees, and the like, publish annual reports. This body of material constitutes a useful primary source of information for research. However, these are so numerous that we have cited annual reports in the *Bibliography* only when they constitute a particularly fruitful source in an area where there are few, if any, other sources available.

Unpublished Materials

Unpublished manuscripts have been cited only where a location could be confirmed. Unpublished papers of individual social workers, reformers, administrators, etc. are included only if they were available at the Public Archives of Canada (Appendix I). University, provincial, church and individual associations' archives represent potentially fertile sources of materials but we did not undertake to detail their holdings.

Government Documents

Given the very large body of literature written both by public servants and private individuals, published anonymously, in the name of government organizations, or by organizations in the name of the individual, we were required to develop an operative definition of what constitutes a government publication. What we were trying to establish was an accurate representation of what constituted government policy in any particular period. The *Bibliography* treats any document published by government, whether by a department, a Royal Commission, or Task Force or by a central agency, as emanating from "government." Consequently, many documents which could have been placed in particular sub-sections were not when they appeared to represent government policy. Thus the subheadings *Government Policy* and *Documentation* appear in sections 6 through 10.

A further problem occurs in the identification of the publisher of government documents. Several types of publications are apparent. First, there are those documents published by the government — The King's Printer, The Queen's Printer, Information Canada or Supply and Services Canada. Second, there are documents published by Commissions, Task Forces, and government departments, which are nonetheless formal publications. Third, there are documents made available by government departments, which are printed by the department in an informal way. Fourthly, there are government documents representing work in progress — working papers — which often lack clear identification. In this latter case we have made every effort to identify the department, branch, section, etc. from which the document emanates.

Local/Regional Government

Thorough coverage of this level of government was difficult. We did not have the resources to check for publications (or archival papers) in each major city. Citations that appear are drawn from coverage given in other sources — periodicals, books, indexes, bibliographies, and catalogues.

Historical Materials

Historical materials have been categorized according to whether they contain an analysis of a particular period of development of social welfare policies, or whether they analyze a particular policy. The former material appears in Part One, the latter in Part Two.

Materials analytic of the longer-term development of social welfare policy in Canada appear in 1.0, *Origins of the Welfare State*, while materials concerned with the ideas of the welfare state that were debated historically appear in 3.0, *The Welfare State in Canada*. Materials listed in the sub-section Historical Development in 6.0 through 10.0 have been judged to be analytic of the history and development of particular policies alone. Under this same sub-section a further distinction has been made between analytic materials of a more general character and materials that are either descriptive of policies historically or constitute descriptive statements of historical interest on a particular policy.

Secondary Sources: Appendices II-IV

The compilation of this *Bibliography* required the collection of many thousands of references to written material on social welfare policy and in related fields. Appendix II contains a listing of *library collections* examined in the process of collecting material. We made ample use of the very extensive library resources in the city of Ottawa as well as the libraries of the universities in Ottawa, Toronto, Montreal, Kingston, and in other areas throughout the country.

An exhaustive review of Canadian periodicals and magazines was undertaken, both through an examination of primary sources and through the use of the *Canadian Periodical Index*. Journals and magazines from the United States, Britain, France, and other countries were also reviewed for material relating to Canadian social welfare policy. A listing of *periodicals* reviewed is contained in Appendix III. Unfortunately, we were not able to undertake a systematic review of newspapers, monthly periodicals, or of more general historical works containing some materials bearing on the topics covered by the *Bibliography*.

In addition to library catalogues and periodicals, we also consulted a wide range of *bibliographies*. These are listed in Appendix IV.

An effort was made to visit special and private collections with material relevant to the study of social welfare policy. In addition, members of the project group visited provincial libraries as well as university and legislative libraries in every province in the country. In every city visited, interviews were arranged with researchers in the field. References obtained were then considered for inclusion in the main body of the *Bibliography*.

The process of searching for materials involved the collective resources of the entire project team for a period of eighteen months, and resulted in the collection of approximately 6,000 citations from which those references that appear in the *Bibliography* were selected. Access to the entire collection of references is available at the Centre for Social Welfare Studies, Carleton University.

Chronology of Social Welfare Legislation: Appendix V

To assist the user in placing literature listed in the *Bibliography* in historical perspective, a *Chronology of Social Welfare Legislation* has been prepared. It appears as Appendix V. In assembling the chronology we have used the same five categories of social welfare policy used in Part Two of the *Bibliography*.

Indexes

Given the detailed, specific subheadings and the cross-referencing in Part Two of the *Bibliography*, a subject index was deemed somewhat redundant and not worth the considerable expense that would have been required to prepare it. The subject index is therefore limited to Part One. It indexes key words in the entries in the *Bibliography* and identifies the entry by the entry number (not the page number). Separate indexes have been prepared for French language and English language citations. A complete author index including individual and corporate authors has also been prepared.

THE BIBLIOGRAPHY

Part One

1.0 Origins of the Welfare State

1.1 General

1 ADAM, G.M. "Comments on the Toronto Conference of the Combined Charities." *Bystander*. 2 (July 1883), p. 206.

2 ALBERTA. Department of Labour, Research Division. *History of Labour and Social Welfare Legislation in Alberta*. Edmonton: Department of Labour, 1971.

3 ARES, Richard. "Le combat de Claude Castonguay pour une politique sociale intégrée." *Relations*. 368 (February 1972), pp. 36-40.

4 ARTIBISE, Alan F.J. *Winnipeg: A Social History of Urban Growth, 1874-1914*. Montreal: McGill-Queen's University Press, 1975.

5 _____, and STELTER, Gilbert A. *The Usable Urban Past: Planning and Politics in the Modern Canadian City*. Carleton Library. Toronto: MacMillan, 1979.

6 BELLA, Leslie. "The Canada Assistance Plan." *Social Worker*. 45:2 (Summer 1977), pp. 86-92.

7 BELLAMY, D. "Social Welfare in Canada." *Encyclopedia of Social Work*. New York: National Association of Social Workers, 1965, pp. 36-48.

8 BERGITHON, C. "The Problem of Social Insurance in Canada." M.A., McGill University, 1931.

9 BLYTH, Jack A. *The Canadian Social Inheritance*. Toronto: Copp Clark, 1972.

10 BOURQUE, Gabrielle, and BROWN, Ruth. *Federal Legislation Related to Social Welfare, 1908-1965: Selected Statutes*. Ottawa: Health and Welfare, 1966.

11 CANADA. Department of National Health and Welfare. Policy and Program Development and Co-ordination Branch. *A Chronology of Social Welfare and Related Legislation 1908-1974; Selected Federal Statutes*. Ottawa: Health and Welfare, 1975.

12 _____. Research and Statistics Directorate. *A Chronology of Social Welfare and Related Legislation 1908-1968; Selected Federal Statutes*. Ottawa: Queen's Printer, 1969.

13 CARIGNAN, Pierre, "Development of Social Security in Canada." Ph.D., Harvard University, 1954.

14 CASSIDY, Harry M. "The Canadian Social Services." *Annals of the American Academy of Political and Social Science*. 253 (September 1947), pp. 190-201.

15 CHARTIER, Roger. *Etude analytique et évolutive des services du ministère du travail et de la législation ouvrière et sociale de la province de Québec, 1885-1952*. Quebec: Ministère du travail, 1953.

16 COLEMAN, Jean Robson. *Welfare Legislation in Canada and Her Provinces*. Ottawa: Canadian Welfare Council, 1936.

17 COLLINS, K. "Three Decades of Social Security in Canada." *Canadian Welfare*. 51:7 (January/February 1976), pp. 5-9.

18 CORBEIL, M. "Historique de l'animation sociale au Québec." *Relations*. 349 (May 1970), pp. 139-147.

19 CORRY, J.A. *The Growth of Government Activities Since Confederation: A Study Prepared for the Royal Commission on Dominion-Provincial Relations*. Ottawa: King's Printer, 1939.

1

20   COWARD, Laurence E. "Pension and Welfare Plans in Canada — History and Trends." Reprinted from *Transactions of the Society of Actuaries*. 10 (June 1958), pp. 174-201.
21   DAVIDSON, George F. *Report on Public Welfare Services*. Royal Commission on Development and Rehabilitation. Halifax: King's Printer, 1944.
22   DAVIS, R.E.G. "Canadian Social Work." Reprinted from *Social Work Year Book*. Ottawa: Canadian Welfare Council, 1954.
23   DENAULT, Hayda. "La pauvreté et le service social en Amérique du Nord." *Service social*. 9:3 (November/December 1960), pp. 50-81.
24   DRAPEAU, Stanislaus. "Etudes historiques et statistiques sur les institutions charitables de bienfaisance et d'éducation au Canada." *Revue canadienne*. 10 (1873), pp. 236-37.
25   _____. *Histoire des institutions de charité, de bienfaisance et d'éducation du Canada, depuis leur fondation jusqu'à nos jours*. Ottawa: Imprimeur du foyer domestique, 1877.
26   ESTIENNE, Henri. "Projet de loi sur l'assistance publique." *Revue trimestrielle canadienne*. 34 (June 1923), pp. 206-13.
27   FINKEL, Alvin. *Business and Social Reform in the Thirties*. Toronto: Lorimer, 1979.
28   _____. "Canadian Business and the 'Reform' Process in the 1930s." Ph.D., University of Toronto, 1976.
29   _____. "Origins of the Welfare State in Canada." *In The Canadian State: Political Economy and Political Power*, edited by L. Panitch. pp. 344-73. University of Toronto Press, 1977.
30   FITZNER, Stan. *The Development of Social Welfare in Nova Scotia*. Halifax: Department of Public Welfare, Nova Scotia, 1967.
31   GERMANO, J. "Histoire de la charité à Montréal, les enfants trouvés." *Revue canadienne*. 32 (1896), pp. 423-38.
32   GIARD, Carmen. "Etude de la législation sociale de la province de Québec, 1900-1921." M.A., Laval University, 1955.
33   GODBOUT, Pauline. "Etude de la législation sociale de la province de Québec, 1921-1939." M.A., Laval University, 1954.
34   GOFFMAN, Irving J. *Some Fiscal Aspects of Public Welfare in Canada*. Toronto: Canadian Tax Foundation, 1965.
35   GORDON, Howard Scott. "The Meaning of Social Security." *Business Quarterly*. 18:4 (Winter 1954), pp. 171-84.
36   GUEST, Dennis. "The Development of Income Maintenance Programmes in Canada, 1945-1967." Ph.D, London School of Economics, 1968.
37   GUILLEMETTE, André M. "Welfare in French Canada." *Canadian Welfare*. 42:1 (January/February 1966), pp. 8-13.
38   HAMEL, M. "Evolution de l'assistance sociale." *Canadian Welfare*. 16:5 (1964), pp. 148-54.
39   HAREVEN, Tamara K. "An Ambiguous Alliance: Some Aspects of American Influences on Canadian Social Welfare." *Social History/Histoire sociale*. 2 (April 1969), pp. 82-98.
40   HERMAN, Kathleen. "The Emerging Welfare State." In *Canadian Perspectives*, edited by D.I. Davies and Kathleen Herman. pp. 131-41. Toronto: New Press, 1971.
41   HORN, Michiel. "The League for Social Reconstruction: Socialism and Nationalism in Canada, 1931-1945." Ph.D., University of Toronto, 1969.

42   _____. "The League for Social Reconstruction and the Development
      of a Canadian Socialism, 1932-1936." *Journal of Canadian Studies*. 7:4
      (November 1972), pp. 3-17.

43   HORNE, G.R. "Labour Legislation and Social Services in the Province
      of Quebec." *Canadian Journal of Economics and Political Science*. 7:2
      (May 1941), pp. 249-59.

44   HOUSTON, Susan Elizabeth. "The Impetus to Reform: Urban Crime,
      Poverty, and Ignorance in Ontario, 1850-1875." Ph.D., University of
      Toronto, 1974.

45   LANG, Vernon. *The Service State Emerges in Ontario 1945-1973*. Toronto:
      Ontario Economic Council, 1974.

46   LAPIERRE, A.M. "Some Aspects of Social Legislation in Canada."
      M.A., Acadia University, 1949.

47   LARIVIERE, Claude. *Crise économique et contrôle social, 1929-1937: le
      cas de Montréal*. Montréal: Editions coopératives A. St. Martin de
      Montréal, 1977.

48   LASKIN, Richard, ed. *Social Problems, A Canadian Profile*. Toronto:
      McGraw-Hill, 1964.

49   LAWSON, Elsie. "Public Welfare in Manitoba." *Canadian Welfare*. 15:3
      (September 1939), pp. 14-23.

50   LAYCOCK, Joseph E. "New Directions for Social Welfare Policy." In
      The Prospect of Change, edited by Abraham Rotstein. pp. 308-27.
      Toronto: McGraw-Hill, 1965.

51   LECLERC, Françoise, and GAUVIN, Ghislaine. "L'évolution de l'assis-
      tance sociale dans la province de Québec." M.A., Laval University,
      1961.

52   LYSNE, David Edgar. "Welfare in Ontario, 1905-1936." M.A., Universi-
      ty of Alberta, 1966.

53   McKENZIE, Betty Ann. "The Impact of Social Change on the Organiza-
      tion of Welfare Services in Ontario 1821-1921: Care of the Poor in
      Toronto." M.S.W., University of Toronto, 1966.

54   McNAUGHT, K.W. "James Shaver Woodsworth: from Social Gospel to
      Social Democracy, 1874-1921." Ph.D., University of Toronto, 1950.

55   _____. *A Prophet in Politics*. Toronto: University of Toronto Press,
      1959.

56   MANHERTZ, H.E.D. "Social Security in the Maritimes, 1939-1958."
      M.A., University of New Brunswick, 1959.

57   MARIER, Roger. "Les objectifs sociaux du Québec." *Canadian Public
      Administration*. 12:2 (Summer 1969), pp. 181-97.

58   MILLER, Orlo. "London, Ontario, Pioneer Welfare Planner." *Canadian
      Welfare*. 36:6 (November 1960), pp. 249-56.

59   MINVILLE, Esdras. *Labour Legislation and Social Services in the Province
      of Quebec*. Royal Commission on Dominion-Provincial Relations (Ap-
      pendix 5). Ottawa: King's Printer, 1939.

60   MONGEAU, Serge. *Evolution de l'assistance au Québec; une étude histo-
      rique des diverses modalités d'assistance au Québec, des origines de la colo-
      nie à nos jours*. Montreal: Editions du Jour, 1967.

61   MORGAN, John S. "Social Welfare Services in Canada." In *Social Pur-
      pose for Canada*, edited by Michael Oliver, pp. 130-67. Toronto: Universi-
      ty of Toronto Press, 1961.

62   MUNRO, Donald Richard. "The Care of the Dependent Poor in Ontario,
      1891-1921: A Study of the Impact of Social Change on the Organiza-
      tion of the Welfare Services in Ontario for the Dependent Poor, Espe-

cially the Unemployed, the Aged and the Mother Raising Children by Herself, between 1891-1921". MSW: University of Toronto. 1966.

63 NEWFOUNDLAND. Royal Commission on Health and Public Charities. *1st Interim Report*. St. John's: King's Printer, 1930.

64 ORMSBY, Margaret. "T. Dufferin Patullo and The Little New Deal." *Canadian Historical Review*. 43:4 (December 1962), pp. 277-297.

65 PEEBLES, A. "Harry Morris Cassidy, 1900-1951." *Canadian Welfare*. 27:6 (December 1951), pp. 3-7.

66 PELLETIER, Michel, and VAILLANCOURT, Yves. *Les politiques sociales et les travailleurs*. 6 vols. Montreal, 1974.

67 POULIN, Gonzalve. "L'assistance sociale dans la province de Québec 1608-1951." Commission royale d'enquête sur les problèmes constitutionnels. *Rapport*, Quebec: Imprimeur de la reine, 1955.

68 _____. "Evolution des services sociaux dans la province de Québec." *Canadian Welfare*. 24:7 (January 1949), pp. 59-62.

69 _____. "Institutions de charité et services sociaux dans la province de Québec." *Service social*. 2:4 (Winter 1952), pp. 146-152.

70 _____. "La socialisation des structures de bien-être: phénomène historique." *Culture*. 25:4 (December 1964), pp. 331-45.

71 PRENTICE, Alison L., and HOUSTON, Susan E., eds. *Family, School and Society in Nineteenth Century Canada*. Toronto: Oxford University Press, 1975.

72 ROY, Hugette Lapointe. "Paupérisme et assistance sociale à Montréal, 1832-1865." M.A., McGill University, 1972.

73 RUBIN, M.W. "The Response of the Bennett Government to the Depression in Saskatchewan, 1930-1935: A Study in Dominion-Provincial Relations." M.A., University of Regina, 1975.

74 SCOTT, F.R. "A Decade of the League for Social Reconstruction." *Saturday Night*. 57 (January 24, 1942), p.8.

75 SHUMIATCHER, Morris C. "Socialism and Social Welfare in Saskatechewan." *Canadian Forum*. 25:293 (June 1945), pp. 60-62.

76 SMALLWOOD, Joseph Roberts, ed. *The Book of Newfoundland*. 6 vols. St. John's: Newfoundland Book Publishers, 1937.

77 SPLANE, Richard B. *Social Welfare in Ontario, 1791-1893*. Toronto: University of Toronto Press, 1965.

78 _____. "The Development of Social Welfare in Ontario, 1791 to 1893: The Role of the Province." D.S.W., University of Toronto, 1961.

79 STELTER, Gilbert A., and ARTIBISE, Alan F.J., eds. *The Canadian City*. Toronto: McClelland and Stewart, 1977.

80 THOMPSON, R.G. "The Development of Welfare Policy in the Maritimes 1945-1960." M.A., University of New Brunswick, 1965.

81 VOYER, Christine. "Etude de la législation sociale du Bas-Canada 1841-1867." M.A., Laval University, 1954.

82 WALLACE, Elizabeth. "The Changing Canadian State: A Study of the Changing Conception of the State as Revealed in Canadian Social Legislation 1867-1948." Ph.D., Columbia University, 1950.

83 _____. "Origin of the Welfare State in Canada, 1867-1900." *Canadian Journal of Economics and Political Science*. 16:3 (August 1950), pp. 383-93.

84 WASTENEYS, Hortense Catherine Fardell. "A History of the University Settlement of Toronto 1910-1958: An Exploration of the Social Objectives of the University Settlement and Their Implementation." D.S.W., University of Toronto, 1975.

85   WHALEN, James M. "Social Welfare in New Brunswick, 1784-1900."
     Acadiensis. 2:1 (Autumn 1977), pp. 54-64.
86   WHITTON, Charlotte, "War and the Social Services in Canada." *Proceedings of the Council of Social Welfare.* 68. pp. 24-31. New York: Columbia University Press, 1941.
87   WILSON, J. "Social Welfare Work in the Maritime Provinces." M.A., Acadia University, 1935.
88   ZIEGLER, Olive. *Woodsworth-Social Pioneer.* Toronto: Ontario Publishing Company, 1934.

1.2   The Relief of the Poor in New France and Early Quebec

89   DROLET, Antonio. "Les conditions de vie d'un engagé du seigneur Taschereau." *Bulletin des recherches historiques.* 68:2 (April/June 1966), pp. 71-76.
90   ECCLES, William John. *Canadian Society During the French Regime.* Montreal: Harvest House, 1968.
91   _____. "Social Welfare Measures and Policies in New France". *Actas y Memorias*, 36° Congreso Internacional de Americanistas, Espana, 1964, vol. 4. Sevilla, 1966, pp. 9-20.
92   HARRIS, C. "Of Poverty and Helplessness in Petite-Nation." *Canadian Historical Review.* 52:1 (1971), pp. 23-50.
93   LACHANCE, André. "Le bureau des pauvres de Montréal 1698-1699. Contribution à l'étude de la société montréalaise de la fin du XVIIe siècle." *Histoire sociale/Social History.* (November 1969), pp. 99-112.
94   LOWER CANADA. Legislative Council. *Report.* Special Committee on the Establishments for the Insane, Foundlings, and Poor. 10 February 1824.
95   MASSICOTTE, E.-Z. "Comment on disposait des enfants du roi." *Bulletin des recherches historiques* (Dec. 1930), pp. 709-12.
96   MATHIEU, Lise. "Etude sur la législation sociale du Bas-Canada 1760-1840." M.A., Laval University, 1953.
97   QUEBEC. Benevolent Society/Société bienveillante. *General Rules of the Quebec Benevolent Society/Règles generales.* Passed 7 August 1805. Quebec: J. Neilson, 1805.
98   _____. Société mécanique, bienveillante et amicale. *Règles et règlements de la société.* Quebec: Imprimé à la nouvelle imprimerie, 1810.
99   REID, Allana G. "The First Poor-Relief System of Canada." *Canadian Historical Review.* 27:4 (1946), pp. 424-31.

1.3   The Relief of the Poor in Nova Scotia and New Brunswick

100 AITON, Grace. "The Selling of Paupers by Public Auction in Sussex Parish." *Collections of the New Brunswick Historical Society.* 16 (1961), pp. 93-110.
101 BELDING, A.M. "The Devil's Poor: A Mild Form of Slavery Practiced in New Brunswick." *Canadian Magazine.* 46:5 (1915-16), pp. 382-84.
102 CAMPBELL, George Allen. "Social Life and Institutions of Nova Scotia in the 1830s." M.A., Dalhousie University, 1949.
103 FINGARD, Judith. "Attitudes Towards the Education of the Poor in Colonial Halifax." *Acadiensis.* 2:2 (Spring 1973), pp. 15-42.

104 _____. "The Relief of the Unemployed Poor in Saint John, Halifax, and St. John's 1815-1860." *Acadiensis.* 5:1 (Autumn 1975), pp. 32-53.

105 GOUETT, Paul Matthew. "The Halifax Orphan House 1752-1787." *Nova Scotia Historical Quarterly.* 6:3 (September 1976), pp. 281-91.

106 GRANT, Marguerite H.L. "Historical Sketches of Hospitals and Alms Houses in Halifax, Nova Scotia, 1749-1859." *Nova Scotia Medical Bulletin.* 27:4, 5, 8 (1938), pp. 229-38, 294-304, 491-512.

107 GREENHAUS, Brereton. "Paupers and Poor Houses: The Development of Poor Relief in Early New Brunswick." *Social History/ Histoire sociale.* 1 (April 1968), pp. 103-28.

108 HART, George. "Early Private Relief in Nova Scotia." *Welfare News.* 2:2 (July 1951), p.4.

109 _____. "The Halifax Poor Man's Friend Society, 1820-1827: An Early Social Experiment." *Canadian Historical Review.* 34:2 (1953), pp. 109-23.

110 _____. "Death of the Poor Law in Nova Scotia." *Canadian Welfare.* 34:5 (Dec. 1958), pp. 226-32.

111 MACDONALD, T.D., "Administration of Poor Relief in Nova Scotia", *Public Affairs,* 1:1 (August 1937), pp. 30-33.

112 _____. "The Nova Scotia Poor Law." *Public Affairs.* 1:2 (August 1937), pp. 30-33.

113 SAUNDERS, Catherine Estelle. "Social Conditions and Legislation in Nova Scotia 1815-1851." M.A., Dalhousie University, 1949.

114 THOMAS, Charles Hubert. "The Administration of the Poor Law in Nova Scotia 1749-1937." M.A., Dalhousie University, 1938.

115 WHALEN, J.M. "New Brunswick Poor Law Policy in the 19th Century." M.A., University of New Brunswick, 1968.

116 _____. "The Nineteenth Century Almshouse System in Saint John County." *Social History/ Historie sociale.* 7 (April 1971), pp. 5-28.

117 WILLIAMS, Relief. "Poor Relief and Medicine in Nova Scotia, 1749-1783." *Nova Scotia Historical Society Collections.* 24 (1938), pp. 33-56.

1.4   Charitable and Benevolent Societies

118 BAMMAN, Haley P. "The Ladies Benevolent Society of Hamilton, Ontario: Form and Function in Mid-Nineteenth Century Urban Philanthropy." *Canadian Social History Project* Interim Report. No. 4. (December 1972), pp. 162-217.

119 BRYCE, Mrs. M.S. *Historical Sketches of Charitable Institutions of Winnipeg.* Winnipeg: Manitoba Free Press, 1899.

120 CHARITY ORGANIZATION SOCIETY OF MONTREAL. *Annual Reports.* (1915-1916), pp. 58; (1916-1917), pp. 40.

121 COMMITTEE OF THE MONTREAL COUNCIL OF SOCIAL AGENCIES. *Report.* Being the findings of a social and financial survey of protestant and non-sectarian social agencies of an undenominational character in the city of Montreal, Quebec. November 1919.

122 COOPER, J.I. "The Quebec Ship Labourer's Benevolent Society." *Canadian Historical Review.* 30 (1949), pp. 336-43.

123 HARRISON, B. "For Church, Queen and Family: The Girl's Friendly Society, 1874-1920." *Past and Present.* 61 (November 1973).

124 LAI, Chuen-Yau. "The Chinese Consolidated Benevolent Association in Victoria: Its Origins and Functions." *British Columbia Studies.* 15 (Autumn 1972), pp. 53-67.

125   PATTERSON, Hartland M. "Montreal Pioneer Welfare Society Founded in 1815." *Canadian Welfare Summary.* 14:5 (January 1939), pp. 43-44.

126   STEWART, Herbert Leslie. *The Irish in Nova Scotia: Annals of the Charitable Irish Society of Halifax, 1786-1836.* Nova Scotia: Kentville Publishing Company, 1949.

1.5   Asylums and Public Charitable Institutions

127   EMERY, George N. "The Methodist Church and the European Foreigners of Winnipeg: The All Peoples Mission, 1889-1914." In *Transactions of the Historical and Scientific Society of Manitoba.* 28:3 (1971-1972), pp. 85-100.

128   JAFFARY, William. "A Day at the Waterloo Poor House and What I Learned There." *Waterloo Historical Society.* 57 (1969), pp. 72-78.

129   NOVA SCOTIA. Royal Commission in the Matter of Certain Charges Affecting the Treatment of the Poor in the County of Digby. "Commissioners Report." *Journals of the Nova Scotia House of Assembly.* Appendix 10, 1886.

130   ONTARIO. Inspector of Prisons and Public Charities. *Annual Report Upon the Hospitals And Charitable Institutions of the Province of Ontario.* 8 vols. Toronto: King's Printer, 1905-1926.

131   PARKER, (Dodds) Ethel. "The Origins and Early History of the Presbyterian Settlement House." In *The Social Gospel in Canada: Papers of the Inter-Disciplinary Conference on the Social Gospel in Canada.* March 21-24, 1973. University of Regina, pp. 86-121. Ottawa: National Museum of Man, 1975.

132   PRISONER'S AID SOCIETY OF CANADA. *County Paupers and County Houses of Industry.* Toronto: Dudley and Burns, 1894.

133   TORONTO INDUSTRIAL REFUGE. *Annual Report.* 1st-86th, 1854-1940. Toronto: Industrial Refuge, 1854.

1.6   Minimum Wages and Limitations on the Hours of Work: General

134   BATTYE, John H. "The Nine-Hour Movement of 1872, Genesis of the Canadian Labour Movement." M.A., University of Waterloo, 1971.

135   CANADA. Department of Labour. *Labour Legislation in Canada: A Historical Outline of the Principal Dominion and Provincial Labour Laws.* Ottawa: Department of Labour, 1945.

136   CHICANOT, E.L. "The Minimum Wage in Canada." *Commonwealth.* 27 (11 February 1938), pp. 430-31.

137   COE, V.F. *Minimum and Fair Wage Legislation. The Economic Aspect.* Kingston: Queen's University Conference on Industrial Relations, 1938.

138   DERRY, K., and DOUGLAS, P.H. "The Minimum Wage in Canada." *Journal of Political Economy.* 30:2 (April 1922), pp. 155-88.

139   DOVER, G.W. "Nine Hours for Canada." *American Federalist.* (September 1901), pp. 341-42.

140   HODGSON, Gordon Walter. "A Study of Canadian Male Minimum Wage Legislation." M.A., McMaster University, 1940.

141   NOVA SCOTIA. Commission of Hours of Labour. "Report." *Journals of the Nova Scotia House of Assembly.* Appendix 26, 1910.

142   RUHLMAN, J. "La question du juste salaire." *Revue canadienne.* 28 (1892), pp. 193-201.

1.7   Minimum Wages and Limitations on the Hours of Work: Women and Children

143   CANADA. Bureau of Statistics. *Children in Gainful Occupations*. Ottawa: King's Printer, 1929.

144   _____. Department of Labour. *The Employment of Children and Young Persons in Canada, December 1930*. Ottawa: King's Printer, 1930.

145   CANADIAN COUNCIL ON CHILD WELFARE. *A Comparative Study of the Child Labour Laws of Canada*. Ottawa: Canadian Council on Child Welfare, 1924.

146   COWLES, J.P. *The Juvenile Employment System of Ontario*. Ottawa: Canadian Council on Child Welfare. 1923.

147   EPSTEIN, E. "The Minimum Wage for Women and Its Application in Canada." M.A., McGill University, 1929.

148   LEGGE, K.B. "Labour Legislation in Canada Affecting Women and Children." M.A., McGill University, 1930.

149   MacDONALD, Dan J. "Into the Mines as a Child." *Atlantic Advocate*. 57:12 (August 1967), pp. 21-23.

150   NOVA SCOTIA. *Commission on the Hours of Labour, Wages and Working Conditions of Women Employed in Industrial Occupations*. Halifax: King's Printer,1920.

151   ONTARIO. Legislative Assembly. Select Committee on Child Labour. "Report" *Journals of the Legislative Assembly*. 1907.

152   QUEBEC. Women's Minimum Wage Commission. 1926-1935. *Report*. Quebec: King's Printer, 1935.

153   STEWART, Annabel M. "Child Labour Standards in Canada." *Social Welfare*. 2:1 (October 1919), pp. 17-20.

154   WHITTON, Charlotte E. *Canada and International Child Labour Conventions*. Canadian Council on Child Welfare, 1926.

155   _____. "The Canadian Provinces and the Child Labour Conventions." *Social Welfare*. 8:9 (August 1926), pp. 239-42.

156   _____. "Child Labour." *Social Welfare*. 1:5 (March 1919), pp. 142-44.

2.0   Organizations and Political Pressure Groups and Social Welfare Policy

2.1   Trade Unions

157   ATKINSON, W.D. "Organized Labour and the Laurier Administration." M.A., Carleton University, 1957.

158   AULD, F.C., and FINKELMAN, Jacob. *Labour and Social Legislation*. Toronto: Workers' Educational Association of Ontario, 1934.

159   BOURGOIN, Louis. "La journée de huit heures et l'organisation industrielle." *Revue trimestielle canadienne*. 21 (March 1920), pp. 3-38.

160   COMEAU, Robert *et al*. *L'action politique des ouvriers québécois fin du XIXe siècle à 1919. Recueil de documents*. Montreal: Les Presses de l'université du Québec, 1976.

161   FRENCH, Doris. *Faith, Sweat and Politics: The Early Trade Union Years in Canada*. Toronto: McClelland and Stewart, 1962.

162   GOLDBERG, Theodore Irving. "Trade Union Interest in Medical Care and Voluntary Health Insurance: A Study of Two Collectively Bargained Programmes." Ph.D., University of Toronto, 1962.

163 JAMIESON, Stuart Marshall. *Times of Trouble: Labour Unrest and Industrial Conflict in Canada, 1900-1966.* Ottawa: Privy Council Task Force on Labour Relations, Study No. 22, 1968.

164 LAZARUS, Morden. *The Long Winding Road: Canadian Labour in Politics.* West Vancouver: Boag Foundation, 1978.

165 _____. *Years of Hard Labour: An Account of the Canadian Working Man, His Organizations and Tribulations Over a Period of More Than A Hundred Years.* Don Mills: Cooperative Press Association for the Ontario Federation of Labour, 1974.

166 LIPTON, Charles. *Histoire du syndicalisme au Canada et au Québec, 1827-1959.* Montreal: Editions Parti pris, 1976.

167 _____. *The Trade Union Movement in Canada, 1827-1959.* Montreal: New Canada Press, 1973.

168 LOGAN, Harold Ames. *The History of Trade Union Organization in Canada.* Chicago: University of Chicago Press, 1928.

169 _____. *Trade Unions in Canada: Their Development and Functioning.* Toronto: Macmillan, 1948.

170 LOOSEMORE, T.R. "The British Columbia Labour Movement and Political Action 1879-1906." M.A., University of British Columbia, 1954.

171 MASTERS, Jane E. "Canadian Labour Press Opinion 1890-1914: A Study in Theoretical Radicalism and Political Conservatism." M.A., University of Western Ontario, 1970.

172 MOORE, Tom. "Trade Unions: Social Forces." *Social Welfare.* 1:10 (August 1919), pp. 259-60.

173 NEW BRUNSWICK FEDERATION OF LABOUR. *History of New Brunswick Federation of Labour.* Saint John: The Federation, 1933.

174 PENNINGTON, Edward, and WALKER, Ian. "The Role of Trade Unions in Social Welfare: An Exploratory Study of the Attitude of Trade Union Members Towards Health and Welfare Services." M.S.W., University of British Columbia, 1962.

175 ROBIN, Martin. *Radical Politics and Canadian Labour 1880-1930.* Kingston: Industrial Relations Centre, Queen's University, 1968.

176 _____. "The Trades and Labour Congress of Canada and Political Action: 1898-1908." *Relations industrielles.* 22:2 (April 1967), pp. 187-214.

2.2 Business and Professional Organizations

177 AKMAN, Dogan D., collector. *Policy Statements and Public Positions of the Canadian Association of Social Workers: A Source Book.* St. John's: Canadian Association of Social Workers, 1972.

178 CANADIAN ASSOCIATION OF SOCIAL WORKERS. *Brief.* Submitted to Rowell-Sirois Commission, 1939.

179 CLARK, S.D. *The Canadian Manufacturers' Association: A Study in Collective Bargaining and Political Pressure.* Toronto: University of Toronto Press, 1939.

180 _____. "The Canadian Manufacturers' Association: Its Economic and Social Implications." In *Essays in Political Economy in Honour of E.J. Urwick,* edited by H.A. Innis, pp. 75-84. Toronto: University of Toronto Press, 1938.

181 DYCK, B. "Attitudes and Actions of Canadian Association of Social Workers Members in the Prairies Towards Political Involvement." M.S.W., University of Calgary, 1972.

182   HELD, Frieda, JENNISON, Mary, and HENDERSON, Lillian. *A Brief History of the Ontario Welfare Council, 1908-1959.* Toronto: Ontario Welfare Council, 1959.

183   HUTT, H.L. "The Civic Improvement Movement in Ontario." *Canadian Municipal Journal.* (February 1909), pp. 65-66.

184   LATIMER, Elspeth Ann. "An Analysis of the Social Action Behaviour of the Canadian Association of Social Workers from its Organizational Beginning to Modern Times." D.S.W., University of Toronto, 1972.

185   SOCIAL SERVICE CONGRESS, Ottawa, 1914. *Proceedings.* Toronto: Social Service Council of Canada, 1914.

186   TAYLOR, M.G. "The Role of the Medical Profession in the Formulation and Execution of Public Policy." *Canadian Journal of Economics and Political Science.* 26:1 (February 1960), pp. 108-27.

187   WHARF, Brian. *The Role of Advisory Councils in Forming Social Policies: A Case Study of the National Council of Welfare.* Hamilton: School of Social Work, McMaster University, 1974.

2.3 Religious Organizations

188   L'ACTION SOCIALE CATHOLIQUE ET L'OEUVRE DE LA PRESSE CATHOLIQUE. *Motifs, programme, organisation, ressources.* Quebec: Marcotte, 1907.

189   ALLEN, H.T. "A View from the Manse: The Social Gospel and Social Crisis in British Columbia, 1929-1945. "In *The Social Gospel in Canada: Papers of the Inter-Disciplinary Conference on the Social Gospel in Canada, March 21-24, 1973. University of Regina,* edited by R. Allen, pp. 151-84. Ottawa: National Museum of Man, 1975.

190   ALLEN, Richard. *The Social Passion. Religion and Social Reform in Canada 1914-1928.* Toronto: University of Toronto Press, 1971.

191   _____. "The Crest and Crisis of the Social Gospel in Canada, 1916-1927." Ph.D., Duke University, 1967.

192   _____. "Salem Bland and the Social Gospel in Canada." M.A., University of Saskatchewan (Saskatoon), 1961.

193   _____. "The Social Gospel and the Reform Tradition in Canada 1890-1928." *Canadian Historical Review.* 49:4 (1968), pp. 381-99.

194   ALLEN, Richard, ed. *The Social Gospel in Canada: Papers of the Inter-Disciplinary Conference on the Social Gospel in Canada, March 21-24, 1973. University of Regina.* Ottawa: National Museum of Man, 1975.

195   ARCHAMBAULT, Joseph-Papin. *Le clergé et l'action sociale.* Montreal: Ecole sociale populaire, 1918.

196   _____. *La question sociale et nos devoirs de catholique.* Montreal: Ecole sociale populaire, 1917.

197   AUCLAIR, E.J. "Le mouvement social catholique canadien." *Revue canadienne.* 26 (1921), pp. 161-74.

198   CHRISTIE, Edward Alexander. "The Presbyterian Church in Canada and Its Official Attitude towards Public Affairs and Social Problems 1875-1925." M.A., University of Toronto Press, 1955.

199   CLARK, S.D. *Church and Sect in Canada.* Toronto: University of Toronto Press, 1948.

200   ECOLE SOCIALE POPULAIRE. *Constitution et programme.* Montreal: Ecole sociale populaire, 1911.

201   FRENCH, Goldwin S. *Parsons and Politics: The Role of the Wesleyan Methodists in Upper Canada and the Maritimes from 1780 to 1855.* Toronto: Ryerson Press, 1962.

202 GAUDREAU, Marie Agnes of Rome. "The Social Thought of French Canada as Reflected in the Semaine Sociale." Ph.D., Catholic University of America, 1946.

203 GAUDREAU, Sr. Agnes-de-Rome. *La pensée sociale du Canada français, telle que reflétée dans les Semaines Sociales.* Montreal: Ecole sociale populaire, 1946.

204 GAUTHIER, Georges. *La doctrine sociale de l'Eglise et la Cooperative Commonwealth Federation (C.C.F.).* Montreal: Ecole sociale populaire, 1934.

205 HARDY, René. "L'activité sociale du curé de Notre-Dame du Québec: aperçu de l'influence du clergé au milieu du XIXe siècle." *Histoire sociale/Social History.* 6 (November 1970), pp. 5-32.

206 JONES, Richard Allan. "L'idéologie de l'action catholique 1917-1939." Ph.D., Laval University, 1971.

207 LEVESQUE, Ernest. "Le rôle de l'action catholique dans la restauration de l'ordre social chrétien." M.A., Laval University, 1945.

208 MAGNEY, William H. "The Methodist Church and the National Gospel 1884-1914." *Bulletin.* Committee on Archives of the United Church of Canada. 20 (1969), pp. 3-95.

209 MONTPETIT, Edouard. *Un programme d'action sociale.* Montreal: Ecole sociale populaire, 1921.

210 _____. "La valeur pratique de la doctrine sociale catholique." *Revue trimestrielle canadienne.* 14 (1928), pp. 248-62.

211 ORLIKOW, Lionel. "A Survey of the Reform Movement in Manitoba, 1910-1920." M.A., University of Manitoba, 1969.

212 PALKER, Edward. "The Anglican Church and the Issue of Capital and Labour in Canada, 1913-1946." Ph.D., University of Ottawa, 1969.

213 PERRAULT, Antonio. *L'action sociale.* Montreal: Ecole sociale populaire, 1920.

214 PERRIER, P. "Le mouvement social catholique." *Revue canadienne.* 3 (1909), pp. 500-509.

215 POULIOT, Léon. "Bishop Bourget: Profiles 2." *Canadian Welfare.* 41:4 (July/August 1965), pp. 180-83.

216 ROYCE, Marion. "The Contribution of the Methodist Church to Social Welfare in Canada." M.A., University of Toronto, 1940.

217 SAINT-PIERRE, Arthur. *L'oeuvre des congrégations religieuses de charité dans la province de Québec.* Montreal: Bibliothèque canadienne, 1932.

218 _____. *Questions et oeuvres sociales de chez nous.* Montreal: Ecole sociale populaire, 1914.

219 _____. "The Charitable Works of Religious Orders." *Revue trimestielle canadienne.* 13 (December 1927), pp. 389-402.

220 SHADD, David Thomas W. "State Aid Versus Voluntarism: Upper Canada Wesleyan Methodist Policy 1832-1855." M.A., University of Toronto, 1957.

221 THOMAS, Ernest. "Social Reform and the Methodist Church." *Canadian Forum.* 1:9 (June 1921), pp. 264-66.

222 UNITED CHURCH OF CANADA. Committee on Economic and Social Research. Brief to Rowell Sirois Commission. *A Brief on Social Security by the Committee on Economic and Social Research of the Board of Evangelism and Social Services of the United Church of Canada.* 11:8, 1938.

2.4 Cooperatives

223 ANSLEM, Sister. *The Antigonish Idea and Social Welfare*. Antigonish: St. Francis Xavier University Press, 1964.

224 ARSENAULT, Ellen. "Le progrès social dans l'est du Canada; le mouvement d'Antigonish." *Education des adultes*. 3:4 (1952), pp. 28-34.

225 BAIN, R.G. "Consumer's Cooperatives in Nova Scotia." M.A., Acadia University, 1968.

226 BIRD, W.R. "Co-op Conquest." *MacLean's Magazine*. 9 (1 August 1936), pp. 32-34.

227 BROWN, Kingsley. "A Tranquil Social Revolution." *Port and Province*. (October 1935), pp. 29-33.

228 CAMERON, Bill, and ROBERTSON, Terry. *Saskatchewan Wheat Pool 1924-1974*. Regina: Saskatchewan Wheat Pool, 1974.

229 COADY, Moses Michael. *Masters of Their Own Destiny: The Story of the Antigonish Movement of Adult Education Through Economic Cooperation*. New York: Harper, 1939.

230 _____. *The Social Significance of the Co-operative Movement*. Antigonish: Extension Department, St. Francis-Xavier University, 1962.

231 COOPERATIVE UNION OF SASKATCHEWAN. *Cooperation and Reconstruction*. Submissions to the Saskatchewan Reconstruction Council. Regina, 1944.

232 DESROCHERS, I. "Une splendide réalisation: l'institut Desjardins." *Relations*. 277 (January 1964), p. 26.

233 GAUVIN-CHOUINARD, M., et al. "Vue d'ensemble sur le mouvement coopératif acadien." *L'Acayen*. 3 (Summer 1976), pp. 10-34.

234 INTERNATIONAL LABOUR ORGANIZATION. *The Co-operative Movement in the Americas: An International Symposium*. Montreal: International Labour Organization, 1943.

235 LAIDLAW, Alexander Fraser. *The Campus and the Community; the Global Impact of the Antigonish Movement*. Montreal: Harvest House, 1961.

236 _____. (ed.) *The Man From Margaree; Writings and Speeches of M.M. Coady, Educator, Reformer, Priest*. Toronto: McClelland and Stewart, 1971.

237 _____. "The Maritime Co-operative Movement Today." *Public Affairs*. 10 (March 1947), pp. 143-46.

238 LAMARCHE, Jacques. *Alphonse Dejardins, un homme au service des autres*. Montreal: Editions du jour, 1977.

239 LAVILLE, Christian. "L'assurance-vie Desjardins 1948-1968." M.A., Laval University, 1971.

240 LOTZ, Jim. "The Historical and Social Setting of the Antigonish Movement." *Nova Scotia Historical Quarterly*. 5:2 (June 1975), pp. 96-116.

241 MacDONALD, C.P. "The Cooperative Movement in Nova Scotia." M.A., McGill University, 1938.

242 MacPHERSON, Ian. "Patterns in the Maritime Cooperative Movement 1900-1945." *Acadiensis*. 5:1 (Autumn 1975), pp. 67-84.

243 MARQUIS, P.E. "Les caisses populaires Desjardins." M.A., Laval University, n.d.

244 MAYO, H.B. "Cooperative Movement in Newfoundland." *Public Affairs*. 4:1 (August 1940), pp. 119-23.

245 MIFFLEN, F.J. "The Antigonish Movement: A Revitalized Movement in Eastern Nova Scotia." Ph.D., Boston College, 1974.

246 ROBY, Yves. *Alphonse Dejardins et les caisses populaires 1854-1920.* Montreal: Fides, 1964.

247 SACOUMAN, Robert James. "Social Origins of Antigonish Movement Cooperative Associations in Eastern Nova Scotia." Ph.D., University of Toronto, 1976.

248 _____. "Underdevelopment and the Structural Origins of Antigonish Movement Cooperatives in Eastern Nova Scotia." *Acadiensis.* 7:1 (Autumn 1977), pp. 66-86.

249 SASKATCHEWAN COOP WHEAT PRODUCERS. *Its Aims, Origins, Operations and Progress.* Saskatoon: Saskatchewan Coop Wheat Producers, Pamphlet No.1, 1928.

250 TUFTS, Evelyn S. "The Cooperative Movement." *Canadian Geographical Journal.* 21:2 (August 1940), pp. 98-105.

251 TURCOTTE, Gaston. "De l'idéologie des caisses populaires Desjardins." M.A., Laval University, 1971.

252 VAILLANCOURT, Cyrille, and FAUCHER, Albert. *Alphonse Dejardins, pionnier de la coopération d'épargne et de crédit en Amérique.* Lévis: Le Quotidien, 1950.

253 WOODSIDE, Willson. "The Co-ops Come to Canada." *Canadian Magazine.* 89:18 (June 1938), pp. 41-42.

254 WRIGHT, James Frederick Church. *Prairie Progress, Consumer Cooperation in Saskatchewan.* Saskatoon: Modern Press, 1956.

2.5 Women's Organizations

255 ABERDEEN, Countess of., ed. *Our Lady of the Sunshine and Her International Visitors.* Toronto: Copp Clark, 1910.

256 BRIGDEN, B. "One Women's Campaign for Social Purity and Social Reform." In *The Social Gospel in Canada: Papers of the Inter-Disciplinary Conference on the Social Gospel in Canada, March 21-24, 1973. University of Regina,* edited by R. Allen, pp. 36-62, Ottawa: National Museum of Man, 1975.

257 CORMACK, B. *Perennials and Politics: The Life Story of the Honorable Irene Parlby.* Sherwood Park, Alberta: Professional Printers, 1968.

258 GIBBON, John Murray. *The Victorian Order of Nurses for Canada, 1897-1947.* Montreal: Southam Press, 1947.

259 GULLEN, Dr. Augusta Stowe. *History of the Formation of the National Council of Women in Canada.* Toronto, 1931.

260 HARSHAW, Josephine. *When Women Work Together: The Story of the Y.W.C.A.* Toronto: Ryerson Press, 1966.

261 INNIS, Mary Quayle. *Unfold the Years: A History of the Young Women's Christian Association in Canada.* Toronto: McClelland and Stewart, 1949.

262 KIDD, Dorothy. "Women's Organizations: Learning From Yesterday." In *Women at Work 1850-1930,* edited by Janice Acton, Bonnie Shepard and Penny Goldsmith, pp. 331-61. Toronto: Canadian Women's Educational Press, 1974.

263 LEAGUE FOR WOMEN'S RIGHTS. *Brief History of the League for Women's Rights.* Montreal: League for Women's Rights, 1941.

264 MacDOUGALL, H.J. "Women's Institutes in Nova Scotia." *Public Affairs.* 2:1 (August 1938), pp. 3-5.

265 OTTY, Marianne T. *Fifty Years of Women's Institutes in New Brunswick 1911-1961. A History.* Frederiction, 1961.

266 SHAW, R. *Proud Heritage: A History of the National Council of Women of Canada*. Toronto: Ryerson Press, 1957.
267 STRONG-BOAG, Veronica. *The Parliament of Women: The National Council of Women of Canada, 1893-1929*. Ottawa: National Museum of Man, 1976.
268 THORPE, W.L. "Lady Aberdeen and the National Council of Women of Canada." M.A., Queen's University, 1973.

3.0   The Welfare State in Canada

3.1   Ideas About the Welfare State

269 ADAM, G.M. "Pauperism and Its Remedies." *Bystander*. 2 (May 1881), p. 246.
270 ARCHAMBAULT, Joseph-Papin. *L'autorité sociale: sa nature, sa nécessité, son origine, son exercice*. Quebec: Action sociale, 1909.
271 _____. *Directives sociales catholiques*. Montreal: Ecole sociale populaire, 1933.
272 BEDARD, M.H., "Le socialisme." *Revue canadienne*. 30 (1894), pp. 82-93.
273 BELANGER, G.M. "La pensée catholique en matière de sécurité sociale." *Service social*. 9:2 (1960), pp. 120-36.
274 BERTRAND, P. "Les doctrines sociales." *Revue canadienne*. 4 (1867), pp. 266-83.
275 BOURASSA, Henri. "Speech of Mr. Henri Bourassa, on Economic and Social Reform." Delivered in the House of Commons on Tuesday, 20 March 1934. Ottawa: King's Printer, 1934.
276 _____. "Une mauvaise loi, l'assistance politique." *Brochures, discours, conférences, causeries 1901-1943*. vol. 3 No. 17.
277 BOUVIER, Emile. *Le samaritanisme moderne ou service social*. Montreal: Ecole sociale populaire, 1940.
278 CAMBRAY, Alfred. "Le socialisme, religion nouvelle." *Revue canadienne*. 50 (1906), pp. 379-96.
279 CANADIAN CONFERENCE ON SOCIAL WELFARE. "Social Evolution: Freedom or Controls?" In *Proceedings*. Ottawa: The Council, 1973.
280 CASSIDY, Harry M. "The Significance of a National Welfare Council in Post War Canada." *Canadian Welfare*. 21:2 (June 1945), pp. 2-6.
281 COBURN, Carrol L. "A Union View of the Security Problem." In *Security in an Industrial Economy*, 8th Annual Conference Industrial Relations Centre, McGill University. Montreal: McGill University, 1956. pp. 72-90.
282 COUSINEAU, Jacques. *L'évolution de la mentalité sociale au Québec depuis 1931*. Montreal: Institut social populaire, 1956.
283 CREALY, Laura May. "Federal Social Welfare Legislation." M.S.W., St. Patrick's College, 1952.
284 DAVIDSON, G.F. "Social Security — Too Much of a Good Thing?" *Canadian Welfare*. 26:8 (March 1951), pp. 3-9.
285 DAVIS, Richard E. "Reflections on Social Welfare Policy in My Time." *Public Welfare*. Number 1 of a special series of supplements. (June 1963), pp. 7-18.

286   DION, G. "La doctrine sociale de l'Eglise dans le Québec." *Perspectives sociales*. 17:1 (1962), pp. 1-5.

287   DIXON, William George, ed. *Social Welfare and the Preservation of Human Values*. Anniversary Papers of the School of Social Work, University of British Columbia. Toronto: J.M. Dent, 1957.

288   DOUGLAS, Monteath. "Economic and Social Consequences of Fringe Benefits." *Relations industrielles*. 15:2 (April 1960), pp. 181-92.

289   DRUMMOND, A.T. "Some Workingmen's Problems." *Queen's Quarterly*. 5:1 (July 1897), pp. 61-66.

290   FOTHERINGHAM, John Brooks, ed. *Transition: Policies for Social Action*. Toronto: McClelland and Stewart, 1966.

291   GOVAN, E.S.L. "Public Assistance in Modern Society." *Canadian Welfare*. 28:1 (May 1952), pp. 5-9.

292   HAMEL, Louis N. "L'Etat et le problème social." *Semaines sociales du Canada*. 7e session, pp. 152-82. Montreal: Bibliothèque de l'action canadienne-française, 1927.

293   HAMEL, M. "L'état et l'assistance sociale." *Service social*. 13:1 (1964), pp. 38-59.

294   HANSON, Eric John. *The Individual and the State*. Ottawa: National Liberal Federation, 1969.

295   HAY, John. "A General View of Socialistic Schemes." *Queen's Quarterly*. 3:4 (April 1896), pp. 283-95.

296   KEAGEY, Joan G. "Desirable Goals in Public Welfare." *Social Worker*. 19:1 (October 1950), pp. 21-23.

297   KENT, Tom. "Welfare in Canada: The Challenge." *Canadian Welfare*. 35:5 (September 1959), pp. 198-209.

298   KING, William Lyon MacKenzie. *Industry and Humanity: A Study in the Principles Underlying Industrial Reconstruction*. Boston and New York: Houghton Mifflin Company, 1918.

299   _____. "Welfare and the Modern State." *Canadian Welfare*. 24:7 (January 1949), pp. 2-3.

300   LEAGUE FOR SOCIAL RECONSTRUCTION. Research Committee. *Social Planning for Canada*. Toronto: Thomas Nelson, 1935.

301   LEMIEUX, Gérard. "Vers une sécurité plus démocratique." *Actualité économique*. 28:1 (April-June, 1952), pp. 90-104.

302   MacMILLAN, John W. *The Limits of Social Legislation*. Toronto: Clark Irwin, 1933.

303   MARSH, Leonard C. "The Welfare State: Is It a Threat to Canada?" In *Proceedings of the Canadian Conference on Social Work, 1950*. pp. 34-44. Ottawa: Canadian Conference on Social Work. 1950.

304   MARTIN, P. "Social Welfare in Canada: A Progress Report." In *Proceedings of Canadian Conference on Social Work*. pp. 11-20. 12th Biennial Meeting. Vancouver, British Columbia, 1950.

305   MAVOR, James. "The Relation of Economic Study to Private and Public Charity." *Annals of American Academy of Political and Social Sciences*. 4 (1893), pp. 34-60.

306   MORGAN, J.S. *Welfare in Canada: Which Way Out of Chaos?* Ottawa: Canadian Welfare Council, 1962.

307   _____. "Social Policies for Canada." *Canada's Mental Health*. Department of National Health and Welfare, 17:2 (1969), pp. 11-13.

308   _____. "Who are the Beneficiaries?" *Social Worker*. 30:1 (January 1962), pp. 4-10.

309   MORIN, C. "Les critères dans la détermination des priorités en bien-être social." *Service social.* 17:1 (1957), pp. 22-27 and 2, pp. 63-75.

310   PAQUET, L.A. "Le rôle social de l'Etat." *Etudes et appréciations IV, Thèmes sociaux.* pp. 263-89. Quebec: Imprimeur franciscaine missionnaire, 1922.

311   _____. "Le rôle social de l'Etat." *Semaines sociales du Canada.* 1re session, (1920), pp. 69-72.

312   _____. "Le socialisme d'Etat." (L'Eglise: les questions ouvrières et l'Etat). *Etudes et appréciations III, nouveaux mélanges canadiens.* pp. 79-106. Quebec: Imprimeur franciscaine missionnaire, 1919.

313   PARIZEAU, Gérard. "Assurance au Canada." *Actualité économique.* 15:1 (November 1939), pp. 1-9.

314   LE PROGRAMME DE RESTAURATION SOCIALE EXPLIQUE ET COMMENTE. Montréal: Ecole sociale populaire, 1934.

315   RIOUX, Marcel. "La valeur du catholicisme dans le service social, étude faite en référence au milieu canadien-français." M.A., Laval University, 1957.

316   ROYAL, Joseph. "Le socialisme aux Etats-Unis et au Canada." *Revue canadienne.* 12 (1894), pp. 49-61.

317   SAINT-PIERRE, Arthur. "Esquisse historique de la pensée sociale au Canada français 1910-1935." *Culture.* 18 (September 1957), pp. 316-25.

318   SEMAINE SOCIALE DE SAINT-JEAN. *La sécurité sociale, rapport de la semaine sociale de Saint-Jean.* Montreal: Edition de l'institut populaire, 1952.

319   SEMAINES SOCIALES DU CANADA. *Le rôle social de la charité.* 28e session. Montreal: Institut social populaire, 1951.

320   SHIFRIN, Leonard. "The Withering Away of Welfare." In *Visions 2020, Fifty Canadians in Search of a Future.* Edited by Stephen Clarkson. Edmonton: Hurtig, 1970, pp. 179-182.

321   SHORTT, Adam. "Recent Phases of Socialism." *Queen's Quarterly.* 5:1 (July 1897), pp. 11-21.

322   TAYLOR, Alice. "The Meaning of Relief." *Social Worker.* 22:3 (March 1954), pp. 3-10.

323   THIBAULT, Gilles. "Evolution de la pensée face aux secours directs pour la période de crise de 1929 à 1938." M.A., University of Montreal, 1969.

324   TOUZEL, Bessie. "Welfare in Canada: The Response." *Canadian Welfare.* 35:5 (September 1959), pp. 199, 210-19.

325   TREMBLAY, M. "Le welfare state et la sécurité sociale." *Service social.* 9:2 (1960), pp. 16-35.

326   TREMBLAY, René. *Plein-emploi, élément fondamental de la sécurité de la famille ouvrière.* pp. 29-51. 6e Congrès des relations industrielles de Laval. Quebec: Les Presses de l'université Laval, 1951.

327   TRIST, Eric. *The Relation of Welfare and Development in the Transition to Post-Industrialism.* Ottawa: Canadian Centre for Community Studies, 1967.

328   UNIVERSITY LEAGUE FOR SOCIAL REFORM. *The Prospect of Change: Proposals for Canada's Future.* edited by Abraham Rotstein. Toronto: McGraw-Hill, 1965.

329   WAISGLASS, Harry. *Goals for Social Policy.* Ottawa: Department of Labour, 1967.

330 WHITELEY, A.S. "The Church and Social Control." *Canadian Forum.* 12:139 (April 1932), pp. 251-53.
331 WOLFENDEN, Hugh Herbert. *The Real Meaning of Social Insurance: Its Present Status and Tendencies.* Toronto: Macmillan, 1932.
332 WOODSWORTH, J.S. *My Neighbour, A Study of City Conditions, A Plea for Social Service.* Toronto: University of Toronto Press, 1972.
333 _____. *Labour's Case in Parliament; A Summary and Compilation of the Speeches of J.S. Woodsworth in the Canadian House of Commons 1921-1928.* Ottawa: Canadian Brotherhood of Railway Employees, 1929.
334 YELAJA, Shankar. "What is Social Policy? Its Assumptions, Definitions and Uses." In *Canadian Social Policy*, edited by S. Yelaja, pp. 3-23. Waterloo: Wilfrid Laurier University Press, 1978.

3.2 Government Policies

3.2.1. Federal

335 CANADA. Advisory Committee on Reconstruction. *Report on Social Security for Canada.* Prepared by L.C. Marsh for Advisory Committee on Reconstruction. Ottawa, 1943.
336 _____. Constitutional Conference. *Income Security and Social Services; Government of Canada Working Paper on the Constitution.* Sécurité du revenu et services sociaux; gouvernement du Canada document de travail sur la constitution. Ottawa: Queen's Printer, 1969.
337 _____. Department of National Health and Welfare. *Income Security for Canadians.* Ottawa: Health and Welfare, 1970.
338 _____. Department of National Health and Welfare. *Federal-Provincial Working Paper on Income Support and Supplementation.* Ottawa: Federal-Provincial Conferences of Ministers of Welfare, 1975.
339 _____. Department of National Health and Welfare. Policy and Program Development and Coordination Branch. *Social Security in Canada, 3rd Edition.* Ottawa: Health and Welfare, 1974.
340 _____. Department of National Health and Welfare. *Social Security Data Book.* Ottawa: Health and Welfare, 1973.
341 _____. Department of National Health and Welfare. *Social Security and Public Welfare Services in Canada 1972.* Ottawa: Health and Welfare, 1973.
342 _____. Department of National Health and Welfare. *Working Paper on Social Security in Canada.* Ottawa: Information Canada, 1973.
343 _____. Government of Canada. *Income Security and Social Services: Working Paper on the Constitution.* Ottawa: Queen's Printer, 1969.
344 _____. House of Commons Special Committee on Social Security. *Minutes of Proceedings and Evidence*, 1944 Session. Ottawa: King's Printer, 1944.
345 _____. Privy Council Special Planning Secretariat. *Meeting Poverty.* Papers from the Canadian Conference on Poverty, December 1965. Ottawa: Queen's Printer, 1966.
346 _____. Senate Special Committee on Poverty. *Report: Poverty in Canada.* Ottawa: Information Canada, 1971.

3.2.2 Provincial

347   ALBERTA. Department of Health and Social Development. *Income Security in Canada. Alberta's Position.* Government of Alberta. Position Paper No. 10. Edmonton: Department of Health and Social Development, 1973.

348   BRITISH COLUMBIA. Department of Human Resources. *Working Paper on Income Security.* Victoria: Government Printer, 1973.

349   BRITISH COLUMBIA'S PROPOSALS ON INCOME SECURITY IN CANADA. First Ministers' Conference, Ottawa, May 23-25, 1973, 1973.

350   ONTARIO. Ministry of Treasury, Economics, and Intergovernmental Affairs. Joint Committee on Economic Policy. *Directions for Economic and Social Policy in Ontario.* Toronto: The Ministry, 1971.

351   _____. Ministry of Treasury, Economics, and Intergovernmental Affairs. Taxation and Fiscal Policy Branch. *Cost of the Federal Guaranteed Annual Income Proposal.* Toronto: The Ministry, 1976.

352   ONTARIO WELFARE COUNCIL. *A Review of Proposed Social Services and Income Security Policies and Legislation.* Toronto: The Council, 1976.

353   QUEBEC. Conseil des Affaires sociales et de la famille. *La notion du revenu minimum: l'état et la question et les recommandations.* Quebec: le Conseil, 1974.

354   _____. Ministère des Affaires sociales. *Analyse du livre blanc fédéral sur la sécurité du revenu.* Quebec: Ministère des Affaires sociales 1971.

355   _____. *Vers un revenu mininum garanti: Discours en deuxième lecture prononcé par Monsieur C. Forget.* Ministère des Affaires sociales. Quebec: Assemblée nationale, 1974.

356   SASKATCHEWAN. Legislative Assembly. Select Special Committee on Social Security and Health Services. *Final Report, Adopted by the Legislative Assembly, March 31, 1944.* Chairman: B.D. Hogarth. 1944.

3.2.3 Intergovernmental

357   DOMINION-PROVINCIAL CONFERENCE ON RECONSTRUCTION, OTTAWA, 1945-1946. *Health, Welfare and Labour;* Reference Book for Dominion-Provincial Conference. Ottawa: King's Printer, 1945.

358   _____. *Dominion and Provincial Submissions and Plenary Conference Discussions.* Ottawa: King's Printer, 1946.

359   FEDERAL-PROVINCIAL CONFERENCE OF MINISTERS OF WELFARE. *A Comprehensive System for Evaluating the Impact of Alternate Welfare Policies.* Ottawa: Information Canada, 1973.

360   WORKING PARTY ON INCOME MAINTENANCE. "Background Paper on Income Support and Supplementation." In *Federal-Provincial Social Security Review.* Ottawa: Information Canada, 1975.

361   _____. "Quantitative Report on Income Support/Supplementation to the Continuing Committee on Social Security." In *Federal-Provincial Social Security Review,* Document No. 264, Ottawa: Information Canada, 1975.

3.3   The Depression, The BNA Act, and Social Welfare Policy

362   BUREAU INTERNATIONAL DU TRAVAIL. *Le rapport Rowell-Sirois: Une affirmation nouvelle de la foi démocratique du Canada dans le progrès social.* Montreal, 1941.

363   CANADA. Royal Commission on Dominion-Provincial Relations. *Report.* Ottawa: King's Printer, 1940.

364   CANADIAN MEDICAL ASSOCIATION. *Submission to the Royal Commission on Dominion-Provincial Relations.* Ottawa: The Association, 1938.

365   CANADIAN WELFARE COUNCIL. *Implications for the Social Services in the Report on Dominion-Provincial Relations.* Ottawa: Canadian Welfare Council. 1940.

366   _____. *Welfare Services for the Canadian People.* Submission to the Royal Commission on Dominion-Provincial Relations. Ottawa: Canadian Welfare Council, 1938.

367   CASSIDY, H.M. *The Problem of Overlapping Services in Health and Welfare as Between the Dominion and the Provinces.* Submission to the Royal Commission on Dominion-Provincial Relations, 1938.

368   _____. "The Rowell-Sirois Report and the Social Services in Summary." In *Implications for the Social Services in the Report on Dominion-Provincial Relations.* Ottawa: Canadian Welfare Council, 1940.

369   _____. "Social Services in a Federal System: Royal Commission on Dominion-Provincial Relations." *Social Service Review.* 14:12 (December 1940), pp. 678-709.

370   CLAXTON, Brooke. "Social Reform and the Constitution." *Canadian Journal of Economics and Political Science.* 1:3 (August 1935), pp. 409-35.

371   CREIGHTON, Donald Grant. *British North America at Confederation.* Appendix 2. Royal Commission on Dominion-Provincial Relations. Ottawa: King's Printer, 1939.

372   GOLDENBERG, H.C. "Social Legislation and the Canadian Constitution." *Canadian Welfare.* 14:4 (November 1938), pp. 1-6.

373   GRAUER, Albert Edward. *Public Assistance and Social Insurance: A Study Prepared for the Royal Commission on Dominion-Provincial Relations.* Ottawa: King's Printer, 1939.

374   LAMBERT, R.S. *Our Other War Aim: The Social Services as Mirrored in the Sirois Report.* Toronto: The Canadian Association for Adult Education, 1941.

375   LEAGUE FOR SOCIAL RECONSTRUCTION. *Canada — One or Nine?* Brief submitted to the Royal Commission on Dominion-Provincial Relations. 1938.

376   MARSH, L.C., and WHITTON, Charlotte. "Administrative Implications Regarding Unemployment Insurance, Employment Services and Unemployment Aid." In *Implications for the Social Services in the Report on Dominion-Provincial Relations.* Ottawa: Canadian Welfare Council, 1940.

377   MENARD, Clément. "Les lois sociales canadiennes de 1935. (Lois Bennett) Contexte dans lequel fut présentée cette législation. Sa nature et ses conséquences." M.A., Laval University, 1961.

378   PURVIS, Arthur B. "Obligations of Government Towards Social Security." *Child and Family Welfare.* 13:3 (September 1937), pp. 1-10.

379   RICHTER, L. "Social Insurance and Politics." *University of Toronto Quarterly.* 6:2 (January 1937), pp. 254-66.

380   SAUNDERS, S.A., and BACK, Eleanor. *The Rowell-Sirois Commission, Part I: A Summary of the Report; Part II: A Criticism of the Report.* Toronto: Ryerson Press, 1940.
381   SCOTT, F.R. *Social Reconstruction and the B.N.A. Act.* League for Social Reconstruction Pamphlet No. 4. Toronto: Nelson, 1934.
382   WELFARE COUNCIL OF TORONTO AND DISTRICT. *Problems of Relief and Assistance of Need and Connected Problems of National, Provincial and Local Administration.* A Brief Presented to the Royal Commission on Dominion-Provincial Relations. The Council, 1938.

3.4   Postwar Reconstruction and Social Security: The Debate

383   ANGERS, François-Albert. "French Canada and Social Security." *Canadian Journal of Economics and Political Science.* 10:3 (1944), pp. 355-64.
384   Brady, Alexander. "Reconstruction in Canada: A Note on Policies and Plans." *Canadian Journal of Economics and Political Science.* 8:3 (1942), pp. 460-68.
385   _____, and SCOTT, Francis Reginald, eds. *Canada after the War. Studies in Political, Social and Economic Policies for Post-War Canada.* Toronto: Macmillan, 1943.
386   CANADA. Advisory Committee on Reconstruction. *Final Report.* Prepared by L.C. Marsh. Ottawa: King's Printer, 1943.
387   _____. Advisory Committee on Reconstruction. *Report on Social Security for Canada.* Prepared by L.C. Marsh. Ottawa: King's Printer, 1943.
388   _____. Parliament. Senate. Special Committee on Economic Reestablishment and Social Security. *Proceedings of the Special Committee on Economic Re-establishment and Social Security.* Ottawa: King's Printer, 1943.
389   CANADIAN WELFARE COUNCIL. *Dominion-Provincial Relations and Social Security.* Ottawa, The Council, 1946.
390   CARMAN, F.A. "Social Security and the B.N.A. Act." *Dalhousie Review.* 23:1 (April 1943), pp. 23-28.
391   CASSIDY, H.M. *Social Security and Reconstruction in Canada.* Toronto: Ryerson Press, 1943.
392   _____. "The Dominion Proposals on Social Security 1945." In *This is the Peace.* pp. 96-118. edited by Violet Anderson. Toronto: Ryerson Press, 1945.
393   _____. "Three Social Security Plans for Canada." *Public Affairs.* 7:2 (March 1944), pp. 67-74.
394   DAVIDSON, George F. "The Future Development of Social Security in Canada." *Canadian Welfare.* 18:7 (January 1943), pp. 2-5, 26-32.
395   _____. "Marsh Report on Social Security for Canada." *Canadian Welfare.* 19:1 (April 1943), pp. 3-6.
396   FERGUSON, M. "Dominion Plan for Social Security." *Canadian Welfare.* 21:6 (December 1945), pp. 17-21.
397   GRAUER, A.E. "Canada's Program of Social Security: The Marsh Report and the Report of the Advisory Committee on Health Insurance." *Public Affairs.* 6:4 (Summer 1943), pp. 181-87.
398   HORN, Michiel. "Leonard Marsh and the Coming of the Welfare State in Canada: A Review Article." *Histoire sociale/ Social History.* 9:7 (1976), pp. 197-204.

399   JAFFARY, S.K. "Social Security: The Beveridge and Marsh Reports." *Canadian Journal of Economics and Political Science.* 9:4 (November 1943), pp. 571-92.

400   JAMES, F.C. "The Planning of Canada's Reconstruction Policies." *Canadian Chartered Accountant.* 41:231 (October 1942), pp. 250-64.

401   KING, William Lyon MacKenzie. "Reconstruction Policy of the Governments of Canada, the Union of South Africa and the United States." *International Labour Review.* 46:6 (December 1942), pp. 718-31.

402   LEVESQUE, Georges-Henri, et DESPRES, J.P. *Mémoire sur la législation du travail et la sécurité sociale dans la province de Québec.* Quebec, 1943.

403   McARTHUR, A. "Canada's Road to Social Security." *Canadian Business.* 17:3 (March 1944), pp. 44-47, 100.

404   MARSH, Leonard. *Social Security for Canada.* Toronto: University of Toronto Press, 1975.

405   ———. "Basis of Social Security." *Canadian Business.* 16:6 (June 1943), p. 6.

406   ———. "Social Security Planning in Canada." *International Labour Review.* 47:5 (May 1943), pp. 591-616.

407   MORGAN, J.S. "A Meeting of Minds: A Report on the Round Table on Social Security Held at the University of Toronto, May 1948." *Canadian Welfare.* 24:3 (July 1948), pp. 2-10.

408   "Report on Social Security for Canada." *Labour Gazette.* 42:7 (April 1943), pp. 429-33.

409   ROWAT, Donald C. "Financing Social Security." *Public Affairs.* 7:2 (Winter 1945), pp. 97-103.

410   SEMAINES SOCIALES DU CANADA. *La restauration sociale; compte rendu des cours et conférences.* Montreal: Ecole sociale populaire, 1944.

411   TOUZEL, Bessie, and CALNAN, Wilfrid. "Social Security — Two Points of View." *Social Worker.* 12:4 (March 1944), pp. 3-8.

412   TUCK, R. "Social Security: An Administrative Solution to the Dominion-Provincial Problem." *Canadian Journal of Economics and Political Science.* 13:2 (May 1947), pp. 256-75.

413   WHITTON, Charlotte. *The Dawn of Ampler Life: Some Aids to Social Security.* Toronto: Macmillan, 1943.

414   ———. *Security for Canadians.* Toronto: Canadian Institute of International Affairs, 1943.

415   ———. *Social Security and Welfare in Canada.* Reprint of a series of articles April 25-June 6, 1945 from the *Family Herald* and *Weekly Star.* Ottawa: Department of Health and Welfare, 1945.

3.5   State Intervention and Social Security: The Debate in the 1960s and the 1970s

3.5.1   Poverty and Social Security

416   ADAMS, Ian, *et al. The Real Poverty Report.* Edmonton: Hurtig, 1971.

417   ———. "Anti-Poverty Policies and Changing Welfare Concepts in Canada." *Social Security Bulletin.* 7 (1970), pp. 13-20.

418   BEAUPRE, Louis. *La guerre à la pauvreté.* Montreal: Editions du Jour, 1968.

419 BENDER, Lloyd D., and GREEN, Bernal L. "Negative Taxation and Poverty." *Canadian Journal of Agricultural Economics.* 16:2 (June 1968), pp. 112-21.

420 BLACK, Edwin R. "Poor Policy: Guaranteed Annual Poverty Proposals." *Queen's Quarterly.* 79:1 (Spring 1972), pp. 17-26.

421 CONSEIL DES OEUVRES DE MONTREAL. *Une politique sociale pour le Québec.* Mémoire préliminaire présenté à la Commission royale d'enquête sur la santé et le bien-être social, pour le Conseil des oeuvres de Montréal et the Montreal Council of Social Agencies, Quebec: Commission d'enquête sur la santé et le bien-être social, 1967.

422 COURCHENE, Thomas J. "The Poverty Reports, Negative Income Taxation and the Constitution: An Analysis and a Compromise Proposal." *Canadian Public Administration.* 16:3 (Fall 1973), pp. 349-69.

423 DALHOUSIE UNIVERSITY. Institute of Public Affairs. *Poverty in Nova Scotia.* Brief for Special Committee on Poverty, Senate of Canada, November 1969. Halifax: Institute of Public Affairs, 1971.

424 DYCK, Perry Rand. "Poverty and Policy-Making in the 1960s: The Canada Assistance Plan." Ph.D., Queen's University, 1973.

425 GILCHRIST, Gayle Marlene. "Poverty in Canada and the United States: A Review and Critique of the Literature With Special Emphasis on Mental and Physical Health and Law Related to Poverty." M.S.W., University of Toronto, 1966.

426 GONICK, C. "Poverty and Capitalism." In *Poverty and Social Policy for Canada.* edited by W.E. Mann, pp. 66-81. Toronto: Copp Clark, 1970.

427 GREEN, Christopher, and LAMPMAN, Robert. "Schemes for Transferring Income to the Poor." *Industrial Relations.* 6:2 (February 1967), pp. 121-37.

428 HETU, Jean, and MARX, H. *Droit et pauvreté au Québec: documents, notes et problèmes.* Montreal: Editions Themis, 1974.

429 KNIGHT, Bryan. "Poverty in Canada". In *Canada and Radical Social Change,* edited by D.I. Roussopoulos, pp. 13-27. Montreal: Black Rose Books, 1973.

430 LARIN, Gilles W. "Poverty in Canada; the Existing Income Security System and the Guaranteed Minimum Income, 1971." M.A., McGill University, 1972.

431 MacRAE, Phyllis. "Hard Times and Social Services: An Examination of the Response of the State in Canada to Economic Recession and Social Service Spending." M.S.W. Carleton University, 1977.

432 MENZIES, M.W. *Poverty in Canada — Its Nature, Significance and Implications for Public Policy.* Winnipeg: Manitoba Wheat Pool, 1965.

433 NATIONAL COUNCIL OF WELFARE. *Poor Kids.* A Report on Children in Poverty in Canada. Ottawa: National Council of Welfare, 1975.

434 OSBORNE, John E. "Canada Combats Poverty through Social Policy." *Public Welfare.* 24:2 (April 1966), pp. 131-39.

435 PARIZEAU, Jacques. "La politique sociale au Québec: d'une étape à l'autre." *Assurances.* 33:2 (1965), pp. 73-85.

436 PEITCHINIS, S.G. "Programs in Aid of the Poor: Let's Plan Rationally." *Canadian Welfare.* 49:3 (May/June 1973), pp. 5-10.

437 SARRISIN, Richard. "Pauvreté et besoins familiaux." *Social Worker.* 33:3 (July 1965), pp. 175-81.

438 WALKER, David Charles. "The Poor People's Conference: A Study of the Relationship Between the Federal Government and Low Income Interest Groups in Canada." M.A., Queen's University, 1972.

3.5.2 Income and Social Security

439 BAETZ, Reuben C., and COLLINS, Kevin. "Equity Aspects of Income Security Programs." *Canadian Public Policy.* 1:4 (Autumn 1975), pp. 489-95.

440 BELLAMY, Donald F. *New Approaches to Welfare: Some Views on Income Security, Work and Leisure.* Toronto: University of Toronto, Faculty of Social Work, 1973.

441 BURNS, Eveline M. "Social Security in Evolution: Towards What?" *Canadian Tax Journal.* 14:4 (1966), pp. 326-36.

442 CANADA. Department of National Health and Welfare. Policy Research and Strategic Planning Branch. *The Federal-Provincial Review of Income Security.* Staff Working Paper by Social Insurance Team. Ottawa: Health and Welfare, August 1974.

443 ————. *Rationalization of Canadian Social Security Programs: A Summary Status Report.* Staff Working Paper by T.R. Robinson. Ottawa: Health and Welfare, October 1976.

444 CANADIAN COUNCIL ON SOCIAL DEVELOPMENT. *Income Supplements for the Working Poor; Proceedings of a Conference on Income Supplementation.* Ottawa: The Council, 1974.

445 ————. Task Force on Social Security. *Social Security for Canada, 1973: A Report of the Task Force on Social Security of the Canadian Council on Social Development.* Ottawa: The Council, 1973.

446 CANADIAN WELFARE COUNCIL. *A Policy Statement on the C.A.P.* Ottawa: The Council, 1966.

447 CARDIN, Jean-Réal. "Convention collective et sécurité-sociale." *Relations industrielles.* 18:1 (January 1963), pp. 3-14.

448 CENTRALE DE L'ENSEIGNEMENT DU QUEBEC. Service des relations de travail. *Sécurité sociale; les fonctions socio-politiques de la sécurité sociale; projet sécurité sociale.* Quebec: Corporation des enseignants du Québec, 1973.

449 CLOUTIER, J.E. *The Distribution of Benefits and Costs of Social Security in Canada, 1971-1975.* Ottawa: Economic Council of Canada, 1978.

450 CONGRES DES RELATIONS INDUSTRIELLES DE LAVAL. *Sécurité de la famille ouvrière.* Par Maurice Tremblay *et al.* Quebec: Les Presses de l'université Laval, 1951.

451 DYCK, Rand. "The Canada Assistance Plan: The Ultimate in Cooperative Federalism." *Canadian Public Administration.* 19:4 (Winter 1976), pp. 587-602.

452 GREEN, Richard A. "The Orange Paper on Social Security: Would Nell Gwynne be Satisfied?" *Canadian Tax Journal.* 21:4 (July/August 1973), pp. 340-46.

453 HINDLE, Colin J. "Income Security and Income Systems." *Conference Report.* pp. 533-41. Toronto: Canadian Tax Foundation, 1972.

454 HULL, Brian. "Equity Aspects of Income Security Programs: A Comment." *Canadian Public Policy.* 1:4 (Autumn 1975), pp. 498-502.

455 JOHNSON, A.W. "Canada's Social Security Review 1973-1975: The Central Issues." *Canadian Public Policy.* 1:4 (Autumn 1975), pp. 456-72.

456 MOORE, A. Milton. "Income Security and Federal Finance." *Canadian Public Policy.* 1:4 (Autumn 1975), pp. 473-80.

457 MORGAN, J.S. "An Emerging System of Income Maintenance: Canada in Transition." In *Social Security in International Perspective, Essays in*

Honour of Eveline M. Burns. edited by Shirley Jenkins, pp. 105-28.
New York: Columbia University Press, 1969.

458 _____. "The Prospect of Welfare." In *Poverty and Social Policy for Canada.* edited by W.E. Mann, pp. 356-64. Toronto: Copp Clark, 1970.

459 _____, and ROSE, A. "The Unfinished Business of Social Security." *Social Worker.* 33:3 (July 1965), pp. 182-89.

460 _____, and ROSE, A. "The Unfinished Business of Welfare Services." *Social Worker.* 33:4 (October 1965), pp. 231-39.

461 MORIN, C. "Caractéristiques du régime canadien de sécurité sociale." *Relations industrielles.* 15:2 (April 1960), pp. 242-46.

462 _____. "La sécurité sociale canadienne: problèmes et perspectives." *Relations industrielles.* 16:1 (January 1961), pp. 3-25.

463 NATIONAL COUNCIL OF WELFARE. *The Federal Government and Social Services.* A Background Paper Prepared by the National Council of Welfare. Ottawa: The Council, March 1978.

464 _____. *Incomes and Opportunities.* A commentary by the National Council of Welfare on the government of Canada's working paper on social security. Ottawa: The Council, 1973.

465 _____. *Statement on Income Security.* Ottawa: The Council, 1971.

466 REA, Samuel A., Jr. *Incentive Effects of Alternative Approaches to Income Supplementation.* Presented to the Canadian Council on Social Development Conference on Income Supplementation, April 8 and 9, 1974. Ottawa: Health and Welfare, 1974.

467 _____. *Incentive Effects of Alternative Negative Income Tax Plans.* Working Paper #7209. Toronto: Institute for the Quantitative Analysis of Social and Economic Policy, University of Toronto, 1972.

468 _____. "The Supply of Labour and the Incentive Effects of Income Maintenance Programs." Ph.D., Harvard University, 1971.

469 ROBINSON, T. Russell. *Alternative Approaches to Income Supplementation.* Ottawa: Research and Long-Range Planning, Department of Health and Welfare, 1974.

470 ROSS, D. "A Critical Look at Present and Future Social Security Policy in Canada." *Social Worker.* 41:4 (Winter 1973), pp. 260-74.

471 _____. "Income Security." In *Canadian Social Policy,* edited by S. Yelaja, pp. 49-69. Waterloo: Wilfrid Laurier University Press, 1978.

472 SAINT-HILAIRE, Lucien. "La sécurité sociale." *Actualité économique.* 31:2 (July-September 1955), pp. 195-217.

473 SMITH, B.A. "Notes on Ontario Income Security Policy." Canadian Tax Foundation. *Conference Report,* pp. 549-54. Toronto: Canadian Tax Foundation, 1972.

474 ULMER, John. "Income Security in Canada: A Review of Changes — 1974 to July 1975." *Bulletin of Canadian Welfare Law.* 4:1 (September 1976), pp. 19-28.

475 "Working Paper on Social Security: The System Under Scrutiny." *Labour Gazette.* 73:10 (October 1973), pp. 671-75.

476 YOUNG, R.G., and BROWN, R.I. *Income Maintenance Measures in Canada — Program Descriptions.* Ottawa: Health and Welfare, 1965.

3.5.3 Guaranteed Annual Income

477 AD HOC COMMITTEE. "Guaranteed Annual Income: Leisure Versus Work." *Canadian Dimension.* 2:1 (November/December 1964), pp. 14-16, 23.

478 BAETZ, Reuben. *A Guaranteed Annual Income: Its Role in an Integrated Social Security System.* Ottawa: Canadian Council on Social Development, 1969.

479 BELL, L. *A Guaranteed Income for British Columbia: An Analysis of the Province's Programs for Supplementation of Low Income Earners.* Vancouver: United Community Services of the Greater Vancouver Area, 1973.

480 BOUVIER, Emile. "Pour un salaire garanti modifié." *Relations.* 149 (May 1953), pp. 133-37.

481 _____. "La salaire annuel garanti." *Relations.* 148 (April 1953), pp. 101-5.

482 BRITISH COLUMBIA ASSOCIATION OF SOCIAL WORKERS. *Guaranteed Annual Income.* Report Prepared for Honorable Norman Levi, Minister of Human Resources of the Province of British Columbia. Vancouver: Association of Social Workers, 1973.

483 BUCHBINDER, H. "Guaranteed Annual Income: The Answer to Poverty for All but the Poor." *Canadian Dimension.* 7 (October/November 1970), pp. 27-28, 30-32.

484 CANADA. Department of National Health and Welfare, Policy Research and Long Range Planning Branch. *The Development and Design of the Basic Guaranteed Annual Income Experiment in Manitoba: A Preliminary Report.* Ottawa: Health and Welfare, 1974.

485 CANADIAN ASSOCIATION OF SOCIAL WORKERS. *Social Policy Statement on Guaranteed Annual Income.* Ottawa: The Association, 1971.

486 CANADIAN COUNCIL ON SOCIAL DEVELOPMENT. *Guaranteed Annual Income: An Integrated Approach.* Ottawa: The Council, 1973.

487 CLARE, James L. "Guaranteed Minimum Income: There's More Than One Answer." *Canadian Business.* 43:8 (August 1970), pp. 32-36.

488 CRAWLEY, Ronald W., and DODGE, D. "Cost of the Guaranteed Annual Income." *Canadian Tax Journal.* 17:6 (November/December 1969), pp. 395-408.

489 CUTT, James. *Guaranteed Annual Income for Canadians.* Toronto: Ontario Woodsworth Memorial Foundation, 1968.

490 _____. *Program Budgeting for Welfare: A Case Study of Canada.* New York: Praeger, 1973.

491 _____. "Guaranteed Income." *Canadian Forum.* 47 (January 1968), pp. 225-29.

492 _____. "A Guaranteed Income — Next Step in the Evolution of Welfare Policy." *Social Service Review.* 42:2 (June 1968), pp. 216-31.

493 _____, and ATKINSON, T. *Public Policy Research and the Guaranteed Annual Income: A Design for the Experimental Evaluation of Income Maintenance Policies in Canada.* Toronto: Institute for Behavioural Research, York University, 1973.

494 _____, TYSALL, John, and BAILEY, Leigh. "Comparative Analysis of Alternative Income Support Programs in Canada." *Canadian Tax Journal.* 20:1 (January/February 1972), pp. 74-104.

495 DESROCHERS, Gilles. "L'insuffisance des revenus au Québec et le coût de la garantie d'un revenu minimum." *Annexe 28.* Quebec: Commission d'enquête sur la santé et le bien-être, 1971.

496 DEUTSCH, Antal, and GREEN, Christopher. "Income Security for Canadians: A Review Article." *Canadian Tax Journal.* 19:1 (January/February 1971), pp. 8-16.

497 DROPPELT, Allen. "Guaranteed Annual Income: The Speenhamland Experience." *Bulletin of Canadian Welfare Law.* 3:2 (Spring 1975), pp. 30-35.

498 _____. "The Evolving Process of Guaranteed Incomes." *Bulletin of Canadian Welfare Law.* 3:2 (1975), pp. 8-10.

499 GOOD, Thomas Henry. "A Guaranteed Minimum Income for Canada." M.A., Queen's University, 1970.

500 "Guaranteed Income and the Will to Work." *Labour Gazette.* 74:5 (May 1974), p. 339.

501 HAMILTON, Neville. "Guaranteed Annual Income." *Canadian Labour.* 13:12 (December 1968), pp. 20-22.

502 HIKEL, R.S., LAUB, M.E., and POWELL, B.J. *Manitoba Basic Annual Income Experiment.* Working Paper No. x-7401. Ottawa: Health and Welfare, 1974.

503 HINDLE, Colin James. "The Negative Income Tax and Canadian Welfare Policy." M.Phil., University of Toronto, 1969.

504 _____. "Negative Income Taxes and the Poverty Problem in Ontario." *Canadian Tax Journal.* 19:2 (March/April 1971), pp. 116-23.

505 HOLMBERG, Ronald. "A Conflict Analysis of the Guaranteed Annual Income." *Social Worker/Le travailleur social.* 39:3 (July 1971), pp. 109-13.

506 "How Much Will Guaranteed Income Affect Social Welfare Costs?" *Labour Gazette.* 70:1 (January 1970), pp. 22-25.

507 JONES, Gregory H. "The Implications of a Guaranteed Annual Income for Employment, Wages and Prices." M.A., University of Calgary, 1972.

508 KEHOE, Mary. "Guaranteed Annual Income." *Canadian Labour.* 16:12 (December 1971), pp. 8-10.

509 McCAFFREY, Gordon. "Guaranteed Annual Income." *Canadian Labour.* 15:4 (April 1970), pp. 37-40.

510 MacLEAN'S MAGAZINE (editorial) "Guaranteed Income? Let's Think Twice." 82:4 (March 1969).

511 MARSH, Leonard. "Guaranteed Annual Income: A New Look at Welfare Policy." *Canadian Welfare.* 49:6 (November/December 1973), pp. 4-6.

512 MARTIN, Nicole V., and BELLEROSE, Pierre-Paul. *Les avantages-coûts du revenu annuel garanti.* Quebec: Ecole nationale d'administration publique, 1973.

513 NATIONAL ANTI-POVERTY ORGANIZATION. *A New Tomorrow for Canada's Poor?* Brief on Guaranteed Income and Social Services. Prepared by Marjorie Hartling. Ottawa: National Anti-Poverty Organization, 1975.

514 _____. *Towards a Guaranteed Income for Canadians. An Analysis of the Three Choices Now Being Considered by the Federal-Provincial Review.* Ottawa: National Anti-Poverty Organization, 1975.

515 NATIONAL COUNCIL OF WELFARE. *Guaranteed Incomes and Guaranteed Jobs.* Ottawa: The Council, 1972.

516 _____. *Guide to the Guaranteed Income.* Ottawa: The Council, Revised. 1976.

517 NUFFIELD CANADIAN SEMINAR. Ste. Adele, 1972. *Guaranteed Annual Income: An Integrated Approach.* Background papers and proceedings of the Seminar. Ottawa: Canadian Council on Social Development, 1973.

518 NYKOR, R. "Negative Tax Weapon Eyed by Taxman and Poverty Fighters." *Financial Post.* 60:1 (March 5, 1966), p. 4.
519 PELLETIER, Michel. "Le revenu minimum garanti: une stratégie de bien-être social ou un instrument de politique économique." *Canadian Public Policy.* 1:4 (August 1975), pp. 503-19.
520 VANDERKAMP, J. "Income Security/Revenu garanti." *Canadian Public Policy.* 1:4 (Autumn 1975), pp. 449-526.

4.0 The Organization and Administration of Social Welfare Policy

4.1 General

521 ARMITAGE, Andrew. *Social Welfare in Canada: Ideals and Realities.* Toronto: McClelland and Stewart, 1975.
522 _____. "A Structural View of Welfare Organization." *Social Worker.* 37:3 (July 1969), pp. 171-76.
523 BELLEAU, Henri-Georges. *Organization of Social Service. New Trends and Directions.* Ottawa: Library of Parliament, 1974.
524 CAMPBELL, Wesley Glen. "Impact of Social Security Expenditures on Canadian Goverment Finance". M.A. Harvard University, 1954.
525 CASSIDY, H.M. *Public Health and Welfare Organization; the Post-War Problems of the Canadian Provinces in Canada.* Toronto: Ryerson Press, 1945.
526 _____. "Public Welfare Reorganization in Canada." *Public Affairs.* 3 (Spring 1942), pp. 143-46.
527 DOUGLAS, Monteath. "Welfare and Redistribution: Economic Implications of the Redistributive Processes Involved in Canadian Social Welfare Policies." *Canadian Journal of Economics and Political Science.* 19:3 (1953), pp. 316-25.
528 GOFFMAN, I.J. "Canadian Social Welfare Policy." In *Contemporary Canada*, edited by R.H. Leach, pp. 191-224. Toronto: University of Toronto Press, 1968.
529 HEPWORTH, H. Philip. *Social Services in Canada: An Introduction; Vol. 1 of Personal Social Services in Canada: A Review.* 1. Ottawa: Canadian Council on Social Development, 1975.
530 NATIONS UNIES. Départment des Affaires d'économiques et sociales. *Organisation et administration des programmes de services sociaux. Serie de monographies par pays: Canada.* New York: Les Nations unies, 1968.
531 ROSE, Albert. "Functional Scope of Social Planning." *Canadian Welfare.* 51:6 (September/October 1975), pp. 9-12.
532 STRONG, Margaret K. *Public Welfare Administration in Canada.* Chicago: University of Chicago Press, 1930.
533 UNITED NATIONS. Department of Economic and Social Affairs. *Organization and Administration of Social Welfare Programmes; a Series of Country Studies: Canada.* New York: United Nations, 1967.
534 WHARF, Brian W.F. *Social Planning Functions and Social Planning Organizations.* Presented at a Seminar on Social Planning. Toronto: Ministry of Community and Social Services, 1973.

4.2   Federal Government

535   CANADA. Statistics Canada. *Social Security: National Programs. A Review for the Period 1946 to 1975/ La sécurité sociale: programmes nationaux; une revue pour la periode 1946 à 1975.* Ottawa: Statistics Canada, 1976. (Annual).

4.3   Provincial Government

536   AULD, Douglas A.L. "Graham Commission: A Reader's Guide." *Canadian Public Policy.* 1:3 (Summer 1975), pp. 343-46.

537   CANADIAN WELFARE COUNCIL. *Public Welfare Services in New Brunswick.* Fredericton: The Council, 1949.

538   CASTONGUAY, Claude. "Pour une politique sociale intégrée, Québec doit avoir le pouvoir prioritaire de légiférer." *Québec aujourd'hui,* 7 (May 1971), pp. 121-31.

539   CHISOLM, James, and FERRIS, Charles. "Social Assistance in New Brunswick." *Bulletin of Canadian Welfare Law.* 2 (1973), pp. 31-36.

540   DULUDE, Louise. "Social Assistance in Quebec." *Bulletin of Canadian Welfare Law.* 3:1 (Spring 1974), pp. 39-49.

541   DENAULT, Hayda. "L'insertion du service social dans le milieu canadien-français." *Service social.* 10:3 (October 1961), pp. 3-30; 11:1 (April 1962), pp. 4-29.

542   FEDERATION DES TRAVAILLEURS DU QUEBEC. *Guide F.T.Q: la sécurité sociale.* Montreal: Féderation des travailleurs du Québec, 1967.

543   GAGNE, Rolande, ed. *Loi sur les services de santé et les services sociaux et règlement; méthode d'étude pour usage et application/ An Act Respecting Health Services and Social Services Regulation; Method of Study for Use and Application.* Montreal: Editions Intermonde, 1973.

544   GALLANT, Marc J. "Social Welfare in Saskatchewan." M.S.W., McGill University, 1963.

545   GILCHRIST, F. Ian. "Public Health, Social Development and Social Welfare." *Report of New Brunswick, Task Force on Social Development.* Fredericton: Queen's Printer, 1971.

546   GODBOUT, Jacques *et al. Participation et innovation: l'implantation des centres locaux des services communautaires: C.S.L.C. et les organismes communautaires autonomes.* Quebec: Les Presses de l'université du Québec, 1974.

547   GREAT BRITAIN. Newfoundland Royal Commission. Chairman: W.W.M. Amulree. *Report.* London: Her Majesty's Stationery Office, 1933.

548   GUILLEMETTE, A.M. "Welfare Organization and Services in the Province of Quebec." *Proceedings in the Ninth Annual Programme Meeting.* Montreal: Council on Social Work Education, 1961.

549   LaFRANCE, Gilles. *Du bill 65 à la fondation d'un centre de service social.* Montreal: Fédération des services sociaux à la famille du Quebec, 1974.

550   LAMARCHE, Rolande. *Une étude sur des organismes de développement social: les conseils de bien-être regionaux.* Quebec: Conseil de bien-être du Québec, 1971.

551   LEIGH, Amy. "Social Welfare Services in Newfoundland." *Social Worker.* 20:3 (February 1952), pp. 9-15.

552   LEMIEUX, Vincent, RENAUD, François, and VON SCHOENBERG, Brigitte. *Les conseils regionaux de la santé et des services sociaux: une*

analyse politique. Quebec: Department of Political Science, Laval University, 1974.

553 MATHIEU, S. "La sécurité sociale au Québec." *Annales de l'Institut d'etudes du travail de la sécurité sociale*. 8 (1968), pp. 101-25.

554 MORGAN, John S. *et al. Public Welfare in New Brunswick*. Fredericton: Department of Health and Social Services, 1952.

555 NEW BRUNSWICK. Legislative Assembly. *White Paper on Social Development and Social Welfare*. Fredericton: Queen's Printer, 1971.

556 NOVA SCOTIA. Department of Public Welfare. *Public Assistance in Nova Scotia*. Halifax: Queen's Printer, 1970.

557 _____. Royal Commission on Education, Public Services, and Provincial-Municipal Relations. *Report*. Halifax: Queen's Printer, 1974.

558 ONTARIO. Royal Commission on Public Welfare. *Report*. Toronto: King's Printer, 1930.

559 _____. Task Force on Community and Social Services. *Report on Selected Issues and Relationships*. Toronto: Ministry of Community and Social Services, 1974.

560 PRINCE EDWARD ISLAND. Department of Development. *The Regional Service Centre Project: An Instrument of Social Development*. Charlottetown: Queen's Printer, 1973.

561 QUEBEC. Commission d'enquête sur la santé et le bien-être sociale. (Castonguay-Nepveu Commission). *Rapport*. Quebec: Queen's Printer, 1967.

562 _____. Commission des allocations sociales. *Rapport sur la mise à execution des lois sociales*. Queen's Printer, 1937, annuel.

563 _____. Commission of Inquiry on Health and Social Welfare. (Castonguay-Nepveu Commission). *Report*. Quebec: 1971.

564 _____. Ministère des Affaires sociales. *Pour une politique de recherche en affaires sociales*. Quebec: Editeur officiel du Québec, February 1974.

565 _____. *Recueil des lois et règlements des affaires sociales*. Quebec: Ministère des Affaires sociales, 1975.

566 _____. Social Allowances Commission. *Report on the Enforcement of the Social Acts*. Quebec: Department of Family and Social Welfare, 1938.

567 ROCHER, Guy. "Le développement des services de bien-être au Québec." *Service social*. 13:2 & 3 (July-December 1964), pp. 2-22.

568 "Saskatchewan Assistance Act." *Bulletin of Canadian Welfare Law*. 2:2 (February 1973), pp. 19-26.

569 SASKATCHEWAN. Legislative Assembly. Special Committee on Welfare. *Final Report*. Legislative Assembly, Regina. 13 November 1973.

570 "Le service social au Canada français." *Service social*. 10:3 (1961-62), pp. 17-21.

571 SHEPPARD, Claude Armand. *L'organisation de la réglementation des professions de la santé et du bien-être au Québec*. Quebec: Gouvernement du Québec, 1970-1973.

572 "Social Assistance in British Columbia." *Bulletin of Canadian Welfare Law*. 1:1 (February 1972), pp. 8-12.

573 "Social Assistance in New Brunswick." *Bulletin of Canadian Welfare Law*. 2:2, (Summer 1973), pp. 31-61.

574 "Social Assistance in Newfoundland." *Bulletin of Canadian Welfare Law*. 2:2 (Summer 1973), pp. 36-41.

575 "Social Assistance in Nova Scotia." *Bulletin of Canadian Welfare Law.* 1:1 (February 1972), pp. 12-16.

576 TOUZEL, Bessie. *The Province of Ontario — Its Welfare Services.* Toronto: Ontario Welfare Council, 1962.

577 ULMER, John. "Provincial Assistance Benefits: A Comparison." *Bulletin of Canadian Welfare Law.* 5:1 (Spring 1976), pp. 34-41.

578 "Welfare Assistance in Prince Edward Island." *Bulletin of Canadian Welfare Law.* 3:1 (Spring 1974), pp. 49-52.

579 ZAY, Nicolas. "Le service social professionnel au Canada français: vingt-cinq ans d'histoire." *Social Worker/ Le travailleur social.* 35:3 (September 1967), pp. 160-67.

4.4   Municipal Government

580 GREGOIRE, Jacques. "Le rôle des municipalités dans le champ du bien-être social." M.A., Laval University, 1966.

581 LEIGH, Amy. "The Contribution of the Municipality to the Administration of Public Welfare." *Canadian Public Administration.* 7:2 (1964), pp. 150-57.

582 _____. "Municipalities and Public Welfare." *Canadian Welfare.* 40:1 (January/February 1964), pp. 16-22.

583 LOEBEL, Peter Bernard. "The Municipal Planning Process, Implications for Social Welfare." D.S.W., University of Toronto, 1976.

584 MacKINNON, F.J. "Local Government and Welfare." *Canadian Public Administration.* 3:1 (March 1960), pp. 31-40; 7:2 (June 1964), pp. 137-49.

585 MORGAN, John S. "Contribution of the Municipality to the Administration of Public Welfare." *Canadian Public Administration.* 7:2 (June 1964), pp. 137-49.

586 ONTARIO. The Royal Commission on Metropolitan Toronto. Background Report. *Social Policy in Metropolitan Toronto.* Toronto: The Commission, 1975.

587 ROSE, Albert. *Welfare Services in Metropolitan Areas. Centennial Study of Training Programme on Metropolitan Problems.* Paper 11, Part B. Toronto: Bureau of Municipal Research, 1967.

588 Social Planning Council of Metropolitan Toronto. *In Search of a Framework: A Review of Trends in the Financing and Delivery of Community Services.* Toronto: The Council, 1976.

589 _____. *Social Policies for Planning in Metropolitan Toronto.* Toronto: The Council, 1976.

590 _____. *Trends Affecting the Development of Social Services in Metropolitan Toronto.* Toronto: The Council, 1970.

591 ZAY, Nicholas. "Assistance publique et service social." *Service social.* 10:3 (October 1961), pp. 17-42; 11:1 (April 1962), pp. 64-85.

4.5   Intergovernmental Relations

592 ANGERS, François-Albert. *La sécurité sociale et les problèmes constitutionnels.* 2 vols. Annexe no. 3, au rapport de la Commission royale d'enquête sur les problèmes constitutionnels. Quebec: Queen's Printer, 1955.

593 ARMITAGE, W.A.J. "Emerging Realignment of Social Policy: A Problem for Federalism." *Canadian Welfare.* 47 (September/October 1971), pp. 4-5.

594 CANADA. Task Force on a Developmental Approach to Public Assistance. *Developmental Approach to Public Assistance: Final Report to the Federal-Provincial Conference of the Ministers of Welfare.* Ottawa: Queen's Printer, 1971.

595 CANADIAN WELFARE COUNCIL. *Guidelines for the Purchase of Services.* A Report on the Canadian Welfare Council's Task Force on Purchase of Service Agreement Between Non-Governmental Agencies and Provincial and Municipal Government Agencies Under the Canada Assistance Plan. Ottawa: Queen's Printer, 1969.

596 GARIGUE, Philippe. "La sécurité sociale, épreuve critique de fédéralisme canadien." In *Vers un meilleur partage des pouvoirs,* Vol. 2 of *Le Québec dans le Canada de demain.* pp. 52-8. Montreal: Editions du Jour, 1967.

597 GOLDENBERG, H. Carl. *Provincial-Municipal Relations in Public Welfare Services.* Ottawa: Canadian Welfare Council, 1949.

598 GROUPE DE TRAVAIL FEDERAL-PROVINCIAL. Pour une approche plus fonctionnelle de l'assistance publique. *Rapport final à la conférence fédérale-provinciale des Ministres du bien-être social.* Ottawa, The Group, 1976.

599 HANES, J.H. "Health and Welfare in the Provinces — Provincial-Municipal Relations." *Canadian Welfare.* 24:1 (January 1945), pp. 14-17.

600 McGILLY, Frank. *Federal and Provincial Jurisdiction in Welfare: A Background Module.* Montreal: McGill University, 1974.

601 SIMEON, Richard. *Federal-Provincial Diplomacy: The Making of Recent Policy in Canada.* Toronto: University of Toronto Press, 1972.

602 ———. "Federalism and Policy-Making: Federal-Provincial Negotiation in Canada." Ph.D., Yale University, 1968.

603 SOCIAL PLANNING AND RESEARCH COUNCIL OF HAMILTON AND DISTRICT. *Split-level Public Assistance; Confusion Masquerading as Policy: A Brief to the Cabinet of the Government of Ontario.* Hamilton: The Council, 1971.

604 STEVENS, Paul, and SAYWELL, John. "Federal-Provincial Relations — Health, Education and Money." *Canadian Annual Review of Politics and Public Affairs.* (1973), pp. 33-39.

605 TUCK, R. "Social Security: An Administrative Solution to the Dominion-Provincial Problem." *Canadian Journal of Economics and Political Science.* 13:2 (May 1947), pp. 256-75.

606 WEEKES, Frances Evelyn. "Provincial-Municipal Relations in Social Service Administration in Ontario." M.A., University of Toronto, 1946.

4.6 Non-Governmental Organizations

607 AKMAN, Dogan D., comp. *Policy Statements and Public Positions of the Canadian Association of Social Workers.* Canadian Association of Social Workers, St. John's: Memorial University, 1972.

608 BAKER, Walter. "The Place of the Private Agency in the Administration of Government Policies." M.A., Queen's University, 1966.

609 BREGHA, F. *Public Participation in Planning, Policy and Programme.* Toronto: Ministry of Community and Social Services, 1973.

610 CARTER, Novia. *Trends in Voluntary Support for Non-Government Social Service Agencies.* Ottawa: Canadian Council on Social Development, 1974.

611   DION, G. *Bénéfices sociaux et initiative privée*. Quebec: Les Presses de l'Université Laval, 1959.

612   MORIN, C. "Le conseil des oeuvres: son rôle et sa fonction dans le champ du bien-être." *Rapport de la journée d'études annuelle du conseil central des oeuvres de Québec*. Quebec: Le Conseil, 15 May 1959, pp. 44-51.

613   ROCHER, G. "Ambiguités et fonctions de l'initiative privée dans le bien-être social." *Service social*. 9:2 (July/August 1960), pp. 62-74.

614   SILCOX, Peter. "The Future Relationships between the Voluntary Social Planning Councils and Local Municipal Governments, Particularly Reformed Regional Governments." *Seminar on Social Planning*. Toronto: Ministry of Community and Social Services, 1975.

615   SPENCER, J.C. "Community Planning Councils and the Making of Social Policy." *Proceedings: Mid-Winter Conference*. Ottawa: Canadian Welfare Council, 1963.

4.7   Bureaucracy and Decision-Making

616   AULD, Douglas A.L. "Social Welfare and Decision-Making in the Public Sector." *Canadian Public Administration*. 16:4 (Winter 1973), pp. 604-12.

617   HICKEY, Paul. *Decision-Making in Ontario's Local Governments with a Summary of the Systems of Local Decision-Making in Other Canadian Provinces, United States and England*. Toronto: Ministry of Treasury, Economics, and Intergovernmental Affairs, 1972.

618   KATZ, Arnold. "Precursor to Policy: A Model for Policy Development." *Social Worker/ Le travailleur social*. 43:2 (Summer 1975), pp. 92-96.

619   ROCHER, Guy. "Bureaucracy and Welfare." *Canadian Welfare*. 2 (1963), pp. 55-60.

4.8   Management of Social Services

620   ARMITAGE, Andrew. "An Analysis of Social Service Delivery Reorganization." *Canadian Journal of Social Work Education*. 2:3 (1976), pp. 59-67.

621   CANADA. Federal-Provincial Conference of the Ministers of Welfare. *A Comprehensive System for Evaluating the Impact of Alternate Welfare Policies*. Ottawa: Information Canada, 1973.

622   CARTER, Novia. *Evaluating Social Development Programs*. Ottawa: Canadian Council on Social Development, 1973.

623   —————. *Perspectives on Planning/ Regards neufs sur planification*. Ottawa: Canadian Council on Social Development, 1973.

624   CASSIDY, H.M. "Public Welfare Reorganizing in Canada." *Public Affairs*. Part 1,5:2 (Winter 1941), pp. 86-90; Part 2,5:3 (Spring 1942), pp. 143-47.

625   COHN, Robert, and WALLACE, Elizabeth. *Some Problems of Administration in Social Work*. Toronto: University of Toronto Press, 1944.

626   DESLAURIERS, Jean-Pierre. "Towards a Self-Management Model of Social Service Organization." D.S.W., University of Toronto, 1976.

627   GANDY, John M. "Some Observations on the Application of Business Management Practices to the Administration of Voluntary Welfare Agencies." *Social Worker*. 33:1 (January/February 1965), pp. 36-42.

628   GUMMER, Burton. *Systems Approach to Inter-organizational Relations among Social Welfare Agencies*. Thunder Bay: Lakehead University, 1972.

629 HATCHER, Gordon Hollett. *Patterns of Administration/Professional Independence*. Canadian Public Welfare Association. Ottawa: Canadian Welfare Council, 1965.

630 HEDDERWICK, W. "A Study of Job Attitudes of Professional Social Workers with Special Reference to Agency Policy and Administration." M.S.W., University of Toronto, 1964.

631 HENRY, Mary. "Development of the Catholic Social Welfare Bureau of Charlottetown, Prince Edward Island." M.S.W., St. Patrick's College, 1956.

632 MORGAN, John S. "Appeals Against Administrative Decisions under Welfare Legislation." *Canadian Public Administration*. 4:1 (March 1961), pp. 44-60.

633 _____. "Staffing the Public Welfare Services." *Canadian Public Administration*. 3 (1960), pp. 157-70.

634 ROBINSON, T. Russell. "A General Framework for the Evaluation of Social Security Policies: A Canadian Overview." *International Social Security Association: Studies and Research, No. 8*. 1976, pp. 14-24.

635 RUTMAN, Leonard. *Social Programme Evaluations in Canada: An Inventory*. Ottawa: Evaluation Research Training Institute, Centre for Social Welfare Studies, School of Social Work, Carleton University: 1977.

636 VEIT, S. "Communities in the Way: The Case for Social Impact Studies in the Preliminary Stages of Project Planning." *Canadian Welfare*. 51:1 (January/February 1975), pp. 9-11.

5.0 Comparative Social Welfare Policy: Canada and Other Countries

637 ADAMS, Thomas. "Town Planning in Canada and the United States." *Town Planning Review*. 5:2 (July 1914), pp. 155-59.

638 ANDREOPOULOS, Spyros, ed. *National Health Insurance: Can We Learn From Canada*. New York: John Wiley and Sons, 1975.

639 AYKROYD, Peter A. *Land Use Control in Britain, the United States and Canada*. Ottawa: Central Mortgage and Housing Corporation, 1969.

640 BIRCH, Anthony Harold. *Federalism, Finance and Social Legislation in Canada, Australia and the United States*. Oxford: Clarendon Press, 1955.

641 BOYD, Monica. "Immigration Policies and Trends: A Comparison of Canada and the United States." *Demography*. 13 (February 1971), pp. 83-104.

642 BRADY, P.E.H. *Relating Public Housing Abroad to the Canadian Scene*. Toronto: Metropolitan Toronto Housing Authority, 1963.

643 BROWN, James S. *Public Housing and Welfare Services; A Review of Developments in Canada, United States and Britain, 1947-1963*. Vancouver: University of British Columbia, 1964.

644 BROWN, Malcolm C. *The Financing of Personal Health Services in New Zealand, Canada and Australia*. Canberra: Centre for Research on Federal Financial Relations, Australian National University, 1977.

645 BURNS, Eveline M. "Post War Planning and the Role of Social Security." *Canadian Welfare*. 19:2, (June 1943), pp. 10-17.

646   BURNS, P. "Planning and Financing for the Future." *Child Welfare.*
      47:6 (1968), pp. 322-30.
647   CANADA. Department of Labour. "Old Age Pension Systems Existing
      in Various Countries." Issued as a supplement to the *Labour Gazette.*
      Ottawa: King's Printer, 1926.
648   CHAMBERS, R. *Family Allowances in Great Britain, Canada, Australia
      and New Zealand.* New York: American Eugenics Society, 1954.
649   CHARRON, Kenneth C. *Health Services, Health Insurance and Their Inter-
      Relationship; A Study of Selected Countries.* Ottawa: Department of
      Health and Welfare, 1963.
650   CLARK, R.M. *Economic Security for the Aged, in United States and
      Canada.* 2 vols. Ottawa: Queen's Printer, 1962.
651   CORBETT, David C. "Immigration and Foreign Policy in Australia and
      Canada." *International Journal.* 6:3 (Spring 1958), pp. 110-23.
652   CUDMORE, James Sedley. "A Comparative Study of Health Insurance
      and Public Medical Care Schemes in Germany, Great Britain, the
      United States of America and Canada." Ph.D., University of
      Toronto, 1951.
653   DOLMAN, Claude Ernest. *Report on a Survey of Medical Education in
      Canada and the United States.* Toronto: University of Toronto Press,
      1946.
654   DORION, Eugène P. *Historique des fonds de retraite en Europe et au
      Canada.* Quebec: Hunter, Rose et Lemieux, 1862.
655   DRIELSMA, H. Albarda-Hankes. *Family and Child Welfare in U.S.A. and
      Canada.* The Hague: International Relations Department, Ministry of
      Social Work, 1965.
656   ECKERSON, Helen F. "United States and Canada: Magnets for Immi-
      gration." *Annals of the American Academy of Political and Social Science.*
      36 (March 1958), pp. 34-42.
657   FARMAN, Carl H. *Health and Maternity Insurance throughout the World,
      1954; Principle Legislative Provision in 48 Countries.* Washington:
      Government Printing Office, 1954.
658   FIFIELD, James Clark, ed. *American and Canadian Hospitals.* Minnea-
      polis: Midwest Publishing, 1933.
659   FLEXNER, Abraham. *Medical Education in the United States and Canada,
      A Report to the Carnegie Foundation for the Advancement of Teaching.*
      New York: Arno Press, 1972.
660   FRY, John, and FARNDALE, W.A.J., eds. *International Medical Care: A
      Comparison and Evaluation of Medical Care Services Throughout the
      World.* Oxford: Medical and Technical Publishing, 1972.
661   GRAY, K.G. "Canadian and American Health Insurance Plans." *Canad-
      ian Journal of Economics and Political Science.* 12 (1946), pp. 505-509.
662   GRUBEL, H.G., and WALKER, M.A. *Unemployment Insurance: Global
      Evidence of its Effects on Unemployment.* Proceedings of a Vancouver
      International Conference. Vancouver: Fraser Institute, 1978.
663   HAWKINS, Freda. *Immigration Policy and Management in Selected Coun-
      tries: A Study of Immigration Policy and Management and Their Implica-
      tions for Population Growth in United States, Australia and Israel.* Ottawa:
      Department of Manpower and Immigration, 1974.
664   HAY, Brian. "Comparative Analysis of Recent Projected Housing Poli-
      cies in Selected Countries." M.E.S., York University, 1973.
665   HURD, Henry M. *et al.*, eds. *The Institutional Care of the Insane in the
      United States and Canada.* Baltimore: Johns Hopkins Press, 1917.

666 KAIM-CAUDLE, P.R. *Comparative Social Policy and Social Security, A Ten Country Study*. London: Martin Robertson, 1973.

667 KOHN, Robert, and RADIUS, Susan. "Two Roads to Health Care: U.S. and Canadian Politics, 1945-1975." *Medical Care*. (March 1974), pp. 189-201.

668 LASKER, Bruno, and "Verax". *Immigration Policies: Canadian and American*. Toronto: Ryerson Press, 1944.

669 MARSHALL, Allen D. "Fundamentals of Economic Security for the Aged — A Look at the Clark Report." Address delivered on 26 May 1959 at annual meeting of the Canadian Life Insurance Association. Toronto, 1959.

670 MERRIAM, I.C., CECILE, L.P., and COWARD, L.E. "The Social Security Systems of Canada and the U.S.A." *Proceedings of the Institute of Public Administration of Canada*. (1958), pp. 11-41.

671 McKENZIE, N.R. "The Education System of Canada and New Zealand." *Queen's Quarterly*. 31:3 (January/February/March 1924), pp. 245-70.

672 RICHARDSON, J. Henry. *Economic and Financial Aspects of Social Security: An International Survey*. Toronto: University of Toronto Press, 1960.

673 RICHTER, L. "Social Insurance and Politics." *University of Toronto Quarterly*. 6:2 (1936-1937), pp. 254-66.

674 _____. "The Employment and Social Insurance Bill I: General Principles and European Experience." *Canadian Journal of Economics and Political Science*. 1:4, (1935), pp. 436-56.

675 ROBERTS, Neal Alison, ed. *The Government Land Developers; Studies of Public Land-Ownership Policy in Seven Countries*. Lexington: Lexington Books, 1977.

676 RODGERS, Barbara N. *Comparative Social Administration*. London: Allen & Unwin, 1968.

677 ROEMER, Milton Irwin. *Health Care Systems in World Perspective*. Ann Arbor: Health Administration Press, 1976.

678 _____. *The Organization of Medical Care Under Social Security; A Study Based on the Experience of 8 Countries*. I.L.O., 1969.

679 SEKINE, Sumie. "A Comparative Study of Social Welfare in Canada and Japan." M.A., University of Victoria, 1976.

680 SIMKIN, Keith A. "The Development of National Education Systems: A Comparative Analysis." M.A., University of Toronto, 1970.

681 STITT, J.M. "Juvenile Delinquency." *Osgoode Hall Law Journal*. 2:3 (1962), pp. 356-69.

682 TAIT, D. Christine. "Migration and Settlement in Australia, New Zealand and Canada." *International Labour Review*. 34:1 (July 1936), pp. 34-65.

683 THOMPSON, A.C. "State Old Age Pension Plans." *Industrial Canada*. 49:5 (September 1948), pp. 91, 142.

684 UNION BANK OF SWITZERLAND. *Social Security in Ten Industrial Nations*. Zurich: The Bank, 1977.

685 UNITED STATES. Children's Bureau. *Laws Relating to Mothers' Pensions, in U.S., Canada, Denmark, and New Zealand*. Washington: Government Printing Office, 1919.

686 WAGGAMAN, Mary T. *Family Allowances in Various Countries*. United States Labour Department. Bureau of Labour Statistics, 1943.

687 WILLARD, Joseph William. "Some Aspects of the Administration of Unemployment Insurance in Canada with Comparative Notes on the Other British Dominions and Great Britain." M.A., University of Toronto, 1944.

688   WINES, Enoch C. *The State of Prisons and of Child Saving Institutions in the Civilised World*. Cambridge: Harvard University Press, 1880.

689   _____, and DWIGHT, T.W. *Report on the Prisons and Reformatories of the United States and Canada*. New York: Van Benthuysen Press, 1867.

690   WOODSWORTH, David E. *Social Security and National Policy: Sweden, Yugoslavia, Japan*. Montreal: McGill-Queen's University Press, 1977.

691   "Workmen's Compensation Legislation in the United States and Canada." *Labour Gazette*. 30:4 (April 1930), pp. 397-99.

Part Two

6.0   Social Welfare Policies for People Out of Work

6.1   Relief

6.1.1   Historical Development

692   CASSIDY, H.M. *Unemployment and Relief in Ontario, 1929-1932*. Toronto: J.M. Dent, 1932.

693   _____. "Relief Works as a Remedy for Unemployment in the Light of Ontario Experience, 1930-1932." *Papers and Proceedings of the 4th Annual Meeting of the Canadian Political Science Association*. 4 (1932), pp. 21-33.

694   _____. "Is Unemployment Relief Enough?" *Canadian Forum*. 14:161 (February 1934), pp. 131-33.

695   DUNCAN, A.S. "Unemployment Relief in the Prairie Provinces, 1930-1937." M.A., McGill University, 1938.

696   "Emergency Relief in Canada." *Labour Gazette*. 33:3 (March 1933), pp. 290-301.

697   FINDLAY, M. "The History of Public Assistance in Newfoundland." M.A., Memorial University, 1964.

698   FRIED, Helen. "An Analysis of Canadian Unemployment Problems and Relief Legislation during the Depression." M.A., Columbia University, 1940.

699   HOPE, A.T. *Canada and the Unemployed Problem; Some Suggestions for its Solution*. London: Simpkin, Marshall, Hamilton Kent, 1910.

700   LAWTON, Alma. "Urban Relief in Saskatchewan in the Depression." M.A., University of Saskatchewan, 1967.

701   MACHAR, Agnes Maude. "Outdoor Relief in Canada." *Review of Historical Publications Relating to Canada*. 11 (1897), pp. 195-96.

702   MacKINNON, Fred S. "From Poor Relief to Social Assistance-Transition in Nova Scotia." *Social Worker*. 29:2 (April 1961), pp. 4-11.

703   MARSH, L.C. "Unemployment and Economic Status: A Study in the Incidence of Unemployment and Relief in Canada." Ph.D., McGill University, 1937.

704   "Methods of Unemployment Relief in Various Cities in Canada." *Labour Gazette*. 32:3 (March 1932), pp. 318-22.

705   NEATBY, H.B. "Saskatchewan Relief Commission, 1931-1934." *Saskatchewan History*. 3:2 (Spring 1950), pp. 41-56.

706   ONTARIO. Advisory Committee on Direct Relief to the Provincial Government of Ontario. *Report on Provincial Policy on Administrative Methods in the Matter of Direct Relief in Ontario*. Toronto: King's Printer, 1932.

707   "Ontario's Experience of Relief Works as a Remedy for Unemployment, 1930-1932." *Labour Gazette.* 32:7 (July 1932), pp. 790-93.
708   "The Relief Act 1933, Report of the Dominion Commission of Unemployment Relief." *Labour Gazette.* 34:4 (April 1934), pp. 342-47.
709   "Single Women on Relief." *Canadian Forum.* 16:194 (March 1937), p.5.
710   SMART, Jane. "The Relief Racket." *Canadian Forum.* 16:193, (February 1937), p.4.
711   STEVENSON, John A. "Canada's Unemployment Problem." *Fortnightly Review.* 130:779 (November 1931), pp. 623-29.
712   STEWART, B.M. "The Employment Service of Canada." *Bulletin of the Departments of History and Political and Economic Science.* Kingston: Queen's University, 1919.
713   STONE, Fred Victor. "Unemployment and Unemployment Relief in Western Canada." M.A., McGill University, 1933.
714   "Survey of Federal Relief Activities Since 1930." *Labour Gazette.* 35:5 (May 1935), pp. 477-503.
715   "Unemployment Relief in Canada, 1930-1932." *Labour Gazette.* 32:12 (December 1932), pp. 1300-1304.
716   WILBUR, J.R.H. *The Bennett Administration, 1930-1935.* Booklet #24, Ottawa: Canadian Historical Association, 1969.

6.1.2   Administration

717   BROWN, Lorne. "Unemployment Relief Camps in Saskatchewan 1933-1936." *Saskatchewan History.* 23:3 (Autumn 1970), pp. 81-104.
718   "Interim Report on Relief Camps in Canada." *Labour Gazette.* 36:2 (February 1936), pp. 141-48.
719   LAWTON, Alma. "Relief Administration in Saskatoon During the Depression." *Saskatchewan History.* 22:2, (Spring 1969), pp. 41-59.
720   "Unemployment Relief Camps in Canada." *Labour Gazette.* 34:3 (March 1934), pp. 228-30.

6.2   Unemployment Insurance

6.2.1   Historical Development

721   ALEXANDRIN, Glen. "Unemployment in Newfoundland, 1949-1951." Ph.D., Clark University, 1964.
722   BOUVIER, Emile. *Unemployment Insurance in Canada, 1940-1950.* Montreal: Industrial Relations. University of Montreal, 1951.
723   _____. "Dix années d'assurance-chômage." *Relations.* (October 1950), pp. 300-304.
724   _____. "Innovation inquietance à l'assurance-chômage." *Relations.* (August 1964), pp. 228-30.
725   BROWN, Gerald H. "The Unemployment Insurance Act." *Labour Review.* 4:2 (November 1940), pp. 261-64.
726   CAIRNS, James P. "Unemployment Insurance in Canada: The Problem of Conflicting Principles." *Canadian Journal of Economics and Political Science.* 28:2 (1962), pp. 262-68.
727   "Canada's Programme for Meeting Unemployment." *Labour Gazette.* 21:1 (January 1921), pp. 43-47.
728   CANE, Thomas Michael. "A Test Case for Canadian Federalism: The Unemployment Insurance Issue, 1919-1940." M.A., University of Western Ontario, 1971.

729 CASSIDY, H.M. "The Case for Unemployment Insurance." *Canadian Forum.* 11:128 (May 1931), pp. 290-93.

730 _____. "Unemployment Insurance for Canada." *Queen's Quarterly.* 38:1 (Spring 1931), pp. 306-34.

731 COHEN, Jacob L. *The Canadian Unemployment Insurance Act — Its Relation to Social Security.* Toronto: Thomas Nelson, 1935.

732 "Commencement of Unemployment Insurance in Canada." *Labour Gazette.* 41:6 (June 1941), pp. 633-38.

733 "Congress Recommendations on Unemployment Insurance." *Canadian Unionist.* 26:7 (August 1952), pp. 238-39.

734 DALY, D.J. "Economic Aspects of Canada's Unemployment Insurance System." M.A., Queen's University, 1948.

735 DESORMEAUX, E.C. "L'assurance-chômage au Canada." M.A., University of Ottawa, 1944.

736 EASTON, D. "Social and Political Roots of the Unemployment Insurance Act." M.A., University of Toronto, 1942.

737 FELTEAU, Cyrille. "Chômage et l'assurance-chômage." M.A., Laval University, 1941.

738 FORTIER, Emilien. "L'assurance-chômage canadienne." M.A., Laval University, 1941.

739 FOWLER, Douglas Weatherbee. "The Unemployment Assistance Act, 1956, its Implications for Social Security and Public Welfare Administration in Canada." M.S.W., University of British Columbia, 1958.

740 GRAHAM, C.R. "Unemployment Insurance in Canada." M.A., McGill University, 1942.

741 GRAUER, A.E. "Is Unemployment Insurance Enough?" *University of Toronto Quarterly.* 4:4 (July 1935), pp. 514-23.

742 "Interim Report of the National Employment Commission, Survey of Relief Situation and Recommendations." *Labour Gazette.* 37:9 (September 1937), pp. 975-79.

743 JACKSON, Gilbert E. "Unemployment." *Canadian Banker.* 21:3 (April 1914), pp. 154-58.

744 KAGE, Joseph. "Some Thoughts on the Report of the Committee of Inquiry into the Unemployment Insurance Act." *Social Worker.* 31:2 (April-May 1963), pp. 27-33.

745 "Legislation Providing for Unemployment Insurance in Canada." *Labour Gazette.* 40:7 (July 1940), pp. 682-86.

746 LOGAN, H.A. "Unemployment Insurance in Canada." *Papers and Proceedings of the 4th Annual Meeting of the Canadian Political Science Association.* 4 (1932), pp. 34-56.

747 MARIER, Roger. "L'assurance sociale est fonction de la prudence politique." M.A., Laval University, 1941.

748 MERRIAM, R.C. "Unemployment Insurance." M.A., Queen's University, 1939.

749 "The National Attack on Unemployment, Review of Unemployment and Relief Situation by Minister of Labour and the Chairman of the National Employment Commission." *Labour Gazette.* 37:1 (January 1937), pp. 25-29.

750 "National Employment Commissioner's Final Report." *Canadian Congress Journal.* 17:4 (April 1938), pp. 11-18.

751 PICARD, R.L.M. "Unemployment Insurance with Special Reference to Canada." M.A., McGill University, 1942.

752   RELPH, H.S. "Goals of Social Legislation with Special Reference to Unemployment Insurance." *Canadian Unionist.* 22:7 (July 1948), pp. 154-56, 158-60.

753   SCHWEITZER, P.R. "Unemployment Insurance in Canada 1941-1958." M.A., McGill University, 1960.
        and Political Science. 1:4, (1935), pp. 436-56.

754   "Special Report of Unemployment Insurance Advisory Committee." *Labour Gazette.* 61:2 (February 1961), pp. 122-30.

755   STEWART, Bryce M. "The Employment Service of Canada." *Queen's Quarterly.* 27:1 (July 1919), pp. 37-61.

756   STRUTHERS, James. "Prelude to Depression: The Federal Government and Unemployment, 1918-1929." *Canadian Historical Review.* 58:3 (September 1977), pp. 277-94.

757   TIMMERMAN, E.D. "Unemployment Insurance — A Sketch." *Child and Family Welfare.* 8:3 (September 1932), pp. 44-50.

758   "20 Years of Unemployment Insurance." *Labour Gazette.* 61:10 (October 1961), pp. 1009-12.

759   "Unemployment and Farm Relief Act, 1931." *Labour Gazette.* 31:9 (September 1931), pp. 1005-1008.

760   "Unemployment and Farm Relief in Canada." *Labour Gazette.* 31:8 (August 1931), pp. 901-904.

761   "An Unemployment Commission." *Canadian Forum.* 17:200, (September 1937), p. 225.

762   "Unemployment Insurance." *Canadian Forum.* 1:12 (September 1921), p. 356.

763   "Unemployment Insurance." *Canadian Forum.* 17:203 (December 1937), pp. 295-96.

764   "Unemployment Insurance in Canada, Historical Background of Legislation — Outline of Administration of Unemployment Insurance Act, 1940-1943." *Labour Gazette.* 43:5 (May 1943), pp. 640-51.

765   "Unemployment Relief Act, 1930." *Labour Gazette.* 30:10 (October 1930), pp. 1140-42.

766   "Unemployment, Sickness and Invalidity Insurance." *Labour Gazette.* 28:4 (April 1928), pp. 361-67.

767   WHITTON, Charlotte. "The Relief of Unemployment." *Child and Family Welfare.* 17:1 (May 1936), pp. 15-33.

768   WON, Shirley. "Canada's Unemployment Insurance Program." *Labour Gazette.* 75:11 (November 1975), pp. 826-30.

6.2.2   Government Policy and Documentation

769   BEAUSOLEIL, Gilles, and BOUCHARD, Maurice. *The Role of the National Employment Service.* Ottawa: Queen's Printer, 1962.

770   BOIVIN, Jean, and SOLASSE, B. *L'assurance-chômage et les services aux travailleurs.* Commission d'enquête sur la santé et le bien-être social, Annexe 21. Quebec: Editeur officiel du Québec, 1970.

771   BROWN, Ray. "Unemployment Insurance and the National Employment Service." *Labour Gazette.* 50:9 (September 1950), pp. 1523-42.

772   CANADA. Committee of Inquiry into the Unemployment Insurance Act. *Report of the Committee of Inquiry into the Unemployment Insurance Act.* Ottawa: Queen's Printer, 1962.

773   CANADA.Parliament. House of Commons. Standing Committee on Labour, Manpower, and Immigration. *Reports Respecting the White Paper on Unemployment Insurance.* Ottawa: Queen's Printer, 1970.

774   CANADA.Unemployment Insurance Commission. *Report on the Comprehensive Review of the Unemployment Insurance Program in Canada.* Ottawa: The Commission, 1977.

775   "Guaranteed Wages and Supplemental Unemployment Benefits." *Labour Gazette.* 56:10 (October 1956), pp. 1244-49.

776   "Interprovincial Conference to Consider Unemployment Insurance in Canada." *Labour Gazette.* 32:12 (December 1932), pp. 1306-1308.

777   MANITOBA. Royal Commission on Seasonal Unemployment. *Report.* Winnipeg: King's Printer, 1928.

778   McLARTY, Norman A. "The Unemployment Insurance Plan." *Labour Review.* 5:5 (May 1941), pp. 68-69.

779   MURCHIE, R.W. *et al. Seasonal Unemployment in Manitoba.* Winnipeg: Legislative Assembly of Province of Manitoba, 1928.

780   "National Employment Commission." *Labour Gazette.* 36:3 (March 1936), pp. 299-300.

781   ONTARIO. Commission on Unemployment. *Report.* Toronto: King's Printer, 1916.

782   "Proposed Federal System of Insurance Against Unemployment, Sickness and Invalidity." *Labour Gazette.* 31:5 (May 1931), pp. 541-43.

783   "Quebec Social Insurance Commission, Reports: No. 5 Old Age Insurance; No. 6 Unemployment Insurance; and No. 7 Sickness and Disability Insurance." *Labour Gazette.* 33:2 (February 1933), pp. 161-66.

784   QUEBEC. Ministère des Affaires sociales. *Analyse du livre blanc fédéral sur l'assurance-chômage.* Quebec: Le ministère, 1971.

785   "Report of Committee of Inquiry into Unemployment Insurance Act." *Labour Gazette.* 63:2 (February 1963), pp. 119-22.

786   "Report of Committee of Inquiry into Unemployment Insurance Act." *Labour Gazette.* 63:4 (April 1963), p. 279.

6.2.3   Special Issues

787   AULD, D.A.L. "Inflation, Unemployment and Incomes Policies in Canada." *Queen's Quarterly.* 84:1 (Summer 1977), pp. 169-77.

788   BAETZ, Reuben C. "Unemployment Insurance and Other Federal Programs." *Conference Report.* Toronto: Canadian Tax Foundation, 1972, pp. 541-49.

789   CUTT, Jim. "Welfare and Unemployment Insurance." *Canadian Annual Review of Politics and Public Affairs.* (ed.) J. Saywell. Toronto: University of Toronto Press, 1972, pp. 348-57.

790   FINE, J.C., and NAGARAJAN, P. *The Impact of Unemployment Insurance on the Economy of Prince Edward Island.* Charlottetown: Department of Economics, University of Prince Edward Island, 1976.

791   GREEN, C., and COUSINEAU, J.M. *Unemployment in Canada: The Impact of Unemployment Insurance.* Ottawa: Economic Council of Canada, 1976.

792   HOUGHAM, George Millard. *The Relationship between Unemployment Insurance and Canada's Other Income Maintenance Programs.* Ottawa: Queen's Printer, 1962.

793   KALISKI, S.F. "Unemployment and Unemployment Insurance: Testing Some Corollaries." *Canadian Journal of Economics.* 9:4 (November 1976), pp. 705-12.

794   OWEN, C.F. "Guaranteed Wages and Unemployment Insurance in Canada." *Relations industrielles.* 10:4 (September 1955), pp. 237-51.

795   "Unemployment Insurance in Seasonal Industries." *Labour Gazette.* 48:6 (July 1948), pp. 752-54.

6.2.4 Financing

796 KELLY, Laurence Alexander. "Unemployment Insurance in Canada: Economic, Social and Financial Aspects." Ph.D., Queen's University, 1967.

797 WOLFENDEN, Hugh Herbert. *Unemployment Funds, A Survey and Proposal: A Study of Unemployment Insurance and Other Types of Funds for the Financial Assistance of the Unemployed.* Toronto: Macmillan, 1934.

6.2.5 Administration

798 BROWN, R. "Unemployment Insurance and the National Employment Service." *Labour Gazette.* 50:9 (September 1950), pp. 1524-42.

799 BUCHANAN, T.D. "The Application of the 1940 Canadian Unemployment Insurance Act in British Columbia." M.A., University of California, 1942.

800 CANADIAN COUNCIL ON CHILD AND FAMILY WELFARE. *Problems in the Social Administration of General and Unemployment Relief of Canada, 1933.* Ottawa: The Council, 1933.

801 *Conseils pratiques sur l'assurance-chômage: ou, comment ne pas se faire fourrez par l'assurance-chômage.* Montreal: Editions Québeçois, 1973.

802 HIDAKA, Kunio. "The Administration of Unemployment Assistance." M.A., Queen's University, 1945.

803 ISSALYS, Pierre, and WATKINS, Gaylord. *Les prestations d'assurance-chômage: une étude de la procedure administrative à la commission d'assurance-chômage.* Ottawa: Ministre des approvisionnements et services, 1977.

804 RELPH, H.S. "Quasi-judicial Powers under the Unemployment Insurance Act." *Canadian Bar Review.* 26:3 (1948), pp. 500-519.

805 ROSEN, E. *A Report on the Comprehensive Review of the Unemployment Insurance Program in Canada.* Ottawa: Advisory Council on the Status of Women, 1977.

806 WHITTON, C.E., and MARSH, L. *Administrative Implications Re: Unemployment Insurance, Employment Services and Unemployment Aid.* Ottawa: Canadian Welfare Council, n.d.

807 WILLARD, J.W. "The Administration of Unemployment Insurance." M.A., University of Toronto, 1942.

6.3 Maternity Benefits

6.3.1 General

808 CANADIAN LABOUR CONGRESS. *Submission to the Committee of Inquiry into the Unemployment Insurance Act.* Ottawa: The Congress, 1961.

809 CANADIAN MANUFACTURERS ASSOCIATION. *Submission to the Committee of Inquiry into the Unemployment Insurance Act.* Toronto: The Association, 1961.

810 CANADIAN PULP AND PAPER ASSOCIATION. *Submission to the Committee of Inquiry into the Unemployment Insurance Act.* Montreal: The Association, 1961.

811 LAVIGNE, E. *Maternity Leave Benefits under the Unemployment Insurance Act, (1971).* Ottawa: Advisory Council on the Status of Women, 1974.

812 NATIONAL COUNCIL OF WOMEN OF CANADA. *Brief Submitted to the Committee of Inquiry into Unemployment Insurance Act.* Ottawa: The Council, 1961.

813   ROBINDAINE Samur, L. *Maternity Leave and Benefits: A Study of Federal Laws and Recent Amendments Concerning Job Security for Pregnant Women and their Entitlement to Maternity Benefits.* Ottawa: Advisory Council on the Status of Women, 1976.

814   WOODSWORTH, S. *Maternity Protection for Women Workers in Canada.* Ottawa: Queen's Printer, 1967.

6.3.2   *Government Policy and Documentation*

6.3.2.1   Federal

815   CANADA. Department of Labour. *Maternity Leave Policies.* Ottawa: Queen's Printer, 1969.

816   CANADA. Department of Labour. Women's Bureau. *International Instruments and Canadian Federal and Provincial Legislation Relating to the Status of Women in Employment.* Ottawa: Queen's Printer, 1972.

817   _____. *Maternity Leave Policies: A Survey.* Queen's Printer, 1969.

6.3.2.2   Provincial

818   ONTARIO. Ministry of Labour. Women's Bureau. *Maternity Leave in the Ontario Public Service.* Toronto, 1972.

819   ONTARIO.Women's Crown Employees Office. *Comparative Survey of Pregnancy and Maternity Policies in the Provincial Governments of Canada and Ontario Crown Agencies.* Toronto: Women's Crown Employees Office, 1974.

7.0   Social Welfare Policies for People Who Cannot Work

7.1   Injured Workers: Workers' Compensation

7.1.1   *Historical Development*

7.1.1.1   General

820   ACTON, Theresa E. "The History of the Workmen's Compensation Movement in Ontario 1900-1930 — A Study in Social Policy Formation." M.S.W., Carleton University, 1977.

821   ARAB, E. "Early History of Workmen's Compensation." *Canadian Congress Journal.* 17:8 (August 1938), pp. 29-30.

822   BEAR, M.R. "The Impact of Social Change on the Organization of Welfare Services in Ontario from 1891-1921; The Development, Organization and Administration of the Workmen's Compensation Act of 1914." M.S.W., University of Toronto, 1966.

823   FINDLAY, Marion. "Protection of Workers in Industry." *Annals of the American Academy of Political and Social Science.* 107 (May 1923), pp. 254-66.

824   PIVA, Michael J. "The Workmen's Compensation Movement in Ontario." *Ontario History.* 67:1 (March 1975), pp. 39-56.

825   "Twenty-five Years of Unemployment Insurance." *Labour Gazette.* 66:11 (December 1966), p. 716.

7.1.1.2   Reviews of Policy

826   "Alberta Special Committee Reports on the Workmen's Compensation Act." *Labour Gazette.* 52:8 (August 1952), pp. 1053-57.

827   GOULD, R.W. "Changes Made in Quebec's Compensation Act." *Industrial Canada*. 26:7 (April 1926), pp. 44-45.

828   "Provisions Existing in Canada for the Rehabilitation of Injured Workmen." *Labour Gazette*. 29:3 (March 1929), pp. 283-86.

829   "Rehabilitation and Workmen's Compensation in Ontario." *Labour Gazette*. 28:6 (June 1928), pp. 598-603.

830   "Report of Commissioner on Workmen's Compensation in Ontario." *Labour Gazette*. 51:3 (March 1951), pp. 315-25.

831   "The Sloan Report." *Labour Gazette*. 53:4 (April 1953), pp. 552-69.

832   "Workmen's Compensation in Alberta and Nova Scotia." *Labour Gazette*. 48:5 (June 1948), pp. 569-70.

833   "Workmen's Compensation in British Columbia." *Labour Gazette*. 42:10 (October 1942), pp. 1158-59.

834   "Workmen's Compensation in Ontario." *Labour Gazette*. 32:4 (March 1932), pp. 407-11.

835   "Workmen's Compensation in the Province of Quebec." *Labour Gazette*. 30:2 (February 1930), pp. 159-61.

836   "Workmen's Compensation Under Review in Three Provinces." *Labour Gazette*. 50:1 (January 1950), pp. 39-42.

7.1.2   Government Policy and Documentation

837   ALBERTA. Legislative Assembly. Select Committee of Assembly. *Report on Workmen's Compensation Act*. Edmonton: Queen's Printer, 1975.

838   ALBERTA. Legislative Assembly. Special Committee Appointed to Inquire into and Make Recommendations on the Subject of Workmen's Compensation and the Workmen's Compensation Act. *Reports*. Edmonton: Legislative Assembly, 1952.

839   BRITISH COLUMBIA. Royal Commissions and Special Commissions of Inquiry into the Workmen's Compensation Act. *Report*. Victoria: Queen's Printer, 1966.

840   BRITISH COLUMBIA. Royal Commissions and Special Commissions. *Report of the Commission Relating to Workmen's Compensation*. Victoria: King's Printer, 1942.

841   BRITISH COLUMBIA. Royal Commission of Inquiry into the Workmen's Compensation Board and Act. *Report*. Vancouver: Queen's Printer, 1963.

842   CANADA. Department of Labour, Legislation Branch. *Workmen's Compensation in Canada*. Ottawa: Department of Labour, 1932.

843   "Legislation with Respect to Workmen's Compensation in Canada." *Labour Gazette*. 11 (November 1910), pp. 546-56.

844   MANITOBA. Commission on the Workmen's Compensation Act. *Report*. Winnipeg: Queen's Printer, 1958.

845   MANITOBA. Special Select Committee on the Adequacy of the Workmen's Compensation Act. *Report*. Winnipeg: Queen's Printer, 1953.

846   MANITOBA. Royal Commission on the Workmen's Compensation Board. *Report*. Winnipeg: King's Printer, 1917.

847   MANITOBA. Royal Commission to Inquire into and Investigate Every Aspect of the Workmen's Compensation Act. *Report*. Winnipeg: Queen's Printer, 1958.

848   MAVOR, James. *Report on Workingmen's Compensation for Industries*. Toronto: Legislative Assembly, 1900.

849   NEWFOUNDLAND. Review Committee Appointed to Review, Consid-
        er, Report Upon, and Make Recommendations Respecting the Work-
        men's Compensation Act. *Report on the Workmen's Compensation Act.*
        St. John's: Queen's Printer, 1966.
850   NOVA SCOTIA. Select Committee on Workmen's Compensation.
        *Report to the House of Assembly of the Select Committee on Workmen's
        Compensation.* Halifax: Queen's Printer, 1974.
851   NOVA SCOTIA. Royal Commission on Workmen's Compensation.
        Report. Halifax: King's Printer, 1937.
852   NOVA SCOTIA. Royal Commission to Inquire into the Workmen's
        Compensation Act of Nova Scotia. *Report.* Halifax: Queen's Printer,
        1958.
853   ONTARIO. Commission on Workmen's Compensation. *Interim Report.*
        Toronto: King's Printer, 1912.
854   ONTARIO. Royal Commission on the Workmen's Compensation Act.
        Report. Toronto: King's Printer, 1932.
855   ONTARIO. Royal Commission on the Workmen's Compensation Act.
        Report. Toronto: King's Printer, 1950.
856   ONTARIO. Royal Commission in the Matter of the Workmen's Com-
        pensation Act. *Report.* Toronto: Legislative Assembly, 1967.
857   ONTARIO. Royal Commission on Workmen's Compensation. *Final
        Report on Laws Relating to the Liability of Employers to Make Compensa-
        tion to Their Employees for Injuries Received in the Course of Their Em-
        ployment Which are in Force in Other Countries.* Toronto: King's Printer,
        1913.
858   ONTARIO. Task Force on the Workmen's Compensation Board. *The Ad-
        ministration of Workmen's Compensation in Ontario.* Toronto: Queen's
        Printer, 1973.
859   QUEBEC. Commission sur les accidents du travail. *Rapport.* Quebec: Im-
        primeur du roi, 1908.
860   QUEBEC. Commission d'étude sur la réparation des accidents du travail.
        Rapport. Quebec: Imprimeur du roi, 1925.
861   QUEBEC. Commission des accidents du travail. *Directives de la Commis-
        sion des accidents du travail du Québec.* Quebec: La commission, 1975.
862   SASKATCHEWAN. Committee of Review Appointed Under Provisions
        of the Workmen's Compensation Act. *Report.* Regina: Queen's Print-
        er, 1968.
863   SASKATCHEWAN. Royal Commission to Enquire into Workmen's
        Compensation for Saskatchewan. *Report.* Regina: King's Printer, 1929.

7.1.3   *General*

864   ASSOCIATION DES MANUFACTURIERS CANADIENS. Division de
        Québec. *Accidents du travail.* Mémoire à l'intention de l'honorable M.
        René Hamel. Quebec: L'association des manufacturiers canadiens,
        1961.
865   "Changes in 1962 in Provincial Workmen's Compensation Laws."
        Labour Gazette. 62:9 (September 1962), pp. 1012-15.
866   "Changes in 1963 in Provincial Workmen's Compensation Laws."
        Labour Gazette. 63:9 (September 1963), pp. 781-83.
867   "Changes in 1964 in Provincial Workmen's Compensation Laws."
        Labour Gazette. 64:10 (October 1964), pp. 856-58.
868   "Changes in Provincial Workmen's Compensation Laws, 1965." *Labour
        Gazette.* 65.11 (November 1965), pp. 1048-52.

869 "Changes in 1966 in Provincial Workmen's Compensation Laws."
     Labour Gazette. 66:9 (October 1966), p. 573.
870 CHARTIER, R. "La réparation des accidents du travail et la commission
     du salaire minimum des femmes, 1925-1931." *Relations industrielles.*
     18:1 (January 1963), pp. 45-58.
871 DEPATIE, Raymond. *Critique des moyens utilisés pour protéger le revenu de
     la famille en cas de décès du travailleur.* Montreal: Institut des recherches
     appliquée sur le travail, 1975.
872 FEDERATION DES TRAVAILLEURS DU QUEBEC. *La sécurité avant
     le travail.* Quebec: La fédération, 1975.
873 GAUVIN, Michel. "Worker's Compensation." *Labour Gazette.* 77:8
     (August 1977), p. 374.
874 HECKER, F.T. "La compensation des accidents du travail." *Bulletin des
     relations industrielles.* 3 (February 1948), pp. 91-95.
875 HOUSE, Milton F. "Labour Legislation in 1973 (Part 2 Workmen's
     Compensation)." *Labour Gazette.* 74:3 (March 1974), pp. 207-13.
876 "Industrial   Safety   and   Workmen's   Compensation   Legislation
     1967-1968." *Labour Gazette.* 69:2 (February 1969), pp. 84-87.
877 ISON, Terence George. *Sickness and Injury Compensation: A Proposal for
     Reform in British Columbia.* Vancouver, 1968.
878 "Labour Legislation in 1968-69 Part 3: Workmen's Compensation."
     Labour Gazette. 70:3 (March 1970), pp. 208-13.
879 "Labour Legislation in 1969-70 Part 3: Workmen's Compensation."
     Labour Gazette. 71:1 (January 1971), pp. 34-38.
880 "Labour Legislation of the Past Decade Part 3: Workmen's Compensa-
     tion." *Labour Gazette.* 61:2 (February 1961), pp. 144-46.
881 "Labour Relations Legislation in 1967 Part 3: Industrial Safety and Work-
     men's Compensation and Industrial Training." *Labour Gazette.* 68:2
     (February 1968), pp. 86-90.
882 LANGFORD, W.H. "Labour Legislation in 1972 Part 2: Workmen's
     Compensation." *Labour Gazette.* 73:3 (March 1973), pp. 162-68.
883 MORRIS, J. "Labour's Role in Rehabilitation." *Canadian Labour.* 18:4
     (April-June 1973), pp. 5-6.
884 SASKATCHEWAN FEDERATION OF LABOUR. *Submissions to Com-
     mittee of Review of Workmen's Compensation Act.* Regina: The Federa-
     tion, 1963.
885 WIRF, Ralph M. "The B.C. Workers' Compensation: A Model for Other
     Jurisdictions." *Labour Gazette.* 77:9 (September 1977), p. 404.

7.1.4 Financing

886 MICHELL, H. "Cost of Workmen's Compensation in Canada." *Industri-
     al Canada.* 28:8 (August 1927), pp. 40-43.

7.1.5 Administration

887 BANCROFT, Fred. "Workmen's Compensation." *"Proceedings of the
     Canadian Club of Toronto."* Toronto: Warwick Bros. & Rutter, 1914,
     pp. 262-69.
888 CANADIAN MANUFACTURERS' ASSOCIATION. *Workmen's Com-
     pensation.* Toronto: The Association, 1914.
889 COMMERCE CLEARING HOUSE CANADIAN. *Canadian Workmen's
     Compensation; Acts, Regulations, and Comparative Summary.* Toronto:
     Commerce Clearing House Canadian, 1958.

890   DALE, Edgar T. *Canadian Workmen's Compensation Acts and Cases*. Winnipeg: Butterworth & Company, 1915.

891   DEAN, T.N. "Workmen's Compensation for Industrial Accidents." M.A., University of Toronto, 1912.

892   EADES, J.E. "The Administrator as Judge as Applied to Workmen's Compensation." *In Proceedings of the 8th Annual Conference of the Institute of Public Administration of Canada*, pp. 289-98. Toronto: University of Toronto Press, 1956.

893   FORAN, T.P. *The Workmen's Compensation Act of Quebec*. Montreal: Wilson and Lafleur, 1910.

894   LAMOTHE, J. Cleophas. *Responsabilité du patron dans les accidents du travail*. Montreal: Carswell, 1905.

895   MASTERS, C.H. "Accident to Workman — Course of the Employment-Negligence." *Canadian Bar Review*. 4:7 (July 1926), pp. 503-506.

896   MERRILL, Walter Alfred, ed. *The Workmen's Compensation Act of Quebec and Reported Decisions*. Montreal: Wilson and Lafleur, 1916.

897   MICHELL, H. "Workmen's Compensation Results in Canada." *Industrial Canada*. 28:6 (June 1927), pp. 40-43.

898   "Report of Inquiry Commission on Manitoba Workmen's Compensation Act." *Labour Gazette*. 60:1 (January 1960), pp. 63-67.

899   "Report of Royal Commission on Nova Scotia Workmen's Compensation Act." *Labour Gazette*. 59:7 (July 1959), pp. 730-37.

900   WALTON, F.P. *The Workmen's Compensation Act, 1909, of the Province of Quebec with a Commentary*. Montreal: John Lovell & Sons, 1910.

901   WEAVER, Roy. "The Ontario Workmen's Compensation Bill." *Journal of Political Economy*. 21:8 (October 1913), pp. 752-61.

902   "Workmen's Compensation." *Canadian Bar Review*. 3:3 (March 1925), p. 144.

903   "Workmen's Compensation." *Canadian Forum*. 1:1 (November 1920), pp. 40-42.

904   "Workmen's Compensation Act." *Canadian Bar Review*. 3:2 (February 1925), pp. 99-101.

905   "Workmen's Compensation Acts Compared." *Industrial Canada*. 29:6 (June 1928), pp. 63-65.

906   "Workmen's Compensation — Disease Slowly Contracted — Accident." *Canadian Bar Review*. 5:10 (October 1926), pp. 710-11.

907   "Workmen's Compensation — Industrial Disease — Lead Poisoning." *Canadian Bar Review*. 5:6 (June 1927).

908   "Workmen's Compensation Legislation 1959." *Labour Gazette*. 59 (July-December 1959) pp. 937-45.

7.2   Retired Persons

7.2.1   Historical Development

909   BAILLIE, Donald Chesley. "Old Age Pensions in Ontario." Ph.D., Columbia University, 1941.

910   BASTEDO, S.T. "Government Annuities." *Queen's Quarterly*. 18:2 (Oct.-Dec. 1910), pp. 87-100.

911   BEGERT, Arline G. "Analysis of the Canadian Old Age Security System." M.A., Cornell University, 1954.

912   BELLAMY, Donald Frank. "A Study in Accommodation: The Development of Income Security for the Aged in Canada." M.A., Columbia University, 1971.

913   BEST, K.E. "Old Age Pension Legislation in Canada." M.A., McGill University, 1930.

914   BRUCE, Geoffrey F. "Development of Canada's Old Age Security Program." M.A., Columbia University, 1952.

915   BRYDEN, Kenneth. *Old Age Pensions and Policy Making in Canada.* Montreal: McGill-Queen's University Press, 1974.

916   _____. "Old Age Pensions and Policy Making in Canada." Ph.D., University of Toronto, 1970.

917   CANADIAN MANUFACTURERS' ASSOCIATION. *Old Age Pensions, Their History and Results.* Toronto: The Association, 1929.

918   _____. *Submissions to the Royal Commission on Dominion/Provincial Relations (Section III, Old Age Pensions and Unemployment Insurance).* Toronto: The Association, 1938.

919   DRUMOND, Andrew T. "A Social Experiment." *Queen's Quarterly.* 8:1 (July 1900), pp. 46-50.

920   HOLMES, Richard A. "Government Assistance to the Aged, with Particular Reference to the Province of Saskatchewan." M.A., University of Saskatchewan, 1956.

921   MacGREGOR, Donald Chalmers. *The Proposed Old Age Pension: The Limitations of a Universal Flat Rate System Supported by Earmarked Revenue.* Toronto: Canadian Tax Foundation, 1951.

922   MacKENZIE, M.A. "Old Age Pensions." *University of Toronto Monthly.* 8:8 (June 1908), pp. 260-66.

923   MAVOR, James. "Old Age Pensions." *University of Toronto Monthly.* 14:6 (April 1913), pp. 275-85.

924   MICHELL, H. "What Will Old Age Pensions Cost Canada?" *Industrial Canada.* 28:10 (October 1928), pp. 41-43.

925   "A National Old Age Pension Plan." *Canadian Forum.* 11:125 (February 1931), p. 65.

926   "Report on Pension Plans and the Employment of Older Workers." *Labour Gazette.* 57:12 (December 1957), pp. 1435-38.

927   STANFORD, Reid W. "An Early French Canadian Pension Agreement." *Canadian Historical Review.* 27:4 (September 1946), pp. 291-94.

928   WILLARD, Joseph W. "Some Aspects of Social Security in Canada: An Analysis of the Growth of Social Security Expenditures and the Development of Family Allowances and Old Age Security Programs in Canada." Ph.D., Harvard University, 1954.

7.2.2   Government Policy and Documentation

7.2.2.1   Federal

929   CANADA. Canada Pension Plan Advisory Committee. *Participation of Housewives in the Canada Pension Plan.* Ottawa: Information Canada, 1976.

930   CANADA. Department of Labour. *Old Age Pensions in Canada together with a Summary of Old Age Pension Systems in Other Countries.* Ottawa: King's Printer, 1929.

931   CANADA. Department of Labour. *Pension Plans and the Employment of Older Workers.* Ottawa: Queen's Printer, 1957.

932   CANADA. Health and Welfare Canada. *Canada Pension Plan: Analysis of Certain Proposals for Amending the Canada Pension Plan.* Ottawa: Information Canada, 1976.

933   CANADA. Parliament. House of Commons. Special Committee on Old
      Age System for Canada. *Proceedings . . . Comprising the Final Report
      and Evidence, May 6-June 30, 1924.* Ottawa. King's Printer, 1924.
934   CANADA. Parliament. Joint Committee on Old Age Security. *Report.*
      Ottawa: King's Printer, 1950.
935   CANADA. Parliament. Special Joint Committee of the Senate and of the
      House of Commons Appointed to Consider and Report upon Bill
      C-136, an Act to Establish a Comprehensive Program of Old Age Pen-
      sions and Supplementary Benefits in Canada. *Minutes of Proceedings
      and Evidence.* Ottawa: Queen's Printer, 1964-65.
936   CANADA. Royal Commission on Pensions and Reestablishment.
      Reports. Ottawa: King's Printer, 1923-24.
937   CANADA. Senate. Special Committee on Aging. *Final Report.* Ottawa:
      Queen's Printer, 1966.

7.2.2.2   Provincial

938   MANITOBA. Department of Health and Social Development. *The Home
      Care Program in Manitoba.* Winnipeg, 1976.
939   MARTIN, Jean-Marie. "Pour une politique de la vieillesse." *Annexe 17.*
      Quebec: Commission d'enqûete sur la santé et le bien-être social,
      1970.
940   NEWFOUNDLAND. Royal Commission on Pensions. *Report.* St.
      John's: Queen's Printer, 1966.
941   NOVA SCOTIA. Royal Commission Appointed to Consider Old Age
      Pensions. *Report.* Halifax: King's Printer, 1930.
942   NOVA SCOTIA. Royal Commission Respecting Old Age Pensions and
      Miners' Relief Societies. *Report.* Halifax: King's Printer, 1908.
943   "Old Age Pensions in Nova Scotia." *Labour Gazette.* 30:5 (May 1930),
      pp. 503-506.
944   ONTARIO. Ministry of Treasury, Economics, and Intergovernmental
      Affairs. *Review of Issues in Financing the Canada Pension Plan.*
      Toronto: The Ministry, 1976.
945   QUEBEC. Commission des pensions de vieillesse. *Pensions de vieillesse et
      pensions aux aveugles.* Quebec: Commission des pensions de vieillesse,
      1938.
946   QUEBEC. Ministère de la famille et du bien-être social. *Hébergement et
      soins spéciaux aux personnes âgées du Québec.* Quebec: Le ministère,
      1964-66.
947   _____. *Le bien-être social des personnes âgées dans la communauté de
      Québec.* Quebec: Le ministère, 1964-66.
948   SASKATCHEWAN. Department of Health. *Adding Life to Years: A
      Report Concerning Services and Facilities for Elderly in Britain and Scan-
      dinavian Countries, Belgium and Holland and Their Relevance to Sas-
      katchewan.* Regina: The Department, 1976.

7.2.3   *Special Issues*

7.2.3.1   General

949   BAUM, Daniel Jay. *The Final Plateau: The Betrayal of Our Older Citizens.*
      Don Mills, Ontario: Burns and MacEachern, 1974.
950   BROWN, Joan C. *How Much Choice? Retirement Policies in Canada.*
      Ottawa: Canadian Council on Social Development, 1975.
951   BUTLER, Peggy. "Pension: Reward or Right?" *Labour Gazette.* 71:7
      (July 1971), pp. 448-55.

952   CARMAN, Francis A. "Canadian Government Annuities." *Political Science Quarterly.* 30:3 (September 1915), pp. 425-47.

953   CLARK, Robert M. "The Pension Benefits Act of Ontario and Its Relation to Federal Proposals." In *Pensions in Canada*, edited by Lawrence E. Coward, pp. 27-44. Don Mills, Ontario: Commerce Clearing House Canadian, 1964.

954   COLLINS, Kevin. *Women and Pensions.* Ottawa: The Council, 1978.

955   COMMERCE CLEARING HOUSE CANADIAN LIMITED. *Canada Pension Plan and Old Age Security Legislation with Regulations.* Don Mills, Ontario: Commerce Clearing House Canadian, 1968.

956   CONFERENCE BOARD IN CANADA. *Perspectives on Pension Planning: A Round Table Discussion: A Report.* Ottawa: Conference Board in Canada, 1977.

957   COWARD, Laurence E. *Mercer Handbook of Canadian Pension and Welfare Plans.* Don Mills, Ontario: Commerce Clearing House Canadian, 1974.

958   ————, ed. *Pensions in Canada: A Compendium of Fact and Opinion.* Don Mills, Ontario: Commerce Clearing House Canadian 1964.

959   DAVIS, R.E.G. "Gearing Social Policy to the Needs of Old People." *Proceedings of the 8th Annual Congress of the Coordinating Council on Rehabilitation.* Regina: Coordinating Council on Rehabiliation, 1957.

960   DUDER, Sydney, and McGILLY, Frank J. *Income Security Programs: Old Age Security, Guaranteed Income Supplement, The Canada and Quebec Pension Plans.* Montreal: School of Social Work, McGill University, 1974. 1974.

961   HOME, George. "C.L.C. Pension Plan Campaign." *Canadian Labour.* 19:1 (March 1974), pp. 34-42.

962   ————. "This 'Free Stuff'/Ces cadeaux gratuits'." *Canadian Labour.* 15:1 (January 1970), pp. 16-26.

963   LaBERGE, Roy. "Canadian Council on Social Development Study: Canadian Retirement Policies." *Labour Gazette.* 76:6 (June 1976), pp. 316-19.

964   NATIONAL TRUST COMPANY. Pension Trust Department. *A Study of Canadian Pension Plans.* Toronto: National Trust Company, 1969.

965   PEDOE, Arthur. *Life Insurance Annuities and Pensions: A Canadian Text.* Toronto: University of Toronto Press, 1970.

966   YUDELMAN, John. *The National Context: A Report on Government Programs Concerning the Elderly.* For Pensioners Concerned (Canada) Inc., Toronto: Hickling-Johnson, 1974.

7.2.3.2   Old Age Pensions

967   ADAMS, W.J. "Old Age Security — An Issue with Conflicting Policies and Programs. *Canadian Business.* 36:8 (August 1963), pp. 66-70.

968   ALLENTUCK, Andrew. *The Cost of Age.* Toronto: Fitzhenry & Whiteside, 1977.

969   "Brief from the Canadian Association of Social Workers to the Parliamentary Committee on Old Age Security." *Social Worker.* 18:4 (April 1950), pp. 8-16.

970   "Canadian Government Annuities." *Labour Gazette.* 63:7 (July 1963), p. 546.

971   CLARK, Robert M. "Some Reflections on Economic Security for the Aged in Canada." In *Canadian Issues: Essays in Honour of Henry F. Angus*, edited by R.M. Clark. pp. 325-66. Toronto: University of Toronto Press, 1961.

972   DOUGLAS, Monteath. "Old Age Security." *Canadian Tax Journal*. 9:4
      (July/August 1961), pp. 309-13.
973   FINN, Ed. "The Debate Over Mandatory Retirement." *Labour Gazette*.
      78:1 (January 1978), p. 9.
974   GUAY, R. Edgar. "Sécurité sociale et pension de vieillesse." *Service
      social*. 1:1 (1951), pp. 91-96.
975   "Labour Congresses Submit Briefs on Old Age Security." *Labour
      Gazette*. 50:7 (July 1950), pp. 1011-13.
976   MacGREGOR, D.C. *The Proposed Old Age Pension, the Limitation of a
      Universal Flat Rate System Supported by Ear-Marked Revenue*. Toronto:
      Canadian Tax Foundation, 1951.
977   _____. "The Old Age Pension Legislation." *Report of the Proceedings
      of the Fifth Tax Conference*. Toronto: Canadian Tax Foundation, 1951.
978   MORGAN, John S. "Old Age Pensions in Canada: A Review and a
      Result." *Social Service Review*. 26:2 (June 1952), pp. 135-52.
979   "Ontario Draft Bill on Portable Pensions." *Labour Gazette*. 61:10 (Octo-
      ber 1961), pp. 1018-24.
980   "Pensions for Canadian Workers." *Labour Gazette*. 77:10 (October
      1977), p. 453.
981   "The Portable Pension Experiment." *Labour Gazette*. 63:5 (May 1963),
      pp. 368-71.
982   WALLACE, Elizabeth. "Old Age Security in Canada: Changing Atti-
      tudes." *Canadian Journal of Economics and Political Science*. 18:2 (May
      1952), pp. 125-34.

7.2.3.3   Canada Pension Plan

983   BELLAMY, Donald F. "The Case for Earning Related Social Security
      Benefits Restated: The Canadian Pension Plan, a Supplementary
      Insurance System." pp. 72-83. In *Old Age Income Assurance*, edited by
      Margaret S. Gordon. Washington: Government Printing Office, 1968.
984   BOSSEN, M. *et al. Sex Discrimination in Fringe Benefits*. Study prepared
      for the Advisory Council on the Status of Women. Ottawa: Queen's
      Printer, 1975.
985   CANADA. Canada Pension Plan Advisory Committee. *A Report to the
      Minister of National Health and Welfare on the Funding Principles of the
      Canada Pension Plan*. Ottawa: The Committee, 1976.
986   CANADA. Department of National Health and Welfare. *The Canada
      Pension Plan*. Ottawa: Queen's Printer, 1965.
987   _____. *Pension Plans; non-Financial Statistics, 1960*. Ottawa: Queen's
      Printer, 1962.
988   CANADIAN LABOUR CONGRESS. *Submissions to the Special Joint
      Committee of the Senate and of the House of Commons on the Canada
      Pension Plan (Bill C-136)*. Ottawa: The Congress, 1965.
989   CANADIAN LIFE INSURANCE OFFICERS ASSOCIATION. *Submis-
      sions to the Special Joint Committee of the Senate and House of Commons
      on the Canada Pension Plan*. Toronto: The Association, 1965.
990   CANADIAN PENSION CONFERENCE. *Symposium of Views on the
      Canada Pension Plan*. Don Mills, Ontario: Commerce Clearing House
      Canadian, 1964.
991   COMMERCE CLEARING HOUSE CANADIAN. *Canadian Pension
      Plan Guide — Laws, Regulations, Rulings, Decisions, Explanations, Orga-
      nized and Annotated by Topic*. Montreal: Commerce Clearing House
      Canadian, 1963.

992 MENZIES, S. June. *A.C.S.W. Recommendation Concerning Inclusion of Housewives in the Canada Pension Plan.* Ottawa: Advisory Council on the Status of Women, 1975.

993 QUEBEC. Department of Finance. Pension Plan Committee. *The Quebec Pension Plan.* Quebec: Pension Plan Committee, 1965.

7.2.4 Services

994 BAUM, Daniel J. *Warehouses for Death.* Don Mills, Ontario: Burns and MacEachern, 1977.

995 CANADIAN COUNCIL ON SOCIAL DEVELOPMENT. Advisory Committee on Visiting Homemaker Services. *Visiting Homemaker Services in Canada;* Report of a Survey with Recommendations, Ottawa: The Council, 1971.

996 _____. *The Visiting Homemaker: Preparation for Service; Proceedings of the National Institute on the Training of Visiting Homemakers.* Ottawa: The Council, 1974.

997 CANADIAN WELFARE COUNCIL. *At Home After 65; Housing and Related Services for the Aging.* Ottawa: The Council, 1964.

998 CASSANO, R. "Changing Trends in the Institutional Care of the Aged: A Study of Institutional Care in Metro with Special Emphasis on Social Policy Development." M.S.W., University of Toronto, 1965.

999 CORMACK, G.C., and HOLLING, S.A. "Homes for Special Care Program, Province of Ontario." *Canadian Journal of Public Health.* 56:11 (November 1965), pp. 469-73.

1000 GUEST, Dennis. "Transportation for the Elderly and Disabled: Social Service or Public Utility." *Canadian Welfare.* 53:2 (May/June 1977), pp. 7-10.

1001 HEPWORTH, H.P. *Residential and Community Services for Old People.* Vol. 6 of *Personal Social Services in Canada: A Review.* Ottawa: Canadian Council on Social Development, 1975.

1002 LYONS, Walter. "The Dynamics of Sheltered Care for the Aged." *Canadian Conference on Aging.* Ottawa: Canadian Council on Social Development, 1966.

1003 _____. "Services to the Aged Beyond the Institutional Setting — What is Our Responsibility." *Canadian Welfare.* 42:1 (January 1966), pp. 2-7.

1004 "Service for Old People." *Labour Gazette.* 75:6 (June 1975), pp. 334-35.

1005 "Vocational Rehabilitation of Older Disabled Persons." *Labour Gazette.* 64:2 (February 1964), p. 116.

1006 ZAY, Nicolas. "Living Arrangements for the Aged." *Canadian Conference on Aging.* Ottawa: Canadian Welfare Council, 1966.

7.2.5 Financing

1007 DOUGLAS, Monteath. *Financing Old Age Pensions: A Personal View.* Toronto: Canadian Tax Foundation, 1951.

1008 PERRY, J.H. "Financing Old Age Security." *Canadian Welfare.* 35:6 (November 1959), pp. 254-58.

7.2.6 Administration

1009 CANADIAN COUNCIL ON SOCIAL DEVELOPMENT. *Administration of Homes for the Aged, A Work Book on the Human Aspects of Administration of Homes for the Aged Based on Presentations Given at the National Seminar for Administrators of Homes for the Aged in Canada.* Ottawa: The Council, 1971.

1010 KLEILER, Frank M. *Canadian Regulation of Pension Plans*. Washington: Department of Labor, Labor Management Sciences Administration, 1970.

1011 YELAJA, Shankar A. "The Elderly and Social Policy." *Canadian Social Policy*, edited by S. A. Yelaja, pp. 147-67. Waterloo: Wilfrid Laurier University Press, 1978.

7.3   Physically Disabled Persons

7.3.1   Historical Development

1012 WHITTON, Charlotte, "Public Liability in Provinces of Canada for Care and Treatment of Crippled Children." *Canadian Child Welfare News*. 4:2 (May 1928), pp. 29-36.

7.3.2   Government Policy and Documentation

1013 ONTARIO. Ministry of Health. *Report of the Task Force on the Development of a Policy Paper on the Future of Services for Physically Handicapped Children*. Toronto: The Ministry. 1976.

7.3.3   Special Issues

7.3.3.1   Rehabilitation of Handicapped

1014 HAMILTON, D.F. "Rehabilitation Services of the Ontario Workmen's Compensation Board." *Canadian Labour*. 18:4 (April-June 1973), pp. 10-14.

1015 HOPPER, R.W. "The Rehabilitation of the Crippled Child." *Social Welfare*. 14:5 (February 1932), pp. 87-90.

1016 ONTARIO MEDICAL ASSOCIATION. Child Welfare Committee. *A Program for Handicapped Children*. Toronto: Ontario Medical Association, Child Welfare Committee, and Atkinson Charitable Foundation, 1962.

1017 PACIFIC REHABILITATION WORKSHOPS ASSOCIATION. *National Guidelines for the Development and Operation of Workshop Programs and Services for the Handicapped: A Handbook*. Vancouver: The Association, 1975.

1018 "Second Meeting, National Advisory Council on the Rehabilitation of Disabled Persons." *Labour Gazette*. 63:6 (June 1963), pp. 478-82.

1019 SHAH, Chandrakant P. "Rehabilitation of Handicapped Children: Hospital, Day Care Unit or Residential Center." *Canadian Journal of Public Health*. 64:5 (May/June 1973), pp. 269-75.

1020 "Vocational Rehabilitation Services for Handicapped to be Extended." *Labour Gazette*. 66:1 (January/February 1966), pp. 18-19.

7.3.3.2   Employment of Handicapped

1021 BOURGEOUS, Paulette. "Employment of the Handicapped in the Federal Public Service." *Labour Gazette*. 78:8 (August 1978), p. 361.

7.3.3.3   Citizen Advocacy

1022 WOLFENSBERGER, Wolf, and ZAUHA, Helen, eds. *Citizen Advocacy and Protective Services for the Impaired and Handicapped*. Downsview, Ontario: National Institute on Mental Retardation, 1973.

7.3.3.4   The Blind

1023 GREENLAND, Cyril. *Vision Canada: The Unmet Needs of Blind Canadians.* Ottawa: Canadian National Institute of the Blind, 1976.
1024 KELLEY, William N. "The Case of the Canadian National Institute of the Blind." *Canadian Forum.* 17:203 (December 1937), pp. 307-309.
1025 NESBIT, Dorothy. "The Plight of the Blind in British Columbia." *Canadian Forum.* 17:200 (September 1937), pp. 204-206.
1026 VERNEY, Allen. "Pensions and the Blind." *Canadian Forum.* 17:200 (September 1937), pp. 235-36.

7.4   Mentally Disabled Persons

7.4.1   Historical Development

1027 ALLODI, Fedrico, and KEDWARD, Henry B. "The Evolution of the Mental Hospital in Canada." *Canadian Journal of Public Health.* 68:3 (May/June 1977), pp. 219-25.
1028 CANADIAN MENTAL HEALTH ASSOCIATION. *Milestones in Mental Health: A Record of Achievements 1918-1958.* Toronto: The Association, 1960.
1029 _____. *More for the Mind: A Study of Psychiatric Services in Canada.* Toronto: The Association, 1963.
1030 CLARKE, Ken H. "Public Provisions for the Mentally Ill in Alberta, 1907-1936." M.A., University of Calgary, 1973.
1031 CURRY, Starr. "Early Efforts to Improve Services for the Mentally Retarded in Nova Scotia." *Nova Scotia Historical Quarterly.* 5:4 (December 1975), pp. 381-90.
1032 FRANCIS, Daniel. "That Prison on the Hill; the Historical Origins of the Lunatic Asylum in the Maritime Provinces." M.A., Carleton University, 1975.
1033 _____. "The Development of the Lunatic Asylum in the Maritime Provinces." *Acadiensis.* 6:2 (Spring 1977), pp. 23-39.
1034 GREENLAND, Cyril. "Services for the Mentally Retarded in Ontario, 1870-1930." *Ontario History.* 54:4 (December, 1962) pp. 267-74.
1035 HACKETT, G.T. "History of Public Education for Mentally Retarded Children in the Province of Ontario, 1867-1964." D.Ed., University of Toronto, 1969.
1036 HAGMAN, R. "Mental Illness; the Mental Health Movement and the Trend Towards a Therapeutic Society." M.A., Simon Fraser University, 1974.
1037 LAVELL, Alfred E. "Beginning of Ontario Mental Hospitals." *Queen's Quarterly.* 49:1 (Spring 1942), pp. 59-67.
1038 MOONEY, Craig M. *Mental Retardation Developments in Canada, 1964-1970.* Ottawa: Department of National Health and Welfare, 1971.
1039 POLLOCK, Sheila Joy. "Social Policy for Mental Health in Ontario, 1930-1967." D.S.W., University of Toronto, 1974.
1040 POULIN, Gonzalve. "L'hygiene mentale dans la province de Québec aux debuts de xixe siécle." *Service social.* 1:2 (June 1951), pp. 86-87.
1041 RYAN, William. "Community Care in Historical Perspective: Implications for Mental Health Services and Professionals." *Canada's Mental Health,* Supplement 60. Ottawa: Department of National Health and Welfare, 1969.
1042 SIMS, Valerie A. *Historical Development of Sheltered Workshops in Canada.* Winnipeg: University of Manitoba Press, 1965.

1043 WOLFENSBERGER, Wolf. *A Look Into the Future for Systems of Human Services with Special Relevance to Mental Retardation.* Toronto: National Institute of Mental Retardation, 1973.

7.4.2   Government Policy and Documentation

7.4.2.1   Federal

1044 CANADA. Department of National Health and Welfare. *Mental Retardation Activities of the Department.* Ottawa: Queen's Printer, 1964.

1045 _____. *Organization and Administration of Rehabilitation Services for the Disabled in Canada, 1970.* Ottawa: Information Canada, 1971.

1046 _____. *Rehabilitation Services in Canada.* Ottawa: Research and Statistics Division, National Health and Welfare, 1959-60.

1047 _____. *The Role of the Federal Government in Mental Health.* Ottawa: The Department, 1973.

1048 _____. *Services for the Care and Training of Mentally Defective Persons in Canada.* Ottawa: The Department, 1953.

1049 _____. *Survey of Provincial Grants in Support of Local Facilities for the Mentally Retarded.* Ottawa: The Department, 1964.

1050 _____. Office of Solicitor General. Task Force on Community-Based Residential Centres. *Report.* Ottawa: Information Canada, 1973.

1051 ISABELLE, P., and DOLAN, W.J. Mental Health in Canada. *Report.* Federal-Provincial Conference on Mental Retardation. Ottawa: Department of National Health and Welfare, 1964.

7.4.2.2   Provincial

1052 BRITISH COLUMBIA. Department of Health Services and Hospital Insurance and Department of Social Welfare. *A Spectrum of Mental Retardation Services.* Prepared for Federal-Provincial Conference on Mental Retardation. Vancouver, 1964.

1053 MANITOBA. Department of Health and Public Welfare. *Manitoba's Mental Retardation Services.* Federal-Provincial Conference on Mental Retardation. Winnipeg: Department of Health and Public Welfare, 1964.

1054 MANITOBA. Department of Health and Social Development. *Mental Health and Retardation Services in Manitoba.* Winnipeg: Department of Health and Social Development, 1973.

1055 NEW BRUNSWICK. Department of Health. *Provincial Report.* Federal-Provincial Conference on Mental Retardation. Fredericton: Department of Health, 1964.

1056 _____. Study Committee on Mental Health Services in the Province of New Brunswick. *Report.* Saint John: Department of Health, 1968.

1057 NEW BRUNSWICK. Office of Mental Retardation. *Mental Retardation in New Brunswick: In Search of a Policy.* Saint John: Office of Mental Retardation, 1975.

1058 NEWFOUNDLAND. *A Spectrum of Mental Retardation Services in the Province of Newfoundland.* Federal-Provincial Conference on Mental Retardation. St. John's: Government of Newfoundland, 1964.

1059 NEWFOUNDLAND. Department of Health. *Report on Services to Children.* St. John's: The Department, 1974.

1060 NOVA SCOTIA. Commission Respecting the Feebleminded in Nova Scotia. *Report.* (Included in the *Journals of the Nova Scotia House of Assembly*, Appendix 33, 1917). Halifax, 1916.

1061 NOVA SCOTIA. Department of Public Welfare. Working Committee. *Report*. Federal-Provincial Conference on Mental Retardation. Halifax: The Department, 1964.

1062 ONTARIO. Department of Education. *Programs and Services for Children and Youth Who are Educationally Retarded*. Toronto: The Department, 1969.

1063 ONTARIO.Department of Health. *A New Day. A New Age (and) Description of the Unit System Within the Residential Facilities for the Mentally Retarded in Ontario*. Toronto: The Department, 1969.

1064 _____. *A Spectrum of Mental Retardation Services in Ontario*. Federal-Provincial Conference on Mental Retardation. Toronto: The Department, 1964.

1065 _____. *Services for Children with Mental and Emotional Disorders*. Toronto: The Department, 1967.

1066 ONTARIO. Ministry of Health. Task Force on Mental Retardation Needs and Services. *Recommendations on Mental Retardation Services and Programs in North-Eastern Ontario*. Toronto: The Ministry, 1972.

1067 ONTARIO. Ministry of Community and Social Services. Advisory Council on Day Care. *Final Report*. Toronto: The Ministry, 1976.

1068 _____. *Community Services for the Mentally Retarded: Detailed Program Proposal and Implementation Plan*. Toronto: The Ministry, 1975.

1069 _____. *Discussion Paper on a New Mental Retardation Program for Ontario*. Toronto: The Ministry, 1974.

1070 _____. *Discussion Paper on Planning and Organizing for Services to the Retarded in Ontario*. Winnipeg: Inter-Provincial Meetings of Ministers of Social Development, 1974.

1071 _____. Inquiry Into the Management and Operation of the Huronia Regional Center. *Report*. Toronto: The Ministry, 1976.

1072 _____. *A New Mental Retardation Program for Ontario*. Toronto: The Ministry, 1974.

1073 _____. *Principles for the Development of Services for the Mentally Retarded in the Province of Ontario*. Toronto: The Ministry, 1976.

1074 _____. *Services for Children with Mental and Emotional Disorders*. Toronto: Queen's Printer, 1966.

1075 PRINCE EDWARD ISLAND. Department of Health. Federal-Provincial Conference on Mental Retardation. *Retardation Services on Prince Edward Island*. Charlottetown: The Department, 1964.

1076 QUEBEC. Ministry of Health. *Un exposé sur la déficience mentale au Québec*. Federal-Provincial Conference on Mental Retardation. Quebec: Ministry of Health, 1964.

1077 SASKATCHEWAN. Department of Public Health. *A Spectrum of Services to the Mentally Retarded in Saskatchewan*. Federal-Provincial Conference on Mental Retardation. Regina: The Department, 1964.

7.4.2.3   Municipal

1078 EDMONTON. Social Services. *Services in Edmonton for the Mentally Retarded*. Edmonton: Social Services, 1974.

7.4.3   Special Issues

7.4.3.1   General

1079 ALBERTA ASSOCIATION FOR RETARDED CHILDREN. *Brief Concerning the Needs of the Mentally Retarded in Alberta*. Edmonton: The Association, 1968.

1080 BECK, M.N. *Retardation Services on Prince Edward Island.* Ottawa: Federal-Provincial Conference on Mental Retardation, 1964. Revised edition 1968, 1972.

1081 BLAIR, W.R.N. Mental Health in Alberta. *A Report to the Alberta Mental Health Study of 1968.* Edmonton: Human Research and Development Executive Council, 1969.

1082 _____. *Mental Health in Alberta.* Vol. II. Edmonton: Queen's Printer, 1973.

1083 BROWN, W.G., and WALKER, Charles. "Mental Hospital Legislation in Ontario." *University of Toronto Law Journal.* 15:1 (1963), pp. 195-224.

1084 CANADIAN ASSOCIATION FOR RETARDED CHILDREN. *Brief Respecting the Disabled Persons Act and Mentally Defective Persons.* Toronto: The Association, 1957.

1085 _____. *Brief to the Royal Commission on Health Services.* Toronto: The Association, 1962.

1086 _____. Nova Scotia Divison. *Brief to the Royal Commission on Health Services concerning Current Problems in the Care, Training and Education of Retarded Persons.* Halifax: The Association, 1961.

1087 _____. *Let's Plan Together; A Brief on Future Planning for the Care, Training and Education of Retarded Persons.* Halifax: The Association, 1971.

1088 _____. Winnipeg Branch. *Policy Paper.* Winnipeg: The Association, 1975.

1089 _____. Winnipeg Branch. *Submission on Canadian Immigration Law As It Pertains to the Mentally Retarded.* Winnipeg: The Association, Manitoba Division, 1976.

1090 CANADIAN MENTAL HEALTH ASSOCIATION. *Mental Health Services in Canada; Hospital Care.* Toronto: The Association, 1956.

1091 _____. *Statement Prepared for Federal-Provincial Conference on Mental Retardation.* Toronto: The Association, 1964.

1092 _____. *Submission to the Royal Commission on Health Services.* Toronto: The Association, 1962.

1093 _____. *Why the Wagon Creaks and Groans: A Report.* Toronto: The Association, 1975.

1094 _____. British Columbia Division. *The Mental Health of Children in British Columbia; Final Report.* Vancouver: The Association, 1966.

1095 _____. Committee on Psychiatric Services. *More for the Mind: A Study of Psychiatric Services in Canada.* Toronto: The Association, 1963.

1096 CANADIAN PSYCHIATRIC ASSOCIATION. *Submission to the Federal-Provincial Conference on Mental Retardation.* Ottawa: The Association, 1964.

1097 CANADIAN REHABILITATION COUNCIL FOR THE DISABLED. *A Submission to the Royal Commission on Human Rights.* Toronto: The Council, 1963.

1098 CARROTHERS, A.W. *A Report on Mental Health Legislation in British Columbia.* Vancouver: Faculty of Law, University of British Columbia, 1959.

1099 CLARKE, C.K. "Ontario's Government Clinic of Nervous and Mental Diseases." *Ontario's Sessional Papers.* 43:21 (1911), pp. 101-102.

1100 CLAYTON, John K. *The Procrustean Bed: Values and Attitudes.* Toronto: Canadian Mental Health Association, 1975.

1101 COMMISSION ON EMOTIONAL AND LEARNING DISORDERS IN CHILDREN. British Columbia Committee. *The Application of the CELDIC (Commission on Emotional and Learning Disabilities in Children) to British Columbia.* British Columbia CELDIC Committee. Vancouver, 1973.

1102 _____. *One Million Children.* Toronto; Leonard Crainford for the CELDIC Commission, 1970.

1103 _____. Ontario Committee. *Report.* Toronto: The Commission, 1970.

1104 THE COUNCIL FOR EXCEPTIONAL CHILDREN IN CANADA. *A Matter of Principle: Principles Governing Legislation for Services for Children with Special Needs.* Regina: The Council, 1974.

1105 CRICHTON, Anne. *Mental Health and Social Policy in Canada.* Vancouver: Department of Health and Epidemiology, University of British Columbia, 1974.

1106 DRAPER, Gary. *Lunacy in Legislation: A Guide to Federal and Alberta Legislation Regarding Idiocy, Imbecility, Insanity and Unsoundness of Mind.* Edmonton: Alberta Law Foundation, 1975.

1107 LINDENFIELD, R. "The New Look in Mental Health Services; Its Implications for Social Work." *Canada's Mental Health.* 12:6 (November/December 1964), pp. 10-16.

1108 METROPOLITAN TORONTO ASSOCIATION FOR RETARDED CHILDREN. *Ontario's New Mental Health Act: Some Highlights.* Toronto: The Association, 1968.

1109 ONTARIO FEDERATION COUNCIL FOR EXCEPTIONAL CHILDREN. *We Are Not Alike: Policies for Education in Our Time.* Ontario: The Council, 1973.

1110 QUEBEC ASSOCIATION FOR THE HELP OF RETARDED CHILDREN. *Brief Respecting a Program for the Care of Mentally Retarded Persons in the Province of Quebec.* Quebec: The Association, 1960.

1111 WOLFENSBERGER, Wolf. *Refections on Reading Old Annual Government Reports on the Lunatic and Idiot Asylums of the Province of Ontario.* Downsview, Ontario: National Institute of Mental Retardation, 1973.

7.4.3.2   Education

1112 BALLANCE, Karoline E. *Legislation for Exceptional Children: Report.* Canadian Committee of the Council for Exceptional Children, 1972.

1113 LAYCOCK, Samuel R. *Special Education/ Facilities d'éducation speciales pour enfants.* Ste. Adele, Quebec: Canadian Conference on Children, 1960.

7.4.3.3   Residential Care and Community Living

1114 BERGMAN, Joel S. ed. *Community Homes for the Retarded.* Toronto: D.C. Heath, 1975.

1115 BOURNEMANN, Steve. *Residential Services for Mentally Retarded Persons in Nova Scotia.* Halifax: Canadian Association for the Mentally Retarded, n.d.

1116 EDMONTON REGIONAL COORDINATOR'S OFFICE. *Edmonton's Residential Services for the Handicapped.* Edmonton: Regional Coordinator's Office, 1976.

1117 ELKIN, Lorne *et al. A Question of Rights: Saskatchewan's Mentally Retarded Move from Institutions to the Community.* Moose Jaw, Saskatchewan, 1976.

1118 GORDON, Peter Allan. *Residential Care of the Mentally Retarded — A Discussion of Some Relevant Factors.* Toronto: York University Press, 1975.

1119 HAYDAY, Bryan. *Residential Services for the Mentally Retarded: A Synthesis of Underlying Principles.* Toronto: York University Press, 1976.

1120 NATIONAL INSTITUTE ON MENTAL RETARDATION. *A Plan for Comprehensive Community Services for the Developmentally Handicapped.* Downsview, Ontario: The Institute, 1973.

1121 _____. Residential Services. *Community Housing Options for Handicapped People.* Downsview, Ontario: The Institute, 1975.

1122 ONTARIO ASSOCIATION FOR THE MENTALLY RETARDED. *A Community Residence — A Community Need.* Toronto: The Association, 1968.

1123 OTTAWA. Social Planning Council. *Planning and Coordination of Community Based Residential Centers.* Ottawa: The Council, 1974.

1124 RAE-GRANT, Quentin, and MOFFAT, Patricia. *Children in Canada, Residential Care.* Toronto: Canadian Mental Health Association, 1971.

1125 ROBERTSON, Angus M. *Problems of Mentally Retarded Persons in Ontario with Regard to Housing.* Toronto: Ontario Association for the Mentally Retarded, 1973.

1126 WELCH, Robert. *Community Living for the Mentally Retarded in Ontario: A New Policy Focus.* Toronto: Cabinet Committee on Social Development, 1973.

7.4.3.4   Sheltered Workshops

1127 ATLANTIC ASSOCIATION OF REHABILITATION WORKSHOPS. *A Paper on Sheltered Workshops in New Brunswick.* Saint John: The Association, 1976.

1128 CANADIAN ASSOCIATION FOR RETARDED CHILDREN. *Position Concerning Government Support for Sheltered Employment.* Toronto: The Association, 1967.

7.4.4   Administration

1129 CARTER, Novia. *Trends in Voluntary Support for Non-Government Social Service Agencies.* Ottawa: Canadian Council on Social Development, 1974.

1130 CONNERY, Robert H. *The Politics of Mental Health; Organizing Community Mental Health in Metropolitan Areas.* Montreal: McGill University Press, 1968.

1131 CRICHTON, Anne. "Mental Health and Social Policies: An Overview." *Canada's Mental Health.* 23:4 (March 1975) pp. 1-4.

1132 MARTEL, Pierre G. *Role of the Federal Government in Mental Health: A Report.* Ottawa: Martel Commission on Mental Health, 1973.

1133 SASKATCHEWAN ASSOCIATION FOR THE MENTALLY RETARDED. *Comprehensive Community Based Services: Public Policy and Legislative Requirements.* Regina: The Association, 1976.

1134 _____. *Governance of Human Services.* Regina: The Association, 1974.

1135 ZARFAS, Donald E. *Organization and Function of the Mental Retardation Services Branch.* Toronto: Mental Health Division, Department of Health, 1970.

8.0   Social Welfare Policies for "Marginal" People

8.1   The Justice and Correctional Systems

8.1.1   Historical Development

8.1.1.1   General

1136 ANDERSON, Frank W. "Prisons and Prison Reforms in the Old Canadian West." *Canadian Journal of Corrections.* 2:2 (April 1960), pp. 209-15.

1137 BADER, Michael, and BURNSTEIN, Edward. "The Supreme Court of Canada 1892-1902: A Study of Men and the Times." *Osgoode Hall Journal.* 8:3 (December 1970), pp. 503-47.

1138 BELLAMO, Gerald J. "Upper Canadian Attitudes towards Crime and Punishment." *Ontario History.* 64:1 (March 1972), pp. 11-26.

1139 BORTHWICK, John Douglas. *From Darkness to Light; History of the Eight Prisons Which Have Been, or Are Now in Montreal, from A.D. 1760 to A.D. 1907 — 'Civil and Military'.* Montreal: Gazette Printing Company, 1907.

1140 CHAMBERS, Capt. Ernest, Jr. *The North West Mounted Police: A Corps History.* Ottawa: Mortimer Press, 1907.

1141 The Commission of the Royal North-West Mounted Police. *Opening Up the West, Being the Official Reports to Parliament of the Activities of the Royal North-West Mounted Police Force, from 1874-1881.* Toronto: Coles Publishing Company, 1973.

1142 _____. *Settlers and Rebels, Being the Official Reports to Parliament of the Activities of the Royal North-West Mounted Police Force from 1882-1885.* Toronto: Coles Publishing Company, 1973.

1143 _____. *Being the Official Reports to Parliament of the Activities of the Royal North-West Mounted Police Force from 1886-1887.* Toronto: Coles Publishing Company, 1973.

1144 _____. *The New West, Being the Official Reports to Parliament of the Activities of the Royal North West Mounted Police Force from 1888-1889.* Toronto: Coles Publishing Company, 1973.

1145 CROUSE, G.H. "The Criminal Code: A Study in the Development of Canadian Criminal Legislation." M.A., Harvard Law School, 1933.

1146 _____. "A Critique of Canadian Criminal Legislation." *Canadian Bar Review.* 12:9 (November 1934), pp. 545-78.

1147 DOUCET, N.B. *Fundamental Principles of Laws of Canada.* Montreal, 1841.

1148 EDMISON, J. Alex. "The History of Kingston Penitentiary." *Historic Kingston.* Kingston Historic Society, 3 (November 1954), pp. 26-35.

1149 _____. "Some Aspects of 19th Century Canadian Prisons." In *Crime and Its Treatment in Canada.* edited by W.T. McGrath. 2nd ed., pp. 279-302. Toronto: Macmillan of Canada, 1976.

1150 FISER, Vladimir. "The Impact of Social Change on the Organization of Welfare Services in Ontario, 1891-1921: Juvenile Delinquency." M.S.W., University of Toronto, 1966.

1151 HAYDON, A.L. *The Riders of the Plains: A Record of the Royal North West Mounted Police of Canada, 1873-1910.* Toronto: Copp Clark, 1910.

1152 HORRALL, S.W. "Sir John A. Macdonald and the Mounted Police Force for the Northwest Territories." *Canadian Historical Review.* 53:2 (June 1972), pp. 179-200.

1153 JOHNSTONE, W.F., and HENHEFFER, B.W. "History of Treatment in Canadian Penitentiaries." *Canadian Welfare.* 29 (September 1953), pp. 5-9.

1154 KAVANAGH, Henry J. *Civil Code of Lower Canada, with the Amendments Effected by Imperial, Federal and Provincial Legislation, up to and including the Fourth Session of 12th Legislature of P.Q. & George V., 1912.* Montreal: John Lowell & Sons, 1912.

1155 KENNY, Wilma L.G. "The Impact of Social Change on the Organization of Welfare Services in Ontario, 1891-1921: Adult Corrections." M.S.W., University of Toronto, 1966.

1156 KIRKPATRICK, A.M. "Jail in Historical Perspective." *Canadian Journal of Corrections.* 6:4 (October 1964), pp. 405-17.

1157 LEON, J.S. "The Development of Juvenile Justice: A Background for Reform." *Osgoode Hall Law Journal.* 15:1 (June 1977), pp. 71-107.

1158 MacBETH, R.G. *Policing the Plains: Being the Real Life Records of the Famous Royal North West Mounted Police.* London: Hodder and Stoughton, 1921.

1159 McCLEOD, R.C. *The North West Mounted Police and Law Enforcement 1873-1905.* Toronto: University of Toronto Press, 1976.

1160 PRINCE, Ellen. "A History of the John Howard Society of Quebec Incorporated." M.S.W., McGill University, 1956.

1161 SENIOR, Elinor. "The Provincial Cavalry in Lower Canada, 1837-1850." *Canadian Historical Review.* 57:1 (March 1976), pp. 1-24.

1162 *The Supreme Court of Canada, 1875-1975/ La cour supreme du Canada, 1875-1975.* Ottawa: Canadian Bar Association, 1975.

1163 TURNER, John Peter. *The North-West Mounted Police 1873-1893.* Ottawa: King's Printer, 1950.

8.1.1.2 Reviews of Policy

1164 ADAM, G.M. "Public Justice in Manitoba." *Bystander.* 2 (April 1881), p. 191.

1165 ARDAGH, W.D., and HARRISON, R.A. "Law Equity and Justice." *Upper Canada Law Journal.* 4:8 (August 1858), pp. 171-72.

1166 CHRISTIE, Hugh G. "Treatment in Provincial Institutions." *Canadian Bar Review.* 27:9 (November 1949), pp. 1052-66.

1167 DYMOND, Allan M. *The Laws of Ontario Relating to Women and Children.* Toronto: Clarkson W. Janus, 1923.

1168 FEATHERSTONHAUGH, R.C. *The Royal Canadian Mounted Police.* Toronto: McClelland and Stewart, 1938.

1169 GIBSON, R.B. "Treatment in Federal Institutions." *Canadian Bar Review.* 27:9 (November 1949), pp. 1041-51.

1170 JENKS, C.W. "The Dominion Jurisdiction in Respect of Criminal Law as a Basis for Social Legislation in Canada." *Canadian Bar Review.* 13:5 (May 1935), pp. 279-89.

1171 JOHNSON, A.W. "Poor Man's Law in Manitoba." *Canadian Bar Review.* 25:5 (May 1947), pp. 478-86.

1172 JOSIE, Svanhuit. "The Purpose and Legal Status of the Family Court." *Annual Report of the Delinquency and Crime Division.* Ottawa: Canadian Welfare Council, 1953.

1173 KIDMAN, John. *The Canadian Prison: The Study of a Tragedy.* Toronto: Ryerson Press, 1947.

1174 KIRKPATRICK, A.M. "The Birth of Prison Reform." *Canadian Welfare.* 33 (May 1959), pp. 3-11.

1175 MacPHAIL, Agnes. *Convict or Citizen: The Urgent Need for Prison Reform.* Toronto: Literature Department, Cooperative Commonwealth Federation, n.d.

1176 RIDDELL, J.H. *A Synopsis of the Report of the Royal Commission Appointed to Inquire Into and Report upon the Penal System of Canada.* Winnipeg: Canadian Welfare Association, 1939.

1177 ROYAL CANADIAN MOUNTED POLICE. *Law and Order in Canadian Democracy.* Ottawa: King's Printer, 1952.

1178 TOPPING, C.W. *Canadian Penal Institutions.* (Rev. Ed., 1943). Toronto: Ryerson Press, 1929.

1179 _____. "Recent Trends in Canadian Penal Institutions." *Prison World.* 6:4 (July-August 1944), pp. 6-7, 18-20.

1180 URWICK, E.J. "The Penal Commissions Report." *Queen's Quarterly.* 46:3 (Autumn 1939), pp. 320-23.

8.1.2 Government Policy and Documentation

8.1.2.1 Federal

1181 ALLMAND, Warren. *The Prevention and Control of Violent Crime in Canada: Some Comments on Violent Crime, Capital Punishment and Other Related Issues.* Ottawa: Solicitor General of Canada, 1975.

1182 CANADA. Comité consultatif national sur la femme delinquante. *Rapport.* Ottawa: Division des affaires publiques du service canadien des penitenciers et le service national des liberations conditionnelles. Ottawa: Approvisionnements et services, 1977.

1183 CANADA. Commission de reforme du droit. *Droit administratif: les commissions d'enquête.* Ottawa: La commission, 1977.

1184 CANADA. Commission of Inquiry into Certain Disturbances at Kingston Penitentiary. (April 1971). *Report.* Ottawa: Information Canada, 1973.

1185 CANADA. Commission of Inquiry on Penitentiary Security within the Quebec Region. *Report.* Ottawa: Information Canada, 1973.

1186 CANADA. Commission on the Penitentiary System of Canada. *Report.* Ottawa: King's Printer, 1947.

1187 CANADA. Commissioner of Penitentiaries. *Annual Reports.* Ottawa: Queen's Printer, 1868-1968.

1188 CANADA. Committee on Corrections. *Towards Unity: Criminal Justice and Corrections, Report.* Ottawa: Queen's Printer, 1969.

1189 CANADA. Department of Justice. Committee on Juvenile Delinquency. Juvenile Delinquency in Canada. *Report.* Ottawa: Queen's Printer, 1965.

1190 CANADA. Department of Justice. *The Delivery of Legal Aid Services in Canada.* Ottawa: Department of Justice, 1974.

1191 CANADA. Department of Solicitor General. *A Summary and Analysis of Some Major Inquiries on Corrections, 1938-1977.* Ottawa: The Department, 1977.

1192 _____. *The Criminal in Canadian Society: A Perspective on Corrections./ Le criminel et la société canadienne: une vue d'ensemble du processus correctionnel.* Ottawa: Information Canada, 1973.

1193 _____. *The General Program for the Development of Psychiatric Services in Federal Correctional Services in Canada.* Ottawa: Information Canada, 1973.

1194 _____. *Young Persons in Conflict with the Law: A Report of the Solicitor General's Committee on Proposals for New Legislation to Replace the Juvenile Delinquents Act./ Loi sur les jeunes qui ont des démêles avec la justice: Rapport du comité du ministère du solliciteur général sur les propositions formuleés en remplacement du loi sur les jeunes délinquants.* Ottawa: Ministry of the Solicitor General, Communication Division/Ministère du solliciteur général, Division des communications, 1975.

1195 CANADA. Law Reform Commission. *The Criminal Process and Mental Disorder.* Ottawa: Information Canada, 1975.

1196 _____. *Report on Family Law.* Ottawa: Information Canada, 1976.

1197 CANADA. Ministère de la justice. Comité sur la délinquance juvenile. *Délinquance juvenile au Canada.* Ottawa: Imprimerie de la Reine, 1965.

1198 CANADA. Ministère du solliciteur général. *Avant-projet aux fins d'étude, Loi concernant les enfants et les adolescents.* Ottawa: Le ministère, 1967.

1199 CANADA. Ministry of the Solicitor General. *Highlights of the Proposed New Legislation for Young Offenders./ Points saillants de l'avant-projet de loi sur les jeunes contrevenants.* Ottawa: Supply and Services Canada/Approvisionnements et services, 1977.

1200 _____. *The Role of Federal Corrections in Canada: A Report of the Task Force on the Creation of an Integrated Canadian Corrections Service./ Le rôle des services correctionnels fédéraux au Canada: rapport du groupe de travail sur la création du service canadien de correction intégré.* Ottawa: The Ministry, 1977.

1201 _____. Economic Division, Task Force on the Creation of an Integrated Canadian Corrections Service. *The Canadian Corrections Service, Organization and Management: A Working Paper.* Ottawa: Supply and Services, 1977.

1202 CANADA. Parlement. Chambre des communes. Comité permanent de la justice et des questions juridiques, 1966-1967. *Procès-verbaux et témoignages.* Ottawa: Imprimerie de la Reine, 1966-67.

1203 CANADA. *Report of a Committee Appointed to Inquire into the Principles and Procedures followed in the Remission Service of the Department of Justice of Canada.* Ottawa: Queen's Printer, 1956.

1204 CANADA. Royal Commission on Law of Insanity as a Defence in Criminal Cases. *Report.* Ottawa: Queen's Printer, 1957.

1205 CANADA. Royal Commission on the Status of Women in Canada. "Le droit criminel et la délinquance feminine." *Rapport.* pp. 413-35. Ottawa: Information Canada, 1970.

1206 CANADA. Royal Commission to Investigate the Penal System of Canada. *Report.* Ottawa: King's Printer, 1938.

1207 "The First Royal Commission Report on the Provincial Penitentiary at Kingston." Appendix to the *Journals of the Legislative Assembly of the Province of Canada, 1849.* 8, Appendix 3, 1849.

8.1.2.2   Provincial

1208 ALBERTA. Board of Review. Administration of Justice in the Provincial Courts of Alberta. *Report.* Edmonton: Queen's Printer, 1974.

1209 BRITISH COLUMBIA. Corrections Branch. *A Five-Year Plan in Corrections.* Victoria: Queen's Printer, 1974.

1210 BRITISH COLUMBIA. Royal Commission on Family and Children's Law. *Report.* Vancouver: The Commission, 1974.

1211 BRITISH COLUMBIA. Task Force on Correctional Services and Facilities. *Report.* Victoria: Department of Attorney General, 1973.

1212 MANITOBA. Department of Attorney General. *Family Law in Manitoba.* Winnipeg: Department of the Attorney General and the Women's Bureau of the Department of Labour, 1977.

1213 MANITOBA. Department of Health and Social Development. *The Rise of the Sparrows: A Paper on Corrections in Manitoba.* Winnipeg: The Deparment, 1972.

1214 MANITOBA. Law Reform Commission. *Report of the Administration of Justice in Manitoba.* Winnipeg: The Commission, 1974.

1215 _____. *Working Paper on Family Law.* Winnipeg: The Commission, 1975.

1216 NEW BRUNSWICK. Department of the Attorney General. *Report of the Commission on the Gaol System.* Fredericton: King's Printer, 1946.

1217 ONTARIO. Department of the Attorney General. *Family Legislation Administered by the Juvenile and Family Courts.* Toronto: The Department, 1959.

1218 ONTARIO. Department of Public Welfare. *Study of the Reformatory Institutions for Juveniles in the Provinces.* Toronto: Queen's Printer, 1933-34.

1219 ONTARIO. Law Reform Commission Report. 5. *Family Court and Special Services.* Toronto: Queen's Printer, 1967-69.

1220 ONTARIO. *The Legal Aid Act 1966 and Ontario Regulation 275/69.* Toronto: Queen's Printer, 1969.

1221 ONTARIO. Legislative Assembly Select Committee. Study and Report Upon Problems of Delinquent Individuals and Custodial Questions and the Place of Reform Institutions Therein. *Report.* Toronto: Queen's Printer, 1954.

1222 ONTARIO. Department of the Attorney General. *White Paper on Courts Administration.* Toronto: The Ministry, 1976.

1223 ONTARIO. Ministry of Correctional Services. *Correctional Programs in Ontario: Adult Male Institutions.* Toronto: The Ministry, 1975.

1224 _____. Planning and Research Branch. *A Review of Alternatives to the Incarceration of the Youthful Offender.* Toronto: The Ministry, 1976.

1225 _____. *Training Schools in Ontario.* Toronto: The Ministry, 1975.

1226 ONTARIO. *Report of the Commissioners Appointed to Enquire into the Prison and Reformatory System of Ontario, 1891.* (Sessional Paper 18) Toronto: Warwick and Sons, 1891.

1227 ONTARIO. Neglected Children's Department. *Report of Superintendent of Neglected and Dependent Children of Ontario.* 1st-37th, 1893-1930. Toronto, n.p., 1894-1931.

1228 ONTARIO. Task Force on Legal Aid. *Report.* Toronto: Ministry of the Attorney General, 1974.

1229 QUEBEC. Civil Code Revision Office. Committee on the Law on Persons and on the Family. *Report on the Family./ Rapport sur la famille.* 2 parts. Montreal: The Office, 1974.

1230 QUEBEC. Commission d'enquête sur l'administration de la justice en matière criminelle et pénale au Québec. *La Société face au crime.* Quebec: Editeur officiel du Québec, 1968.

1231 QUEBEC. Department of Justice. *The Judicial System/ Le système judiciaire.* Ministère de la justice. Service de l'information. Quebec: Ministère de la Justice, 1975.

1232 SASKATCHEWAN. Department of Welfare. Corrections Study Committee. *Report of the Saskatchewan Corrections Study Committee.* Regina: The Department, 1971.

1233 SASKATCHEWAN. Penal Commission. *Report.* Regina: King's Printer, 1946.

8.1.3   Special Issues

8.1.3.1   The Justice System

1234 CANADA. Department of the Solicitor General. *The Criminal in Canadian Society: A Perspective on Corrections.* Ottawa: Information Canada, 1973.
1235 CANADIAN CONGRESS OF CORRECTIONS. *Concepts of Treatment and Training in the Field of Corrections.* Ottawa: Canadian Corrections Association, 1968.
1236 CORMIER, B. "Pour une politique criminelle du Québec." *Cité libre.* 15:79 (August-September 1965), pp. 15-23.
1237 CORRECTIONAL CONSULTATION COMMITTEE. *Report of the Correctional Consultation Committee Appointed to Study Correctional Service for Women in the Maritime Provinces.* Moncton: Correctional Consultation Committee, 1972.
1238 COTLER, Irwin, and MARX, Herbert, eds. *The Law and the Poor in Canada.* Montreal: Black Rose Books and Editions Themis, 1977.
1239 EVANS, Robert, Jr. *Developing Policies for Public Security and Criminal Justice.* Special Study No. 23 prepared for Economic Council of Canada. Ottawa: Information Canada, 1973.
1240 FAGUY, Paul A. "The Canadian Penal System of the Seventies." *Canadian Journal of Criminology and Corrections.* 15:1 (January 1973), pp. 7-13.
1241 GALL, Gerald L. *The Canadian Legal System.* Toronto: Carswell Company, 1977.
1242 JAFFARY, Stuart K. *Sentencing of Adults in Canada.* Toronto: University of Toronto Press, 1963.
1243 JAYEWARDENE, C.H.S., ed. *The Criminal Justice System in Canada: The Proceedings of a Colloquium.* Ottawa: Department of Criminology, University of Ottawa, 1975.
1244 KALIEL, B. "Civil Rights in Juvenile Courts." *Alberta Law Review.* 12 (1974), p. 341.
1245 KIRKPATRICK, A.M. "Correcting Corrections." *Criminal Law Quarterly.* 2 (1959-60), pp. 152-63.
1246 MacLEOD, A.J. "Criminal Legislation." In *Crime and Its Treatment in Canada,* edited by W.T. McGrath. pp. 91-109. Toronto: Macmillan of Canada, 1965.
1247 McGRATH, W.T., ed. *Crime and Its Treatment in Canada.* 2nd ed. 1976. Toronto: Macmillan of Canada, 1976.
1248 McILRAITH, G.J. "Developments in Federal Corrections in Canada." *Canadian Journal of Corrections.* 12:4 (October 1970), pp. 526-33.
1249 RYAN, Stuart. "Adult Court." In *Crime and Its Treatment in Canada,* edited by W.T. McGrath. pp. 136-209. Toronto: Macmillan of Canada, 1965.
1250 STREET, T.G. "Canada's Correctional System." *Proceedings of the American Corrections Association.* pp. 165-70. Washington, D.C.: The Association, 1962.
1251 VANCOUVER PEOPLE'S LAW SCHOOL. *The Canadian Court System.* Vancouver: The School, 1972.

8.1.3.2 Probation, Parole and After-Care

1252 CANADIAN CRIMINOLOGY AND CORRECTIONS ASSOCIATION. "The Parole System in Canada." *Canadian Journal of Criminology and Corrections.* 15:2 (April 1973), pp. 144-70.

1253 CARABINE, W.F. "Parole as an Alternative to Prison." Paper delivered to 3rd Canadian Congress of Corrections. Toronto, June 1961.

1254 EDMISON, J.A. "Minimum Parole Experiment in Canada." *Proceedings of the American Corrections Association.* pp. 249-53. Washington, D.C.: The Association, 1966.

1255 _____. "The Prison After-Care Problem." *Canadian Bar Review.* 24:5 (May 1946), pp. 389-92.

1256 HART, Rev. Wm. Edward. *What is a John Howard Society.* Ottawa: Canadian Welfare Council, 1952.

1257 JACKSON, J. "Rehabilitation After Prison." M.S.W., University of Toronto, 1957.

1258 JAFFARY, Stuart K. "Probation for the Adult Offender." *Canadian Bar Review.* 27:9 (November 1949), pp. 1020-40.

1259 KIRKPATRICK, A.M. "After-Care and Prisoners Aid Societies." In *Crime and Its Treatment in Canada,* edited by W.T. McGrath. pp. 384-410. Toronto: Macmillan of Canada. 1965.

1260 MALONEY, Arthur E. "Remission, Ticket of Leave and Parole." *Canadian Bar Review.* 27:9 (November 1949), pp. 1067-91.

1261 MILLER, Frank P. "Parole." In *Crime and Its Treatment in Canada,* edited by W.T. McGrath. pp. 326-84. Toronto: Macmillan of Canada. 1965.

1262 REID, D.C.S. "After-Care Pre-Release Preparation of Prison Inmates." *Canadian Journal of Corrections.* 1:1, 1:2 (1958-59), pp. 42-49; pp. 47-56.

1263 ST.JOHN, Madeley. "Probation." In *Crime and Its Treatment in Canada,* edited by W.T. McGrath. pp. 220-44. Toronto: Macmillan of Canada. 1965.

1264 STREET, T.G. "The National Parole Board." *Canadian Journal of Corrections.* 7:3 (July 1965), pp. 283-88.

1265 WILTON, Jean B. *May I Talk to John Howard: The Story of J.D. Hobden; A Friend to Prisoners.* Vancouver: John Howard Society of British Columbia, 1973.

8.1.3.3 Prisons and Prisoners' Rights

1266 CANADIAN CORRECTIONS ASSOCIATION. *Prison Pay and Discharge Provisions in Canada.* Ottawa: The Association, 1964.

1267 CARON, Roger. *Go-Boy! Memoirs of a Life Behind Bars.* Toronto: McGraw-Hill Ryerson, 1978.

1268 FORNESET, G.R. "Prisons are Outmoded." *Canadian Bar Review.* 24:6 (June-July 1946), pp. 471-80.

1269 JAFFARY, Stuart K. "Saskatchewan Examines Penal Reform." *Canadian Bar Review.* 24:10 (1946), pp. 908-15.

1270 MacLEOD, A. *The Changing Canadian Prison.* Toronto: John Howard Society of Ontario, 1962.

1271 RICHMOND, Guy. *Prison Doctor: One Man's Story that Must be Told in Canada Today.* British Columbia: Nugana Publishing, 1975.

1272 ROSENBLUTH, Vera. "Women in Prisons." In *Women in Canada,* edited by Mary Lee Stephenson. pp. 209-27. Toronto: General Publishing Company, 1973.

1273 SCHROEDER, Andreas. *Shaking it Rough: A Prison Memoir.* Toronto: Doubleday Canada, 1976.

8.1.3.4   Family Court

1274 BAXTER, I.F.G. "Family Welfare and the Courts." *Canadian Bar Review.* 56:1 (March 1978), pp. 37-48.
1275 CANADIAN CORRECTIONS ASSOCIATION. *Family Court in Canada.* Ottawa: The Association, 1960.
1276 COLE, P.J.E. "Family Courts — Their Nature and Function." *Manitoba Law Journal.* 4:2 (1971), pp. 317-46.
1277 HALL, Emmett M. *Study of the Organization of the Courts in Saskatchewan: Interim Report for a Unified Family Court.* Regina: Department of the Attorney General, 1974.
1278 HOSKING, R. *The Family Court.* Ottawa: Canadian Council on Child and Family Welfare, 1930.
1279 LITSKY, H. "Family Courts Belong to the Poor." *Canadian Welfare.* 47:5 (September-October 1971), pp. 6-9.
1280 McGRATH, W.T. "Juvenile and Family Court." In *Crime and Its Treatment in Canada,* edited by W.T. McGrath. pp. 209-20. 2nd ed., 1976. Toronto: Macmillan of Canada, 1976.
1281 REAGH, Fred. "The Need for a Comprehensive Family Court System." *University of British Columbia Law Review.* 5:1 (June 1970), pp. 13-42.
1282 SANDERS, Douglas. *Family Law and Native People.* Ottawa: Law Reform Commission of Canada, 1975.
1283 STUBBS, Roy St. George. "A View of the Family Court." *Manitoba Law Journal.* 5:2 (1973), pp. 333-57.
1284 TOWARD, L.M. "A Case for a Family Court in Nova Scotia." L.L.M., Dalhousie University, 1958.
1285 UNIVERSITY OF ALBERTA. *Family Court.* Edmonton: Institute of Law Research and Reform, 1976.

8.1.3.5   Juvenile Justice

1286 BABCOCK, Kathy. "The Development and Implementation of the Juvenile Delinquents Act of 1908 — A Study in Social Policy Formulation." M.S.W., Carleton University, 1977.
1287 BAXTER, I.F.G., and EBERTS, M.A. *The Child and the Courts.* Toronto: Carswell Company, 1978.
1288 BOWERS, Gregory Martin. "Juvenile Correctional Services in Nova Scotia: A Study Tracing the Development of Juvenile Correctional Services from 1867-1967, with a Critical Analysis of Present Day Services." M.S.W., St. Mary's University, 1969.
1289 CATTON, Katherine, and LEON, Jeffrey S. "Legal Representation and the Proposed Young Persons In Conflict with the Law Act." *Osgoode Hall Law Journal.* 15:1 (June 1977), pp. 107-37.
1290 CANADIAN ASSOCIATION OF SOCIAL WORKERS. "Brief in Response to the Proposed Legislation Regarding Young Persons in Conflict with the Law." *Social Worker.* 44:2,3 (Fall 1976), pp. 1-4.
1291 CANADIAN BAR ASSOCIATION. "Being a Report of a Committee of the Canadian Bar Association to Review Legislation on Punishment of Juveniles and Young Persons." *Canadian Bar Review.* 22:7 (August-September 1944), pp. 585-97.
1292 CANADIAN CORRECTIONS ASSOCIATION. *The Child Offender and the Law: A Brief Presented to the Department of Justice Committee on Juvenile Delinquency.* Ottawa: Canadian Welfare Council, 1963.

1293 _____. Report of the Committee Established to Consider Child Welfare and Related Implications Arising from the Department of Justice. *Report on Juvenile Delinquency*. Ottawa: The Association, 1967.

1294 CANADIAN CRIMINOLOGY AND CORRECTIONS ASSOCIATION. "Brief on the Young Offenders Act (Bill C-1972)." *Canadian Journal of Criminology and Corrections*. 13 (1971), pp. 307-18.

1295 CANADIAN WELFARE COUNCIL. *The Juvenile Court in Law*. 4th ed. Ottawa: The Council, 1952.

1296 _____. *Juvenile Courts in Canada*. Ottawa: The Council, 1943.

1297 CHRISTIE, Hugh. "Recent Trends in the Treatment of Juvenile Delinquents in Canada." M.A., University of British Columbia, 1946.

1298 ERICKSON, P.C. "The Defence Lawyer's Role in Juvenile Court: An Empirical Investigation into Judges' and Social Workers' Points of View." *University of Toronto Law Journal*. 24:2 (1974), pp. 126-48.

1299 GIFFEN, P.J. "Official Rates of Crime and Delinquency." In *Crime and Its Treatment in Canada*. edited by W.T. McGrath, pp. 66-110. 2nd ed. Toronto: Macmillan of Canada, 1976.

1300 HOOPER, H. *Rehabilitating Youthful Offenders*. Toronto: John Howard Society of Ontario, 1967.

1301 "Juvenile Courts — Proclamation — Habeas Corpus — Jurisdiction — Evidence." *Canadian Bar Review*. 5:3 (March 1937), pp. 214-15.

1302 "The Juvenile Delinquents Act, 1908, in Vancouver." *Canadian Bar Review*. 4:5 (May 1926), pp. 342-44.

1303 KELLY, Maurice, BEDARD, G.M., BEGG, C.M., MURPHY, Ambrose. "Brief on Corrections Policy in Ontario." *Canadian Journal of Criminology and Corrections*. 13:4 (1971), pp. 346-52.

1304 LAYCOCK, Joseph E. "Juvenile Courts in Canada." *Canadian Bar Review*. 21:1 (January 1943), pp. 1-22.

1305 LEON, J.S. "New and Old Themes in Canadian Juvenile Justice: The Origins of Delinquency Legislation and the Prospects for Recognition of Children's Rights." *Interchange*. 8:1,2 (1977), pp. 151-75.

1306 MacDONALD, John A. "A Critique of Bill C-192: The Young Offenders Act." *Canadian Journal of Criminology and Corrections*. 13:2 (1971), pp. 166-79.

1307 MacGILL, Helen G. *Juvenile Court in Canada, Origin, Underlying Principles, Governing Legislation and Practise*. Ottawa: Canadian Council on Child Welfare, 1925.

1308 _____. *The Work of the Juvenile Court and How to Secure such a Court in a Canadian Community*. Vancouver: Juvenile Court of Vancouver, 1943.

1309 McNAIRN, Colin H. "Constitutional Law — Juvenile Delinquents Act Characterized as Criminal Law Legislation." *Canadian Bar Review*. 46:3 (September 1968), pp. 473-82.

1310 PARKER, Graham. "Juvenile Delinquency — Transfer of Juvenile Cases to Adult Courts — Factors to be Considered under the Juvenile Delinquents Act." *Canadian Bar Review*. 48:2 (May 1970), pp. 336-46.

1311 PEPLER, E. "The Juvenile Delinquents Act, 1929." *Canadian Bar Review*. 30:8 (October 1952), pp. 819-31.

1312 ROBERTSON, R.S. "Juvenile Delinquency." *Canadian Bar Review*. 21:8 (October 1943), pp. 601-4.

1313 SCHRIEBER, J.R.G. "Comments upon Indictable Offenses in the Juvenile Delinquents Act." *Canadian Bar Review*. 35:9 (November 1957), pp. 1073-86.

1314 SCOTT, W.L. *The Genesis of the Juvenile Delinquents Act.* Ottawa, 1939.

1315 _____. *The Juvenile Court in Law.* 3rd ed. Ottawa: Canadian Welfare Council, 1941.

1316 _____. *The Juvenile Court in Law and the Juvenile Court in Action.* 2nd ed. Ottawa: Canadian Council on Child Welfare, 1930.

1317 SOCIAL PLANNING COUNCIL OF WINNIPEG. *Children's Rights within the Child Welfare-Juvenile Corrections Systems.* Winnipeg: The Council, 1976.

1318 STITT, J.M. "Correction Facilities for the Juvenile Offender — A Comparison of Ontario and the U.K." *Osgoode Hall Law Journal.* 2:3 (April 1962), pp. 356-69.

1319 TADMAN, M. "A Critical Analysis of Bill C-192: The Young Offenders Act." *Manitoba Law Journal.* 4:2 (1971), pp. 371-79.

1320 WILSON, H.J. "The Problem of Juvenile Crime and Penal Reform." *Canadian Bar Review.* 24:4 (April 1946), pp. 276-83.

1321 WILSON, Lawrence Charles. "Juvenile Justice in Canada: The End of the Experiment." M.A., University of Manitoba, 1976.

8.1.3.6   Legal Aid

1322 BRITISH COLUMBIA CIVIL LIBERTIES ASSOCIATION. *Brief in Support of a Comprehensive Provincial Legal Aid Plan.* Vancouver: The Association, 1972.

1323 FAIRBAIRN, L.S. "Legal Aid Clinics for Ontario Law Schools." *Osgoode Hall Law Journal.* 3:2 (April 1965), pp. 316-30.

1324 _____. "Student Legal Aid — The Search for Legitimacy." *Osgoode Hall Law Journal.* 12:3 (December 1974), pp. 627-43.

1325 JONES, James E. "Legal Aid for the Poor." *Canadian Bar Review.* 9:4 (April 1931), pp. 271-76.

1326 LUKES, Dorothy J. "Legal Aid in Canada." M.A., McGill University, 1969.

1327 NELLIGAN, John P. "Legal Aid in Canada: Existing Facilities." *Canadian Bar Review.* 29:6 (June-July 1951), pp. 589-620.

1328 _____. "Legal Aid in Canada: The Need." *Canadian Bar Review.* 31:7 (August-September 1953), pp. 752-69.

1329 PARKER, G.E. "Legal Aid — Canadian Style." In *Poverty in Canada*, edited by John Harp and J.R. Hofley. pp. 305-25. Scarborough: Prentice-Hall, 1971.

1330 PRUD'HOMME, Jules. "Legal Aid Societies." *Canadian Bar Review.* 2:3 (March 1924), pp. 181-86.

1331 SCOTT, Cuthbert. "Free Law for the Poor." *Canadian Bar Review.* 13:3 (March 1935), pp. 152-63.

8.1.3.7   Training Schools

1332 CANADIAN CORRECTIONS ASSOCIATION. Ninth National Conference on Training Schools. *Proceedings.* Montreal (August 1965), Ottawa, The Association, 1965.

1333 SINCLAIR, Donald. "Training Schools in Canada." In *Crime and Its Treatment in Canada*, edited by W.T. McGrath. pp. 244-79. Toronto: Macmillan of Canada, 1965.

1334 WALKER, J., and GLASNER, A. "The Process of Juvenile Detention: The Training School Act, The Child Welfare Act." *Osgoode Hall Law Journal.* 3:2 (April 1965), pp. 343-61.

8.1.3.8 Justice and Mental Health

1335 CANADIAN MENTAL HEALTH ASSOCIATION. Committee on Legislation and Psychiatric Disorder. *The Law and Mental Disorder; A Report on the Legislation and Psychiatric Disorder in Canada.* 3 vols. Toronto: The Association, 1964-69.

1336 MOHR, Johann W. *Prison or Hospital — Some Problems in the Relationship Between Criminal Law and Mental Illness.* (Paper presented to the Journal Club of the Toronto Psychiatric Hospital. 25 September 1962). Toronto, 1962.

1337 PAGE, Stewart. *Mental Patients and the Law.* Toronto: Self-Counsel Press, 1973.

1338 VANCOUVER PEOPLE'S LAW SCHOOL. *Mental Patients and the Law.* Vancouver: The School, 1974.

8.1.4 Administration

1339 BERNIER, Robert, and GAGNON, Rosette. *Les services correctionnels et la police au Canada.* Montreal: University of Montreal, 1975.

1340 BOYDELL, Craig L., GRINDSTAFF, C.F., WHITEHEAD, R.C., eds. *The Administration of Criminal Justice in Canada.* Toronto: Holt, Rinehart & Winston of Canada, 1974.

1341 BOYDELL, Craig L., and CONNIDIS, Ingrid A. "The Administration of Criminal Justice: Continuity Versus Conflict." *Canadian Journal of Criminology and Corrections.* 18:2 (April 1976), pp. 161-67.

1342 GANDY, John M. "The Exercise of Discretion by the Police as a Decision Making Process in the Disposition of Juvenile Offenders." *Osgoode Hall Law Journal.* 8:2 (November 1970), pp. 329-46.

1343 GREEN, Bernard. "Juvenile Delinquents Act (Can) — Meaning of Support — A Case Study in the Administration of Juvenile Justice." *Canadian Bar Review.* 44:1 (March 1966), pp. 152-58.

1344 MAJOR, Henri. *Background Notes on Areas of Federal and Provincial Jurisdiction in Relation to Family Law; A Draft Paper.* Ottawa: Advisory Council on the Status of Women, 1974.

1345 MURPHY, E.F. "The Administration of Criminal Justice in Canada." National Council of Social Work. *Proceedings*, 55, pp. 176-80. Chicago: University of Chicago Press, 1924.

1346 RICO, José M. "Le livre blanc sur la justice au Québec et les principes de base pour une reforme de l'administration de la justice." *Canadian Journal of Criminology and Corrections.* 18:3 (July 1976), pp. 258-66.

1347 RUSSELL, Peter H. "The Jurisdiction of the Supreme Court of Canada: Present Policies and a Programme for Reform." *Osgoode Hall Law Journal.* 6:1 (October 1968), pp. 1-38.

1348 THOMAS, Paul. "The Manitoba Law Reform Commission: A Critical Evaluation." *Dalhousie Law Journal.* 2:2 (September 1975), pp. 417-43.

8.2 Immigration Policy

8.2.1 Historical Development

8.2.1.1 General

1349 ALLYN, N.C. "History of Canadian Immigration, 1932-1952." Ph.D., Stanford University, 1952.

1350 ARTIBISE, Alan F.J. "Advertising Winnipeg: The Campaign for Immigrants and Industry, 1874-1914." Manitoba Historical Society, *Transactions*. Series 3, No. 27 (1970-71), pp. 75-106.

1351 AVERY, Donald Howard. "Canadian Immigration Policy and the Alien Question, 1896-1919: The Anglo-Canadian Perspective." Ph.D., University of Western Ontario, 1973.

1352 BEST, J.C. "Canadian Immigration Patterns and Policies." *Labour Gazette*. 50:8 (September 1970), pp. 1512-22.

1353 CAMERON, J.D. "The Law Relating to Immigration, 1867-1935." Ph.D., University of Toronto, 1936.

1354 _____. "Legislation Relating to Immigration to Canada Prior to Confederation." M.A., University of Toronto, 1935.

1355 CAMPBELL, Bonnie. "Immigration: Four Options for Canada." *Labour Gazette*. 75:5 (May 1975), pp. 297-99.

1356 CORBETT, David. *Canada's Immigration Policies; A Critique*. Toronto: University of Toronto Press, 1957.

1357 _____. "A Study of Factors Governing Canada's Absorption of Immigrants from 1867-1914 with Suggestions towards a Definition of Absorptive Capacity." M.A., University of Toronto, 1949.

1358 COX, R. "Short History of Canadian Immigration." *Canada and the World*. 39 (February 1974), pp. 18-19.

1359 DORVAL, Simon. "Attitude du gouvernement du Canada concernant l'immigration, dans les années qui suivirent la guerre, 1939-1945." M.A., Laval University, 1960.

1360 GATES, Paul W. "Official Encouragement of Immigration by the Province of Canada." *Canadian Historical Review*. 15:1 (March 1934), pp. 24-38.

1361 HARRIS, Evelyn L.K. "The Restriction of Immigration between the United States and Canada, 1927-1945." M.A., Columbia University, 1946.

1362 HAWKINS, Freda. *Canada and Immigration: Public Policy and Public Concern*. Montreal: McGill-Queen's University Press, 1972.

1363 _____. "Canadian Immigration. A Study in Public Policy, 1946-1968." Ph.D., University of Toronto, 1969.

1364 KAGE, Joseph, ed. *Studies and Documents on Immigration and Integration in Canada*. Montreal: Jewish Immigrant Aid Services of Canada, 1964.

1365 KALBACH, W.E. "The Evolution of an Immigration Policy." In *Critical Issues in Canadian Society*, edited by C.L. Boydell *et al.* pp. 312-13. Toronto: Holt, Rinehart & Winston, 1971.

1366 LAJOIE-ROBICHAUD, Andrée. *Politiques et attitudes à l'égard de l'immigration depuis la confédération au Québec*. Royal Commission on Bilingualism and Biculturalism. Research Reports, No. 17. Ottawa: The Commission, 1965.

1367 LINDEN, Allen M. "Race and Nationality Restrictions in the Immigration Act: Is a Revision Overdue." *Osgoode Hall Law Journal*. 2:2 (April 1961), pp. 243-53.

1368 McDOUGALL, Duncan M. "Immigration Into Canada, 1850-1920." *Canadian Journal of Economics and Political Science*. 27:2 (May 1961), pp. 162-75.

1369 MacGILL, Helen Gregory. "Anti-Chinese Immigration Legislation in British Columbia, 1876-1903." B.A. Essay, University of British Columbia, 1925.

1370 PARAI, Louis. "Canada's Immigration Policy, 1962-1974." *International Migration Review*. 9:4 (Winter 1975), pp. 449-77.

1371 _____. "Canadian International Immigration, 1953-1965: An Empirical Study." Ph.D., Yale University, 1969.

1372 PIGGOTT, Eleanora. "Dominion Government Policy on Immigration and Colonization, 1867-1937." M.A., University of British Columbia, 1950.

1373 RAWLYK, George A. "Canada's Immigration Policy, 1945-1962." *Dalhousie Review*. 42:3 (Autumn 1962-63), pp. 287-300.

1374 REUTER, W.C. "The Promotion of Immigration by the Government of Canada, 1896-1914." M.A., University of California, 1961.

1375 SANDERSON, George. "Immigration: A Look at Present Trends." *Labour Gazette*. 75:1 (January 1975), pp. 31-39.

1376 SMELTZER, M.F. "Saskatchewan Opinion on Immigration from 1925-1939." M.A., University of Saskatchewan, 1950.

1377 STEVENS, R.C. "Western Canadian Immigration in Sir Clifford Sifton's Time." M.A., University of Western Ontario, 1963.

1378 SZOHNER, Gabriel. *The Immigrant*. Vancouver: Intermedia Press, 1977.

1379 TIMLIN, Mabel F. "Canada's Immigration Policy, 1896-1910." *Canadian Journal of Economics and Political Science*. 26:4 (November 1960), pp. 517-32.

1380 TROPER, Harold M. *Only Farmers Need Apply: Official Canadian Government Encouragement of Immigration from the United States, 1896-1911.* Toronto: Griffin House, 1972.

1381 _____. "Official Canadian Government Encouragement of American Immigration, 1896-1911." Ph.D., University of Toronto, 1971.

8.2.1.2 Reviews of Policy

1382 ADAM, G.M. "Immigration Into the Northwest." *Bystander*. 2 (June 1881), p. 267.

1383 "The Alien Labour Act." *Labour Gazette*. 1:10 (June 1901), pp. 552-55.

1384 AMERICAN COUNCIL FOR NATIONALITIES SERVICE. "Canada's New Immigration Policy." *Interpreter Releases*. 39 (23 March 1962), pp. 86-92.

1385 ANGUS, H.F. "The Future of Immigration into Canada." *Canadian Journal of Economics and Political Science*. 12:3 (August 1946), pp. 379-86.

1386 _____. "Need for an Immigration Policy." *Annals of the American Academy of Political and Social Science*. 253 (September 1947), pp. 16-21.

1387 "Asiatic Immigration into Canada." *Round Table*. 13:50 (1923) pp. 398-404.

1388 BEAUDIN, Dominique. "Le Canada français et l'immigration." *L'Action nationale*. 31:3 (March 1948), pp. 161-65.

1389 BEST, J. C. "Canadian Immigration Patterns and Policies." *Labour Gazette*. 50:9 (September 1950), pp. 1512-22.

1390 BODSWORTH, Fred. "What's behind the Immigration Wrangle." *MacLean's Magazine*. 68 (1955), p. 13, 127-130.

1391 "Canada's Immigration Policy." *Commonwealth*. 45 (1946), pp. 181-82.

1392 "The Canadian Citizenship Act." *Canadian Bar Review*. 25:4 (April 1947), pp. 364-72.

1393 CANADIAN CITIZENSHIP COUNCIL. *Policy Statements and Resolutions of Some Canadian Organizations on Immigration*. Ottawa: The Council, 1955.

1394 CARROTHERS, W.A. "Immigration Problem in Canada." *Queen's Quarterly*. 36:3 (Summer 1929), pp. 517-31.

1395 CH'ENG, T'ien-Fang. "Oriental Immigration in Canada." Ph.D., University of Toronto, 1926.

1396 CHICANOT, E. "The Future of Immigration." *Dalhousie Review*. 16:1 (1936-37), pp. 28-34.

1397 CHOW, W.S. "History of Chinese Immigration." *China Town News*. (Vancouver, British Columbia.) 9 (18 February 1962), pp. 9-11; 9 (3 March 1962), pp. 9-11, 14.

1398 CORBETT, David. "Immigration and Canadian Politics." *International Journal*. 6:3 (Summer 1951), pp. 207-16.

1399 COUSINEAU, René. "Pour une politique canadienne d'immigration." *Actualité économique*. 23:3 (October 1947), pp. 541-58; 24:3 (October 1948), pp. 544-49.

1400 CRICHTON, Robert. *How Canada Welcomes Immigrants: A United States Opinion on Canada's Immigration Policy and Practices*. Ottawa: Department of Citizenship and Immigration, 1956.

1401 CULLITON, J.T. *Assisted Emigration and Land Settlement with Specific Reference to Western Canada*. McGill University Economic Studies, No. 9. Montreal: Federation Press, 1928.

1402 DeBRISAY, Richard. "A New Immigration Policy." *Canadian Forum*. 8:85 (October 1927), pp. 394-96.

1403 "The Determinants of Canada's Immigration Policy." *Round Table*. 37:145 (1946), pp. 51-57.

1404 "Encouragement of Immigration to Canada." *Labour Gazette*. 47:5 (May 1947), pp. 644-47.

1405 "Evidence Presented before Senate Standing Committee on Immigration and Labour." *Labour Gazette*. 47:8 (August 1947), pp. 1108-13.

1406 FLUX, A.W. "Canada's Gain by Immigration." *Canadian Banker*. 15:2 (January 1908), pp. 127-43.

1407 GAUTIER, Charles. "L'immigration et son enquête." *Action française*. 20:7 (1928), pp. 4-17.

1408 GIBBON, J. Murray. "The Foreign Born." *Queen's Quarterly*. 27 (April/May/June 1920), pp. 331-52.

1409 GLYNN-WARD, Hilda. *The Writing on the Wall: Chinese and Japanese Immigration to British Columbia, 1920*. Toronto: University of Toronto Press, 1974.

1410 GORDON, Honorable N.A. "Canadian Immigration." *Canadian Club of Toronto Addresses*. 28 (1930-31), pp. 177-84.

1411 GRAVES, John. "Dealing in Futures." *Canadian Geographical Journal*. 40:6 (June 1950), pp. 274-82.

1412 HURD, W. Burton. "The Case for a Quota." *Queen's Quarterly*. 36:4 (Winter 1929), pp. 145-59.

1413 _____. "The Immigrant Problem." *Canadian Club of Toronto Addresses*. 34 (1936-37), pp. 249-63.

1414 "Immigration: (I) A Negative View; (II) Another View." *Round Table*. 29:44 (March 1939), pp. 398-404, 404-11.

1415 INTERNATIONAL LABOUR OFFICE. "Immigration to Canada." *Migration*. 1:6 (November/December 1952), pp. 17-22.

1416 JENKINS, Joseph. "Canadian Immigration." *Municipal Review of Canada*. 32:11 (December 1936), pp. 20-24.

1417 KEENLEYSIDE, H.L. "Canadian Immigration." *Trades and Labour Congress Journal*. 27:10 (October 1948), pp. 22-23.

1418 _____. "Canadian Immigration Policy." *International Journal.* 3:3 (1947-48), pp. 222-38.

1419 KING, W.L.M. *Report on Mission to England to Confer with the British Authorities on the Subject of Immigration to Canada from the Orient and Immigration from India in Particular.* Ottawa: King's Printer, 1908.

1420 KIRKCONNEL, Watson. "Canada and Immigration." *Empire Club of Canada Addresses.* (1943-44), pp. 374-91.

1421 KLOK, Pierre. "Diriger l'immigration: est-ce possible?" *Relations.* 13:148 (September 1953), pp. 107-08.

1422 _____. "Dangers de l'immigration au Canada." *Relations.* 13:156 (December 1953), pp. 316-18.

1423 LAMOUREUX, Pierre. "Les premières années de l'immigration chinoise au Canada." *Revue canadienne de geographie.* 9:2 (January/March 1955), pp. 9-28.

1424 LOWER, Arthur R.M. "Case against Immigration." *Queen's Quarterly.* 37:3 (Summer 1930), pp. 557-74.

1425 McARTHUR, Duncan. "What is the Problem?" *Queen's Quarterly.* 35 (Autumn 1928), pp. 603-14.

1426 MacDONALD, Donald C. "We Need an Immigration Policy." *Canadian Business.* 19:9 (September 1946), pp. 15-17, 84-88.

1427 MacINNIS, Grace. "Immigration? On What Basis?" *Canadian Forum.* 27:315 (April 1947), pp. 7-8.

1428 MERCIER, Jean. "Immigration and Provincial Rights." *Canadian Bar Review.* 22:9 (December 1944), pp. 856-69.

1429 MESSIER, Emilien. "Immigration: pensée de l'Eglise." *L'Action nationale.* 43:5 (May/June 1954), pp. 387-94.

1430 PLUMPTRE, H.P. "The Canadian Immigration Law and the Trend of Public Opinion." *Proceedings.* National Council of Social Welfare, 51 (1924), pp. 598-603.

1431 REID, E.B. "Canada's Immigration Policy." *Industrial Canada.* 53:94 (Summer 1952), p. 96.

1432 RODDICK, Paul M. "Canadian Immigration Policy; The Hard Facts." *International Journal.* 11:2 (Spring 1955-56), pp. 122-29.

1433 _____. "Canadian Immigration — Policy and Practice." *Queen's Quarterly.* 62:4 (Winter 1956), pp. 529-38.

1434 "Senate Studies Immigration Problem." *Labour Gazette.* 47:6 (June 1947), pp. 779-85.

1435 STEAD, Robert J.C. "Canada's Immigration Policy." *Annals of the American Academy of Political and Social Science.* 107 (May 1923), pp. 56-62.

1436 STEVENSON, J.A. "Immigration." *Canadian Forum.* 4:47 (August 1924), pp. 328-39.

1437 STEWART, Wallace W. "The Canadian Immigration Policy." *Canadian Magazine.* 30:4 (February 1908), pp. 358-61.

1438 THOMAS, E. "Wanted — An Immigration Policy." *Canadian Forum.* 2:18 (March 1922), pp. 550-52.

1439 TIMLIN, Mabel F. *Does Canada Need More People?* Toronto: Oxford University Press, 1951.

1440 _____. "Recent Changes in Government Attitudes towards Immigration." *Proceedings and Transactions.* The Royal Society of Canada. 3rd series 49 (June 1955), sec. 2, pp. 95-105.

1441 TROPER, H.M. "Creek — Negroes of Oklahoma and Canadian Immigration, 1909-1911." *Canadian Historical Review.* 53:3 (September 1972), pp. 272-88.

1442 WAINES, W.J. "Post-war Immigration Policy." *Canadian Banker.* 51 (1944), pp. 87-98.

1443 WALLACE, W.S. "An Examination of Our Immigration Policy." *University of Toronto Monthly.* 6 (April 1906), pp. 150-55.

1444 WHITTON, Charlotte. "The Immigration Problem for Canada." *Queen's Quarterly.* 31 (April/June 1924), pp. 388-420.

8.2.2 Government Policy and Documentation

8.2.2.1 Federal

1445 ANDRAS, Robert. "Recent Trends and Future Immigration Policy in Canada." *Journal of Comparative Sociology.* 2 & 3 (1974-75), pp. 10-20.

1446 CANADA. Commission de l'emploi et de l'immigration. *Immigration au Canada: renseignements préalables à l'intention des requerants.* Ottawa: La commission, 1978.

1447 CANADA. Commission of Inquiry Relating to the Department of Manpower and Immigration in Montreal. *Report.* Ottawa: Information Canada, 1975.

1448 CANADA. Department of Agriculture. *Reception and Protection of Female Immigrants in Canada.* Ottawa, 1879.

1449 CANADA. Department of Citizenship and Immigration. Immigration Branch. *Canadian Immigration Aims and Objectives, 1946-1955.* Ottawa: The Department, 1956.

1450 _____. *The Sedgewick Report.* 2 parts. Ottawa: The Department, 1965.

1451 CANADA. Department of Employment and Immigration. *Immigration Act Regulations: Information Kit.* Ottawa: Employment and Immigration, 1978.

1452 _____. *Twenty Questions About Canada's New Immigration Act.* Ottawa: Department of Employment and Immigration, 1977.

1453 CANADA. Department of Manpower and Immigration. *Canadian Immigration Policy, 1966.* Ottawa: Queen's Printer, 1966; reprinted 1975.

1454 _____. *Highlights from the Green Paper on Immigration and Population.* Ottawa: Information Canada, 1975.

1455 _____. *Immigration Regulations*: Text and Comments. Ottawa, 1965.

1456 _____. Canadian Immigration and Population Study. *Immigration Policy Perspectives.* (Vol. 1 of Green Paper). Ottawa: Information Canada, 1974..

1457 _____. Canadian Immigration and Population Study. *The Immigration Program.* (Vol. 2 of Green Paper). Ottawa: Information Canada, 1974.

1458 _____. Canadian Immigration and Population Study. *Immigration and Population Statistics.* (Vol. 3 of Green Paper). Ottawa: Information Canada, 1974.

1459 _____. Canadian Immigration and Population Study. *Three Years in Canada: First Report of the Longitudinal Survey on the Economic and Social Adaptation of Immigrants.* (Vol. 4 of Green Paper). Ottawa: Information Canada, 1974.

1460 CANADA. Ministère de la main d'oeuvre et de l'immigration. *Perspectives de la politique d'immigration, étude sur l'immigration et les objectifs demographiques du Canada* (dossier 1, livre vert). Ottawa: Information Canada, 1974.

1461 _____. Etude sur l'immigration et les objectifs. *Le programme de l'immigration.* (dossier 2, livre vert), Ottawa: Information Canada, 1974.

1462 _____. Etude sur l'immigration et les objectifs demographiques du Canada. *Statistiques sur l'immigration et la population.* (dossier 3, livre vert). Ottawa: Information Canada, 1974.

1463 _____. Etude sur l'immigration et les objectifs demographiques du Canada. *Trois ans de vie au Canada.* (dossier 4, livre vert). Ottawa: Information Canada, 1974.

1464 _____. *Le projet de loi concernant l'immigration:* dossier. Ottawa: Le ministère, 1976.

1465 _____. *Règlement sur l'immigration:* dossier. Ottawa: Le ministère, 1977.

1466 CANADA. Law Reform Commission. *The Immigration Appeal Board: A Study.* Ottawa: Supply and Services, 1976.

1467 CANADA. Laws, Statutes, etc . . . *Chinese Immigration Act, 1923 and Regulations.* Minister of Immigration and Colonization. Ottawa: King's Printer, 1926.

1468 CANADA. Parliament. House of Commons. Select Standing Committee on Agriculture and Colonization. *Minutes of Proceedings and Evidence and Report.* Ottawa: King's Printer, 1928.

1469 CANADA. Parliament. House of Commons. Standing Committee on Labour Manpower and Immigration 1968-1969. *Minutes of Proceedings and Evidence.* Ottawa: Queen's Printer, 1968-69.

1470 CANADA. Parliament. Senate. Standing Committee on Immigration and Labour. *Proceedings on the Operation and Administration of the Immigration Act.* Ottawa: King's Printer, 1946; 1949; 1951.

1471 _____. *Proceedings (1), Bill Q-5, An Act to Amend the Canadian Citizenship Act (2), on the Operation and Administration of the Immigration Act.* Ottawa: Queen's Printer, 1953.

1472 _____. *Proceedings (1), Bill C-2, An Act to Amend Fair Wages and Hours of Labour Act (2), Bill C-220, An Act to Make Provision for Appeal to an Immigration Appeal Board in Respect of Certain Matters Relating to Immigration.* Ottawa: Queen's Printer, 1966, 1967.

1473 CANADA. Parliament. Special Joint Committee on Immigration Policy, 1974-76. *Minutes of Proceedings and Evidence* of the Special Joint Committee of the Senate and the House of Commons on Immigration Policy/*Procès-verbaux et témoignages* du Comité mixte spécial du Sénat et de la Chambre des communes sur la Politique de l'immigration. (Nos. 1-53). Ottawa: Queen's Printer, 1975.

1474 CANADA. Royal Commission on Chinese Immigration. *Report and Evidence.* Ottawa, 1885.

1475 CANADA. Royal Commission on Chinese and Japanese Immigration. *Report.* Ottawa: King's Printer, 1902.

1476 CANADA. *White Paper on Canadian Immigration Policy.* Ottawa: Queen's Printer, 1966.

1477 MARCHAND, Jean. "White Paper on Immigration." *External Affairs.* 19:3 (March 1967), pp. 97-100.

1478 MARTIN, Paul. "Canada's Immigration Policy." *University of Toronto Quarterly.* 13:2 (1943-44), pp. 196-206.

1479 WALMSLEY, Norma E. "Some Aspects of Canada's Immigration Policy." Unpublished report prepared for the Royal Commission on Bilingualism and Biculturalism. 2 vols. Ottawa, 1966.

1480 WOODSWORTH, Charles J. "Canada's Oriental Immigrants." *Canadian Forum.* 17:202 (November 1937), pp. 268-70.

8.2.2.2 Provincial

1481 SASKATCHEWAN. Royal Commission on Immigration and Settlement. *Report*. Regina: King's Printer, 1930.

8.2.3 Special Issues

8.2.3.1 General

1482 ANGERS, François-Albert. "Le Canada français et l'immigration." *L'Action nationale*. 43:5 (1954), pp. 423-40.

1483 ARES, Richard. "L'immigration et l'avenir du français au Québec." *L'Action nationale*. 59:3 (1969/70), pp. 209-29.

1484 BONIN, Bernard, ed. *Immigration: Policy-Making Process and Results/ Processus d'élaboration de la politique et résultats*. Toronto: Institute of Public Administration of Canada, 1976.

1485 _____. "L'immigration étrangère au Québec." *Canadian Public Policy/ Analyse de politique*. 1:3 (Summer 1975), pp. 296-301.

1486 BROSSARD, Jacques. *L'immigration; les droits et pouvoirs du Canada et du Québec*. Montreal: Presses de l'université de Montréal, 1967.

1487 CAMPBELL, B. "Immigration: Four Options for Canada." *Labour Gazette*. 75:5 (May 1975), pp. 297-99.

1488 CRAN, Mrs. George. *A Woman in Canada*. Toronto: Mussan Book Company, 1910.

1489 GODLER, Zlata. "Doctors and the New Immigrants." *Canadian Ethnic Studies*. 9:1 (1977), pp. 6-15.

1490 HAWKINS, Freda. "The Canadian Experience." *Venture*. 23:1 (January 1971), pp.32-35.

1491 HUCKER, John. "Immigration — Deportation — Bill of Rights — Audi Alteram Partem Rule — National Interest and the Immigrants' Right to a Hearing." *Canadian Bar Review*. 53:3 (September 1975), pp. 810-19.

1492 JENNESS, R.A. "Canadian Migration and Immigration Patterns and Government Policy." *International Migration Review*. 8:1 (Spring 1974), pp. 5-22.

1493 KAGE, Joseph. "The Recent Changes in Canadian Immigration Legislation." *International Migration Review*. 2:1 (Fall 1967), pp. 47-50.

1494 LONEY, M. "Canada's Immigration Policy." *Race Today*. 3:9 (September 1971), pp. 303-4.

1495 _____. "A Consumer Perspective on Canadian Immigration Policy." *Race Today*. 4:4 (April 1972), pp. 117-20.

1496 MARR, William. "Canada's Immigration Policies since 1962." *Canadian Public Policy*. 1:2 (Spring 1975), pp. 196-203.

1497 MERCIER, Jean. "Immigration and Provincial Rights." *Canadian Bar Review*. 22:10 (December 1944), pp. 856-69.

1498 MOLDOFSKY, N. "Planning in Immigration? The Canadian Experience." *Australian Outlook*. 26:1 (April 1972), pp. 67-82.

1499 SANDERSON, George. "Immigration Policy: A Labour Related Issue." *Labour Gazette*. 76:3 (March 1976), pp. 138-43.

1500 THOMAS, D. "How We Keep Out the Black and the Yellow." *Saturday Night*. 87:6 (June 1972), pp. 12-15.

1501 TIMLIN, Mabel F. "Canadian Immigration Policy: An Analysis." *International Migration*. 3:1 & 2 (1965), pp. 52-72.

8.2.3.2   Green Paper

1502 ALLEN, Jeremiah. "Labour Market Analysis in The Green Paper."
       Canadian Ethnic Studies. 7:1 (1975), pp. 65-70.
1503 *Canada's Racist Immigration Policy.* Toronto: Pathfinder Press, 1975.
1504 CAPPON, Paul. "The Green Paper: Immigration as a Tool of Profit."
       Canadian Ethnic Studies. 7:1 (1975), pp. 50-54.
1505 DIRKS, Gerald. "The Green Paper and Canadian Refugee Policy."
       Canadian Ethnic Studies. 7:1 (1975), pp. 61-64.
1506 DOBELL, Peter C., and d'AQUINS, Susan. *The Special Joint Committee
       on Immigration Policy 1975: An Exercise in Participatory Democracy.*
       Toronto: Canadian Institute of International Affairs, 1976.
1507 GRAFFTEY, W.H. "Quest for an Immigration Policy." *Canadian Busi-
       ness.* 48 (May 1975), p. 60.
1508 GUNTER, Peter. "Canada's Immigration Policy: Some Comments."
       Canadian Public Policy. 1:4 (Autumn 1975), pp. 580-83.
1509 HAWKINS, Freda. "Immigrants and Cities: A Report on the Green
       Paper on Immigration Policy." *Urban Forum.* 1:1 (Spring 1975), pp.
       7-13.
1510 _____. "Immigration and Population: The Canadian Approach."
       Canadian Public Policy. 1:3 (Summer 1975), pp. 285-95.
1511 KALBACH, Warren. "Demographic Concerns and the Control of Immi-
       gration." *Canadian Public Policy.* 1:3 (Summer 1975), pp. 302-10.
1512 _____. "The National Conference on Canadian Immigration and the
       Green Paper in Retrospect." *Canadian Ethnic Studies.* 7:1 (1975), pp.
       71-93.
1513 LONEY, M., and MOSCOVITCH, A. "Immigration Green Paper in
       Black and White." *Canadian Dimension.* 10:7 (March 1975), pp. 4-8.
1514 NATIONAL CONFERENCE ON IMMIGRATION POLICY,
       TORONTO, 1975. *Immigration 1975-2001; Report of the National Con-
       ference on Immigration Policy, May 22-24, 1975.* Toronto: Canadian
       Association for Adult Education, 1975.
1515 PAUL, Gurbachan Sing. "The Green Paper and Third World Immigrants
       — A Subjective Analysis." *Canadian Ethnic Studies.* 7:1 (1975), pp.
       40-49.
1516 SOCIAL PLANNING COUNCIL OF METROPOLITAN TORONTO.
       Immigration Policy Project. *Report.* Toronto: The Council, 1975.

8.2.3.3   Child Immigration

1517 ASHWORTH, Mary. *Immigrant Children and Canadian Schools.* Toronto:
       McClelland and Stewart, 1975.
1518 KIRKPATRICK, P.T. "Nobody's Children in New Lands: The Empire
       Work of Dr. Barnardo's Homes." *United Empire.* 27:10 (October
       1936), pp. 567-70.
1519 MacGREGOR, H. *Several Years After.* Ottawa: Canadian Council on
       Child Welfare; 1928.
1520 RUTMAN, Leonard. "Importation of British Waifs into Canada,
       1868-1916." *Child Welfare.* 52:3 (March 1973), pp. 158-66.
1521 TURNER, W.B. "Miss Rye's Children and the Ontario Press, 1875." *On-
       tario History.* 68:3 (September 1976), pp. 169-203.
1522 WHITTON, C.E. "Juvenile Immigration." *Proceedings.* National Confer-
       ence of Social Work. 51 (1924), pp. 609-613.

8.2.3.4 Labour and Immigration

1523 "Canadian Labour Congress Brief on Immigration." *Canadian Labour.* 20:4 (December 1975), pp. 34-38, 40.

1524 MacDONALD, D. "Congress Policy on Immigration." *Canadian Unionist.* 29:7-8 (July/August 1955), pp. 238-39, 249-50.

1525 "Mémoire du CTC sur l'immigration." *Le Travailleur canadien.* 20:4 (December 1975), pp. 38-42.

1526 MILLING, Gordon B. "Immigration and Labour: Critic or Catalyst." *Canadian Public Policy.* 1:3 (Summer 1975), pp. 311-16.

1527 ORLIKOW, David. "Labour and Immigration." *Canadian Labour.* 9:2 (February 1964), pp. 17-18.

1528 "Statements of Labour Organizations on Immigration." *Labour Gazette.* 46:8 (August 1946), pp. 1034-36.

8.2.3.5 Economic Impact of Immigration

1529 CORBETT, David C. "Immigration, Population Growth and Canadian Economic Development." Ph.D., McGill University, 1954.

1530 _____. "Immigration, Population Growth and Canadian Economic Development." *Canadian Journal of Economics and Political Science.* 17:3 (August 1951), pp. 360-68.

1531 COWAN, A.W. "Immigration and the Labour Force, 1966-1969." *Canada Manpower Review.* 3 (Second Quarter 1970), pp. 15-25.

1532 EPSTEIN, Larry. *Immigration and Inflation.* Ottawa: Information Canada, 1974.

1533 GREEN, Allan G. *Immigration and the Post-war Canadian Economy.* Toronto: Macmillan of Canada, 1976.

1534 JOHNSON, Caswell Lewington. "Immigration and the Labour Market: A Study of Some Economic Aspects of Canada's Post-war Immigration Policy and Practice." Ph.D., Columbia University, 1964.

1535 LEVESQUE, Robert. "Immigration, main-d'oeuvre et chômage." M.A., University of Montreal, 1961.

1536 MARR, William L. *Labour Market and Other Implications of Immigration Policy for Ontario.* Toronto: Ontario Economic Council, 1976.

1537 MELTZ, N.M. "Implications of Manpower and Immigration Policy." In *Issues in Canadian Economics*, edited by L.H. Officer and L.B. Smith. pp. 245-75. Toronto: McGraw-Hill Ryerson, 1974.

1538 PARAI, Louis. *The Economic Impact of Immigration.* Ottawa: Information Canada, 1974.

1539 _____. *Immigration and Emigration of Professional and Skilled Manpower during the Post-war Period.* Ottawa: Queen's Printer, 1965.

1540 STAR, Spencer. "In Search of a Rational Immigration Policy." *Canadian Public Policy.* 1:3 (Summer 1975), pp. 328-42.

1541 TIMLIN, Mabel F. "Economic Theory and Immigration Policy." *Canadian Journal of Economics and Political Science.* 16:3 (August 1950), pp. 375-82.

8.2.4 Administration

1542 ANDERSON, Grace. "Immigration and Social Policy." In *Canadian Social Policy*, edited by Shankar A. Yelaja. pp. 107-33. Waterloo: Wilfrid Laurier University Press, 1978.

1543 ANGUS, H.F. "Canadian Immigration: The Law and Its Administration." *American Journal of International Law.* 28:1 (January 1934), pp. 74-89.

1544 BELKIN, Simon. *Through Narrow Gates: A Review of Jewish Immigration, Colonization and Immigration Work in Canada, 1840-1940*. Montreal: Canadian Jewish Congress and Jewish Colonization Association, 1968.

1545 BERGER, Michael. "Canadian Immigration Procedure and Practise." *Interpreter Releases*. 38 (17 May 1961), pp. 125-29.

1546 DIRKS, Gerald E. "Canadian Policies and Programmes Towards Political Refugees." Ph.D., University of Toronto, 1972.

1547 FRASER, C.F. "Administrative Control Over Aliens in Canada." *George Washington Law Review*. 7:3 (Fall 1939), pp. 433-74.

1548 GREEN, L.C. "Immigration, Extradition and Asylum in Canadian Law and Practice." In *Canadian Perspectives on International Law and Organization*, edited by R. St.J. MacDonald, Gerald l. Morris and Douglas M. Johnston. pp. 244-303. Toronto: University of Toronto Press, 1974.

1549 HUNTER, Ian A. *The Immigration Appeal Board: A Study*. Law Reform Commission. Ottawa: Supply and Services, 1976.

1550 "Implementing Immigration Policy." *Canadian Welfare*. 51:7 (January/February 1976), pp. 26-27.

1551 KEENLEYSIDE, H.L. "Canadian Immigration Policy and Its Administration." *External Affairs*. 1:5 (May 1949), pp. 3-11.

1552 KRONBY, Malcolm. "Administration of the Immigration Act." *Osgoode Hall Law Journal*. 1:2 (April 1959), pp. 1-9.

1553 PARENT, Marc A. "Affaires d'immigration en appel (la Commission d'appel de l'immigration)." *La Revue du barreau*. 32:3 (May 1972), pp. 194-228.

1554 PHELAN, V.C. "L'organisation de l'immigration au Canada." *Revue international du travail*. 65:3 (March 1952), pp. 335-64.

1555 SCOTT, F.R. "Immigration Act — False Arrest — Illegal Treatment of Arrested Person." *Canadian Bar Review*. 14:1 (January 1936), pp. 62-67.

1556 SESSING, Trevor S. "How They Kept Canada Almost Lily White: The Previously Untold Story of Canadian Immigration Officials Who Stopped American Blacks from Coming to Canada." *Saturday Night*. 85:9 (September 1970), pp. 30-32.

1557 WOODSWORTH, J.S. "Immigration Legislation and Its Administration as It Bears upon the Problem of Assimilation in Canada." *Proceedings*. National Conference of Social Work. 51 (1924), pp. 92-101.

8.3 Intergroup Relations and Policy

8.3.1 Historical Development

8.3.1.1 General

1558 ADACHI, Ken. *The Enemy That Never Was: A History of the Japanese Canadians*. Toronto: McClelland and Stewart, 1976.

1559 ADAM, G.M. "Equal Rights Movement." *Bystander*. (November 1889), pp. 40-44.

1560 BROADFOOT, Barry. *Years of Sorrow, Years of Shame: The Story of the Japanese Canadians in World War II*. Toronto: Doubleday Canada, 1977.

1561 CLAIRMONT, D., and MAGILL, D. *Nova Scotia Blacks: An Historical and Structural Over-View*. Halifax: Institute of Public Affairs, Dalhousie University, 1970.

1562 HAAS, Theodore H. "The Legal Aspects of Indian Affairs from 1887-1957." *Annals of the American Academy of Political and Social Science.* 311 (May 1957), pp. 12-22.

1563 LARNER, John William. "The Kootenay Plains (Alberta) Land Question and Canadian Indian Policy 1799-1947." Ph.D., West Virginia University, 1972.

1564 MUNRO, J.A. "British Columbia and the 'Chinese-Evil': Canada's First Anti-Asiatic Immigration Law." *Journal of Canadian Studies.* 6 (May 1971), pp. 42-51.

1565 SCOTT, Duncan C. "Indian Affairs, 1840-1867." In *Canada and Its Provinces,* edited by A. Shortt and A.G. Doughty. pp. 331-64. Toronto: Publishers Association of Canada, 1913.

1566 SHANKEL, George Edgar. "The Development of Indian Policy in British Columbia." Ph.D., University of Washington (Seattle), 1945.

1567 SHIBATA, Yuko Y., *et al. The Forgotten History of the Japanese Canadians.* Vancouver: New Sun Books, 1977.

1568 SPRAY, W.A. "The Settlement of the Black Refugees in New Brunswick 1815-1836." *Acadiensis.* 6:2 (Spring 1977), pp. 64-80.

1569 SURTEES, Robert J. "Indian Reserve Policy in Upper Canada, 1830-1845." M.A., Carleton University, 1966.

1570 TAYLOR, John L. "The Development of an Indian Policy for the North-West, 1869-1879." Ph.D., Queen's University, 1975.

1571 UPTON, L.F.S. "Indian Affairs in Colonial New Brunswick." *Acadiensis.* 3:2 (Spring 1974), pp. 3-26.

1572 _____. "Indian Affairs in Colonial Nova Scotia, 1783-1871." *Acadiensis.* 5:1 (Autumn 1975), pp. 3-32.

1573 _____. "The Origins of Canadian Indian Policy." *Journal of Canadian Studies.* 8:4 (November 1973), pp. 51-61.

1574 WARD, William Peter. "White Canada Forever; British Columbia's Response to Orientals, 1858-1914." Ph.D., Queen's University, 1972.

1575 _____. "British Columbia and the Japanese Evacuation." *Canadian Historical Review.* 57:3 (September 1976), pp. 289-309.

8.3.1.2   Reviews of Policy

1576 "Anti-Chinese Legislation." *The Week.* 7:21 (Friday, 25 April 1890), p. 324.

1577 BRYCE, P.H. *The Story of a National Crime: An Appeal for Justice to the Indians of Canada.* Ottawa: James Hope & Sons, 1922.

1578 CALDWELL, George, *et al.* "An Island between Two Cultures: The Residential Indian School." *Canadian Welfare.* 43:4 (July/August 1967), pp. 12-32.

1579 CARDINAL, Harold. "Canadian Indians and the Federal Government." *Western Canadian Journal of Anthropology.* 1:1 (1969), pp. 90-97.

1580 COLVILLE, K.N. "Indian Reform." *Queen's Quarterly.* 26:2 (October/November/December 1918), pp. 191-94.

1581 "Commission on Chinese and Japanese Immigration." *Labour Gazette.* 1:2 (October 1900), p. 52.

1582 DAVIS, Arthur K. "Urban Indians in Western Canada: Implications for Social Theory and Social Policy." *Proceedings and Transactions.* Royal Society of Canada. 6:4 (June 1968), pp. 217-28.

1583 DEPREZ, Paul, and SIGURDSON, Glenn. *The Economic Status of the Canadian Indian: A Re-examination.* Winnipeg: Centre for Settlement Studies, University of Manitoba, 1969.

1584 FOWKE, Edith Margaret. *They Made Democracy Work; The Story of the Cooperative Committee on Japanese Canadians.* Toronto: Japanese Canadian Citizen's Association, 1951.

1585 _____. "Justice and Japanese Canadians." *Canadian Forum.* 26:312 (January 1947), pp. 225-26.

1586 GIRAUD, Marcel. "A Note on the Half-Breed Problem in Manitoba." *Canadian Journal of Economics and Political Science.* 3:4 (November 1937), pp. 541-49.

1587 "The Indian Policy." *The Week.* 8:40 (4 September 1891), p. 636.

1588 INSTITUTE OF PUBLIC AFFAIRS. *The Condition of Negroes of Halifax City.* Publication #27. Halifax: Institute of Public Affairs, 1962.

1589 JAMIESON, Stuart. "Native Indians and the Trade Union Movement in British Columbia." *Human Organization.* 20:4 (Winter 1961-62), pp. 219-25.

1590 JENNESS, D. "Canada's Eskimo Problem." *Queen's Quarterly.* 32:4 (April/May/June 1925), pp. 317-29.

1591 JOHNSTON, Lubin. "British Columbia's Oriental Problem." *United Empire.* 13:9 (September 1922), pp. 570-76.

1592 JUDD, David. "Canada's Northern Policy: Retrospect and Prospect." *Polar Record.* 14:92 (May 1969), pp. 593-602.

1593 LaFOREST, Gerard U. *Natural Resources and Public Property under the Canadian Constitution.* Toronto: University of Toronto Press, 1969.

1594 McGILP, J.G. "The Relations of Canada's Indians and Canadian Governments." *Canadian Public Administration.* 6:3 (September 1963), pp. 299-308.

1595 McNICKLE, D'Arcy. "Private Intervention." *Human Organization.* 20:4 (Winter 1961), pp. 208-15.

1596 McNIVEN, J.D. "Oriental Immigration Commission." *Labour Gazette.* 1:9 (May 1901), pp. 508-11.

1597 MELLING, John. "Recent Developments in Official Policy Towards Canadian Indians and Eskimos." *Race.* 7:4 (April 1966), pp. 379-99.

1598 "The Negro Problem." *The Week.* 7:25 (23 May 1890), pp. 133, 452.

1599 RUSSEL, Nelson Vance. "The Indian Policy of Henry Hamilton: A Revaluation." *Canadian Historical Review.* 11:1 (March 1930), pp. 20-38.

1600 SALYSYN, Vladimir. "Goals in Indian Affairs." *Canadian Welfare.* 42:2 (March/April 1966), pp. 79-81.

1601 SYMINGTON, D.F. "Metis Rehabilitation." *Canadian Geographical Journal.* 46:4 (April 1953), pp. 128-39.

8.3.2   Government Policy and Documentation

8.3.2.1   Federal

1602 ADAMSON, Christopher R., FINDLAY, P., OLIVER, M., and SOLBERG, J. "The Unpublished Research of the Royal Commission on Bilingualism and Biculturalism." *Canadian Journal of Political Science.* 7:4 (December 1974), pp. 709-20.

1603 BATTLE, R. "An Historical Review of Indian Affairs Policies and New Directions for the Future." Ottawa: Department of Northern Affairs and National Resources, 1966.

1604 CANADA. Department of Citizenship and Immigration, Indian Affairs Branch. "The Administration of Indian Affairs." Unpublished. Ottawa, 1964.

1605 CANADA. Department of Indian Affairs and Northern Development. *History of Indian Policy*. Background Paper No. 2. Ottawa: Information Canada, 1972.

1606 ———. *Indians and the Law*. Ottawa: Information Canada, 1971.

1607 ———. *Statement of the Government of Canada on Indian Policy*. Ottawa: Information Canada, 1969.

1608 CANADA. Department of Justice. *A Canadian Charter of Human Rights*. Ottawa: Queen's Printer, 1968.

1609 CANADA. Department of Labour. Legislative Research Branch. *Human Rights in Canada, 1975*. Ottawa: Information Canada, 1975.

1610 ———. *Human Rights in Canada 1976*. Ottawa: Supply and Services, 1976.

1611 CANADA. Department of Secretary of State. *Decade for Action to Combat Racism and Racial Discrimination, 1973-1983*. Ottawa: Information Canada, 1975.

1612 ———. *Federal-Provincial Programme of Co-operation for the Development of Bilingualism in Education at the Pre-university Levels: Provincial Reports/ Programme féderal-provincial de co-opération pour la promotion du bilingisme dans le domaine de l'éducation aux niveaux pré-universitaires: rapports provinciaux*. Ottawa: The Department, 1973.

1613 ———. *Official Languages Programmes/ Programmes des langues officielles*. Ottawa: Information Canada, 1973.

1614 ———. *Prejudice and Discrimination: A Study Guide*. Ottawa: Information Canada, 1975.

1615 CANADA. *Indian Treaties and Surrenders: From 1680-1890*. 2 vols. Ottawa: Queen's Printer, 1891.

1616 CANADA. *Indian Treaties and Surrenders: From No. 281 to No. 483*. Vol. 3. Ottawa: King's Printer, 1912.

1617 CANADA. Labour Canada. Legislative Analysis. *Human Rights in Canada, 1977*. Ottawa: Supply and Services, 1977.

1618 CANADA. Law Reform Commission. *Family Law and Native People*. Background Paper. Ottawa: The Commission, 1975.

1619 CANADA. *A National Understanding: Statement of the Government of Canada on the Official Languages Policy: The Official Languages of Canada./ Un choix national: Exposé du Gouvernement du Canada sur une politique linguistique nationale: Les langues officielles du Canada*. Ottawa: Supply and Services, 1977.

1620 CANADA. Royal Commission on Bilingualism and Biculturalism. *An Abridged Version of the Royal Commission Report*. By Hugh R. Innis. Toronto: McClelland and Stewart, in cooperation with the Secretary of State, 1973.

1621 ———. "Briefs Submitted to the Royal Commission on Bilingualism and Biculturalism." Unpublished. Ottawa: Library of Parliament, 1973.

1622 ———. *Documents of the Royal Commission on Bilingualism and Biculturalism*. (13 Documents). Ottawa: Information Canada, 1969-72.

1623 ———. *Index to Briefs and Transcripts of Public Hearings*. Toronto: Micromedia Ltd., 1972.

1624 ———. *Preliminary Report/ Rapport préliminaire*. Ottawa: Queen's Printer, 1965.

1625 ———. *Report*. Vol. I. (Book I — *The Official Languages*). Ottawa: Queen's Printer, 1967.

1626 ———. *Report*. Vol. 2. (Book 2 — *Education*). Ottawa: Queen's Printer, 1968.

1627 _____. *Report*. Vol. 3. (Book 3 — *The Work World*). Ottawa: Queen's Printer, 1969.
1628 _____. *Report*. Vol. 4. (Book 4 — *The Cultural Contribution of Other Ethnic Groups*). Ottawa: Queen's Printer, 1969.
1629 _____. *Report*. Vol. 5. (Book 5 — *The Federal Capital*, Book 6 — *Voluntary Associations*). Ottawa: Queen's Printer, 1969.
1630 _____. *Resumé of Report*. Toronto: Canadian Association for Adult Education, 1968-1970.
1631 _____. *Studies of the Royal Commission on Bilingualism and Biculturalism*. (11 Studies). Ottawa: Information Canada, 1969-1970.
1632 CANADA. Treasury Board. Official Languages Branch. *Revisions of the Official Language Policies in the Public Service/Révision aux politiques des langues officielles dans la fonction publique*. Ottawa: The Board, 1977.
1633 CHRETIEN, Honourable Jean. "Indian Policy: A Reply." *Canadian Forum*. 49:590 (March 1970), pp. 279-80.
1634 HAWTHORN, Harry Bertram, ed. *A Survey of the Contemporary Indians of Canada: A Report on Economic, Political, Educational Needs and Policies*. Vol. 1. Ottawa: Queen's Printer, 1966; Vol. 2. Ottawa: Queen's Printer, 1967.
1635 POTTER, H.H., and HILL, D.G. "Negro Settlement in Canada, 1628-1965." Unpublished Research Report for the Royal Commission on Bilingualism and Biculturalism. Ottawa, 1967.
1636 VALLEE, Frank G. *Indians and Eskimos of Canada: An Overview of Studies of Relevance for the Royal Commission on Bilingualism and Biculturalism, Report*. Ottawa: Queen's Printer, 1966.

8.3.2.2 Provincial

1637 BRITISH COLUMBIA. Law Reform Commission. *Report on Civil Rights*. Vancouver: Queen's Printer, 1972.
1638 MANITOBA. Law Reform Commission. *Working Paper on the Case for a Provincial Bill of Rights*. Winnipeg: The Commission, 1974.
1639 NEW BRUNSWICK. Human Rights Commission. *A Selection of Human Rights Laws in Canada, 1973*. Fredericton: The Commission, 1973.
1640 ONTARIO FEDERATION OF LABOUR. *Brief to the Government of Ontario Concerning Human Rights*. Don Mills: The Federation, 1971.
1641 ONTARIO. Ministry of Culture and Recreation. Multicultural Development Branch. *Papers on the Black Community*. Toronto: The Ministry, 1976.
1642 ONTARIO. Ontario Human Rights Commission. *Life Together: A Report on Human Rights in Ontario*. Toronto: The Commission, 1977.

8.3.3 Social Welfare Policies and Minority Groups

8.3.3.1 Native Peoples

1643 ADAMS, Howard. *Prison of Grass: Canada from the Native Point of View*. Toronto: New Press, 1975.
1644 BAILEY, Stanley. "The Welfare and Training Services Supplied to the Indians of Canada." M.A., University of British Columbia, 1946.
1645 CARDINAL, Harold. *The Unjust Society: The Tragedy of Canada's Indians*. Edmonton: M.G. Hurtig, 1969.
1646 _____. "Policy Statement from Harold Cardinal." *Native People*. 10:4 (22 April 1977), p. 4.
1647 DOSMAN, Edgar J. *Indians: The Urban Dilemma*. Toronto: McClelland and Stewart, 1972.

1648 DUNNING, R.W. "Indian Policy — A Proposal for Autonomy." *Canadian Forum*. 49:587 (December 1969), pp. 206-07.

1649 DURAN, James A. "The New Indian Policy: Lessons from the U.S." *Canadian Dimension*. 6:6 (December/January 1969-70), pp. 21-23.

1650 GRAHAM, W.R. "Indian Treaties and the Settlement of the North-West." *Saskatchewan History*. 2:1 (January 1949), pp. 19-22.

1651 HARKER, Brent. "Alberta Government Preparing a Policy." *Native People*. 9:49 (24 December 1976), pp. 2-3.

1652 _____. "Government Prepares Native Policy." *Native People*. 10:1 (7 January 1977), p. 10.

1653 McGEE, H.F., ed. *The Native Peoples of Atlantic Canada — A History of Ethnic Interaction*. Toronto: McClelland and Stewart, 1973.

1654 MARSZOWSKI, Eva. "Welfare Services for Indians." *Bulletin of Canadian Welfare Law*. 2:2 (Summer 1973), pp. 24-31.

1655 METIS AND NON-STATUS INDIAN CRIME AND JUSTICE COMMISSION. *Report*. Cutler, Ontario: Woodland Studio, 1977.

1656 MORISSONNEAU, Christian. "Bien-être de consommation chez les esquimaux du Nouveau Québec: Une probleme communautaire." *Cahiers de Géographie de Québec*. 17:41 (September 1973), pp. 265-81.

1657 "Native Development Policies Begin." *Native People*. 9:40 (29 October 1976), p. 15.

1658 "The New Policy for Canada's Indians." *Labour Gazette*. 69:9 (September 1969), p. 513.

1659 ROBERTSON, Heather. *Reservations are for Indians*. Toronto: James, Lewis and Samuel, 1970.

1660 SHUMIATCHER, Morris C. *Welfare: Hidden Backlash*. Toronto: McClelland and Stewart, 1971.

1661 SIMON, Sir John. "The Indian Problem." *Canadian Bar Review*. 8:9 (November 1930), pp. 633-42.

1662 STEFFE, Norman, ed. *Issues for the Seventies: Canada's Indians*. Toronto: McGraw-Hill, 1970.

1663 TREMAUDAN, Auguste-Henri de. *Histoire de la nation métisse dans l'ouest canadien*. (Documents historiquees). Montreal: Levesque, 1935. 1935.

1664 WATKINS, Mel. *Dene Nation: The Colony Within*. Toronto: University of Toronto Press, 1977.

1665 WAUBAGESHIG, ed. *The Only Good Indian: Essays by Canadian Indians*. Toronto: New Press, 1970.

1666 WHITE, C.A. "Canada's Indians: A New Policy." *Canada and the World*. 37:7 (March 1972), pp. 6-7.

8.3.3.2 Black Peoples

1667 ARTHURS, H.W. "Civil Liberties — Public Schools — Segregation of Negro Students." *Canadian Bar Review*. 60:3 (September 1963), pp. 453-57.

1668 CLAIRMONT, Donald H., and MAGILL, Dennis W. *Africville: The Life and Death of a Canadian Black Community*. Toronto: McClelland and Stewart, 1974.

1669 _____. *Africville, Relocation Report*. Halifax: Institute of Public Affairs, Dalhousie University, 1971.

1670 WINKS, R.W. "Negro School Segregation in Ontario and Nova Scotia." *Canadian Historical Review*. 50:2 (June 1969), pp. 164-91.

8.3.3.3   Chinese

1671 ANGUS, H.F. "The Legal Status in British Columbia of Residents of Oriental Race and Their Descendants." *Canadian Bar Review.* 9:1 (January 1931), pp. 1-12.

1672 ROY, Patricia E. "The Oriental 'Menace' in British Columbia." In *Studies in Canadian Social History*, edited by M. Horn and R. Sabourin. pp. 287-97. Toronto: McClelland and Stewart, 1974.

8.3.3.4   Others

1673 WOODCOCK, George, and AVAKUMOVIC, Ivan. *The Doukhobors.* Toronto: Oxford University Press, 1968.

8.3.4   Special Issues

8.3.4.1   Native Rights

1674 ASSOCIATION OF IROQUOIS AND ALLIED INDIANS. *Immigration, Taxation, Jay Treaty, Treaty of Ghent.* Brantford, Ontario: The Association, 1974.

1675 BADCOCK, William T. *Who Owns Canada? Aboriginal Title and Canadian Courts.* Ottawa: Canadian Association in Support of Native Peoples, 1976.

1676 BAUER, G.W. "Aboriginal Rights in Canada." *Canadian Forum.* 53:628 (May 1973), pp. 15-20.

1677 CANADA. Indian-Eskimo Association of Canada. *Native Rights in Canada.* Toronto: The Association, 1970.

1678 CANADIAN CORRECTIONS ASSOCIATION. *Indians and the Law, A Survey Prepared for the Department of Indian Affairs and Northern Development.* Ottawa: Queen's Printer, 1967.

1679 CUMMING, P.A. "Native Rights and Laws in An Age of Protest." *Alberta Law Review.* 11:2 (1973), pp. 238-59.

1680 CUMMING, Peter, and MICKENBERG, Neil H., eds. *Native Rights in Canada.* 2nd ed. Toronto: Indian-Eskimo Association of Canada and General Publishing Company, 1972.

1681 DANIELS, Christine. *The White Man's Laws.* Edmonton: M.G. Hurtig, 1975.

1682 GOODFELLOW, W.A. *Civil Liberties and Rights of Indians in Ontario.* Toronto: Select Committee on Indian Affairs of the Legislative Assembly of Ontario, 1954.

1683 GREEN, L.C. "Canada's Indians: Federal Policy, International and Constitutional Law." *Ottawa Law Review.* 4:1 (Summer 1970), pp. 101-31.

1684 _____. "The Canadian Bill of Rights, Indian Rights and the United Nations." *Chitty's Law Journal.* 22 (January 1974), pp. 22-28.

1685 INUIT TAPIRISAT OF CANADA. *Inuit and the Law.* Produced by Inuit Tapirisat of Canada; Peter A. Cumming *et al.* Translation into syllabics by Jeela Moss Davies, Sarah Seeloo, Domina Uvilluk. Ottawa, 1974.

1686 JAMIESON, Kathleen. *Indian Women and the Law in Canada: Citizen's Menu.* Ottawa: Supply and Services, 1978.

1687 LEIGH, L.H. "The Indian Act: The Supremacy of Parliament, and the Equal Protection of the Laws." *McGill Law Journal.* 16:2 (June 1970), pp. 389-98.

1688 LYSYK, Kenneth. *Resource Paper on Human Rights and Canada's Native People.* Toronto: Indian-Eskimo Association of Canada, 1968.

1689 _____. "Human Rights and the Native Peoples of Canada." *Canadian Bar Review.* 46:4 (December 1968), pp. 695-705.

1690 MacKENZIE, N.A.M. "Indians and Treaties in Law." *Canadian Bar Review.* 7:8 (October 1929), pp. 561-68.

1691 MICKENBERG, Neil. H. "Aboriginal Rights in Canada and the United States." *Osgoode Hall Law Journal.* 9:1 (August 1971), pp. 119-56.

1692 MONTGOMERY, Malcolm. "The Legal Status of the Six Nations Indians in Canada." *Ontario History.* 55:2 (June 1963), pp. 93-105.

1693 SANDERS, D.E. "The Bill of Rights and Indian Status." *University of British Columbia Law Review.* 7:1 (Summer 1972), pp. 81-105.

1694 SMITH, Derek. *Canadian Indians and the Law: Selected Documents, 1663-1972.* Toronto: McClelland and Stewart, 1975.

1695 STAATZ, Howard. *Some Aspects of the Legal Status of Indians.* Toronto: Indian-Eskimo Association of Canada, 1971.

8.3.4.2 Human Rights

1696 ADAM, G.M. "Equal Rights in Society." *Bystander.* (February 1890) pp. 163-64.

1697 ANGUS, H.F. "Underprivileged Canadians." *Queen's Quarterly.* 38:3 (Summer 1931), pp. 445-60.

1698 "Anti-discrimination Legislation in Canada, 1964." *Labour Gazette.* 64:11 (November 1964), pp. 939-43.

1699 "Anti-discrimination Legislation Enacted in 1966: Alberta Adopts Human Rights Act, Ontario Passes the Age Discrimination Act." *Labour Gazette.* 66:6 (June 1966), pp. 598-99.

1700 "Anti-discrimination Legislation in 1963 (Human Rights Act, Nova Scotia, Hotels Act, Quebec)." *Labour Gazette.* 63:10 (October 1963), pp. 877-78.

1701 BOWKER, W.F. "Fundamental Rights in Canada." M.A., University of Minnesota, 1949.

1702 CANADIAN LABOUR CONGRESS. *Submission on Bill C-25 'Canadian Human Rights Act'.* Ottawa: The Congress, 1977.

1703 EBERLEE, T. "Ontario's Program for Human Rights." *Canadian Labour.* 7:1 (January 1962), pp. 8-10.

1704 _____, and HILL, D.G. "The Ontario Human Rights Code." *University of Toronto Law Journal.* 15:2 (1964), pp. 448-55.

1705 "Federal Human Rights Legislation." *Canadian Welfare.* 52:25 (March/April 1976), pp. 25-26.

1706 FERRARI, Leo. *The Rise of Human Rights, a Canadian Outline.* Fredericton: New Brunswick Human Rights Commission, 1973.

1707 GOTLIEB, Allan, ed. *Human Rights, Federalism and Minorities/ Les droits de l'homme, la fédéralisme et les minorités.* Toronto: Canadian Institute of International Affairs, 1970.

1708 HILL, Daniel G. *Human Rights in Canada: A Focus on Racism.* Ottawa: Canadian Labour Congress, 1977.

1709 HOGY, P.W. "The Canadian Bill of Rights — Equality before the Law." *Canadian Bar Review.* 52:2 (May 1974), pp. 263-80.

1710 HUCKER, John, and McDONALD, Bruce C. "Securing Human Rights in Canada." *McGill Law Journal.* 15:2 (June 1969), pp. 220-43.

1711 HUNTER, Ian A. "The Development of the Ontario Human Rights Code: A Decade in Retrospect." *University of Toronto Law Journal.* 22:4 (Autumn 1972), pp. 237-57.

1712 INTERNATIONAL COUNCIL ON SOCIAL WELFARE. Canadian Committee. *Human Rights and Social Welfare in Canada, Report.* Ottawa: Canadian Welfare Council, 1968.

1713 MacDONALD, P.V. "Race Relations and Canadian Law." *University of Toronto Faculty of Law Review.* 18 (April 1960), pp. 115-27.

1714 McNEILLY, Russell A. *Strategies for Human Rights Education in New Brunswick: A Report Prepared for the New Brunswick Human Rights Commission.* Fredericton: The Commission, 1974.

1715 SANDWELL, B.K. "The State and Human Rights." *Behind the Headlines.* 7:2 (1947), pp. 1-16.

1716 SASKATCHEWAN ASSOCIATION ON HUMAN RIGHTS. *A Brief in Support of a Saskatchewan Human Rights Commission.* Saskatoon: The Association, 1971.

1717 SCOTT, Frank R. *The Canadian Constitution and Human Rights.* Toronto: Canadian Broadcasting Corporation, 1959.

1718 _____. "Dominion Jurisdiction over Human Rights." *Canadian Bar Review.* 27:5 (May 1949), pp. 497-536.

1719 SIGSWORTH, D.F. "Some Considerations Relating to Jurisdiction over Fundamental Human Rights under the Canadian Constitution." L.L.M., Dalhousie University, 1960.

1720 SOHN, Herbert Alvin. "Human Rights Legislation in Ontario: A Study of Social Action." D.S.W., University of Toronto, 1976.

1721 TARNOPOLSKY, W.S. "The Supreme Court and the Canadian Bill of Rights." *Canadian Bar Review.* 53:4 (December 1975), pp. 649-714.

8.3.4.3   Civil Liberties

1722 BOLTON, Philip Michael. *Civil Rights in Canada.* 2nd ed. Vancouver: Self Counsel Press, 1972.

1723 CORRY, James Alexander. *Civil Liberties in Trying Times.* (The Bryan Priestman Memorial Lecture, 1953). Fredericton: University of New Brunswick, 1953.

1724 DELEURY, Edith, and RIVET, Michèle. *Droit civil: Droit des personnes et de la famille.* Quebec: Presses de l'université Laval, 1974.

1725 KRAUTER, Joseph Francis. "Civil Liberties and the Canadian Minorities." Ph.D., University of Illinois, 1968.

1726 LASKIN, Bora. "Our Civil Liberties: The Role of the Supreme Court." *Queen's Quarterly.* 61:4 (Winter 1955), pp. 455-71.

1727 MONETTE, Gustave. "Report of Committee on Civil Liberties." *Canadian Bar Review.* 22:1 (August/September 1944), pp. 598-617.

1728 SCHMEISER, D.A. *Civil Liberties in Canada.* Toronto: Oxford University Press, 1964.

8.3.5   Administration

8.3.5.1   Native Policy

1729 ABBOT, F.H. "The Administration of Indian Affairs in Canada." (Report of an investigation made in 1914 under the direction of the Board of Indian Commissioners). Washington: The Board, 1915.

1730 DUNNING, R.W. "Some Aspects of Government Indian Policy and Administration." *Anthropologica.* 4:2 (1962), pp. 209-31.

1731 _____. "Some Problems of Reserve Indian Communities: A Case Study." *Anthropologica.* 6:1 (1964), pp. 3-38.

1732 DYCK, Noel E. "The Administration of Federal Indian Aid in the Northwest Territories, 1879-1885." M.A., University of Saskatchewan, 1970.

1733 HARPER, Allan G. "Canada's Indian Administration: Basic Concepts and Objectives." *America Indigena*. 5:2 (April 1945), pp. 119-32.

1734 _____. "Canada's Indian Administration: the 'Indian Act'." *America Indigena*. 6:4 (October 1946), pp. 297-314.

1735 _____. "Canada's Indian Administration: The Treaty System." *America Indigena*. 7:2 (April 1947), pp. 129-48.

1736 HOLMES, Alvin Ishmael. "The Social Welfare Aspects and Implications of the Indian Act." M.S.W.. University of British Columbia, 1961.

1737 JENNESS, Diamond. *Eskimo Administration 1. Alaska*. Montreal: Arctic Institute of North America, July 1962.

1738 _____. *Eskimo Administration 2. Canada*. Montreal: Arctic Institute of North America, May 1964.

1739 _____. *Eskimo Administration 3. Labrador*. Montreal: Arctic Institute of North America, May 1965.

1740 _____. *Eskimo Administration 4. Greenland*. Montreal: Arctic Institute of North America, May 1967.

1741 _____. *Eskimo Administration 5. Analysis and Reflections*. Montreal: Arctic Institute of North America, March 1968.

1742 MacINNES, T.R.L. "History of Indian Administration in Canada." *Annual Report of the Smithsonian Institute*. Washington, 1942.

1743 _____. "History of Indian Administration in Canada." *Canadian Journal of Economics and Political Science*. 12:3 (August 1946), pp. 387-94.

1744 _____. "History and Policies of Indian Administration in Canada." In *The North American Indian Today*, edited by Charles T. Loram and Thomas F. McIlwraith. pp. 143-167. Toronto: University of Toronto Press, 1943.

1745 MARSHALL, Brian David. "Some Problems in Indian Affairs Field Administration." M.A., Carleton University, 1962.

1746 PATTERSON, E. Palmer. "Native Peoples and Social Policy." In *Canadian Social Policy*, edited by Shankar Yelaja. pp. 167-87. Waterloo: Wilfrid Laurier University Press, 1978.

1747 SCOTT, D.C. *The Administration of Indian Affairs in Canada*. Toronto: Canadian Institute of International Affairs, 1931.

9.0   Social Welfare Policies for Women, Children and the Family

9.1   Historical Development

9.1.1   General

1748 ANGUS, Anne Margaret. *Children's Aid Society of Vancouver, British Columbia, 1901-1951*. Vancouver, 1951.

1749 _____. "Profiles 3: Winona D. Armitage." *Canadian Welfare*. 41:1 (September/October 1965), pp. 226-31.

1750 ANGUS, H.F. "Vancouver Children's Aid Society, 1901-1951." *Canadian Welfare*. 27:1 (April 1951), pp. 20-24.

1751 ARMITAGE, W.A.J. "The Family and Canadian Social Policy: Background Paper for the Conference on Family Policy." *Proceedings. Conference on Family Policy.* Ottawa, 24-26 April, 1977, pp. 187-233. Ottawa: Canadian Council on Social Development, 1977.

1752 ARMSTRONG, Pat, and ARMSTRONG, Hugh. *The Double Ghetto: Canadian Women and Their Segregated Work.* Toronto: McClelland and Stewart, 1978.

1753 BAIN, Ian. "The Role of J.J. Kelso in the Launching of the Child Welfare Movement in Ontario." M.S.W., University of Toronto, 1955.

1754 BREWER, Brian. *A Discussion of the Role of the Community and the Role of the Government in the Early Development of the Regina Children's Aid Society, 1895-1917.* Regina: School of Social Work; University of Regina, 1976.

1755 CANADIAN COUNCIL ON CHILD WELFARE. *Report of the New Brunswick Child Welfare Survey.* Saint John: Kiwanis Club and Central Welfare Council of Saint John, 1928-29.

1756 CLEVERDON, Catherine Lyle. *The Woman Suffrage Movement in Canada.* Toronto: University of Toronto Press, 1950.

1757 COHN, T.M.L. "Child Welfare Legislation in Canada." M.A., University of Toronto, 1935.

1758 COOK, R., and MITCHINSON, W., eds. *Their Proper Sphere: Woman's Place in Canadian Society.* Toronto: Oxford University Press, 1976.

1759 DAWE, Jane-Alice Kathleen. "The Impact of Social Change on the Development of Welfare Services in Ontario, 1891-1921: An Historical Study of the Transition from Institutional to Foster Care of Children in Ontario, 1891-1921." M.S.W., University of Toronto, 1966.

1760 DOUGLAS, Muriel H. "History of the Society for the Protection of Women and Children from 1882 to 1966." M.S.W., McGill University, 1967.

1761 EICHLER, M. "Social Policy Concerning Women." In *Canadian Social Policy*, edited by Shankar Yelaja. pp. 133-46. Waterloo: Wilfrid Laurier University Press, 1978.

1762 FORTIER, de la Broquerie. *Au service de l'enfance, l'association québéçoise de la goutte de lait, 1915-1965.* Quebec: Edition Garneau, 1966.

1763 HAMLET, Elizabeth. "Charlotte Whitton and the Growth of the Canadian Council on Child Welfare, 1926-1941. A Study of the Role of Social Reformers in Social Policy Making in Canada." M.S.W., Carleton University, 1978.

1764 JOHNSON, Helen. *The Development of Public Child Welfare Programs in Saskatchewan.* Vancouver: School of Social Work, University of British Columbia, 1952.

1765 JOLLIFE, Russell. "The History of the Children's Aid Society of Toronto, 1891-1947." M.S.W., University of Toronto, 1950.

1766 KELSO, John Joseph. *Early History of the Humane and Children's Aid Movement in Ontario, 1886-1893.* Toronto: King's Printer, 1911.

1767 KITCHEN, Brigitte. "Canadian Controversy over Family Income Support Programs, 1928-1976." Ph.D., London School of Economics, 1977.

1768 MacDONNELL, Mary K., et al. *The Decision-Making Process in the Formulation of Social Policy, Ontario Child Welfare, 1960-1965.* Toronto: School of Social Work, 1969.

1769 MELICHERCIK, J. "Child Welfare in Ontario." In *Canadian Social Policy*, edited by Shankar Yelaja. pp. 187-205. Waterloo: Wilfrid Laurier University Press, 1978.

1770 MORRISON, T.R. "'Their Proper Sphere' Feminism, the Family, and Child-Centred Social Reform in Ontario, 1875-1900." Part I, *Ontario History*, 48:1, (March 1976), pp. 45-64. Part II, 48:2, (June 1976), pp. 67-74.

1771 ———. "Ways of Seeing Children." In *Children and the State*. Proceedings of a Conference held 16-18 April, 1978 School of Social Work, Carleton University, pp. 5-43. Ottawa: Centre for Social Welfare Studies, Carleton University, 1978.

1772 ———. "The Child and Urban Social Reform in Late Nineteenth Century Ontario, 1875-1900." Ph.D., University of Toronto, 1970.

1773 ONTARIO. Committee on Child Labour. *Report*. Toronto: King's Printer, 1907.

1774 PARKER, G. "The Century of the Child." *Canadian Bar Review*. 45:4 (1967), pp. 741-63.

1775 PELLETIER, Gérard. *Histoire des enfants tristes, un reportage sur l'enfance sans soutien dans la province du Québec*. Montreal: L'Action nationale, 1950.

1776 PIERSON, R. "Women's Emancipation and the Recruitment of Women into the Labour Force in World War II." In *The Neglected Majority: Essays in Canadian Women's History*, edited by A. Prentice and S.M. Trofimenkoff. pp. 125-46. Toronto: McClelland and Stewart, 1976.

1777 "Pioneering Family Welfare in Toronto." *Canadian Welfare Summary*. 15 (September 1939), pp. 49-55.

1778 POLLOCK, Sheila Joy. "A Study of the Impact of Social Change on Developments in the Philosophy of Child Welfare in Ontario between 1891-1921." M.S.W., University of Toronto, 1966.

1779 POULIN, Gonzalve. "Vers la stabilité de la famille ouvrière." *Sécurité de la famille ouvrière*. Conference Rapport 6ᵉ. Congrés des relations industrielles de Laval. Quebec: Presses de l'université Laval, 1951.

1780 PYL, J. "The Development of Daycare in Ontario." M.S.W., Carleton University, 1977.

1781 QUEBEC. Civil Code Revision Office. *Report on the Legal Position of the Married Women*. Quebec: Official Publisher, 1964.

1782 RAMSAY, Dean. "Development of Child Welfare Legislation in Ontario." M.S.W., University of Toronto, 1949.

1783 SCHLESINGER, B., and GODFREY, E.R. *Child Welfare Services: Winding Paths to Maturity*. Toronto: Canadian Conference on Children, 1965.

1784 SMYSER, Martha Marbury. "Protective Services for Children; Changing Patterns in Children's Protective Services in the U.S. and Canada 1874-1954." M.S.W., University of British Columbia, 1954.

1785 SOCIETY FOR THE PROTECTION OF WOMEN AND CHILDREN. *A History of Seventy-Five Years Operations in the Service of the Community*. Montreal: The Society, 1956.

1786 SPETTIGUE, C. *An Historical Review of Ontario Legislation on Child Welfare*. Toronto: Department of Public Welfare, 1957.

1787 SPLANE, R.B. "Evolution and Application in Canada of Rights relating to Motherhood and Childhood." *Labour Gazette*. 58:11 (November 1958), pp. 1236-40.

1788 SUTHERLAND, Neil. *Children in English-Canadian Society: Framing the Twentieth-Century Consensus*. Toronto: University of Toronto Press, 1976.

1789 TORONTO POLICE FORCE. *Treatment of Neglected Children: Report*. Toronto: Arcade Printing, 1907.

1790 WHITTON, Charlotte. "The Canadian Council on Child Welfare, 1920." *Canadian Welfare.* 32:1 (May 1956), pp. 3-7.
1791 _____. "Child Welfare Legislation in Canada 1920-1925." *Social Welfare.* 7 (January 1926), pp. 79-86.
1792 _____. "A Children's Aid or Community Aid Society." *Canadian Welfare.* 17:6 (November 1941), pp. 10-13.

9.1.2   Reviews of Policy

1793 ALBERTA. Commission Relating to the Child Welfare Branch of the Department of Public Welfare. *Welfare in Alberta: The Report of a Study Undertaken by the Imperial Order, Daughters of the Empire.* Alberta Provincial Chapter. Edmonton: The Order, 1947.
1794 CANADA. Department of Health. *Handbook of Child Welfare Work in Canada.* Ottawa: King's Printer, 1925.
1795 CANADA. Department of Labour. Women's Bureau. *Day Care Services for Children of Working Mothers.* Ottawa: Women's Bureau Bulletin, 11 January 1964.
1796 CANADIAN CONFERENCE OF CATHOLIC BISHOPS. Administrative Board. *The Family and the Family Law Report: A Brief Presented to the Honorable S.R. Basford, Minister of Justice and Attorney General of Canada.* Ottawa: The Conference, 1977.
1797 COMMUNITY CHEST AND COUNCIL OF GREATER VANCOUVER. *Child Welfare Legislation in British Columbia. A Summary of Federal, Provincial and Vancouver City Legislation.* Vancouver, 1947.
1798 COSTIN, Lela B. *Child Welfare: Policies and Practice.* Toronto: McGraw-Hill, 1972.
1799 "Day Nurseries for Children of War Workers." *Public Affairs.* 6:1 (Autumn 1942), pp. 29-30.
1800 EDWARDS, H.M. *Legal Status of Canadian Women as Shown by Extracts from Dominion and Provincial Laws relating to Marriage, Property, Dower, Descent of Land, Franchise, Crime and Other Subjects.* Calgary: National Council of Women of Canada, 1908.
1801 _____. ed. *Legal Status of Women in Alberta.* 2nd ed. n.p. 1921.
1802 FOX, Nora M. "New Policies in Child Welfare." *Canadian Welfare.* 32:2 (June 1956), pp. 60-64.
1803 GIBSON, J.M. "The Children's Act." *Methodist Magazine.* 39 (1894), pp. 39-48.
1804 HEPWORTH, H. Philip. *Personal Social Services in Canada: A Review.* 9 Vols. Ottawa: Canadian Council on Social Development, 1975.
1805 McMURCHY, Helen. "Canadian Day Nurseries: Well — Baby Centre." *Canadian Home Journal.* 39:6 (October 1942), pp. 42-43.
1806 TOWARD, L.M. *Development of Matrimonial Property Law in England and Nova Scotia, An Historic Perspective.* Halifax: Nova Scotia Law Reform Advisory Commission, 1975.
1807 WHITTON, C.E. *Canada and the World's Child Welfare Work.* Ottawa: Social Service Council of Canada and Canadian Council on Child Welfare, 1927.
1808 WINNIPEG FREE PRESS. *Welfare in Alberta.* Pamphlet #17. Winnipeg, 1947.

9.2   Government Policy and Documentation

9.2.1   Federal

1809 CANADA. Advisory Committee on Reconstruction. Final Report of the Sub-Committee. *Post War Problems of Women*. Ottawa: King's Printer, 1944.

1810 CANADA. Advisory Council on the Status of Women. *One Parent Family: Principles and Recommendations*. Ottawa: The Council, January 1977.

1811 ————. *"What's Been Done?"* Assessment of the Federal Government's Implementation of the Recommendations of the Royal Commission on the Status of Women: *Report*. Ottawa: The Council, March 1974.

1812 CANADA. Commission de reforme du droit. *Rapport: Le droit de la famille*. Ottawa: Information Canada, 1976.

1813 CANADA. Commission de reforme du droit. Section de recherches sur le droit de la famille. *Etude de droit de la famille: bulletin d'information*. Ottawa: La commission, 1972.

1814 CANADA. Department of Labour. *Legal Status of Women in Canada*. Ottawa: The Department, 1924.

1815 CANADA. Department of Labour. Women's Bureau. *Consultation on the Employment of Women with Family Responsibilities*. Ottawa: The Department, 1965.

1816 ————. *Working Mothers and Their Child Care Arrangements*. Ottawa: Queen's Printer, 1970.

1817 CANADA. Department of National Health and Welfare. *Canadian Day Care Survey*. Ottawa: The Department, 1972.

1818 ————. *Day Care; A Resource for the Contemporary Family*. Papers and Proceedings of a seminar held in Ottawa, 1969. Ottawa: Information Canada, 1974.

1819 ————. *Status of Day Care in Canada*. Ottawa: The Department, 1973.

1820 CANADA. Department of National Health and Welfare. Policy Research Planning and Evaluation Branch. *Deserted Wives' and Children's Maintenance Legislation in Canada*. Ottawa: The Department, 1973.

1821 CANADA. Department of National Health and Welfare. Research Division. *Changes and Developments in Child Welfare Services in Canada*. General Series Memo #7, 1949-53. Ottawa: The Department, 1954.

1822 ————. *Day Care Legislation in Canada*. Ottawa: The Department, 1972.

1823 CANADA. Department of National Health and Welfare. Research and Statistics Division. *Changes in Legislation in General Assistance, Mothers' Allowances and Living Accommodation for the Elderly in Canada*. General Series Memo #19, 1962-63. Ottawa: The Department, 1964.

1824 ————. *Changes in Legislation in General Assistance, Mothers' Allowances and Living Accommodation for the Elderly in Canada*. General Series Memo #21, 1964-65. Ottawa: The Department, 1966.

1825 ————. *Changes in Legislation in General Assistance, Mothers' Allowances and Living Accommodation for the Elderly in Canada*. General Series Memo #22, 1966. Ottawa: The Department, 1967.

1826 ————. *Mothers' Allowances Legislation in Canada*. Ottawa: The Department, 1960.

1827 CANADA. Department of National Health and Welfare. Social Allowances and Service Branch. *Policy Guidelines relating to the Provision of Day Care Services for Children under the Canada Assistance Plan.* Ottawa: The Department, 1974.

1828 CANADA. House of Commons. Standing Committee on Health, Welfare and Social Affairs. *Child Abuse and Neglect.* Ottawa: Queen's Printer, 1976.

1829 CANADA. Law Reform Commission. *Maintenance on Divorce.* Canada Law Reform Commission Working Papers #12. Ottawa: Information Canada, 1975.

1830 _____. *Report on Family Law.* Ottawa: Information Canada, 1976.

1831 _____. *Studies on Divorce.* Ottawa: Information Canada, 1975.

1832 CANADA. National Ad Hoc Advisory Committee on Child Battering. *Report.* Department of National Health and Welfare. Ottawa: The Committee, 1973.

1833 CANADA. Royal Commission on the Status of Women in Canada. *Report of the Royal Commission on the Status of Women in Canada.* Ottawa: Information Canada, 1970.

1834 CANADA. Special Joint Committee of the Senate and House of Commons on Divorce. *Report.* Ottawa: Queen's Printer, 1967.

1835 McARTON, Dorothy. *Canadian Policy and the One-Parent Family.* Ottawa: Advisory Council on the Status of Women, 1975.

1836 MAJOR, H. *Background Notes on Areas of Federal and Provincial Jurisdiction in Relation to Family Law.* A draft paper prepared for the Advisory Council on the Status of Women. Ottawa: Advisory Council on the Status of Women, 1974.

1837 MENZIES, S.J. *The Canada Pension Plan and Women.* Ottawa: Advisory Council on the Status of Women, 1974.

1838 _____. *New Directions for Public Policy: A Position Paper on the One-Parent Family.* Ottawa: Advisory Council on the Status of Women, 1976.

9.2.2   Provincial

1839 ALBERTA. Committee to Investigate Child Welfare and Juvenile Delinquency. *Report.* Edmonton: The Committee, 1943.

1840 ALBERTA. Department of Public Welfare. *Child Welfare Work in the Province of Alberta.* Edmonton: The Department, 1946.

1841 _____. *Public Welfare in Alberta: Child Welfare is Given Much Thoughtful Study.* Edmonton: The Department, 1950.

1842 ALBERTA. Royal Commission on the Child Welfare Branch, Department of Welfare. *Report.* Edmonton: The Department, 1948.

1843 BRITISH COLUMBIA. Commission on Health Insurance. *Report on Mothers' Pensions.* Victoria: King's Printer, 1920.

1844 BRITISH COLUMBIA. Conference on the Family, 1975-76. *Recommendations.* Victoria: Ministry of Human Resources, 1977.

1845 BRITISH COLUMBIA. Department of Human Resources. *Towards a Youth and Family Service System.* Report prepared for the Minister of Human Resources. Victoria: The Ministry, 1973.

1846 BRITISH COLUMBIA. Department of Social Welfare. *Circular Letter to All Municipalities, and Officials of the Department of Social Welfare, Re: Daycare Services.* Serial No. 401. Victoria: The Department, 1966.

1847 BRITISH COLUMBIA. Department of Health, Division of Child Welfare. *Plan of Work and General Policy.* Victoria: The Department, 1920.

1848 BRITISH COLUMBIA. Royal Commission on Family and Children's Law. *Thirteen Reports and Summary of Recommendations.* Vancouver: The Commission, 1975-76.

1st Report:	*Unified Family Court Pilot Project*
2nd Report:	*The Use of Lay Panels in the Unified Family Court*
3rd Report:	*The Role of the Family Advocate*
4th Report:	*The Family, the Courts and the Community*
5th Report:	Part 1. *The Legislative Framework*
	Part 2. *The Status of Children Born Outside Marriage*
	Part 3. *Children's Rights*
	Part 4. *The Special Needs of Special Children*
	Part 5. *The Protection of Children (Child Care)*
	Part 6. *Custody, Access, and Guardianship*
	Part 7. *Adoption*
Supplement:	*The Children's Act, 1976: Draft Model Act.*
6th Report:	*Report on Matrimonial Property*
7th Report:	*Maintenance*
8th Report:	*Preparation for Marriage*
9th Report:	*Artificial Insemination*
10th Report:	*Native Families and the Law*
11th Report:	*Change of Name*
12th Report:	*Medical Consent*
13th Report:	*Community Consultation*

1849 GREENLAND, C. *Child Abuse in Ontario.* Toronto: Ministry of Community and Social Services, 1973.

1850 HENNESSEY, G. A Policy Context for the Welfare of Tomorrow's Children in Quebec. *Report.* Commission of Inquiry on Health and Social Welfare. Quebec: Official Publisher, 1970.

1851 HOGAN, Phyllis Williams. *Mothers in the Labour Force: Their Child Care Arrangements.* Study Commissioned by the Women's Bureau, Department of Labour and Planning Priorities Committee of Cabinet Secretariat. Winnipeg: Women's Bureau, 1974.

1852 JAMES, J.M. *Family Benefits for Mothers in Metropolitan Toronto.* Toronto: Ministry of Community and Social Services, 1973.

1853 MacFARLANE, Andrew. *The Neverland of the Neglected Child.* Toronto: Department of Public Welfare, 1958.

1854 McGUIGAN, Lorne. *Report on a Study of Social Services to Children.* Fredericton: Department of Social Services, 1975.

1855 MANITOBA. Department of the Attorney General. *Family Law in Manitoba.* Winnipeg: Department of the Attorney General, Women's Bureau, 1977.

1856 MANITOBA. Department of Health and Social Development. *A Review of Child Welfare Policies, Programs and Services in Manitoba; A Report of the Ministers of Health and Social Development.* Winnipeg: Department of Health and Welfare, 1975.

1857 MANITOBA. Law Reform Commission. *Reports on Family Law.* Winnipeg: The Commission, 1976.

1858 _____. *Working Paper on Family Law.* Winnipeg: The Commission, 1975.

1859 MANITOBA. Royal Commission of Inquiry into the Administration of the Child Welfare Division of the Department of Health and Public Welfare. *Report, Findings and Recommendations.* Winnipeg: Department of Health and Public Welfare, 1929.

1860 MANITOBA. Women's Bureau. *Women's Place in Manitoba: Their Legal Rights.* Commissioned by the Women's Bureau, Department of Labour and the Planning Committee of the Cabinet Secretariat. Winnipeg: Women's Bureau, 1975.

1861 NEW BRUNSWICK. Advisory Committee on Family and Child Services. *Report.* Fredericton: The Committee, 1973.

1862 NEW BRUNSWICK. Department of Health and Social Services. *Report on the Administration of Old Age Assistance, Blind Allowances, Mothers' Allowances.* Frederiction: The Department, 1955.

1863 NEW BRUNSWICK. Interdepartmental Committee on the Role of Women in the New Brunswick Economy and Society. *Report.* Fredericton: The Committee, 1975.

1864 NEW BRUNSWICK. Royal Commission Appointed to Consider the Payment of Mothers' Allowances. *Report.* Fredericton: The Commission, 1930.

1865 NEW BRUNSWICK. Royal Commission on Mothers' Allowance and Minimum Wage. *Report.* Fredericton: The Commission, 1924.

1866 NOVA SCOTIA. Royal Commission on Mothers' Allowances. *Report.* In Journals of the House of Assembly. Halifax: King's Printer, 1921.

1867 NOVA SCOTIA. Task Force on Child Abuse. *Final Report.* Halifax: The Task Force, 1974.

1868 ONTARIO. Advisory Council on Daycare. *Report.* Toronto: Minister of Community and Social Services, 1975-76.

1869 ONTARIO. Committee to Study Standards for Children's Institutions. *Children's Institutions' Needs: Resources and Standards for Service.* A Report to the Minister of Public Welfare. Toronto, 1961.

1870 ONTARIO. Department of Public Welfare. *Suggestions for the Organization of a Children's Aid Society.* Toronto: King's Printer, 1893.

1871 ONTARIO. Law Reform Commission. *Report on the Status of Adopted Children.* Toronto: Department of the Attorney General, 1969.

1872 _____. *Study of Family Law Project.* Working Papers. Toronto: Department of Justice, 1968.

1873 ONTARIO. Ministry of the Attorney General. *Family Law Reform.* Toronto: The Ministry, 1976.

1874 ONTARIO. Task Force on Community and Social Services. *Report on Ministry Goals and Objectives.* Toronto: The Task Force, 1973.

1875 ONTARIO. Department of Labour. Women's Bureau. *Law and the Woman in Ontario.* Toronto: The Women's Bureau, 1972.

1876 PRINCE EDWARD ISLAND. Provincial Advisory Committee on the Status of Women in the Province of Prince Edward Island. *Report.* Charlottetown: The Committee, 1973.

1877 QUEBEC. Civil Code Revision Office. Committee on the Law of Persons and the Family. *Preliminary Report Granting Recognition to Certain Rights of Parents and Natural Children.* Montreal: The Office, 1969.

1878 _____. *Report on a Draft Law of Adoption Presented to the Civil Code Reform Commission on the Law of Persons and the Family.* Montreal: The Office, 1966.

1879 _____. *Report on the Family.* Part 1, 2. Montreal: The Office, 1974, 1975.

1880 QUEBEC. Comité pour la protection de la jeunesse. *Rapport d'activité.* Quebec: Editeur officiel, 1977.

1881 QUEBEC. Comité d'étude sur l'assistance publique. *Rapport.* Quebec: Editeur officiel du Québec, 1963.

1882 QUEBEC. Commission d'assurance-maladie du Québec sur le problème des garderies et de la protection de l'enfance. *Rapport de la commission d'assurance-maladie du Québec.* Quebec: La commission, 1944.

1883 QUEBEC. Ministère des affaires sociales. *Avant-projet de loi sur la protection de la jeunesse.* Quebec: Le ministère, 1975.

1884 _____. Mémoires de programmes; *Les services à l'enfance.* Quebec: Le ministère, 1973.

1985 CAMERON, Barbara. *The Day Care Book.* Toronto: Canadian Womens' Educational Press, 1972.

ministère, 1970.

1886 _____. *Compilation de la jurisprudence canadienne sur l'enfance 1959-1967.* Quebec: Le ministère, 1977.

1887 QUEBEC. Ministry of Family and Social Welfare. *Guidelines For a New Quebec Family Allowance Policy.* Quebec: The Ministry, 1969.

1888 QUEBEC. Social Allowances Commission. *Report on the Enforcement of the Social Acts.* Quebec: The Commission, 1938.

1889 RUTMAN, L. *Daycare Services in Manitoba.* Winnipeg: Queen's Printer, 1971.

1890 SASKATCHEWAN. *Women's and Children's Rights in Saskatchewan.* Regina: Bureau of Publications, 1954.

1891 SASKATCHEWAN. Law Reform Commission. *Children's Maintenance.* A Background Paper. Saskatoon: The Commission, 1976.

1892 SASKATCHEWAN. *Some Saskatchewan Legislation affecting Women and Children.* Regina: Government Printer, 1920.

1893 SASKATCHEWAN. Task Force Report on the Status of Women. *Saskatchewan Women 1973.* Regina: The Task Force, 1973.

1894 STAPLEFORD, E.M. *History of the Day Nurseries Branch.* Toronto: Ministry of Community and Social Services, 1976.

1895 STRONG, Margaret, comp. *Mothers' Allowance: An Investigation.* Toronto: King's Printer, 1920.

9.3 Special Issues

9.3.1 Children's Services

1896 BOURGEOIS, Mgr. Charles Edward. *The Protection of Children in the Province of Quebec.* Trois-Rivières, 1948.

1897 CANADIAN WELFARE COUNCIL. Family and Child Welfare Division. Committee on Child Protection. *Child Protection in Canada.* Ottawa: The Council, 1954.

1898 DICKENS, B.M. *Legal Issues in Child Abuse.* Toronto: University of Toronto, 1976.

1899 DOYON, Lise. "Efficacité des plans de traitement établis par la clinique d'aide à l'enfance en rapport avec la disponibilité des ressources communautaires." Quebec: Laval University, 1966.

1900 FLINT, Margaret. *The Security of Infants.* Toronto: University of Toronto Press, 1959.

1901 FRASER, Murray F., ANDERSON, J.P., BURNS, Kevin. *Child Abuse in Nova Scotia, a Research Project about Battered and Maternally Deprived Children.* Halifax, 1973.

1902 GREENLAND, C. "Reporting Child Abuse in Ontario." *Reports of Family Law.* 10:1 (July 1973), p. 50.

1903 HEPWORTH, H. Philip. *Residential Services for Children in Care.* Ottawa: Canadian Council on Social Development, 1975.

1904 _____. *Services for Abused and Battered Children.* Ottawa: Canadian Council on Social Development, 1975.

1905 KINNEY, B.D. "Child Neglect." *Manitoba Law Journal.* 3:1 (1968), pp. 31-47.

1906 LARIN, Jacques, ed. *La réforme de système de protection.* Montréal: Association des Centres de services sociaux du Québec, 1977.

1907 ———. *Le système québécois de protection de l'enfance.* Montréal: Association des Centres de services sociaux du Québec, 1976.

1908 LETARTE, Pierrette D. "L'histoire de l'assistance aux enfants abandonnés dans le Québec." M.A., Laval University, 1958.

1909 MONTREAL COUNCIL OF SOCIAL AGENCIES. "Brief to the Ministry of Family and Social Welfare, Province of Quebec on Services to Protect Abused and Neglected Children." Montreal: The Council, 1965.

1910 PROVERBS, Trevor B., and KOENIG, Daniel J. *Social Services for Children: The Public Speaks: Part 2 of the Final Report.* Victoria: Elector Concern and Satisfaction Surveys, University of Victoria, 1977.

1911 RAE-GRANT, Quentin L., and MOFFAT, Patricia J. *Children in Canada in Residential Care.* Toronto: Canadian Mental Health Association, 1971.

1912 VAN STOLK, Mary. *The Battered Child in Canada.* Toronto: McClelland and Stewart, 1972.

9.3.2   Adoption

1913 BLATZ, M.W. "Aspects of Adoption Laws in Canada." M.A., University of Toronto, 1931.

1914 CANADIAN COUNCIL ON CHILD WELFARE. *Comparative Study of the Canadian Adoption Laws as in Force, November 1, 1924.* Ottawa: The Council, 1924.

1915 CANADIAN COUNCIL ON SOCIAL DEVELOPMENT. *Foster Care — A New Look.* Workshop Papers presented at the Canadian Conference on Social Welfare, Laval University. Ottawa: The Council, 1972.

1916 DANIELS, C.P. "Adoption — Consent of Natural Parent-Revocation." *Canadian Bar Review.* 35:7 (1957), pp. 836-38.

1917 DAVIES, C. "Custody and Adoption: Some Interrelated Problems." *University of Toronto Law Journal.* 23:1 (1973), pp. 88-110.

1918 KENNEDY, Gilbert D. "Adoption in the Conflict of Laws." *Canadian Bar Review.* 34:5 (1956), pp. 507-63.

1919 ———. "British Columbia's New Adoption Legislation." *University of Toronto Law Journal.* 12:2 (1958), pp. 296-99.

1920 ———. "The Legal Effects of Adoption." *Canadian Bar Review.* 33:7 (1955), pp. 751-874.

1921 "La loi de la protection de la jeunesse et la loi de l'adoption." *L'Action nationale.* 55:9-10 (May/June 1966), pp. 1171-76.

1922 READ, F. "Absolute Adoption." *Canadian Bar Review.* 6:2 (1928), pp. 166-70.

1923 SMITH, G., and DICK, A. "Recent Changes in Ontario Adoption Legislation." *Osgoode Hall Law Journal.* 2:1 (1960), pp. 130-39.

1924 TUCK, G.S., and BURGESS, R.B. "A Separation of Church and State in Ontario: Adoption Procedure." *Osgoode Hall Law Journal.* 2:2 (1961), pp. 216-30.

9.3.3   Children's Rights

1925 ARMOUR, A.D. "The Legitimation and Adoption Act." *Canadian Bar Review.* 5:3 (1927), pp. 186-89.

1926 CASTONGUAY, Claude *et al. The Legal Rights of Children: Every Child has the Right to be Happy.* Quebec: Canadian Mental Health Association, 1974.

1927 "The Evolution and Application in Canada of Rights relating to Motherhood and Childhood." *Labour Gazette.* 58:11 (November 1958), pp. 1236-41.

1928 MORSE, C., ed. "Legitimation Act — Esheat — Bona Vacantia." *Canadian Bar Review.* 6:10 (1928), pp. 795-96.

1929 READ, F. "The Legal Position of the Child of Unmarried Parents." *Canadian Bar Review.* 9:9 (1931), pp. 609-18 and 9:10 (1931), pp. 729-36.

1930 UNIFORM LAW CONFERENCE OF CANADA. "Children Born outside Marriage." In *Proceedings of the 58th Annual Meetings of the Uniform Law Conference of Canada,* pp. 90-126. Yellowknife, 19-27 August, 1976. Toronto: The Conference, 1976.

1931 UNIVERSITY OF ALBERTA. Institute of Law Research and Reform. *Illegitimacy.* Paper #10. Edmonton: University of Alberta, 1974.

1932 ―――. *Status of Children.* Report #20. Edmonton: University of Alberta, 1976.

9.3.4 Women's Rights

1933 BAUDOUIN, Jean-Louis. "Examen critique de la réforme sur la capacité de la femme mariée Québécoise." *Canadian Bar Review.* 43:3 (1965), pp. 393-413.

1934 BIRD, F.B.K. *The Rights of Women.* Toronto: Canadian Association for Adult Education, 1950.

1935 BOURNE, P. *Women in Canadian Society.* Toronto: Ontario Institute for Secondary Education, 1976.

1936 CASGRAIN, Thérèse. *Comparative Study of Women's Rights in Canada.* Ottawa: Women's Rights Organization, 1968.

1937 COOK, G.A., ed. *Opportunity for Choice: A Goal for Women in Canada.* Ottawa: Statistics Canada in Association with the C.D. Howe Research Institute, 1976.

1938 CROSSROADS '75. *Round Table Report and Papers.* Quebec: The Council on the Status of Women of Quebec, 1975.

1939 FEDERATION DES FEMMES DU QUEBEC. *Guide de discussion et résumé du rapport de la commission royale d'enquête sur la situation de la femme au Canada.* Quebec: La fédération, 1971.

1940 FREDERICTON WOMEN'S ACTION COALITION. *Women and the Law in New Brunswick.* Fredericton: The Coalition, 1973.

1941 GINSBURG, M., and GUIJANO, G. *Canadian Women and the Law.* Toronto: Osgoode Hall Law School, 1974.

1942 KERR, W. "The Canadian Bill of Rights and Sex Based Differentials in the Canadian Federal Law." *Osgoode Hall Law Journal.* 12:2 (October 1974), pp. 357-87.

1943 LIBERAL PARTY (CANADA) TASK FORCE ON THE STATUS OF WOMEN. *Final Report.* Ottawa: The Task Force, 1972.

1944 McEWAN, J. *Women and the Law.* Vancouver: Vancouver Peoples' Law School, 1973.

1945 PESTIEAU, C. "Women in Quebec." In *Women in the Canadian Mosaic,* edited by Gwen Matheson, pp. 57-70. Toronto: Peter Martin Associates, 1976.

1946 REYNOLDS, B.P. *Status of Women in Canada.* Ottawa: Library of Parliament Research Branch, 1974.

1947 WEISSTUB, D.N., ed. *Law and Policy.* Toronto: Osgoode Hall Law School, 1976.

1948 "Women and the Law. La femme et le droit." *McGill Law Journal.* 21:4 (1975), pp. 476-707.
1949 ZUKER, M.A., and CALLWOOD, J. *Canadian Women and the Law.* Toronto: Copp Clark, 1971.

9.3.5 Family Law Reform

1950 BAXTER, I. "Family Law Reform in Ontario." *Canadian Bar Review.* 55:1 (1977), pp. 187-96.
1951 _____. "Family Law Reform in Ontario." *University of Toronto Law Journal.* 25:3 (Summer 1975), pp. 236-80.
1952 BUSHNELL, S. Ian. "Family Law and the Constitution." *Canadian Journal of Family Law.* 1:2 (April 1978), pp. 203-31.
1953 CANADA. Law Reform Commission. *Studies in Family Property Law.* Ottawa: Information Canada, 1975.
1954 _____. *Working Paper 8: Family Property.* Ottawa: Information Canada, 1975.
1955 GROFFIER, Ethel. "La réforme du droit familial et la condition de la femme au Canada." *McGill Law Journal.* 2:4 (Winter 1975), pp. 495-517.
1956 KOULACK, E., and McEVOY, L. "Family Law Reform." *Canadian Dimension.* 12:4-5, (September 1977), pp. 22-23.
1957 MacDOUGALL, D. *Developments in Family Law.* Vancouver: Centre for Continuing Education, University of British Columbia, 1974.
1958 NEWFOUNDLAND. Family Law Study. *Family Law in Newfoundland.* Prepared at Dalhousie Law School. St. John's, 1973.
1959 WUESTER, Terrance J., and PAYNE, Julien D. *Family Property Law: Proposals for Reform.* Ottawa: Law Reform Commission of Canada, 1975.

9.3.6 Single Parents, Divorce, Separation, Marriage

1960 BATES, Frank. "Behind the Law of Divorce: A Modern Perspective." *Manitoba Law Journal.* 17:1 (1976), pp. 39-56.
1961 BAXTER, I.F.G. "The Law of Domestic Relations." *Canadian Bar Review.* 36:3 (1958), pp. 299-332.
1962 CANADIAN COUNCIL ON SOCIAL DEVELOPMENT. *The One-Parent Family in Canada; Report of an Inquiry on One-Parent Families in Canada.* Ottawa: The Council, 1971.
1963 CANADA. Law Reform Commission. *Divorce.* Ottawa: Information Canada, 1975.
1964 CANADIAN WELFARE COUNCIL. Family and Child Welfare Division. *Social Policy Implications of the Unmarried Parent.* Ottawa: The Council, 1966.
1965 CHERNIACK, L., and FEIN, C. "Common Law Marriages in Manitoba." *Manitoba Law Journal.* 6:1 (1974), pp. 85-116.
1966 CULLITY, M.C. "Property Rights during the Subsistence of Marriage." In *Studies in Canadian Family Law.* edited by D. Mendes da Costa, pp. 179-283. Toronto: Butterworths, 1972.
1967 DA COSTA, D. Mendes. "Some Comments on the Conflict of Laws Provisions of the Divorce Act, 1968." *Canadian Bar Review.* 46:2 (1968), pp. 252-92.
1968 DAVIDSON, J.F. "Marriage and Divorce." *Canadian Bar Review.* 5:9 (1927), pp. 654-63.

1969 GUYATT, D. *The One-Parent Family in Canada.* Ottawa: Vanier Institute of the Family, 1971.

1970 MORSE, C. "Husband and Wife and Custody of Infants." *Canadian Bar Review.* 1:7 (1923), pp. 551-54.

1971 ————, ed. "The Interest of the Child — Can a Good Father be Deprived of his Daughter?" *Canadian Bar Review.* 5:3 (1927), pp. 216-18.

1972 NATIONAL COUNCIL OF WELFARE. *One in a World of Two's: A Report of the National Council of Welfare on One-Parent Families in Canada.* Ottawa: The Council, 1976.

1973 NEAVE, D.C., and MATHESON, K.D. "Questions about Policies and Practise in Parent-Child Separation." *Canadian Welfare.* 46:6 (November/December 1970), pp. 15-17, 22.

1974 PAYNE, Julien. "Divorce Reform in Canada." *Buffalo Law Review.* 18:1 (1968-69), pp. 119-52.

1975 RIOUX, M.H. *Study Paper on Divorce.* Ottawa: Advisory Council on the Status of Women, 1976.

1976 SCHLESINGER, B. "The Unmarried Mother Who Keeps Her Child." *Social Worker.* 44:4 (Winter 1976), pp. 108-13.

1977 SCHROEDER, F.A. "Matrimonial Property Law Reform: Evaluating the Alternatives." *University of British Columbia Law Review.* 11:1 (1977), pp. 24-39.

1978 SCOTT, W.S. "Powers of Provincial Legislatures as to Marriage." *Canadian Bar Review.* 2:6 (1924), pp. 381-90.

1979 SOPINKA, J. "The Divorce Act, 1968: Collusion Confirmed." *Canadian Bar Review.* 47:1 (1969), pp. 31-39.

1980 TAYLOR, G.E. "Divorce in Canada." *Canadian Bar Review.* 23:6 (1945), pp. 495-98.

1981 WHITTON, C.E. "Unmarried Parenthood and the Social Order." *Social Welfare.* Part 1. 2:7 (April 1920), pp. 184-87; Part 2. 2:8 (May 1920), pp. 222-23.

9.3.7 Day Care

1982 BAAR, E. "Provincial Regulation of Day Care: Child Protection or Child Growth? *Canadian Welfare.* 49:2 (March/April 1973), pp. 12-17.

1983 BURSHTYN, Roslyn. "Day Care: A Resource for the Contemporary Family." *Papers and Proceedings of a Seminar.* Ottawa: Vanier Institute of the Family, 1970.

1984 CALGARY. Social Service Department. *Day Care Policy and Guidelines.* Calgary: Social Service Department, 1975.

1985 CAMERON, B. *The Day Care Book.* Toronto: Canadian Womens' Educational Press, 1972.

1986 CANADIAN CONFERENCE ON DAY CARE. *Proceedings.* Ottawa: Canadian Council on Social Development, 1972.

1987 CANADIAN COUNCIL ON SOCIAL DEVELOPMENT. Ad Hoc Policy Committee on Day Care Standards. *Day Care: Growing, Learning, Caring: National Guidelines for the Development of Day Care Services for Children.* Ottawa: The Council, 1975.

1988 CANADIAN LABOUR CONGRESS. "Canadian Labour Congress Urges Local Day Care Centres." *Canadian Labour.* 13:10 (October 1968), p. 40.

1989 CANADIAN WELFARE COUNCIL. Research Branch. *The Daycare of Children in Canada.* Ottawa: The Council, 1968.

1990 CHISHOLM, B.A. "Foster Day Care." *Canada's Mental Health.* 13:2 (1965), pp. 14-17.

1991 CLIFFORD, Howard. *Let's Talk Daycare*. Edmonton: Canadian Mental Health Association, 1972.

1992 _____. "Family Day Care: A Fast Growing Resource." *Canadian Welfare*. 50:5 (September/October 1974), pp. 7-10.

1993 _____. "Judging Staff Competence in Day Care." *Canadian Welfare*. 51:3 (May/June 1975), pp. 10-11.

1994 COHEN, Marcy *et al. Cuz There Ain't No Daycare (Or Almost None She Said) A Book About Daycare in British Columbia*. Vancouver: Press Gang Publishers, 1973.

1995 CONSEIL CANADIEN DE DEVELOPPEMENT SOCIAL. *Garde de jour: Croissance, apprentissage, protection*. Ottawa: Le conseil, 1973.

1996 "Des logements et des crèches en commun aideraient les mères 'travailleuses.'" *Trades and Labour Congress Journal*. 30:45 (August 1951), p. 45.

1997 FEIN, Greta G., and CLARKE-STEWART, Alison. *Day Care in Context*. Toronto: John Wiley, 1973.

1998 FREEMAN, J. Seymour Trieger. *The Duke of York Day Care Project*. Toronto: Toronto Board of Education, 1968.

1999 HARRISON, Joan M. "Daycare in Ontario." *Faculty of Law Review, University of Toronto*. 34:1 (1976), pp. 74-83.

2000 HEPWORTH, Philip. *Canadian Daycare Standards 1976: Better Daycare, Slowly but Surely*. Ottawa: Canadian Council on Social Development, 1976.

2001 _____. *Day Care Services for Children*. Vol. 2: *Personal Social Services*. Ottawa: Canadian Council on Social Development, 1975.

2002 KRASHINSKY, Michael. *Day Care and Public Policy in Ontario*. Toronto: University of Toronto Press, 1977.

2003 McLEOD, E.M. *Study of Child Care Services at Canadian Universities*. Ottawa: Association of Universities and Colleges of Canada, 1975.

2004 ONTARIO INSTITUTE FOR STUDIES IN EDUCATION. *Development of a Prototype Infant Preschool and Child Daycare Centre in Metropolitan Toronto. Year I, Progress Report; Program Development*. Toronto: The Institute, 1972.

2005 SOCIAL PLANNING COUNCIL OF METRO TORONTO. *Brief on Day Care Services*. Toronto: The Council, 1967.

2006 _____. *Working Papers for Day Care Study*. Toronto: The Council, 1968.

9.4 Administration

9.4.1 State

2007 "Administration of Family Allowances in Canada." *Labour Gazette*. 46:1 (January 1946), pp. 17-19.

2008 BINGHAM, Thomas Donald. "Desertion: Legislation and Administration; A Comparative Review of Desertion Legislation in B.C., Saskatchewan and Ontario; Administration of Desertion Legislation by Family Courts, Implications for Social Work Practice in British Columbia." M.S.W., University of British Columbia, 1956.

2009 CANADIAN CIVIL LIBERTIES EDUCATION TRUST. *Welfare Practises and Civil Liberties: A Canadian Survey*. Toronto: The Trust, 1975.

2010 CHARDON DU RANQUET, Mathilde. "Le placement d'enfant dans le diocèse de Québec; coordination existant entre le service de la protection de la sauvegarde et les agences familiales." M.A., Laval University, 1959.

2011 ERRINGTON, Barbara Gene, FREEMAN, Ruth, GREENWELL, Gail. "Public and Private Responsibilities in Child Welfare; A Review of the Distribution of Functions in Child Welfare between Public and Private Agencies in Four Canadian Provinces." M.S.W., University of British Columbia, 1964.

2012 FLINT, Betty Margaret. *The Child and the Institution: A Study of Deprivation and Recovery.* Toronto: University of Toronto Press, 1966.

2013 HEPWORTH, Philip. *Community Multi-Service Centres: Summary of Recent Developments in the Delivery of Personal Health and Social Services and Report of Meeting of the Committee of Multi-Service Centres.* Ottawa: Canadian Council on Social Development, 1976.

2014 KELSO, J.J. "Some First Principles in Social Welfare Work." 21st Annual Report of the Superintendent of Neglected and Dependent Children. *Ontario Sessional Papers.* Toronto: King's Printer, 1910.

2015 LATIMER, E.A. "Methods of Child Care as Reflected in the Infants Home of Toronto 1875-1920." M.S.W., University of Toronto, 1953.

2016 SPLANE, Richard B. "The Administration of the Children of Unmarried Parents Act of the Province of Ontario." M.S.W., University of Toronto, 1951.

2017 WILLMS, Abraham Martin. "Setting Up Family Allowances, 1944-1955." M.A., Carleton University, 1962.

9.4.2   Voluntary

2018 DAHL, Norman. "Why the Voluntary Welfare Agency?" *Canadian Labour.* 10:11 (November 1965), pp. 5-8.

2019 HARDY, J.M.R. "Family Endowment." *Canadian Forum.* 6:55 (April 1925), pp. 204-205.

9.4.3   Regulation of Social Work Profession

2020 CANADIAN ASSOCIATION OF SOCIAL WORKERS. "Canadian Association of Social Workers Code of Ethics." *Ontario Association of Professional Social Workers Journal.* 3:3 (August 1975), pp. 18-19.

2021 _____. *The Profession of Social Work: Aims, Qualifications, Opportunities.* Ottawa: The Association, 1959.

2022 CANADIAN ASSOCIATION OF SOCIAL WORKERS. Ontario Branches. *Principles and Standards with Reference to Public Child Welfare Programs in Ontario.* Ottawa: The Association, 1954.

2023 HAMILTON, G. "Registration and Professional Accountability." *Social Worker.* 41:2 (Summer 1973), pp. 73-76.

2024 LANDAUER, M. *Social Work in Ontario.* A Study for the Committee on the Healing Arts. Toronto: Queen's Printer, 1970.

2025 LEIBOVITCH, P. "The Politics of Practice — Quebec 1973." *Social Worker.* 41:2 (Summer 1973), pp. 160-66.

2026 ONTARIO ASSOCIATION OF PROFESSIONAL SOCIAL WORKERS. *Background Material on Registration — Licensing.* Annual Meeting and Conference, 17-18 June 1975. Toronto: The Association, 1975.

9.5   Benefits

9.5.1   Mothers' Allowances

2027 ADAMOWSKI, K. *et al. Women on Welfare.* Ottawa: School of Social Work, Carleton University, 1975.

2028 "Alberta: Social Allowances." *Bulletin of Canadian Welfare Law.* 2:1 (February 1973), pp. 26-30.

2029 COHEN, J.L. *Mothers' Allowance Legislation in Canada.* Toronto: Macmillan, 1927.
2030 "La loi de l'assistance publique et l'enfance malheureuse." *L'Action nationale.* 55:1 (April 1966), pp. 1006-1009.
2031 MOSS, T. "Dependents' Allowances and Alimony Provisions for Divorced and Separated Wives." *Canadian Bar Review.* 22:10 (1944), pp. 903-908.
2032 NEWTON, L. *Employment, Social Assistance and Sole Support Mothers in Ontario.* Toronto: Toronto Board of Education, 1978.
2033 SOCIAL PLANNING COUNCIL OF METROPOLITAN TORONTO. *Social Allowances in Ontario: An Historical Analysis of General Welfare Assistance and Family Benefits, 1961-1976.* Toronto: The Council, 1977.
2034 TURGEON, Gisèle. "Appréciation de la loi de l'assistance aux mères nécessiteuses, à la lumière des statistiques de la sauvegarde de l'enfance de 1948-1953." M.A., Laval University, 1954.

9.5.2 Family Allowances

2035 "Les allocations familiales et l'agriculture." *Actualité économique.* 9:3, 4 (June/July 1933) pp. 181-82.
2036 ANGERS, François-Albert. "Les allocations familiales fédérales de 1944." *Actualité économique.* 21:3 (1945-46), pp. 228-62.
2037 _____. "Secours direct familial." *L'Action nationale.* 25:5 (May 1945), pp. 330-53.
2038 BELZILE, T. "Les allocations familiales au Canada." *Revue trimestrielle-canadienne.* 16 (1930), pp. 237-68; 445-56.
2039 BLOUIN, Claude T. "L'allocation familiale, mesure de protection de la famille." M.A., Laval University, 1964.
2040 BOUVIER, Emile. "Les allocations familiales à Ottawa." *Relations.* 45 (September 1944), pp. 240-42.
2041 _____. "Un projet d'allocations familiales." *Relations.* 44 (August 1944), pp. 202-205.
2042 BRUEL, F.R. "The Genesis of Family Allowances in Canada." *Social Service Review.* 27:3 (September 1953), pp. 269-80.
2043 _____. "Family Allowances in Canada." Ph.D., McGill University, 1951.
2044 BUNN, R.F. "The Family Allowance System in Canada." M.A., Duke University, 1952.
2045 CASSIDY, H.M. "Children's Allowances in Canada." *Public Welfare.* 3:8 (August 1945), pp. 171-77.
2046 _____. "Family Allowances in Canada." *National Council of Social Workers Proceedings*, pp. 169-81. New York: Columbia University Press, 1945.
2047 CLAXTON, Brooke. *Family Allowances in Canada.* Washington: National Catholic Welfare Council, 1946.
2048 CONSEIL DE DEVELOPPEMENT SOCIAL DU MONTREAL METROPOLITAIN. *Le régime des allocations familiales vu par la famille.* Montreal: Le Conseil, 1970.
2049 COTE, A. "Le régime des allocations familiales au Canada, sa raison d'être, son rôle économique et social, son effet de redistribution et ses faiblesses." M.A., University of Montreal, 1961.
2050 CURRY, R.B. "Family Allowances in Canada." *Public Welfare.* 6:1 (1948), pp. 50-55.

2051 DAVIDSON, G.F. *Family Allowances — an Instalment on Social Security.* Ottawa: Canadian Welfare Council, 1944.

2052 DEUTSCH, Antal. *Income Redistribution through Canadian Federal Family Allowances and Old Age Benefits.* Toronto: Canadian Tax Foundation, 1968.

2053 DEXTER, Grant. *Family Allowances: An Analysis.* Winnipeg: Free Press, 1944.

2054 FLEMING, M. "Family Allowances in Canada." *Canadian Welfare.* 22:6 (December 1946), pp. 11-12.

2055 GOULD, Margaret. *Family Allowances in Canada, Facts Versus Fiction.* Toronto: Ryerson Press, 1945.

2056 JEAN, Luce. "Les allocations familiales à Québec." *Service social.* 2:2 (1952), pp. 75-80.

2057 KELLY, Laurence A. *Family Allowances and the Tax System.* Kingston: Industrial Relations Centre, Queen's University, 1971.

2058 KING, W.L. MacKenzie. "Family Allowances." *Labour Review.* 6:18 (August/September 1944), pp. 311-19.

2059 KITCHEN, Brigitte. "The Principles and Aims of Family Allowances; A Policy Discussion." M.S.W., University of British Columbia, 1973.

2060 LaMARSH, Judy. "Family and Youth Allowances in Canada." *Public Welfare.* 23:4 (1965), pp. 223-26.

2061 LEBEL, Léon. "Les allocations familiales au Canada." *Relations.* 122 (February 1951), pp. 47-51.

2062 _____. "Les allocations familiales et les hommes d'affaires." *Actualité économique.* 6:10 (January 1931), pp. 354-60.

2063 _____. *Les allocations familiales; solution du problème des familles nombreuses.* Montreal: L'Ecole sociale populaire, 1927.

2064 _____. "Après deux ans d'allocations familiales." *Relations.* 80 (August 1947), pp. 228-31.

2065 _____. "Notre système d'allocations familiales." *Relations.* 124 (April 1951), pp. 91-93.

2066 _____. "Notre système d'allocations familiales." *Relations.* 126 (June 1951), pp. 158-62.

2067 MADISON, Bernice. "Canadian Family Allowances and Their Major Social Implications." *Journal of Marriage and the Family.* 26:2 (May 1964), pp. 134-41.

2068 NAPIER, Joseph. "L'assurance familiale." *Bulletin des relations industrielles.* 8:4 (September 1953), pp. 388-96.

2069 NATIONAL ANTI-POVERTY ORGANIZATION. *Critique of the New Family Allowances.* Ottawa: The Organization, 1974.

2070 "Ontario Family Benefits and General Welfare Assistance." *Bulletin of Canadian Welfare Law.* 2 (1972), pp. 15-22.

2071 ORGANISMES FAMILIAUX ASSOCIES DU QUEBEC. *Mémoire des organismes familiaux associés du Québec présenté à messieurs Denis Lazure et Marc Lalonde, ministres responsables: objet, les allocations aux familles.* Montreal: Les organismes, 1977.

2072 PARKINSON, R.H. "Ten Years of Family Allowances." *Canadian Welfare.* 31:4 (November 1955), pp. 195-200.

2073 ROY, L.E. "Le régime des allocations familiales et scolaires au Québec." *Annales de l'Institut d'études du travail de la sécurité sociale.* 9 (1970), pp. 103-13.

2074 ROY, T. "Influence économique et sociale des allocations familiales." M.A., University of Montreal, 1948.

2075 RYAN, M.T. "Canada's Family Allowance Program." *Revue de l'Université d'Ottawa*. 34:4 (1964), pp. 427-38.

2076 SCHWARTZ, E. "Some Observations on the Canadian Family Allowances Programme." *Social Service Review*. 20:4 (1946), pp. 451-74.

2077 SILCOX, C.E. *The Revenge of the Cradles*. Toronto: Ryerson Press, 1945.

2078 STEPLER, Dorothy. *Family Allowances for Canada*. Toronto: Canadian Institute of International Affairs, 1943.

2079 THOORENS, Léon. "Les allocations familiales." *Relations*. 140 (August 1952), pp. 220-22.

2080 USHER, T.H. "An Appraisal of the Canadian Family Allowance System." *Review of Social Economy*. 9 (September 1951), pp. 124-36.

2081 WHITTON, Charlotte E. *Baby Bonuses: Dollars or Sense*. Toronto: Ryerson Press, 1946.

2082 _____. "Baby Bonus Plan Involves Waste and Duplication." *Saturday Night*. (17 March 1945), p. 6.

2083 _____. "The Family Allowances Controversy in Canada." *Social Service Review*. 18:4 (December 1944), pp. 413-32.

2084 _____. *Welfare Must be Planned and Paid For*. Ottawa: Privately printed, 1944.

2085 WILLARD, J.W. *Some Aspects of Family Allowances and Income Redistribution in Canada*. Cambridge: School of Public Administration, Cambridge University, 1954.

2086 _____. "Family Allowances in Canada, Background and Evolution since 1945." *International Labour Review*. 75 (1957), pp. 207-29.

2087 _____. "Some Aspects of Social Security; An Analysis of the Growth of Social Security Expenditures and the Development of Family Allowances and Old Age Security Programs in Canada." Ph.D., Harvard University, 1954.

9.5.3   Alimony and Dependents' Allowances

2088 CAPARROS, E. "La détermination conventionnelle de la contribution des époux aux besoins de la famille." *Cahiers de droit*. 17:3 (1976), pp. 603-32.

2089 GOURLAY, Margaret. "Deserted Wives Maintenance Act." *Social Worker*. 17:1 (October 1948), pp. 4-11.

2090 KONDO, V.A. "No Fault Maintenance for Spouses." *Canadian Journal of Family Law*. 1:1 (January 1978), pp. 57-87.

2091 LUPIEN, Michel. *La pension alimentaire*. Quebec: M. Lupien, 1977.

2092 McGREGOR, G. "Alimony and Maintenance Payments." *Canadian Tax Journal*. 27 (November/December 1969), pp. 453-60.

2093 RYAN, Edward F. *Enforcement of Maintenance Orders*. Ottawa: Law Reform Commission of Canada, 1976.

2094 SILVERBERG, M.M. "Variations of Maintenance Awards under Section 11 (2), of the Divorce Act." *Family Law Reports*. 25 (1977), pp. 180-209.

2095 UNIFORM LAW CONFERENCE OF CANADA. "Support Obligations: Maintenance Orders." *Proceedings of 58th Annual Meeting of the Uniform Law Conference of Canada*. pp. 245-84. Yellowknife, 19-17 August, 1976. Toronto: The Conference, 1976.

9.5.4   Public Welfare Assistance

2096 ALBERTA. Department of Public Welfare. *Public Welfare for the Province of Alberta*. Edmonton: The Department, 1955.

2097 CASSIDY, H.M. *Canada's Public Welfare Bill, Facing Up to Public Welfare Costs and Services.* Ottawa: Canadian Welfare Council, 1939.
2098 CHEVALIER, Albert. "Social Assistance in the Metropolis of Canada." *Canadian Welfare.* 9:4 (November 1933), pp. 50-55.
2099 DESROCHERS, Monique Frappier. *Problèmes et limites des programmes actuels d'assistance sociale.* Ottawa: Conseil economique du Canada, 1976.
2100 GRIPTON, James. "Blue-Print for Revolution in Public Welfare in Quebec: An Essay Review." *Social Service Review.* 39:3 (1965), pp. 320-32.
2101 HAY, (Mrs.) B. Stewart. "Social Welfare in Winnipeg." *Canadian Welfare.* 9:5 (January 1934), pp. 50-57.
2102 JACQUES, Barbara E. "A Study of Social Assistance in Alberta." M.A., University of Calgary, 1970.
2103 LEIGH, A. "Developments in British Columbia's Public Welfare Program." *Canadian Welfare.* 19:3 (July 1943), pp. 10-12.
2104 _____. "Municipalities and Public Welfare." *Canadian Welfare.* 40 (January/February 1964), pp. 16-22.
2105 McARTON, Sidney P. "Public Welfare in Manitoba." *Social Worker.* 15:4 (April 1974), pp. 18-24.
2106 McINNES, Ronald W. *Welfare Legislation and Benefit Plans in Canada.* Toronto: Law Society of Upper Canada, 1974.
2107 POULIN, Gonzalve. "Evolution historique des services d'assistance de la province de Québec." *Service social.* 4:3 (Autumn 1954), pp. 112-126. problèmes constitutionnels, Quebec: Imprimeur de la Reine, 1955-56.
2108 WIEDEMAN, Frank Victor. "Municipal Policy in Social Assistance: A Comparative Review of Social Assistance Policy in Selected Major Cities of Western Canada, 1959." M.S.W., University of British Columbia, 1959.

9.5.5   Family Income Security Plans

2109 CANADIAN COUNCIL ON SOCIAL DEVELOPMENT. *Comments and Recommendations on the Family Income Security Plan, Proposed in the Federal Government White Paper, "Income Security for Canadians 1970, a Policy Statement."* Ottawa: The Council, 1971.
2110 _____. Conference on Family Policy. *Proceedings.* 24-26 April 1977. Ottawa: The Council, 1977.
2111 _____. *The Family Income Security Plan.* Ottawa: The Council, 1976.
2112 CUTT, J. "Income Support Programmes for Families With Children: Alternatives for Canada." *International Social Service Review.* 23:1 (1970), pp. 100-112.
2113 _____. "Selectivity or Universality? Income Support Alternatives for Families with Children." In *Poverty in Canada,* edited by J. Harp and J.R. Hofley. pp. 337-47. Scarborough: Prentice Hall, 1971.
2114 GARIGUE, Philippe. "The Real Problems of the Family." *Transition.* 2:2 (July 1971), pp. 1-3.
2115 HENRIPIN, J. "Besoins économiques des familles et prestations familiales." *Relations.* 305 (May 1966), pp. 138-40.
2116 MORGAN, John S. "The White Paper on Income Security: Another Family Assistance Plan?" *Social Worker.* 39:1 (1971), pp. 21-25.
2117 SOCIAL PLANNING COUNCIL OF METROPOLITAN TORONTO. *Family Income Security Issues.* Toronto: The Council, 1976.

10.0   Social Welfare Policies for Maintaining the Labour Force

10.1   Housing Policy

10.1.1   Historical Development

10.1.1.1   General

2118 ADAM, G.M. "The Building Societies." *Bystander*. 1 (April 1880), pp. 180-84.

2119 ARMSTRONG, A.H. "Thomas Adams and the Commission of Conservation." *Plan Canada*. 1:1 (1959), pp. 14-32.

2120 BELL, Edwin. *A Treatise on the Law of Landlord and Tenant in Canada*. Toronto: The Canada Law Book Co., 1904.

2121 BERRINGTON, Adrian. "Town Planning." *Canadian Forum*. 1:9 (June 1921), pp. 269-71.

2122 BETTISON, David G. *The Politics of Canadian Urban Development*. Edmonton: University of Alberta Press, 1975.

2123 CARVER, Humphrey. *Compassionate Landscape*. Toronto: University of Toronto Press, 1975.

2124 _____. "Still No Housing." *Canadian Forum*. 18:215 (December 1938), pp. 267-69.

2125 _____. "Utopia and the City Hall." *Canadian Forum*. 15:181 (February 1936), pp. 922-23.

2126 CLARKE, Samuel. *A Treatise on the Law of Landlord and Tenant Applicable to the Dominion of Canada*. Toronto: Carswell, 1895.

2127 COREA, Larry. "Thomas Adams: Town Planner as Social Reformer." M.S.W., Carleton University, 1979.

2128 FIRESTONE, O.J. *Residential Real Estate in Canada*. Toronto: University of Toronto Press, 1951.

2129 GOLDBERG, J. "Canadian Housing Policy, 1960-1970." M.A., McGill University, 1970.

2130 HISELER, L. "Wartime Housing Policy; Case Study of Halifax." Ph.D., University of Guelph, 1975.

2131 INSTITUTE OF PUBLIC ADMINISTRATION OF CANADA. *Shaping the Canadian City: Essays on Urban Politics and Policy 1890-1920*. Institute of Local Government. [n.p., n.d.]

2132 JONES, Andrew Eric. "The Beginnings of Canadian Government Housing Policy, 1918-1924." Ottawa: Centre for Social Welfare Studies, Carleton University (1978).

2133 KINGSFORD, Rupert. *Manual of the Law of Landlord and Tenant*. Toronto: Carswell, 1904.

2134 LARSEN, Peter. "Quelques aspects sur l'histoire de la politique du logement de l'état Canadien." Ph.D., Université de Grenoble, 1976.

2135 NUNN, Phyllis M. "The History of the Movement for Housing Reform in Ontario." M.A., Queen's University, 1938.

2136 RICHARDS, J. Howard. "Lands and Policies: Attitudes and Controls in the Alienation of Lands in Ontario during the First Century of Settlement." *Ontario History*. 50:4 (Autumn 1958), pp. 193-209.

2137 ROSE, Albert. *Canadian Housing Policies*. Ottawa: Canadian Welfare Council, 1968.

2138 _____. "Canadian Housing Policies". *In The Right to Housing*, edited by Michael Wheeler. pp. 63-128. Montreal: Harvest House, 1969.

2139 SHOSTACK, Hannah. "Business and Reform: The Lost History of the Toronto Housing Company." *City Magazine*. 3:7 (September 1978), pp. 24-31.

2140 SMITH, L.B. "Housing Policy in Post-War Canada." In *Urban and Social Economics in Market and Planned Economies: Housing, Income, Environment*. edited by A.A. Brown, J.A. Liccri and E. Neuberger. pp. 31-51. New York: Praeger, 1974.

2141 _____. "Post-War Canadian Housing Policy in Theory and Practice." *Land Economics*. 44:3 (August 1968), pp. 338-50.

2142 UNDERHILL, Frank H. "The Housing Fiasco in Canada." *Canadian Forum*. 17:201 (October 1937), pp. 228-29.

2143 WEAVER, J.C. "Reconstruction of the Richmond District in Halifax: A Canadian Episode in Public Housing and Town Planning, 1918-1921." *Plan Canada*. 16:1 (1975), pp. 36-47.

2144 WILSON, A.D. "Canadian Housing Legislation." *Canadian Public Administration*. 2:4 (December 1959), pp. 214-228.

10.1.1.2   Reviews of Policy

2145 ADAMS, Thomas. "Bad Housing Conditions: Private and Public Responsibility in Canada." *Town Planning and Conservation of Life*. 7:1 (January-March 1921), pp. 12-15.

2146 _____. "Canada's Drive for Better Housing." *National Municipal Review*. 8 (July 1919), pp. 354-59).

2147 _____. "Civic and Social Questions in Canada: Home Problems During the War." *Conservation of Life*. 2:3 (April-June 1916), pp. 53-61.

2148 _____. "Government Housing during War." *Conservation of Life*. 4:2 (April 1918), pp. 25-33.

2149 _____. *Housing in Canada: The General Project of the Federal Government*. Ottawa: King's Printer, 1919.

2150 _____. "Housing and Social Reconstruction." *Landscape Architecture*. 9 (January 1919), pp. 41-62.

2151 _____. "Housing and Town Planning in Canada." *American City*. 12 (April 1915), pp. 334-37.

2152 _____. "Housing and Town Planning in Canada." *Report*. Sixth Annual Meeting of the Commission of Conservation. Ottawa: The Commission, 1915, pp. 158-79.

2153 _____. "Housing and Town Planning in Canada." *Town Planning Review*. 6:1 (July 1915), pp. 20-6.

2154 _____. "Housing, Town Planning and Municipal Government." *Report*. Tenth Annual Meeting of the Commission of Conservation. Ottawa: The Commisssion, 1919, pp. 95-105.

2155 _____. "Improvement of Slum Areas." *Town Planning and Conservation of Life*. 6:2 (April 1920), pp. 36-39.

2156 _____. "The Need for Scientific Investigation of Garden Cities and Town Planning Problems." *Garden Cities and Town Planning*. 10:9 (September 1920), pp. 191-99.

2157 _____. "The Need of Town-Planning Legislation and Procedure for Control of Land as a Factor in House-Building Development." *Journal of the American Institute of Architects*. 6 (February 1918), pp. 68-70.

2158 _____. "Planning New Towns in Canada: Ojibway." *Conservation of Life*. 4:4 (October 1918), pp. 73-80.

2159 _____. "Review of Town Planning in Canada." *Canadian Engineer*. 46:26 (June 1924), pp. 651-53.

2160 _____. "Should Governments Conscript Land or Regulate Its Use?" *Conservation of Life*. 4:3 (July 1918), pp. 59-61.

2161 _____. "Some Provisions of the Nova Scotia Town Planning Act, 1915." *Town Planning Institute, Papers and Discussions*. 1 (1914-15), pp. 150-52.

2162 _____. "Some Recent Developments in Town Planning." *Town Planning Institute: Papers and Discussions*. 1 (1914-15), pp. 141-49.

2163 _____. "Town and Country Planning in Quebec." *Town Planning and the Conservation of Life*. 6:4 (October-December 1920), pp. 77-79.

2164 _____. "Town Planning and Land Development." *Report*. Ninth Annual Meeting of the Commission of Conservation. Ottawa: The Commission, 1918, pp. 194-203.

2165 ADAMSON, Anthony, ed. *Homes or Hovels? Some Authoritative Views on Canadian Housing*. Toronto: Canadian Institute of International Affairs, 1943.

2166 BEGG, W.A. "Town Planning and Development in Saskatchewan." *Canadian Engineer*. 40 (February 1921), pp. 239-43.

2167 BEST, W.L. "National Housing Act." *Canadian Congress Journal*. 17 (November 1938), pp. 18-20.

2168 BRYCE, P.H. "The Land Problem in Relation to Housing." *Public Health Journal*. 6:12 (December 1915), pp. 608-13.

2169 BUCKLEY, A. "Town Planning in Saskatchewan." *Town Planning and Conservation of Life*. 6:3 (July-September 1920), pp. 48-50.

2170 _____. "Women and Town Planning." *Social Welfare* (December 1926), pp. 320-21.

2171 BURDITT, W.F. "Civic Efficiency and Social Welfare in Planning of Land." In *Urban and Rural Development in Canada: Report of Conference Held at Winnipeg*. Ottawa: Commission of Conservation, 1917, pp. 71-78.

2172 BURLAND, J.H. "Preliminary Report of the Committee on Town Planning Legislation." *Report*. Fifth Annual Meeting of the Commission of Conservation. Ottawa: The Commission, 1914, pp. 121-25.

2173 _____. "A Town Planning Act for Canada." Address to Sixth National Conference on City Planning. *Report*. Sixth Annual Meeting of the Commission of Conservation. Ottawa: The Commission, 1915, pp. 245-84.

2174 CANADIAN YOUTH COUNCIL. *Report on Slums and Re-housing in Toronto*. Toronto: The Council, 1936.

2175 CARVER, Humphrey. "A Housing Policy for Canada." In *Rights and Liberties in Our Times*. edited by Martyn Estall. pp. 54-71. Toronto: Ryerson Press for the Canadian Institute on Public Affairs, 1947.

2176 CLARK, W.C. "Low-Rent Housing Legislation." *Royal Architectural Institute of Canada Journal*. 14:4 (April 1939), pp. 72-73.

2177 COUGHLIN, J.F. *New Housing in Canada and Other British Nations*. Toronto: The Author, 1937.

2178 CREED, George E. "Future Housing in Canada." *Food for Thought*. 3:5 (January 1943), pp. 9-11.

2179 DAVIDSON, J.W. "The New Alberta, Canada, Town Planning Act." *Proceedings*. Fifth National Conference on City Planning. Chicago, 1913, pp. 68-73.

2180 DAVIS, R.E.G. "Housing Legislation in Canada." *Canadian Welfare*. 28:6 (December 1952), pp. 12-17.

2181 FALUDI, E.G. "Housing in Canada and the Shape of Things to Come." *Food for Thought.* 11:8 (April 1942), pp. 10-19.

2182 "The First Canadian Town Planning Regulations." *Conservation of Life.* 1:1 (August 1914), pp. 14-16.

2183 GOFORTH, W.W. "How Business Can Make Housing Pay." *Canadian Business.* 12:6 (June 1939), pp. 16-19.

2184 HASTINGS, Charles J.C.O. "Suggestions for the Housing Problem." *Industrial Canada.* 13:1 (August 1912), pp. 66-69.

2185 HIGGINS, B.H. "Appraisals of the Canadian Housing Act." *Public Affairs.* 7:2 (Winter, 1945), pp. 167-71.

2186 *Housing and Community Planning.* A series of lectures delivered at McGill University 2 November 1943-21 March 1944. Montreal: McGill University, 1944.

2187 LEONARD, T. D'Arcy. "The Dominion Housing Act 1935." *Canadian Banker.* 43:3 (April 1936), pp. 297-304.

2188 LORRAIN, Léon. "Les logements ouvrières et notre loi provinciale." *Revue trimestrielle canadienne.* 1:3 (November 1915), pp. 244-55.

2189 MOONEY, George S. "A Post-War Housing Program for Canada." *Canadian Welfare.* 19:3 (July 1943), pp. 3-9.

2190 PARENTEAU, R. "La législation fédérale sur l'habitation." *Actualité économique.* 32:2 (1956), pp. 210-30.

2191 PRINCE, Samuel Henry. *Society and the Housing Crisis; an Introduction to the Study of Housing.* n.p.: The Council for Social Service, 1936.

2192 SEYMOUR, Horace L. "The National Housing Act, 1938." *Public Affairs.* 2:3 (March 1939), pp. 127-31.

2193 SISSONS, C.B. "A Housing Policy for Ontario." *Canadian Magazine.* 53:3 (July 1919), pp. 241-48.

2194 VIVIAN, H. "Town Planning and Town Housing." *Canadian Municipal Journal.* (October 1910), pp. 400-404.

2195 WALKER, J.A. "Planning of Company Towns in Canada." *Canadian Engineer.* 53:3 (1927), pp. 147-50.

2196 WODLINGER, David B. "Housing and Community Planning in Canada." *Canadian Welfare.* 20:4 (September 1944), pp. 25-31.

2197 YOUNG, S. "Controlling the Subdivision of Land." *Canadian Engineer.* 57:8 (August 1929), pp. 334-35.

10.1.2   Government Policy and Documentation

10.1.2.1   Federal

2198 ACQUAUH-HARRISON, Richard. *Residential Development Approval Processes in Canada.* Ottawa: Policy Planning Division, Central Mortgage and Housing Corporation, 1974.

2199 ANDREWS, H.F. *Co-operative Housing: A Case Study of Decision-Making in Design and User Satisfaction.* Ottawa: Ministry of State for Urban Affairs, n.d.

2200 ARCHER, P. *Urbanization on Agricultural Land: Trends and Implications for National Housing Policies.* Ottawa: Central Mortgage and Housing Corporation, 1976.

2201 BATES, S. "La construction de maisons et le gouvernement." *Royal Architectural Institute of Canada Journal.* 35 (August 1958), pp. 305-309.

2202 CANADA. Advisory Committee on Reconstruction. Housing and Community Planning. *Final Report of the Subcommittee.* Ottawa: King's Printer, 1946.

2203 CANADA. Commission d'étude sur le logement et l'aménagement urbain. *Rapport de la commission fédérale d'étude sur le logement et l'aménagement urbain.* Ottawa: Imprimeur de la Reine, 1969.

2204 CANADA. Department of Labour. *Joint Conference of the Building and Construction Industries in Canada Held at Ottawa, May 3-6, 1921.* (Industrial Relations Series Bulletin No. 3). Ottawa: King's Printer, 1921.

2205 CANADA. Department of Munitions and Supply. *Preliminary Report on the Housing Situation in Canada and Suggestions for Its Improvement.* Ottawa: Department of Munitions and Supply, 1942.

2206 CANADA. Department of National Health and Welfare. Research and Statistics Division. *Legislative Measures Affecting Living Accommodations for Elderly Persons in Canada.* Ottawa: The Department, 1961.

2207 CANADA. Department of Reconstruction. Housing Division. *Manpower and Material Requirements for a Housing Program in Canada.* Ottawa: King's Printer, 1946.

2208 _____. *A Report on the Immediate Housing Needs and a Tentative Five Year Canadian Housing Programme and How the Needs of Low Rental Housing May Be Met.* Ottawa: King's Printer, 1945.

2209 CANADA. Federal Task Force on Housing and Urban Development. *Report of the Federal Task Force on Housing and Urban Development.* Ottawa: Queen's Printer, 1969.

2210 CANADA. Northwest Territories Council. *Report of the Northwest Territories Council Task Force on Housing.* Yellowknife: Department of Local Government, 1972.

2211 CENTRAL MORTGAGE AND HOUSING CORPORATION. *A Catalogue of Housing Programs.* Ottawa: The Corporation, 1977.

2212 _____. *Current Trends and Policies in the Field of Housing, Building and Planning, Canada 1974-1975/ Tendances et politiques actuelles dans les domaines de l'habitation, de la construction et de la planification.* Ottawa: The Corporation, 1975.

2213 _____. *Developing the Residential Mortgage Market.* Ottawa: The Corporation, 1973.

2214 _____. "Evolution of the Federal Governments' Participation in Housing and Urban Development." Background paper for the Federal-Provincial Conference. Ottawa: The Corporation, 1967.

2215 _____. *Federal Housing Programs: A Quick Review for Ready Reference/ Programmes fédéraux du logement: Exposé succinct facile à consulter.* Ottawa: The Corporation, 1976.

2216 _____. *Housing in Canada 1946-1970: A Supplement to the 25th Annual Report of Central Mortgage and Housing Corporation/ L'habitation au Canada 1946-1970: Supplément au 25ième Rapport annuel de la société centrale.* Ottawa: The Corporation, 1970.

2217 _____. *Housing the Handicapped/ Pour les handicapés.* Ottawa: The Corporation, 1974.

2218 _____. *Low Rental Housing; a Statement of Principles and Policy.* Ottawa: The Corporation, 1956.

2219 _____. *Post War Housebuilding in Canada; Cost and Supply Problems.* Ottawa: The Corporation, 1951.

2220 _____. *Report of the Committee to Study the Federal Provincial Rental Scale.* Ottawa: The Corporation, 1960.

2221 _____. Advisory Group. *Public Housing Policy.* Ottawa: The Corporation, 1962.

2222 _____. Policy Research Coordination. *Report of the Task Force on Shelter and Incomes.* Ottawa: The Corporation, 1976.

2223 _____. Prairie Regional Office. *Proceedings: Design and Construction Workshop: Rural and Native Housing.* Winnipeg: The Corporation, 1974.

2224 DUBE, Yves, HOWES, J.E., and McQUEEN, D.L. *Housing and Social Capital.* (Special Study for the Royal Commission on Canada's Economic Prospects). Ottawa: Queen's Printer, 1957.

2225 FIRESTONE, O.J. *The Labour Value of the Building Dollar: Some Aspects of the Results of Eight Years Administration.* Ottawa: King's Printer, 1943.

2226 GRAUER, A. E. *Housing: A Study Prepared for the Royal Commission on Dominion-Provinical Relations.* Ottawa: King's Printer, 1939.

2227 KIRKLAND, John S. *Demand for Housing in Canada.* Ottawa: Central Mortgage and Housing Corporation, 1973.

2228 SHOYAMA, T.R. *Rental Housing in Canada; a Study of the Federal Government's Programme, 1941-1949.* Ottawa: The Corporation, 1949.

2229 SIFTON, Clifford. "Inaugural Address" *Report.* First Annual Meeting of the Commission of Conservation. Ottawa: King's Printer, 1910. pp. 1-27.

2230 STREICH, Patricia. *Home Ownership for Low Income Canadians.* A Report Prepared for the Task Force on Shelter and Incomes. Ottawa: The Corporation, 1976.

2231 WINTERS, R.W. "Federal Housing Policy." *Public Affairs.* 12:2 (Winter 1949) pp. 71-78.

10.1.2.2   Provincial

2232 ALBERTA. Alberta Housing Corporation. *Analysis of the Social Development Housing Program.* Edmonton: The Corporation, 1972.

2233 ALBERTA. Department of Housing and Public Works. *Housing for Albertans: A Review of Alberta Housing Programs Planned, Administered and Financed Through Alberta Government Crown Corporations.* Edmonton: The Department; Alberta Home Mortgage Corporation; Alberta Housing Corporation, 1976.

2234 ALBERTA. Department of Municipal Affairs. Alberta Housing and Urban Renewal Corporation. *Alberta Housing Profile.* Edmonton, The Department, 1968.

2235 _____. Regional Planning Section. *Provincial Land Use Policies Background Paper.* Edmonton, The Department, 1976.

2236 ALBERTA. Royal Commission Into the Affairs of the Alberta Housing Corporation. *Report.* Calgary: The Commission, 1975.

2237 BRITISH COLUMBIA. Department of Housing. *Housing for People; Program of the British Columbia Department of Housing.* Victoria: The Department, 1975.

2238 BRITISH COLUMBIA. Interdepartmental Study Team on Housing and Rents. *A Comprehensive Social Housing Policy for British Columbia.* Vancouver, 1975.

2239 _____. *Housing and Rent Control in British Columbia.* Vancouver, 1975.

2240 BRITISH COLUMBIA. Ministry of Municipal Affairs and Housing. *ARP: Assisted Rental Program; A Program of the British Columbia Ministry of Municipal Affairs and Housing.* Victoria, 1976.

2241 _____. *Cooperative Housing Assistance; A Programme of the British Columbia Ministry of Municipal Affairs and Housing.* Victoria, 1976.

2242 _____. *Rental Programs for Senior Citizens; A Program of the British Columbia Ministry of Municipal Affairs and Housing and C.M.H.C.* Victoria, 1977.

2243 _____. *SAFER: Shelter Aid for Elderly Renters; A Programme of the Province of British Columbia.* Victoria: The Ministry, 1977.

2244 COOK, Gail C.A. *Municipal Finances and Housing Development.* Background Report for Advisory Task Force on Housing Policy. Report No. 2. Toronto: Queen's Printer, 1974.

2245 GORDON, Peter, and CROOK, Andrew J. *Report of the Gordon-Crook Commission on Homes for the Disabled in Nova Scotia.* Halifax: Department of Public Welfare, 1970.

2246 LEAL, Allan H. "The Condominium Act: A Disarmingly Simple Legislative Fiat." *Ontario Housing.* 13:3 (February 1968), pp. 13-18.

2247 MANITOBA. Department of Health and Public Welfare. Elderly Persons Housing Authority. *Hostels or Residences for Elderly Persons.* Winnipeg, 1961.

2248 MANITOBA. Manitoba Housing and Renewal Corporation. *Housing Conditions, Requirements and Supply; A Profile of Housing in the Province of Manitoba.* Winnipeg, 1968.

2249 MILLIGAN, P.A. *Home Purchaser Protection.* Background Report for the Advisory Task Force on Housing Policy. Toronto: Queen's Printer, 1973.

2250 ONTARIO. Advisory Task Force on Housing Policy. *Background Report: The Housing Production Process in Ontario.* Toronto: Queen's Printer, 1973.

2251 _____. *Report.* Toronto: Queen's Printer, 1973.

2252 _____. *Working Papers: Housing Issues and Housing Programs.* Vol. 1A. Toronto: Queen's Printer, 1973.

2253 _____. *Working Papers: Housing Supply.* Toronto: Queen's Printer, 1973.

2254 _____. *Working Papers: Land For Housing.* Vol.2C. Toronto: Queen's Printer, 1973.

2255 _____. *Working Papers: Housing Assistance.* Vol. 2D. Toronto: Queen's Printer, 1973.

2256 _____. *Working Papers: Government and Housing.* Toronto: Queen's Printer, 1973.

2257 ONTARIO. Bureau of Municipal Affairs. *Report: Housing for 1919.* Toronto: King's Printer, 1920.

2258 ONTARIO. Department of Economics and Development. Research and Planning Section, Housing Branch. *Report on the Need and Demand for Federal-Provincial Public Rental Housing.* Toronto, 1963.

2259 ONTARIO. Housing Committee. *Report: Including Standards for Inexpensive Houses Adopted for Ontario and Typical Plans.* Toronto: King's Printer, 1919.

2260 ONTARIO. *Policies, Programs and Structure.* Toronto: Ontario Housing Corporation, 1972.

2261 ONTARIO. Ministry of Community and Social Services. *Housing and Social Policy in Ontario.* Toronto: The Ministry, 1973.

2262 ONTARIO. Ministry of Consumer and Commercial Relations. *Policy Options for Continuing Tenant Protection.* Toronto: The Ministry, 1978.

2263 ONTARIO. Ministry of Housing. *Housing Ontario '74: An Initial Statement of Policies, Programs and Partnerships.* Toronto: The Ministry, 1974.

2264 _____. Ontario Housing Corporation. *The Housing of Handicapped Persons in Ontario.* Toronto: The Ministry, 1977.

2265 ONTARIO. *Report.* Lieutenant Governor's Commission on Housing Conditions in Toronto. Toronto: Hunter-Rose, 1934.

2266 ————. Planning Act Review Committee. *Report.* Toronto: The Ministry, 1977.

2267 ONTARIO WELFARE COUNCIL. *Community Studies: Background Report for the Advisory Task Force on Housing Policy.* Toronto: The Council, 1973.

2268 PETER BARNARD ASSOCIATES. *Developments in the Cost, Supply and Need for Housing in Ontario.* Background Report for The Advisory Task Force on Housing Policy. Toronto: Peter Barnard Associates, 1973.

2269 QUEBEC. Commission d'enquête sur le probleme de logement dans la province. *Rapport.* Quebec, 1949.

2270 QUEBEC. Groupe de travail sur l'habitation. *Avis concernant le controle des loyers.* Quebec: Editeur Officiel du Québec, 1976.

2271 QUEBEC. Groupe de travail sur l'habitation. *Habiter au Québec.* Quebec: Editeur Officiel du Québec, 1976.

2272 ————. *Habiter au Québec: annexe 2. Etudes sur les co-opératives d'habitation.* Quebec: Editeur officiel du Québec, 1976.

2273 ————. *Habiter au Québec: annexe 3. Propositions pour une nouvelle formule de co-opératives d'habitation au Québec: les aspects juridiques.* Quebec: Editeur officiel du Québec, 1975.

2274 ————. *Les programmes d'habitation de l'Ontario.* Quebec: Editeur Officiel du Québec, 1976.

2275 ————. *Livre blanc sur les relations entre locateurs et locataires.* Quebec: Editeur officiel du Québec, 1978.

2276 SASKATCHEWAN. Department of Social Services. *Housing and Welfare: An Analysis of the Living Accommodations of Public Assistance Recipients in Saskatchewan.* Regina: The Department, 1972.

2277 ————. Planning and Evaluation. *Proposals for Shelter Allowance Program.* Regina: The Department, 1976.

2278 SASKATCHEWAN. Department of Welfare. Program Division. *Housing and Special Care Home Program.* Regina, The Department, 1969.

2279 SASKATCHEWAN. Interdepartmental Committee on Housing. *Housing Policy for Northern Administration District.* Regina, 1976.

10.1.2.3 Municipal

2280 TORONTO CONSULTATIVE COMMITTEE ON HOUSING POLICIES. *Final Report.* Toronto, 1966.

10.1.2.4 Intergovernmental

2281 L'ECUYER, Gilbért. "La compétence législative en matière d'habitation." M.A., Laval University, 1975.

2282 McFARLANE, Ivan D. "Housing Policy: Three Levels of Government Action." M.A., Carleton University, 1969.

2283 FEDERAL/PROVINCIAL TASK FORCE ON THE SUPPLY AND PRICE OF SERVICED RESIDENTIAL LAND. *Report.* Ottawa, 1978.

10.1.3 Special Issues

10.1.3.1 Public Housing

2284 ANDREW, Caroline; BLAIS, André; DesROSIERS, Rachel. *Les élites politiques, les bas-salariés et la politique du logement à Hull.* Ottawa: Editions de l'université d'Ottawa, 1976.

2285 AUDAIN, Michael. "The C.M.H.C. Task Force on Low Income Housing." *Housing and People.* 2:4 (December 1971), pp. 1-5.

2286 AUDET, Jules. "Impact of a Public Housing Program on the Users: A Study of Three Ottawa Public Housing Projects." M.A., Carleton University, 1972.

2287 BLUMENFELD, H. *Housing of Low-Income Persons in Ontario.* Background Report for Advisory Task Force on Housing Policy. Toronto, 1973.

2288 BOSSE, Michaud Arcand. *Le logement pour les ménages à faible revenu: une analyse des besoins, des ressources et des programes de logement pour les ménages à faible revenu (du Québec).* Quebec: Laval University, 1972.

2289 CANADIAN WELFARE COUNCIL. *Special Project on Social Aspects of Low-Income Housing and Social Planning, with Special Reference to Public Housing and Urban Renewal.* Ottawa: The Council, 1968.

2290 ————. *Who Should Manage Public Housing?* Report of a Workshop held at Pointe-Claire, Quebec, 19-21 June 1970. Ottawa: The Council, 1970.

2291 CARVER, Humphrey, and HOPWOOD, A.L. *Rents for Regent Park; A Rent-Scale System for a Public Housing Project, A Study for the Toronto Metropolitan Housing Research Project.* Toronto: Civic Advisory Council of Toronto, 1948.

2292 CHARNEY, Melvin. *The Adequacy and Production of Low Income Housing.* Ottawa: Central Mortgage and Housing Corporation, Task Force on Low Income Housing, 1971.

2293 DENNIS, Michael, and FISH, Susan. *Programs in Search of a Policy: Low Income Housing in Canada.* Toronto: Hakkert, 1972.

2294 DEVINE, George. "Social Housing Management/L'administration des logement sociaux." *Housing and People/ L'habitation et les citoyens.* 6:2 (Summer 1975), pp. 3-7.

2295 DIVAY, Gérard, and GODBOUT, Jacques. *Le logement des ménages à faible revenu au Québec: situation, problèmes, perspectives, solutions.* Montreal: Institut national de la recherche scientifique, urbanisation, 1975.

2296 DROVER, Glenn. "Low Income Housing in Nova Scotia." *Housing and People.* 4:2 (Summer 1973), pp. 10-11.

2297 LA FEDERATION DES UNIONS DE FAMILLES. *Avant de se retrouver tout nu dans la rue: le problème du logement.* Montreal: Editions Parti Pris, 1977.

2298 FELDMAN, L.D. "A Housing Project Wends its Weary Way." *Canadian Public Administration.* 6:2 (June 1963), pp. 221-32.

2299 ————. "The Provision of Public Housing in Canada." M.A., Carleton University, 1962.

2300 FISH, Susan A. "Low Income Housing in Ontario: Some Hidden Agendas and Basic Beliefs." In *The City: Attacking Modern Myths,* edited by Allan Powell. pp. 47-60. Toronto: McClelland and Stewart, 1972.

2301 GODBOUT, Jacques. "Ménages à faible revenu: développement et politiques gouvernmentales de l'habitation." *Sociologie et sociétés.* 4:1 (May 1972), pp. 43-54.

2302 GOLDFARB CONSULTANTS. *Public Housing: A Research Report for Central Mortgage and Housing Corporation.* Toronto: Central Mortgage and Housing Corporation, 1968.

2303 GRAHAM, T.A. "Slums vs Public Housing; A Cost-Benefit Analysis." M.A., University of Manitoba, 1964.

2304 KINZEL, Mary Josephine. "Living Space and Tenant Strategies: A Case Study of a Public Housing Project." Ottawa: Carleton University, 1974.

2305 McGILLY, Frank J. *Housing Programs: Public Housing.* Montreal: McGill University, 1974.

2306 MacMILLAN, James A., and NICKEL, Edith. "An Economic Appraisal of Urban Housing Assistance: Rental Supplements Versus Public Housing. *Canadian Public Administration.* 17:3 (Fall 1974), pp. 443-60.

2307 MARSH, Leonard C. "The Economics of Low-rent Housing." *Canadian Journal of Economics and Political Science.* 15:1 (Feb. 1949), pp. 14-33.

2308 ONIBOKUN, A.G. "Housing for Low Income Groups, Some Realities and Misconceptions." *Community Planning Review.* 22:1 (Spring 1972), pp. 23-27.

2309 _____. "Public Housing Habitability Study." *Housing and People.* 3:1 (April 1972), p. 10.

2310 _____. "Public Housing in Canada: A Synthesis of Research Efforts." *Urban Renewal and Low Income Housing.* 8:3 (1972), pp. 2-13.

2311 _____. "Some Insights to Guide the Design and Management of Public Housing." *Plan Canada.* 13:2, (1973), pp. 163-72.

2312 _____. "Relative Habitability of Public Housing in Canada: A Comparative Analysis." Ph.D., Waterloo University, 1971.

2313 PETER BARNARD ASSOCIATES. *Managing Public Housing in the Province of Ontario.* Toronto: Peter Barnard Associates, 1971.

2314 POULTER, Christine. "Public Housing in Canada: Institutional Control and Tenant Action." M.S.W. Carleton University, 1975.

2315 RINGER, Paul. *The Social Implications of Public Housing in Metropolitan Toronto.* Toronto: Metropolitan Toronto Housing Authority, 1963.

2316 ROSE, Albert. *Regent Park; A Study in Slum Clearance.* Toronto: University of Toronto Press, 1958.

2317 _____. "Housing Low Income Families. Welfare and Community Planning Implications." *Social Worker.* 25:1 (October 1956), pp. 9-18.

2318 _____. "The Social Philosophy Underlying Public Housing." *Ontario Housing.* 16:6 (May 1972), pp. 7-9.

2319 SNIDER, Earle L. "Buying is Not Enough for Low Income Families." *Housing and People.* 8:3 (Spring 1978), pp. 11-14.

2320 STREICH, P. *Housing the Elderly: An Examination of the Rationale for Using the Existing Rent-Income Scale for Elderly Tenants in Public Housing.* Ottawa: Economics and Statistics Division, Central Mortgage and Housing Corporation, 1970.

2321 _____. *A Review of the Rent-to-Income Scale for Public Housing Units.* Ottawa: Economics and Statistics Division, Central Mortgage and Housing Corporation, 1972.

2322 THURINGER, H.P. "Low Income Families and Public Housing." M.S.W., University of Toronto, 1959.

2323 WEST, Margaret. *A Study of Two Forms of Low Income Housing Tenure.* Ottawa: Central Mortgage and Housing Corporation, 1973.

2324 WHEELER, Michael. "Evaluating the Need for Low-Rental Housing: A Review of Conditions among Family Applications for the Little Mountain Low-Rental Housing Project, Vancouver, and Consideration of Criteria for Future Housing Projects." M.S.W., University of British Columbia, 1955.

10.1.3.2   Cooperatives

2325 ANDREWS, Howard F., and BRESLAUER, Helen J. *Co-operative Housing Project: An Overview of a Case Study, Methods and Findings.* Toronto: Centre for Urban and Community Studies, 1976. Research Paper 73.

2326 _____. *Reflections on the Housing Process: Implications from a Case Study of Co-operative Housing.* Toronto: Centre for Urban and Community Studies, 1976. Research Paper 74.

2327 ARNOLD, Mary Ellicott. *The Story of Tompkinsville.* New York: The Co-operative League, 1940.

2328 CANADIAN INTERNATIONAL CENTRE OF RESEARCH AND INFORMATION ON PUBLIC AND COOPERATIVE ECONOMY. *Background Papers for Seminar on Public and Cooperative Housing.* Montreal: The Centre, 1967.

2329 CENTRAL MORTGAGE AND HOUSING CORPORATION. Task Force on Low Income Housing. *Cooperative Housing Program Review and Proposal.* Ottawa: The Corporation, 1971.

2330 CHEN, Patrick. "The Economics of a Continuing Housing Co-operative." M.A., University of Ottawa, 1971.

2331 CHUNG, Joseph H. *Le mouvement des caisses populaires Desjardins et l'habitation au Québec.* Montreal: Laboratoire de recherche en sciences immobilières, Université du Québec à Montréal, 1975.

2332 CLARKE, Gerald E., and MOORMAN, James D. *Co-operative Housing Administration Manual.* Ottawa: Institute for Social Action, 1961.

2333 CONSEIL DE LA COOPERATION DU QUEBEC. *Les coopératives d'habitation: rapport de la commission de l'habitation du conseil de la coopération du québec.* Levis: Le conseil, 1968.

2334 DINEEN, Janice. *The Trouble with Co-ops.* Toronto: Green Tree Publishing, 1974.

2335 DREYFUSS, A.E. *City Villages: The Cooperative Quest.* Toronto: New Press, 1973.

2336 DROVER, Glenn, and JORDAN, John. "New View of Co-ops." *Canadian Welfare.* 45:5 (September/October 1969), pp. 18-20.

2337 GODBOUT, Jacques. "L'échec récent des co-opératives d'habitation au Québec." *Housing and People.* 5:4 (Winter 1975), pp. 1-5.

2338 HADDRELL, Glenn. "What's Happening in Co-operative Housing." *Housing and People.* 2:1 (March/April 1971), p. 8.

2339 HUNTER, Donna. "DACHI: Problems of a Struggling Coop." *Living Places/Cadres de Vie.* 11:2 (1975), pp. 2-9.

2340 JORDAN, John E. *Co-operative Housing: Program Review and Proposal.* Ottawa: Central Mortgage and Housing Corporation, 1971.

2341 _____. "Canadian Policy Toward Co-operative Housing: A Study of Values in Conflict." M.E.S., York University, 1973.

2342 LABEN, Joe. *Co-operative Housing Manual: Steps to Co-operative Housing in Nova Scotia.* Antigonish: Extension Department, St. Francis-Xavier University, 1958.

2343 LAIDLAW, Alex. *A Roof Over Your Head; Co-op Housing.* Winnipeg: Department of Co-operative Development, 1975.

2344 _____. *Housing You Can Afford.* Toronto: Green Tree Publishing, 1977.

2345 _____. "Cooperative Housing: An Alternative." *Housing and People.* 3:1 (Winter/Spring 1972), pp. 8-10.

2346 _____. "Co-operative Housing in Canada." *Canadian Labour.* 11:3 (March 1966), pp. 5-7.

2347 _____. "Cooperatives as Third Sector Housing." *Housing and People.* 5:2, 3 (Summer/Fall 1974), pp. 1-6.

2348 _____. "Focus on Co-op Housing." *Ontario Housing.* 10:3 (June 1964), pp. 4-6.

2349 MIDMORE, J.F. *Report on Co-operative Housing.* Ottawa: Co-operative Union of Canada, 1962.

2350 PRINCE, S.H. "Co-operative Housing." *Royal Architectural Institute of Canada Journal.* 20:9 (September 1943), pp. 156-58.

2351 RICHARD, Jean d'Auteuil. "Cooperative Housing." *Public Affairs.* 10:4 (October 1947), pp. 239-45.

2352 ROACH, William M. *Co-operative Housing in Nova Scotia, 1938-1973.* Halifax: Nova Scotia Housing Commission, 1974.

2353 UNIVERSITY OF TORONTO. Centre for Urban and Community Studies. *Cooperative Housing Project; An Overview of a Case Study, Methods and Findings.* Toronto: The Centre, 1976.

2354 _____. *Residential Movement Choice of a Co-operative Housing Project.* Toronto: The Centre, 1976.

10.1.3.3   Senior Citizens

2355 AUDAIN, Michael *et al. Beyond Shelter; A Study of the National Housing Act financed housing for the Elderly.* Ottawa: Canadian Council on Social Development, 1973.

2356 _____. "A Study of Canada's Housing Developments for the Elderly." *Housing and People.* 4:2 (Summer 1973), pp. 1-7.

2357 CANADIAN WELFARE COUNCIL. *Study on Housing for the Aged: Final Report.* Ottawa: The Council, 1964.

2358 ENVIRONICS RESEARCH GROUP. *The Elderly and Their Environment: A Pilot Enquiry Into Senior Citizen's Housing Satisfaction.* Toronto: Central Mortgage and Housing Corporation, 1971.

2359 EPSTEIN, Don. *Retirement Housing in Urban Neighbourhoods; Some Inner City Options.* Winnipeg: Institute for Urban Studies, University of Winnipeg, 1976.

2360 *L'habitation et les personnes âgées.* Comptes-rendus des colloques régionaux et des ateliers tenus à Winnipeg, Vancouver, Toronto, Montréal et Halifax. 1974-75, 2nd Ed. Ottawa: Conseil canadien de devéloppement social, 1976.

2361 HART, George. *Non-profit Housing for the Aged and Other Special Care Groups; A Policy Study for the Central Mortgage and Housing Corporation.* Ottawa: Central Mortgage and Housing Corporation, 1976.

2362 O'GORMAN, Denis Keith Patrick. "Housing the Elderly: A Comprehensive Policy and Coordinated Program." M.A., University of British Columbia, 1965.

2363 PASSMORE, G.W. *Development of Homes for the Aged in Ontario.* Toronto: Ontario Department of Social and Family Services, 1967.

2364 PRIEST, Gordon Edward. "An Investigation of the Elderly in Their Urban Environment with Special Reference to Their Housing." M.A., Simon Fraser University, 1970.

2365 WARRILOW, D. *Building for Older People: A Study of Living Accommodation in Ontario for Elderly Persons of Low Income.* Toronto: University of Toronto, 1962.

10.1.3.4   Non-Profit and Social Housing

2366 FISH, Susan A. "Administrative Discretion on Social Housing Policy." *Osgoode Hall Law Journal.* 15:1 (June 1977), pp. 209-15.

2367 GODBOUT, Jacques, ed. *L'aspect institutionnel de la production du "logement social" au Québec.* Montreal: Centre de recherches urbaines et régionales, Université du Québec, 1971.

2368 HAIRE, Christopher P. *In Want of a Policy: A Survey of the Needs of Non-Profit Housing Companies and Co-operative Housing Societies.* Ottawa: Canadian Council on Social Development, 1975.

2369 _____. "New Housing Programs and the Development of Non Profit Housing/Les nouveaux programmes d'habitation et le logement non lucratif" *Housing and People.* 5:2,3 (Summer/Fall 1974) pp. 7-12.

2370 HOUSE, Jeffrey. "Third Force Housing in Canada: Problems and Prospects." *Osgoode Hall Law Journal.* 14:1 (June 1976), pp. 49-63.

2371 MATHEWS, Georges. *Besoins en logement sociaux en 1976, 1981 et 1986 dans les régions métropolitaines de Montréal, Québec, Hull et dans la municipalité de Sept-Iles.* Montreal: Institut national de la recherche scientifique, Urbanisation, 1974.

2372 ONTARIO HABITAT FOUNDATION. *Voluntary Activity in Housing: A Policy and Program for the Third Sector.* Prepared for the Advisory Task Force on Housing Policy. Toronto, 1972.

2373 ONTARIO WELFARE COUNCIL. *Municipal Action in Non-Profit Housing.* Toronto: The Council, 1977.

2374 PATTERSON, Jeffrey, and STREICH, Patricia. *A Review of Canadian Social Housing Policy.* Ottawa: Canadian Council on Social Development, 1977.

10.1.3.5   Urban Renewal

2375 ADAMSON, R.T. "Housing Policy and Urban Renewal." In *Urban Studies: A Canadian Perspective,* edited by N.H. Lithwick and Gilles Paquet, pp. 222-39. Toronto: Methuen, 1968.

2376 AXWORTHY, Lloyd. *The Citizen and Neighbourhood Renewal.* Winnipeg: Institute of Urban Studies, University of Manitoba, 1973.

2377 _____. "A Strategy for Self-Help Housing and Renewal." *Plan Canada.* 13:2 (August 1973), pp. 141-44.

2378 BIRINGEN, Turgut. "Rehabilitation of Housing." M.A., University of Toronto, 1969.

2379 BOURNE, Larry S. *Private Redevelopment of the Central City.* Chicago: University of Chicago Press, 1967.

2380 _____. *Urban System Development in Central Canada.* Toronto: University of Toronto Press, 1972.

2381 COLLIER, Robert W. *Administrative Aspects of Urban Renewal.* Ottawa: Central Mortgage and Housing Corporation, 1967.

2382 CROSS, K.J. "Urban Redevelopment in Canada." Ph.D., Cornell University, 1958.

2383 _____, and COLLIER, Robert W. *The Urban Renewal Process in Canada: An Analysis of Current Practice.* Vancouver: School of Community and Regional Planning Studies, University of British Columbia, 1967.

2384 DANSEREAU, Francine; DIVAY, Gérard; LEONARD, Jean-François. *Analyse des agents d'intervention impliqués dans le redéveloppement des zones periphériques du centre-ville à Montréal. Rapport d'étape.* Montreal: Institut national de la recherche scientifique, urbanisation, 1972.

2385 DORE, G., and MAYER, R. *L'idéologie du reaménagement urbain à Québec.* Quebec: Conseil des oeuvres et du bien-être du Québec, 1972.

2386 FLEMING, Chris. "Demand for Housing in Ontario: A Government Response through Rehabilitation." *Ontario Economic Review.* 12:2 (March/April 1974), pp. 3-8.

2387 FRASER, Graham. *Fighting Back — Urban Renewal in Trefann Court.* Toronto: Hakkert, 1972.

2388 FREEMAN, Bill. "Hamilton's Civic Square: The First 11 Years." *City Magazine.* 1:8 (January/February 1976), pp. 26-41.

2389 GRANATSTEIN, J.L. *Marlborough Marathon.* Toronto: Hakkert, 1971.

2390 GUTSTEIN, Donald; LANG, Jack; McINTOSH, Dorothy. "Neighbourhood Improvement: What it Means in Calgary, Vancouver and Toronto." *City Magazine.* 1:5,6 (August/September 1973), pp. 15-28.

2391 JONES, Murray V. *The Role of Private Enterprise in Urban Renewal.* A Study prepared for the Metropolitan Toronto Planning Board. Toronto: The Board, 1966.

2392 KRUEGER, Ralph R. "The Kitchener Market Fight: Another View." *Urban Forum.* 2:2 (Summer 1976), pp. 40-47.

2393 LORIMER, James. *A Citizen's Guide to City Politics.* Toronto: James, Lewis and Samuel, 1972.

2394 McKAY, Angus. "Government Land Development for Private Housing." *Plan Canada.* 3:1 (May 1962), pp. 30-35.

2395 McLEMORE, Reginald. "Three Approaches to Effecting Change in Low-Income Areas a Case Study of La Petite Bourgoyne Renewal Area, Montreal." M.A. University of Waterloo, 1972.

2396 MARSH, Leonard. "Rebuilding a Neighbourhood." *Report on Demonstration Slum Clearance.* Vancouver: University of British Columbia, 1950.

2397 MARTIN, Frank S. "The Development of Urban Renewal Policy for Older Residential Areas in the City of Toronto." M.A. University of Toronto, 1972.

2398 PASTERNAK, J. *The Kitchener Market Fight.* Toronto: Samuel Stevens and Hakkert, 1975.

2399 PETER BARNARD ASSOCIATES. *Residential Rehabilitation in Canada — A Survey of Projects: A Report Prepared for the Central Mortgage and Housing Corporation.* Toronto: Peter Barnard Associates, 1973.

2400 RICHARDSON, Boyce. *The Future of Canadian Cities.* Toronto: New Press, 1972.

2401 ROBERT, L. "La rénovation urbaine et la stratégie fiscale des municipalités." *Sociologie et sociétés.* 4:1 (1972), pp. 55-82.

2402 _____, and RACIOT, P. *La politique de rénovation urbaine: le cas québeçois.* Quebec: Conseil des oeuvres et du bien-être du Québec, 1972.

2403 ROSE, Albert. *Citizen Participation in Urban Renewal.* Toronto: Centre for Urban and Community Studies, University of Toronto, 1974.

2404 _____. *Prospects for Rehabilitation of Housing in Central Toronto.* Report of Research Submitted to the City of Toronto Planning Board and Central Mortgage and Housing Corporation, September 1966.

2405 _____. "The Crisis in Urban Renewal." In *Social and Cultural Change in Canada,* edited by W.E. Mann. pp. 193-205. vol. 1, Toronto: Copp Clark, 1970.

2406 SEWELL, John. *Up Against City Hall.* Toronto: James, Lewis and Samuel, 1972.

2407 STEIN, David Lewis. *Toronto for Sale.* Toronto: New Press, 1972.

10.1.3.6   Native Housing

2408 ALBERTA. Indian and Metis Housing Advisory Committee. *Opportunity Housing; A Review and Evaluation of the Indian and Metis Housing Program.* Edmonton, 1968.

2409 "Aspects of Northern Housing Policy in Ontario by Ontario Welfare Council." *Housing and People.* 6:2 (Summer 1976), p. 19.

2410 BAILEY, Richard W. "Housing for Indians and Metis in Northern Saskatchewan." *Habitat.* 11:4 (1968), pp. 18-23.

2411 BUFFALO, Y. "New Housing Policy for Indian Reserves." *Native People.* 10 (March 1977), pp. 1-2.

2412 CANADIAN ASSOCIATION IN SUPPORT OF THE NATIVE PEOPLES. "Native Housing: Overcoming Government Neglect." *Bulletin.* 17:2 (August 1976).

2413 CAVERHILL, Wilma. "New Housing for Northern Indians." *North.* 16:6 (November/December 1969), pp. 8-12.

2414 CLICHE, David. "De la tente au bungalow." M.A., University of Montreal, 1977.

2415 DE JOURDAN, Alan. "Native Housing: The Focus is Self-Help." *Habitat.* 18:2 (1975), pp. 13-15.

2416 DIETZ, S.H. "Housing in the Canadian North." M.A., University of Toronto, 1967.

2417 GLOVER, Michael. ed. *Building in Northern Communities.* Report on a Conference Workshop held in Inuvik, N.W.T., February 1974. Montreal: Arctic Institute, 1974.

2418 "Housing for Metis and Non Status Indians." *Housing and People.* 7:3 (Fall 1976), pp. 1-8.

2419 "Indian and Metis Housing in Northern Saskatchewan Communities." *Urban Renewal and Low Income Housing.* 6:3 (1970), pp. 13-18.

2420 MANITOBA METIS FOUNDATION. *The Human Element in Housing: An Evaluation of the Manitoba Remote Housing Program.* Winnipeg: The Federation, 1971.

2421 O'CONNELL, Martin P. *Canadian Standards of Housing in Indian Reserve Communities.* Toronto: Indian-Eskimo Association of Canada, 1965.

2422 ONTARIO WELFARE COUNCIL. *Aspects of Northern Housing Policy in Ontario.* Toronto: The Council, 1975.

2423 YATES, A.B. "Housing Programmes for Eskimos in Northern Canada." *Polar Record.* 15:94 (January 1970), pp. 45-50.

10.1.3.7   Handicapped Housing

2424 CAMERON, Jean. *A Study of Housing for the Disabled, Together with a Report of Housing for the Blind in Montreal.* Ottawa: Central Mortgage and Housing Corporation, 1955.

2425 CANADIAN PARAPLEGIC ASSOCIATION. Quebec Division. *Integrated Housing for the Severely Physically Disabled.* Montreal: The Association, 1974.

2426 CANADIAN REHABILITATION COUNCIL FOR THE DISABLED. *A National Conference on Housing and Essential Support Services for the Physically Disabled.* Toronto: The Council, 1976.

2427 CLARK, Alex. *Housing Needs for Handicapped Canadians.* Vancouver: Central Mortgage and Housing Corporation, 1972.

2428 COOPER, Claire. *Housing the Handicapped.* Ottawa: Central Mortgage and Housing Corporation, 1974.

2429 FALTA, Patricia. "Beyond Tokenism." *Housing and People*. 7:2 (Summer 1976), pp. 1-8.
2430 _____, and CAYOUETTE, Ghislain. *Integrated Housing for the Severely Physically Handicapped*. Ottawa: Central Mortgage and Housing Corporation, 1974.
2431 HANDICAPPED HOUSING SOCIETY OF ALBERTA. *Access Housing*. Edmonton: The Society, 1975.
2432 _____. *Handicapped Housing: Charette Report*. Edmonton: The Society, 1973.
2433 NATIONAL INSTITUTE ON MENTAL RETARDATION. *Residential Services Community Housing Options for Handicapped People*. Downsview: The Institute, 1975.
2434 PINE, Michael. *Housing the Disabled — Design of the Unit*. Ottawa: Central Mortgage and Housing Corporation, 1970.
2435 TORONTO. Mayor's Task Force Regarding the Disabled and Elderly. *Report*. Toronto: City of Toronto, 1975.

10.1.3.8   Land and Land Use

2436 ADAMS, Thomas. "The Purchase of Land for Building Purposes: A Problem that Needs Investigation in the Public Interest." *Conservation of Life*. Part I, 2:4 (July/September 1916), pp. 73-80; Part 2, 3:1 (December 1916), pp. 13-16.
2437 ADLER, G.M. *Land Planning by Administration Regulation: The Policies of the Ontario Municipal Board*. Toronto: University of Toronto Press, 1971.
2438 ALBERTA LAND USE FORUM. *Report and Recommendations*. Edmonton: The Forum, 1976.
2439 BEAUCHAMP, Kenneth P. *Land Management in the Canadian North*. Ottawa: Canadian Arctic Resources Committee, 1976.
2440 BLUMENFELD, Hans. *Land Control and Land Prices*. Ottawa: Community Planning Association of Canada, 1973.
2441 BRYANT, R.W.G. *Land: Private Property, Public Control*. Montreal: Harvest House, 1972.
2442 _____. *Land Speculation and Municipal Real Estate Policy*. Montreal: Institut d'urbanisme de l'université de Montréal, 1964.
2443 BUREAU OF MUNICIPAL RESEARCH. "Land Banking: Investment in the Future." *Civic Affairs*, 1 (1973).
2444 BURY, Duncan, and PIPER, John. "Saskatoon: How do You Make a Land Bank Work?" *City Magazine*. 2:7 (March 1977), pp. 28-35.
2445 CANADIAN COUNCIL ON SOCIAL DEVELOPMENT. *Urban Land Symposia: Proceedings*. Ottawa: The Council, 1977.
2446 CASSIDY, Michael. "Crownhold: A New Form of Land Tenure." *Housing and People*. 4:1 (Spring 1973), pp. 5-9.
2447 CHUNG, Joseph H. *Land Market and Land Speculation*. Montreal: Ecole des hautes etudes commerciales, 1969.
2448 CLIBBON, Peter Brooke, *et al*. *Structure and Dynamics of Land Use*. Montreal: Les presses de l'université de Montréal, 1975.
2449 COLE, Dennis. "The City of Red Deer." *Habitat*. 6:4 (1963), pp. 28-33.
2450 COMMUNITY PLANNING ASSOCIATION OF CANADA. Manitoba Division. *Planning and Land Use under the City of Winnipeg Act and the Newly Proclaimed Planning Act*. Winnipeg: The Association, 1976.
2451 CROOK, Raymond L. *Towards a Land Use Management Philosophy in British Columbia*. Vancouver: University of British Columbia, 1976.

2452 DERKOWSKI, Andrzej. *Costs in the Land Development Process*. Toronto: Housing and Urban Development Association of Canada, 1976.

2453 DILLON, M.M. *The Effects of Land Development Control on Housing Supply in Ontario*. Prepared for the Advisory Task Force on Housing Policy. Toronto, 1973.

2454 GOLDBERG, Michael A., ed. *Recent Perspectives in Urban Land Economics: Essays in Honour of Richard U. Ratcliff and Paul F. Wendt*. Vancouver: University of British Columbia, 1976.

2455 GREINER, A.J. *Land Policy in Canada*. Paper submitted to the Urban Land Policy Seminar. Vienna: 27 February to 17 March 1974. Ottawa: Policy Branch, Ministry of State for Urban Affairs, 1974.

2456 GUNTON, Tom. "The Urban Land Question: Who is Right?" *City Magazine*. 3:3 (February 1978), pp. 39-45.

2457 HAMILTON, S.W. *Public Land Banking — Real or Illusionary Benefits?* Vancouver: University of British Columbia, 1974.

2458 HELLYER, Paul. "How They Killed Public Land Banking: A Political Memoir." *City Magazine*. 3:2 (December 1977), pp. 31-38.

2459 JORDAN, John. "The Case for Public Land Assembly." *Housing and People*. 2:3 (October 1971), pp. 1-7.

2460 KEHOE, Dalton; MORLEY, David; PROUDFOOT, Stuart and ROBERTS, Neal. *Public Land Ownership: The Arguments Pro and Con*. Toronto: Lexington Books, 1976.

2461 LAMONT, Glenda R. *Land Use Policy — Population Growth*. Edmonton: Alberta Land Use Forum, 1974.

2462 "Land and City Politics in Winnipeg." *City Magazine*. 2:8 (June 1977), pp. 21-29.

2463 LAPOINTE, Linda. "Residential Land Use Patterns, Problems and Policy Direction." M.E.S., York University, 1976.

2464 LAW SOCIETY OF UPPER CANADA. *The Changing Face of Land Use and Development; Special Lectures*. Toronto: De Boo, 1974.

2465 LEDGERWOOD, Grant, and STREET, Elizabeth. "Central Government Office Location and Design: Recent Experience in Government Management of Land in Cities." *Plan Canada*. (September/December 1977), pp. 184-99.

2466 McCANDLESS, Michael. "Land Use Planning: The Financial Implications." *Housing and People*. 7:4 (Winter/Spring 1977), pp. 8-11.

2467 McCANN, Lawrence D. *Neighbourhoods in Transition: Processes of Land Use and Physical Change in Edmonton's Residential Areas*. Edmonton: Department of Geography, University of Alberta, 1975.

2468 MAKUCH, S.M. "Legal Authority and Land Uses in Central Toronto." *Urban Forum* 2:3 (Fall 1976), pp. 23-33.

2469 MANITOBA. Winnipeg Land Prices Inquiry Commission. *Report and Recommendations*. Winnipeg, 1977.

2470 MURCHISON, Wayne. "Land Banking Makes Sense." *Ontario Housing*. 14:1 (June 1968), p. 10.

2471 NAYSMITH, John Kennedy. "Land Use and Public Policy in Northern Canada." Ph.D., University of British Columbia, 1975.

2472 NELSON, J.G.; SCACE, R.C.; KOURI, R., eds. *Canadian Public Land Use in Perspective*. Ottawa: Social Science Research Council of Canada, 1976.

2473 PEARSON, Norman. *Land Banking: Principles and Practice*. Winnipeg: Research and Development Fund, Appraisal Institute of Canada, 1975.

2474 _____. *Towards a Methodology for Housing and Land-Bank Needs Analysis.* Toronto: Ontario Housing Corporation, 1973.

2475 PHELPS, G. "Need for Government Organization of Land Settlement." *Conservation of Life.* 4:1 (January 1918), pp. 3-8.

2476 PIPER, John. "Saskatoon Robs the Bank." *City Magazine.* 1:1 (October 1974), pp. 16-20.

2477 RAVIS, Don. *Advanced Land Acquisition by Local Government: The Saskatoon Experience.* Ottawa: Community Planning Association of Canada, 1973.

2478 RICHARDSON, Boyce. "Saskatoon: The City as Landowner." *Canadian Forum.* 52:616 (May 1972), pp. 42-44.

2479 ROBINSON, Ira M. "Trends in Provincial Land Planning, Control and Management." *Plan Canada.* 17:3, 4 (September/December 1977), pp. 166-83.

2480 SMITH, Lawrence B., and WALKER, Michael, eds. *Public Property? The Habitat Debate Continued.* Vancouver: The Fraser Institute, 1977.

2481 SPURR, Peter. *Land and Urban Development: A Preliminary Study.* Toronto: James Lorimer, 1976.

2482 TORONTO. City Planning Board. *Built-form Analysis: A Working Paper on the Implications for Built-form of Land-use Policies Relating to Housing, Mixed-uses, and Recreation Space in the Inner Core Area.* Toronto: The Board, 1975.

2483 WATSON, Kenneth Frank. "Landbanking in Red Deer." M.A., University of British Columbia, 1974.

10.1.3.9   Town Planning and Zoning

2484 BARRECA, Donna. "Housing Code Enforcement in Montreal." M.S.W., Carleton University, 1975.

2485 CARVER, Humphrey. "Housing Needs and Community Planning." *Canadian Welfare.* 24:7 (January 1949), pp. 35-40.

2486 CAUCHON, Noulan. "Town Planning For Canada: Address to the Social Service Council of Canada." *Social Welfare.* 8:5 (February/March 1926), pp. 92-95.

2487 CHARLES, Réjane. *Le zonage au Québec, un mort en sursis.* Montreal: Les Presses de l'université de Montréal, 1974.

2488 "Criticism of the Toronto Building By-Law." *Contract Record.* 25:20 (1911), pp. 42-51.

2489 DONALD, W.J. "Zoning Cities for Tomorrow." *Canadian Engineer.* 4 (December 1919), pp. 510-12.

2490 GERTLER, L.O. *The Process of New City Planning and Building.* Waterloo: School of Urban and Regional Planning, University of Waterloo, 1971.

2491 "Grants and the Housing Code, Montreal." *Urban Renewal and Low Income Housing.* 7:2 (1971), pp. 14-18.

2492 HANCOCK, Macklin L. "Policies for New Towns: Policies, Problems and Prospects in Legislation, Design and Administration." *Ontario Housing.* 11:3 (Summer 1965), pp. 4-11.

2493 HASON, Nino. *The Emergence and Development of Zoning Controls in North American Municipalities: A Critical Analysis.* Toronto: Department of Urban and Regional Planning, Toronto: University of Toronto, 1977.

2494 HODGETTS, C.A. "Town Planning and Housing." *Public Health Journal.* 3:2 (February 1912), pp. 61-63.

2495 _____. "Town Planning and Housing." *The Contract Record.* 25:52 (1911), pp. 52-53.

2496 LAW SOCIETY OF UPPER CANADA. *Current Problems in Development, Planning and Zoning.* Toronto: The Society. Department of Continuing Education, 1976.

2497 "New Building By-Law for Toronto." *Canadian Engineer.* 22:22 (1912), pp. 736-39.

2498 OBERLANDER, H.P. "Community Planning and Housing: An Aspect of Canadian Federalism." Ph.D., Harvard University, 1957.

2499 _____. "Community Planning and Housing: Step-Children of Canadian Federalism." *Queen's Quarterly.* 67:4 (Winter 1960-61), pp. 663-72.

2500 ONTARIO ECONOMIC COUNCIL. *Subject to Approval: A Review of Municipal Planning in Ontario.* Toronto: The Council, 1973.

2501 "Recent Town Planning Progress in Maritime Provinces." *Report.* Sixth Annual Meeting of the Commission of Conservation. Ottawa: The Commission, 1915, pp. 285-302.

2502 "Revision of the Toronto Building By-Law." *Canadian Engineer.* 26:26 (1911), pp. 713-14; 721-23.

2503 ROGERS, Ian MacFee. *Canadian Law of Planning and Zoning.* Toronto: Carswell, 1973.

2504 ROYAL ARCHITECTURAL INSTITUTE OF CANADA. *Reflections on Zoning: The Report of the Zoning Study Committee.* Ottawa: Study Committee, The Institute, 1964.

10.1.4   Policy Analysis

10.1.4.1   General

2505 AUDAIN, Michael. "Transforming Housing Into A Social Service." *Plan Canada.* 13:2 (1973), pp. 91-111.

2506 AXWORTHY, L., and GILLIES, James H. *Canada's Prospects, Canada's Problems.* Toronto: Butterworth, 1973.

2507 BLAND, J., and SCHOENAVER, Naber. *University Housing in Canada.* Montreal: McGill University Press, 1966.

2508 BOURNE, L.S. *The Housing Supply and Price Debate: Divergent Views and Policy Consequences.* Toronto: Centre for Urban and Community Studies, University of Toronto, 1977.

2509 *Canadian Labour.* Issue on Housing. 11:3 (March 1966).

2510 CARVER, Humphrey. *Houses for Canadians: A Study of Housing Problems in the Toronto Area.* Toronto: University of Toronto Press, 1948.

2511 CHUNG, Joseph H., and ANH, T.M. *Cyclical Instability in Residential Construction in Canada.* Ottawa: Economic Council of Canada, 1976.

2512 CLARKSON, Stephen. *City Lib.* Toronto: Hakkert, 1972.

2513 DALE-JOHNSON, David Terrance. "Housing Policy, Tenure Choice and the Demand for Housing in Greater Vancouver." M.Sc., University of British Columbia, 1975.

2514 _____. "Government Housing Policies and Programs: Their Impact on Housing Demand in British Columbia." In *Housing: Its Your Move,* A Report Prepared by a Study Team in the Urban Land Economics Division, Faculty of Commerce and Business Administration, University of British Columbia. pp. Vancouver, 1976.

2515 DIAMOND, A.E. *Le logement au cours des années soixante-dix: une perspective du secteur privé/ Housing in the Nineteen-Seventies: A View From the Private Sector.* Ottawa: Canadian Housing Design Council, 1970.

2516 DONNISON, D.V. *Housing Problems and Policies: An Introduction.* Background Paper prepared for the Canadian Conference on Housing, 20-23 October 1968. Ottawa: Canadian Welfare Council, 1968.

2517 _____. "A Housing Policy." *Canadian Welfare.* 44:5 (September/October 1978), pp. 5-9.

2518 FELDMAN, L.D., and GOLDRICK, M.D., eds. *Politics and Government of Urban Canada: Selected Readings.* Toronto: Methuen, 1969.

2519 FREEMAN, Wylie. "The Housing Crisis and Government Response." *Architecture Canada.* 4:45 (April 1968), pp. 69-71.

2520 GOLDSMITH, M.J. *Housing Demands and Housing Policy — A Case Study.* Kingston: Queen's University, 1972.

2521 GUTSTEIN, Donald. *Vancouver Ltd.* Toronto: James Lorimer, 1975.

2522 HAMILTON-WRIGHT, Heather Jane. "Canadian Housing Policy and the Future Demand for Housing: A Demographic Analysis and a Look Into the Future." M.Sc., University of British Columbia, 1977.

2523 LACASSE, François D. *Politiques du logement: analyse économique.* Montreal: Conseil de bien-être du Québec, 1971.

2524 LORIMER, James, and ROSS, Evelyn, eds. *The City Book: The Politics and Planning of Canada's Cities.* Toronto: James Lorimer, 1976.

2525 _____. *The Second City Book: Studies in Urban and Suburban Canada.* Toronto: James Lorimer, 1977.

2526 MATSUSHITA, Ronald, ed. *Housing: Issues for the Seventies.* Toronto: McGraw-Hill, 1971.

2527 MORTON, Desmond, and KUMOVE, Leon. *Housing: The Predictable Crisis.* Toronto: Woodsworth Memorial Foundation, 1967.

2528 MURPHY, Rae. "Home is Where the $50,000 Mortgage Is." *Last Post.* 4:2 (August 1974), pp. 29-33.

2529 OBERLANDER, Peter H., ed. *Canada: An Urban Agenda: A Collection of Papers.* Ottawa: Community Planning Press, 1976.

2530 ONTARIO ASSOCIATION OF HOUSING AUTHORITIES. *Good Housing for Canadians.* A Study by the Ontario Association of Housing Authorities. Ottawa: The Association, 1964.

2531 "Pour une politique nouvelle de l'habitation." *Revue maintenant.* 113 (February 1972), p. 34.

2532 ROSE, Albert. "Housing and Social Welfare." In *Trans-Disciplinary Issues in Social Welfare,* edited by Paul C. Vrooman, pp. 37-52. Waterloo: Graduate School of Social Work, 1973.

2533 SAYEGH, Karnal S., ed. *Canadian Housing: A Reader.* Waterloo: University of Waterloo Press, 1972.

2534 SMART, Alice. "Housing and Social Work." *Canadian Welfare.* 37:5 (September 1961), pp. 228-33.

2535 SMITH, James. "What To Do (Or Not To Do) About the High Price of Houses." *Saturday Night.* 88:11 (November 1973), pp. 15-19.

2536 SMITH, L.B. "Housing Issues and Housing Policy." In *Issues in Canadian Economics,* edited by L.H. Officer and L.B. Smith, pp. 383-94. Toronto: McGraw-Hill Ryerson, 1974.

2537 STEWART, Walter. "The Wrong Way to Solve the Housing Crisis." *Maclean's.* 83:2 (February 1970), pp. 23-27.

2538 WRIGHT, R.W. "Housing as an Instrument of Social Policy." *Journal of Canadian Studies.* 4:2 (May 1969), pp. 19-30.

10.1.4.2 Federal

2539 AXWORTHY, Lloyd. "The Task Force on Housing: A Case Study." In *The Structure of Policy-Making in Canada*, edited by G. Bruce Doern and Peter Aucoin. pp. 130-53. Toronto: Macmillan, 1971.

2540 _____. "The Task Force on Housing and Urban Development: A Study of Democratic Decision-Making in Canada." Ph.D., Princeton University, 1972.

2541 BARKER, Graham; PENNEY, Jennifer; SECCOMBE, Wally. *Highrise and Superprofits*. Kitchener: Dumont Press Graphix, 1973.

2542 _____. "The Developers." *Canadian Dimension*, 9:2 (January 1973), pp. 19-50.

2543 BARROW, Malcolm McDonald. "Federal Housing Policies and the Developing Urban Structure, Conflict and Resolution." M.A., University of British Columbia, 1967.

2544 BERGER, Sara. "The House that CMHC Built." *Canadian Dimension*, 8:8 (August 1972), pp. 11-18.

2545 BINHAMMER, H.H. "The Fiscal Implications of a Housing Program." *Canadian Journal of Economics and Political Science*. 29:3 (August 1963), pp. 336-47.

2546 CANADIAN COUNCIL ON SOCIAL DEVELOPMENT. *Where the $200 Million Went*. Ottawa: The Council, 1971.

2547 CLAYTON, Frank. "The Dennis Report — Another Point of View." *Housing and People*. 4:1 (Spring 1973), p. 11.

2548 DIAMOND, A.J. *Housing in Canada: Problems and Possibilities*. Toronto: University of Toronto, 1973.

2549 GERMAIN, Denis. "La politique fédérale du logement." *Actualité économique*. 39:1 (April/June 1963), pp. 96-107.

2550 JACKSON, Roger. *Housing Study: A Partial Review of Federal, Provincial and Municipal Housing Policies and Programs*. Edmonton: Roger Jackson, 1972.

2551 KURTZ, Larry Robert. "Public Policy and the Housing Problem: Goals, Programs and Policy Constraints." Ph.D., University of Toronto, 1977.

2552 RENY, Paul. "Le problème du logement au Canada: analyse du discours politique." M.A., Laval University, 1974.

2553 SHAFFNER, Richard. *Housing Policy in Canada; Learning from Recent Problems*. Montreal: C.D. Howe Research Institute, 1975.

2554 SMITH, L.B. *Anatomy of a Crisis: Canadian Housing Policy in the Seventies*. Vancouver: Fraser Institute, 1977.

2555 _____. *Housing in Canada: Market Structure and Policy Performance*. Ottawa: Central Mortgage and Housing Corporation, 1971.

2556 _____. *Le logement au Canada: structure du marché et application et resultats des politiques*. Ottawa: Société centrale d'hypothèques et de logement, 1971.

2557 _____. "The Housing Market, the Housing Problem and Government Policy." edited by L.H. Officer and L.B. Smith. In *Canadian Economic Problems and Policies*. McGraw-Hill Ryerson, 1970. pp. 242-57.

2558 _____. "Housing Task Force." *Canadian Banker*. 76 (March/April 1969), pp. 42-43.

2559 SMITH, R.T. "The Politics of Housing and Urban Development: A Case Study of the Central Mortgage and Housing Corporation." M.A., University of Waterloo, 1972.

2560 "William Teron vs. Walter Rudnicki: How Ottawa Does Its Business."
     City Magazine. 2:5 (November 1976), pp. 14-24.

10.1.4.3   Provincial and Municipal

2561 ANTOFT, Kell. "Recommendations of the Graham Commission with
     Respect to Housing." *Housing and People*. 7:1 (Spring 1976), p. 8-11.
2562 AQUIN, Thérèse. "Task Force Studies Quebec Housing/Le groupe de
     travail sur l'habitation au Québec." *Living Places/ Cadres de vie*. 1:1
     (1975), pp. 26-29.
2563 BENJAMIN, Jacques. *Planification et politique au Québec*. Montreal: Les
     Presses de l'université de Montréal, 1974.
2564 CAULFIELD, John. "Making Toronto Safe-Once More-for the Develo-
     pers." *City Magazine*. 1:2 (December/January 1975), pp. 29-38.
2565 CHUNG, Joseph H. *Une politique de l'habitation au Québec*. Montreal:
     Université du Québec à Montréal, 1976.
2566 CONFEDERATION DES SYNDICATS NATIONAUX. Comité central
     d'action, Secretariat. *Le logement au Québec*. Montreal, 1970.
2567 DERKOWSKI, Andrzej. "The Effects of Planning Controls on Housing
     Prices." *Housing and People*. 7:4 (Winter/Spring 1977), pp. 5-8.
2568 DIVAY, Gérard. "Les rapports Legault et Castonguay: perspectives
     montréalaise et provinciale sur l'habitation au Québec." *Housing and
     People*. 7:1 (Spring 1976) pp. 1-7.
2569 _____, and GODBOUT, Jacques. *Les interventions gouvernementales
     dans le domaine de l'habitation*. Montreal: Institute de la recherche
     scientifique, Urbanisation, 1975.
2570 _____. Une politique de logement au Québec? Montréal: les Presses
     de l'université du Québec, 1973.
2571 GODBOUT, Jacques. *Des conséquences sociales de l'intervention publique
     sur le logement locatif au Québec*. Montreal: Institut de la recherche
     scientifique, urbanisation, 1974.
2572 HEUNG, Raymond. *The Do's and Don'ts of Housing Policy: The Case of
     British Columbia*. Vancouver: Fraser Institute, 1976.
2573 LEGAULT, J.R., ed. *Le programme de logement de l'Ontario*. Quebec: Edi-
     teur officiel du Québec, 1976.
2574 LOGAN, C. Orton. "Area Housing Authorities: Quality and Flexibility."
     Ontario Housing. 16:1 (March 1971), pp. 21-22.
2575 McAFEE, Ann. "The Vancouver City Non-Profit Housing Experience."
     Housing and People. 7:1 (Spring 1976), pp. 21-25.
2576 McGUIRE, John., comp. and ed. *The Housing Problem in Manitoba —
     What Can Be Done!* Proceedings of a seminar sponsored by the
     Manitoba Economic Development Advisory Board. Winnipeg, 1976.
2577 McKENNA, B. "The OMB: Citizens as Losers." In *The City Book; The
     Politics and Planning of Canada's Cities*, edited by James Lorimer and
     Evelyn Ross, pp. 197-203. Toronto: James Lorimer, 1976.
2578 MARKUSEN, J.R., and SCHEFFMAN, D.T. *Speculation and Monopoly
     in Urban Development: Analytical Foundations with Evidence for Toronto*.
     Toronto: University of Toronto Press, 1977.
2579 ONTARIO ECONOMIC COUNCIL. *Housing: Issues and Alternatives
     1976*. Toronto: The Council, 1976.
2580 ONTARIO WELFARE COUNCIL. *Housing in Ontario: A sourcebook*.
     Toronto: The Council, 1973.
2581 _____. *The Municipal Role in Housing*. Toronto: The Council, 1974.
2582 _____. *A Study of Housing Policies in Ontario: General Report*. Toronto:
     The Council, 1973.

2583 PETER BARNARD ASSOCIATES. *The Role of the Ontario Housing Corporation in System Building.* Toronto: Queen's Printer, 1970.

2584 SETH, Ram P., and DICKSON, Janet J. *Evaluation of the Housing Programmes Embodied in the Prince Edward Island Development Plan.* Halifax: Institute of Public Affairs, Dalhousie University, 1974.

2585 SHARPE, Christopher Andrew. *Public Policy and the Apartment Development Process.* Toronto: Centre for Urban and Community Studies, University of Toronto, 1970.

2586 SOCIAL PLANNING AND REVIEW COUNCIL OF BRITISH COLUMBIA HOUSING COMMITTEE. *Housing Programs in British Columbia.* Vancouver: Housing Committee of Social Planning and Review Council of British Columbia and Students at the School of Community and Regional Planning, University of British Columbia, 1975.

10.1.5 Finance

2587 CANADIAN ECONOMIC SERVICES. *An Analysis of the Role of Central Mortgage and Housing Corporation and the Mortgage Insurance Fund in the Residential Mortgage Market in Canada and the Development of Criteria for Approval of Central Mortgage and Housing Corporation Approved Lenders.* Ottawa, 1975.

2588 CANADIAN LIFE INSURANCE ASSOCIATION. *Implications of the Report of the Royal Commission on Taxation for Housing and The Mortgage Market.* Toronto: The Association, 1967.

2589 CHUNG, Joseph H. "Housing and Mortgage Loans: Postwar Canadian Experience." Ph.D., University of Toronto, 1967.

2590 CLINTON, K.J. "Portfolio Behaviour of the Trust and Mortgage Loan Companies of Canada, 1967-1972: A Theoretical and Econometric Analysis." Ph.D., University of Western Ontario, 1973.

2591 D'ANDREA, John T. *The Canadian Mortgage Market.* Ottawa: Bank of Canada, 1975.

2592 GILLIES, J. "Some Financial Aspects of the Canadian Government Housing Program: History and Prospective Developments." *Journal of Finance.* 8:1 (March 1953), pp. 22-33.

2593 HATCH, James E. *The Canadian Mortgage Market.* Toronto: Queen's Printer, 1975.

2594 ONTARIO WELFARE COUNCIL. *Community Housing Interim Finance Problems.* Toronto: The Council, 1976.

2595 POAPST, J.V. "New Pillars of the Home Mortgage Market." *Canadian Banker.* 81:4 (1974), pp. 10-13.

2596 SMITH, L.B. *The Post-War Canadian Housing and Residential Mortgage Markets and the Role of the Government.* Toronto: University of Toronto Press, 1974.

2597 _____. "A Model of the Canadian Housing and Mortgage Markets." *Journal of Political Economy.* 77:5 (September/October 1969), pp. 795-816.

2598 _____. "The Post-War Residential Mortgage Market and the Role of the Government." Ph.D., Harvard University, 1966.

2599 _____, and SPARKS, Gordon R. *Institutional Mortgage Lending in Canada, 1954-1968: An Econometric Analysis.* Ottawa: Bank of Canada, 1973.

2600 SUSSMAN, Edward. "The Evolving Mortgage Market." *Canadian Banker.* 72:1 (Spring 1965), pp. 43-55.

10.1.6   Market Relations

10.1.6.1   Rent Control

2601 BRENNER, Joel F., and FRANKLIN, Herbert M. *Rent Control in North America and Four European Countries.* Washington: Council for International Urban Liaison, 1977.

2602 BUCKNALL, Brian. "Rent Review in Ontario: Policy, Politics and the Well-Paved Road." *Housing and People.* 8:2 (Fall/Winter 1977), pp. 8-12.

2603 CANADIAN COUNCIL ON SOCIAL DEVELOPMENT. *Is There a Case for Rent Control?* Background Papers and Proceedings of a Canadian Council on Social Development Seminar on Rent Policy. Ottawa: The Council, 1973.

2604 DONNISON, David. "Rent Regulation: Guidelines for Policy?" *Housing and People.* 3:3, 4 (Fall/Winter 1972), pp. 7-10.

2605 FRANKENA, Mark W. *Alternative Models of Rent Control.* London: Department of Economics, University of Western Ontario, 1975.

2606 HAMILTON, S.W., and BAXTER, David. *Landlords and Tenants in Danger.* Winnipeg: Appraisal Institute of Canada, 1975.

2607 HAYEK, F.A. *et al. Rent Control: A Popular Paradox: Evidence on the Economic Effect of Rent Control.* Vancouver: Fraser Institute, 1975.

2608 MATHEWS, Georges. *La théorie économique et le contrôle des loyers.* Montreal: Institut national de la recherche scientifique, Urbanisation, 1978.

2609 Ontario. Law Reform Commission. "Rent Control." *Interim Report on Landlord and Tenant Law Applicable to Residential Tenancies.* Toronto: The Commission, 1968.

2610 OWEN, David. "Rent Controls: Solution or Problem." *Saskatchewan Law Review.* 41:3 (1976-77), pp. 3-18.

2611 PATTERSON, Jeffrey, and WATSON, Ken. *Rent Stabilization: A Review of Current Policies in Canada.* Ottawa: Canadian Council on Social Development, 1976.

2612 "A Reponse to Rent Control From Legal Aid Societies." *Housing and People.* 8:2 (Fall/Winter 1977), pp. 16-17.

2613 SOCIAL PLANNING COUNCIL OF METROPOLITAN TORONTO. Community Review and Research Group. *Rent Controls: Why We Need Them, What Kind, How Long: A Background Analysis.* Toronto, The Council, 1975.

2614 WATSON, Ken. "Rent De-Control." *Housing and People.* 8:2 (Fall/Winter 1977), pp. 3-7.

2615 WHITELAW, John. "Taking the Teeth Out of the Ontario Rent Review." *City Magazine.* 4:1 (January 1979), pp. 41-45.

10.1.6.2   Taxation

2616 BIRD, R.M. "The Incidence of the Property Tax: Old Wine in New Bottles?" *Canadian Public Policy.* II Supplement (1976), pp. 323-34.

2617 _____, and SLACK, N.E. *Residential and Property Tax Relief in Ontario.* Toronto: University of Toronto Press, 1978.

2618 BUREAU OF MUNICIPAL RESEARCH. "Property Taxation and Land Development." *Civic Affairs.* 2 (1973).

2619 CANADIAN PUBLIC POLICY. "Property Tax Reform." II Supplement, 1976.

2620 CANADIAN TAX FOUNDATION. Corporate Management Tax Conference 1977. *Income Tax Treatment of Real Estate Transactions.* Toronto: The Foundation, 1978.

2621 CLAYTON, Frank. "Income Taxes and Subsidies to Homeowners and Renters: A Comparison to United States and Canadian Experience." *Canadian Tax Journal.* 16:3 (May/June 1974), pp. 295-305.

2622 _____. "Real Property Tax Assessment Practices in Canada." *Canadian Public Policy.* II Supplement (1976), pp. 347-62.

2623 _____. "Taxation and Urban Policy in Canada." *Housing and People.* 7:4, (Winter/Spring 1977), pp. 11-14.

2624 FINNIS, Federic H. *Property Assessment in Canada.* Toronto: Canadian Tax Foundation, 1970.

2625 _____. "Slums and Property Taxation." *Canadian Tax Journal.* 16:2 (March 1968), pp. 154-58.

2626 GLASSMAN, Martyn, and JAWOSIK, George. "Social Costs and Lost Revenue: The Tax Shelter Game." *Housing and People.* 8:3 (Spring 1978) pp. 3-7.

2627 HUDSON, Clayton A. *The Land Transfer Tax Act 1974.* Toronto: Butterworth, 1975.

2628 JOHNSON, J.A. "Municipal Tax Reform — Alternative to the Real Property Tax." *Canadian Public Policy.* 2 Supplement (1976), pp. 335-45.

2629 MacKENZIE, Hugh. "Ontario's Land Speculation Tax." *City Magazine.* 1:1 (October 1974), pp. 31-36.

2630 MARTIN, Joe. "Real Property Taxation: Stirrings of Reform." *Canadian Tax Journal.* 20:5 (September/October 1972), pp. 437-52.

2631 ONTARIO. Commission on the Reform of Property Taxation. *Report.* Toronto: The Commission, 1977.

2632 ONTARIO. Department of Municipal Affairs. *Real Property Taxation: History, Theory and Administration.* Toronto, 1971.

2633 SANTOS, Benjamin R. "Property Taxation and Housing Market Analysis." Ph.D., University of Manitoba, 1974.

2634 WOLFF, Horst G. "The White Paper: Tax Treatment of Principal Residences." *Canadian Tax Journal.* 18:4 (July/August 1970), pp. 263-76.

10.1.6.3 Housing Subsidies

2635 ANGUS, H.F. "The Great Canadian Housing Subsidy." *Canadian Tax Journal.* 3:3 (May/June 1955), pp. 178-80.

2636 BELLA, Leslie, and PATTERSON, Jeffrey. "The Assisted Home Ownership Program: How it Doesn't Help Those Whose Need is Greatest." *Canadian Welfare.* 50:4 (July/August 1974), pp. 20-21.

2637 KITCHEN, Harry. "Imputed Rent on Owner-Occupied Dwellings." *Canadian Tax Journal.* 15:5 (September/October 1967), pp. 482-91.

2638 _____. "Homeowner grants." *Canadian Tax Journal.* 15:1 (January/February 1967), pp. 63-67.

2639 McFADYEN, Stuart. "British Columbia's Home-Owner Grant Program: Has it Reduced Property Taxes?" *Canadian Tax Journal.* 18:5 (September/October 1970), pp. 420-34; 18:6 (November/December 1970), pp. 533-39.

2640 PATTERSON, Jeffrey. "Housing and Income Security: A Look at Shelter Allowances." *Canadian Welfare.* 50:2 (March/April 1974), pp. 9-12.

2641 WHEELER, Michael. "Why Not a National Housing Allowance?" *Canadian Welfare.* 44:4 (September/October 1968), pp. 9-12.

10.1.6.4 Landlord-Tenant Relations

2642 AUDAIN, Michael, and BRADSHAW, Chris. *Tenant Rights in Canada.* Ottawa: Canadian Council on Social Development, 1971.

2643 BRACE, Paul. *Guide to Landlord and Tenant Law in Ontario.* Toronto: Coles Publishing, 1977.

2644 CAMPFENS, Hubert. "Landlord-Tenant Relations in High Rise Apartments." *Housing and People.* 3:3,4 (Fall/Winter 1972), pp. 16-18.

2645 DAVIS, Donald. "Tenant Associations: In Search of the Elusive Quality of Life." *Ontario Housing.* 16:1 (March 1971), p. 13.

2646 FAYERS, Heather. *Landlord Tenant Relations for British Columbia.* Vancouver: International Self-Counsel Press, 1976.

2647 FEDERATION OF METRO TENANTS' ASSOCIATIONS. *Your Rights As A Tenant.* Toronto: The Federation, n.d.

2648 FODDEN, S.R. "The Landlord-Tenant Act Since 1970." *Osgoode Hall Law Journal.* 12:2 (November 1974), pp. 441-74.

2649 HILL, P. Adrian. *Landlord and Tenant Rights and Responsibilities in Ontario.* Background Report for the Advisory Task Force on Housing Policy. Toronto, 1973.

2650 KROHN, Roger G., *et al. The Other Economy; the Internal Logic of Local Rental Housing.* Toronto: Peter Martin, 1977.

2651 LAMONT, Donald H.L. *Residential Tenancies — The Landlord and Tenant Act.* Toronto: Carswell, 1973.

2652 McINNES, Ron. *Ontario Landlord Tenant Relations.* Toronto: International Self-Counsel Press, 1972.

2653 MARTIN, D.L. "Civil Remedies Available to Residential Tenants in Ontario: The Case for Assertive Action." *Osgoode Hall Law Journal.* 14:1 (1976), pp. 65-92.

2654 NORTH YORK BOROUGH. *Report.* Special Task Force on Tenant and Landlord Obligations. Willowdale, Ontario, 1976.

2655 UNIVERSITY OF ALBERTA. Institute of Law Research and Reform. *Residential Tenancies Project.* Edmonton: Institute of Law Research and Reform, University of Alberta, 1975.

2656 WEINRIB, Arnold. "The Ontario Landlord and Tenant Amendment Act." *University of Toronto Law Journal.* 21:1 (1971), pp. 93-98.

10.2 Education Policy and Administration

10.2.1 *Historical Development*

10.2.1.1 General

2657 ADAMS, Howard. *The Education of Canadians 1800-1867: The Roots of Separatism.* Montreal: Harvest House, 1968.

2658 ADAMS, Howard Joseph. "The Role of Church and State in Canadian Education, 1800-1967." Ph.D., University of California (Berkeley), 1966.

2658 AUDET, Louis-Philippe. *Histoire de l'enseignement du Québec.* 2 vols. Toronto: Holt, Rinehart and Winston, 1971.

2659 BAIN, M. "1848-1966, du gouvernement responsable à l'éducation responsable." *Cahiers de Cité libre*. 17 (July/August 1966), pp. 10-13.

2660 BRETT, G.S. "Canada: Higher Education." *Annals of the American Academy of Political and Social Science*. 107 (May 1923), pp. 126-30.

2661 CHALMERS, John West. *Schools of the Foothills Province: The Story of Public Education in Alberta*. Toronto: University of Toronto Press, 1967.

2662 CHARBONNEAU, Jean Claude. "The Lay School Movement in Quebec since 1840." M.A., McGill University, 1972.

2663 CHAUVEAU, Pierre Joseph Olivier. *L'instruction publique au Canada: précis historique et statistique*. Quebec: Imprimeur A. Coté, 1876.

2664 CLAGUE, Robert E. "The Political Aspects of the Manitoba School Question 1890-1896." M.A., University of Manitoba, 1939.

2665 CLARK, Lovell, ed. *The Manitoba School Question: Majority Rule or Minority Rights?* Toronto: Copp Clark, 1968.

2666 COOK, G.R. "Church, Schools and Politics in Manitoba, 1903-1912." *Canadian Historical Review*. 39:1 (March 1958), pp. 1-23.

2667 CRUNICAN, Paul. *Priests and Politicians: Manitoba Schools and the Election of 1896*. Toronto: University of Toronto Press, 1974.

2668 _____. "The Manitoba School Question and Canadian Federal Politics, 1890-1896: A Study of Church-State Relations." Ph.D., University of Toronto, 1968.

2669 DENT, Melville, *et al. The Story of the Women Teachers' Association of Toronto*. Vol. 1. Toronto: Thomas Nelson, 1963.

2670 DHILLON, Pritman S. "An Historical Study of Aims of Education in Ontario 1800-1900." Ed.D., University of Toronto, 1961.

2671 "Enquête royale sur l'éducation en Ontario." *Culture*. 7 (March 1946), pp. 3-76.

2672 FIRESTONE, O.J. *Industry and Education: A Century of Canadian Development*. Ottawa: University of Ottawa Press, 1969.

2673 FLETCHER, B.A. "A Century of Educational Organization, 1838-1938." *Public Affairs*. 1 (August 1938), pp. 18-22.

2674 FRENCH, Doris. *High Button Bootstraps: Federation of Women Teachers' Associations of Ontario, 1918-1968*. Toronto: Ryerson, 1968.

2675 GOULSON, Carlyn Floyd. "An Historical Survey of Royal Commissions and Other Major Government Inquiries in Canadian Education." Ed.D., University of Toronto, 1966.

2676 HAMILTON, William Baille. "Education, Politics and Reform in Nova Scotia, 1800-1848." Ph.D., University of Western Ontario, 1970.

2677 HARRIS, Robin S. *Quiet Revolution: A Study of the Educational System of Ontario*. Toronto: University of Toronto, 1967.

2678 HODGINS, J.G. *Documentary History of Education in Upper Canada from the Passing of the Constitutional Act of 1971 to the Close of the Rev. Dr. Ryerson's Administration of the Education Department in 1876*. Toronto: King's Printer, 1902.

2679 _____. *Historical and Other Papers and Documents Illustrative of the Educational System of Ontario 1856-1872*. Six vols. Toronto: King's Printer, 1911-12.

2680 _____. *The Legislation and History of Separate Schools in Upper Canada from 1841 to 1876*. Toronto: William Briggs, 1897.

2681 HOUSTON, Susan Elizabeth. "Politics, Schools and Social Change in Upper Canada between 1836 and 1846." M.A., University of Toronto, 1967.

2682 HUNTE, Keith D. "The Development of the System of Education in Canada East 1841-1867; An Historical Study." M.A., McGill University, 1962.

2683 _____. "The Ministry of Public Instruction in Quebec, 1867-1875: A Historical Study." Ph.D., McGill University, 1964.

2684 JOHNSON, F.H. *A Brief History of Canadian Education.* Toronto: McGraw-Hill, 1968.

2685 _____. *A History of Public Education in British Columbia.* Vancouver: University of British Columbia, 1964.

2686 _____. "Canadian Public Education at the Time of Confederation." *Journal of Education in British Columbia.* 13 (May 1967), pp. 40-48.

2687 JONES, Alan H. "The Role of Pressure Groups in the Educational System of the Province of Ontario." M.A., University of Michigan, 1961.

2688 KEANE, P. "A Study in Early Problems and Policies in Adult Education: The Halifax Mechanic's Institute." *Histoire sociale/ Social History.* 8:16 (November 1975), pp. 225-75.

2689 KIDD, J.R. "A Study of the Influence of Dr. H.M. Tory on Educational Policy in Canada." M.A., McGill University, 1945.

2690 LAJEUNESSE, Marcel. *L'éducation au Québec. [19ᵉ — 20ᵉ siècles.]* Montreal: Editions du Boréal Express, 1971.

2691 LAROSE, Wesley Allan. "The Struggle for a Federal Office of Education for Canada." M.A., McGill University, 1975.

2692 LAWR, Douglas Archie, and GIDNEY, Robert D. *Educating Canadians: A Documentary History of Public Education.* Toronto: Van Nostrand Reinhold, 1973.

2693 LEES, J.G. *et al.,* eds. *An Educational Quo Vadis: Development of Education in the Atlantic Provinces and Future Trends.* Toronto: Ryerson, 1969.

2694 McFATRIDGE, W., comp. "A Documentary Study of Early Educational Policy." *Nova Scotia: Public Archives Bulletin.* 1:1 (1937), pp. 1-60.

2695 MacKENZIE, Eric Duncan. "The Historical Development of the New Brusnwick Teacher's Association, 1902-1954." M.Ed., University of New Brunswick, 1971.

2696 McLEOD, Keith A. "Politics, Schools and the French Language, 1881-1931." In *Politics in Saskatchewan,* edited by Norman Ward and D.S. Spafford. pp. 124-50. Longmans, 1968.

2697 MacNAUGHTON, Katherine C. *The Development of the Theory and Practice of Education in New Brunswick, 1784-1900: A Study in Historical Background.* Fredericton: University of New Brunswick Press, 1947.

2698 McQUEEN, J. "The Development of the Technical and Vocational Schools of Ontario." M.A., Columbia University, 1935.

2699 MAKOON-SINGH, Jerome Ambrose. "An Investigation into the School Acts of Nova Scotia Between 1808 and 1867 with Specific Reference to School Administration." M.A., Dalhousie University, 1971.

2700 NASON, Gerald. "The Canadian Teachers' Federation: A Study of Its Historical Development, Interests and Activities from 1919-1960." Ed.D., Toronto University, 1964.

2701 NICHOLSON, Kenneth Maxwell. "Policies of the Ontario Department of Education during the Administration of Premier E.C. Drury, 1919-1923." M.A., University of Toronto, 1972.

2702 "Papers on Teachers Associations." *Journal of Education for Ontario.* 18:10 (October 1965), pp. 146-55.

2703 PATTERSON, Robert Steven. "The Establishment of Progressive Education in Alberta." Ph.D., Michigan State University, 1968.

2704 PERRAULT, M.J. "Enquête royale sur l'éducation." *Culture* 7 (September 1946), pp. 342-52.

2705 PHILLIPS, C.E. *The Development of Education in Canada.* Toronto: W.J. Gage, 1957.

2706 PRENTICE, Alison L. *From Private Servant to Public Servant: Status, Sex and Hierarchy in the Mid-Nineteenth Century Ontario Teaching Profession.* Toronto: Ontario Institute for Studies in Education, 1976.

2707 _____. *The School Promoters. Education and Social Class in Mid-Nineteenth Century Upper Canada.* Toronto: McClelland and Stewart, 1977.

2708 PURDY, Judson Douglas. "John Strachan and Education in Canada 1800-1851." Ph.D., University of Toronto, 1962.

2709 _____. "John Strachan's Educational Policies, 1815-1841." *Ontario History.* 64:1 (March 1972), pp. 45-64.

2710 PUTMAN, J. Harold. *Egerton Ryerson and Education in Upper Canada.* Toronto: William Briggs, 1912.

2711 READY, William Bernard. "The Political Implications of the Manitoba School Question 1896-1916." M.A., University of Manitoba, 1948.

2712 ROWE, Frederick William. *The Development of Education in Newfoundland.* Toronto: Ryerson Press, 1964.

2713 _____. *History of Education in Newfoundland.* Toronto: Ryerson, 1952.

2714 _____. "History of Education in Newfoundland." *Canadian College of Teachers.* 8 (1965), pp. 40-56.

2715 RUSAK, Stephen T. "Archbishop Adelard Langevin and the Manitoba School Question, 1895-1915." Ph.D., University of Alberta, 1975.

2716 SISSONS, C.B. *Church and State in Canadian Education: A Historical Study.* Toronto: Ryerson, 1959.

2717 SPRAGGE, George W. "The Upper Canada Central School." *Papers and Records, Ontario Historical Society.* 32 (1937), pp. 171-91.

2718 STEWART, Freeman K. "The Canadian Education Association: Its History and Role." M.Ed., University of Toronto, 1956.

2719 TALLENTIRE, Rex. "The Development of National Purpose in Canadian Education, 1945-1967." M.A., McGill University, 1971.

2720 TOOMBS, Morley Preston. "The Control and Support of Public Education in Rupert's Land and the North West Territories to 1905 and in Saskatchewan to 1960." Ph.D., University of Minnesota, 1962.

2721 TURNER, Allan R. "W.R. Motherwell and Agricultural Education, 1905-1918." *Saskatchewan History.* 12:3 (Autumn 1959), pp. 81-97.

2722 WALKER, Bernal Ernest. "Public Secondary Education in Alberta: Organization and Curriculum 1889-1951." Ph.D., Stanford University, 1955.

2723 WALKER, Eva K. *The Story of the Women Teachers' Association of Toronto.* Vol. 2. Toronto: Copp Clark, 1963.

2724 WALLACE, R.C. "Education in Canada." *Annals of American Academy of Political and Social Science.* 253 (September 1947), pp. 176-83.

2725 WILSON, J.D. "The Teacher in Early Ontario." In *Aspects of Nineteenth Century Ontario,* edited by F.A. Armstrong, H.A. Stevenson, and J.D. Wilson. pp. 223-29. Toronto: University of Toronto Press, 1974.

2726 _____, STAMP, R.M., and AUDET, L.P. *Canadian Education: A History.* Scarborough: Prentice Hall, 1970.

2727 WILSON, Keith. "The Development of Education in Manitoba." Ph.D., Michigan State University, 1967.

10.2.1.2 Reviews of Policy

2728 ADAM, G.M. "Coeducation." *Bystander.* 1 (November 1880), pp. 591-92, 633-37.

2729 _____. "Coeducation." *Bystander.* 2 (April 1883), p. 103.

2730 _____. "The Education Depository." *Bystander.* 2 (April 1881), p. 184.

2731 _____. "The Education Imbroglio." *Bystander.* 1 (August 1880), p. 416.

2732 _____. "The Education Report." *Bystander.* (May 1890), p. 267.

2733 _____. "Educational Reforms." *Bystander.* 1 (March 1880), p. 128.

2734 _____. "Our Educational System." *Bystander.* 2 (January 1881), p. 16.

2735 _____. "Improvements in the Endowments to Universities." *Bystander.* 2 (January 1883), p. 68.

2736 _____. "Public School Expenditure." *Bystander.* (July 1890), p. 317.

2737 _____. "Separate Schools." *Bystander.* 2 (June 1881), p. 308.

2738 _____. "Separate Schools." *Bystander.* (October 1889), p. 17.

2739 _____. "Separate Schools." *Bystander.* (May 1890), p. 243.

2740 ALTHOUSE, J.G. *Structure and Aims of Canadian Education.* Toronto: W.J. Gage, 1949.

2741 ARES, Richard. "L'aide fédérale à l'éducation." *Relations.* 188 (September 1956), pp. 211-14; 189 (December 1956), pp. 236-38.

2742 BYRNE, T.C. "Role of the Province in Instructional Improvement." *Canadian Education.* 13 (1958), pp. 52-67.

2743 BUSH, Douglas. "Some Notes on University Education." *Canadian Forum.* 6:69 (June 1926), pp. 272-74.

2744 CAMERON, M.A. "Education and the Rowell-Sirois Report." *School Secondary Edition.* 29:5 (January 1941), pp. 424-27.

2745 CANADIAN SUPERINTENDENT. *Secondary Education in Canada.* Toronto: Ryerson Press, 1964.

2746 CANADIAN TEACHERS' FEDERATION. *A Brief Presented by the Canadian Teachers' Federation to the Royal Commission on Dominion-Provincial Relations.* Toronto: The Federation, 1938.

2747 CASSELMAN, Hubert. *The Middle Way to School and Economic Reconstruction.* M.A., University of Ottawa, 1940.

2748 CISTONE, Peter J. *School Boards and the Political Fact: A Report on the Conference; The Politics of Education; Some Main Themes and Issues.* Toronto: Ontario Institute for Studies in Education, 1972.

2749 CUDMORE, S.A. "Primary and Secondary Education in Canada." *Annals of the American Academy of Political and Social Science.* 107 (May 1923), pp. 120-25.

2750 ERICSON, D.E. "The Significance of State Education." *Canadian Forum.* 13:145 (October 1932), pp. 14-18.

2751 FLEMMING, William Gerald. *Ontario's Educative Society.* 7 vols. Toronto: University of Toronto Press, 1971.

2752 HART, Thomas. "The Educational System of Manitoba." *Queen's Quarterly.* 12:3 (January 1905), pp. 240-52.

2753 HOLLAND, John W., and McDIARMID, Garnet. "Education, Public Policy, and Personal Choice." In *From Quantitative to Qualitative Change in Ontario Education: A Festschrift for R.W.B. Jackson,* pp. 67-100. Toronto: Ontario Institute for Studies in Education, 1976.

2754 LANGFORD, Howard David. *Educational Service: It's Functions and Possibilities.* New York: Arno Press, 1972.

2755 LINGWOOD, F. Houchen. "The State Control of Education." D.Paed., Queen's University, 1911.

2756 LLOYD, Woodrow S. *The Role of the Government in Canadian Education.* Toronto: W.J. Gage, 1959.

2757 LUCAS, Barry Gillespie. "Federal Relations to Education in Canada, 1970: An Investigation of Programs, Policies and Directions." Ph.D., University of Michigan, 1971.

2758 MAGNUSON, Roger. *Education in the Province of Quebec.* United States Office of Education, Washington, D.C., 1969.

2759 MARCOTTE, Marcel. "Les devoirs de l'Etat dans l'éducation." *Relations.* 1:211 (July 1958), pp. 174-77; 2:212 (August 1958), pp. 200-204.

2760 _____. "Les droits de l'Etat dans l'éducation." *Relations.* 1:210 (June 1958), pp. 145-49.

2761 MARTELL, George, ed. *The Politics of the Canadian Public School.* Toronto: James, Lewis and Samuel, 1974.

2762 McCREADY, S.B. "Rural Education in Ontario." *Canadian Forum.* 13:154 (July 1933), pp. 376-78.

2763 McKINNON, Donald Taylor. "An Analysis of the Educational Effort of the Province of Manitoba." M.Ed., University of Manitoba, 1971.

2764 McPHEDRAN, Mary. "The Development of Professional Education for Social Work in Canada since 1928." *Social Worker.* 12:1 (September 1943), pp. 14-16.

2765 MEEK, Edward. *The Legal and Constitutional Aspects of the Manitoba School Question; the Statutes; the Privy Council Decisions; the Remedial Order and the Answer of Manitoba Considered.* Toronto: Hunter Rose, 1895.

2766 MERCHANT, F.W. *Report on the Condition of English-French Schools in the Province of Ontario.* Toronto: King's Printer, 1912.

2767 MITCHELL, G.W. "The New Ontario School Regulations." *Queen's Quarterly.* 12:1 (July 1904), pp. 28-34.

2768 MORSE, Charles, ed. "School Laws — Catholic Separate Schools in Ontario." *Canadian Bar Review.* 4:8 (1926), pp. 592-96; 5:3 (1927), p. 219.

2769 "Our Schools Serve the Ruling Class." *Community Schools* (May/June 1973), pp. 52-62.

2770 PATTERSON, Robert S., *et al.*, eds. *Profiles of Canadian Education.* Toronto: Heath, 1974.

2771 PUTMAN, J.H., and WEIR, G.M. *Survey of the School System.* Victoria: Charles F. Banfield, 1925.

2772 ROBBINS, J.E. "Canadian Education Viewed in the Light of Social Needs." *The Yearbook of Education, 1936.* (1936), pp. 601-17.

2773 SPRY, G. "University Control in Ontario." *Canadian Forum.* 6:68 (May 1926), pp. 234-35.

2774 STEVENSON, Hugh A., and WILSON, J. Donald, eds. *Precepts, Policy and Process: Perspective on Contemporary Canadian Education.* London, Ontario: Alexander, Blake Associates, 1977.

2775 SWIFT, William Herbert. *Trends in Canadian Education.* Toronto: W.J. Gage, 1958.

2776 VANDERBERG, D. "Ideology and Educational Policy." *Journal of Educational Thought.* (April 1967), pp. 38-50.

2777 WEIR, G.M. *The Separate School Question in Canada.* Toronto: Ryerson, 1934.

2778 WHITTON, Charlotte. "Education — Strengthening the Compulsory School Law in New Brunswick." *Canadian Child Welfare News.* 4:2 (May 1928), pp. 19-23.

2779 WISEMAN, E. "Protestant Education in Quebec." *Canadian Forum.* Toronto: 17:203 (December 1937), pp. 303-306.

10.2.2   Government Policy and Documentation

10.2.2.1   Federal

2780 CANADA. Department of Labour. *Training Canada's Young Unemployed: Facts, Figures and Objectives of the Dominion-Provincial Youth Training Program.* Ottawa: The Department, 1938.

2781 CANADA. Dominion Bureau of Statistics, Education Division. *Education Planning and the Expanding Economy.* Ottawa: Queen's Printer, 1964.

2782 _____. *The Organization and Administration of Public Schools in Canada.* Ottawa: Queen's Printer, 1960.

2783 CANADA. Privy Council. *Papers in Reference to the Manitoba School Case Presented to Parliament During the Session of 1895.* Ottawa: Queen's Printer, 1895.

2784 CANADA. Secretary of State. Education Support Branch. *Federal Expenditures on Post-Secondary Education, 1966-1967, 1967-1968.* Ottawa: Queen's Printer, 1969.

2785 _____. *Federal and Provincial Student Aid in Canada, 1966-1967, 1967-1968.* Ottawa: Secretary of State, 1970.

2786 PROVINCE OF CANADA. (1841-1867). Department of Public Instruction for Upper Canada. *Acts, Forms and General Regulations and Instructions for the Better Organization and Better Establishment and Maintenance of Common Schools in Upper Canada, 1841-1855.* Toronto: 1841-55.

10.2.2.2   Provincial

2787 ALBERTA. Commission on Educational Planning. *A Choice of Futures; A Future of Choices.* Edmonton: Queen's Printer, 1972.

2788 ALBERTA. Department of Education. *The Alberta Special Education Study.* Edmonton: Queen's Printer, 1977.

2789 ALBERTA. Royal Commission on Education in Alberta. *Report.* Edmonton: Queen's Printer, 1959.

2790 ATHERTON, P.J. "Education: Radical Reform in Nova Scotia." *Canadian Public Policy.* 1:3 (Summer 1975), pp. 384-92.

2791 BRITISH COLUMBIA. Commission of Inquiry into Educational Finance. *Report.* Victoria: King's Printer, 1945.

2792 BRITISH COLUMBIA. Commission on School Taxation. *Report.* Vancouver: 1947.

2793 BRITISH COLUMBIA. Ministry of Education. *Report.* Committee on Continuing and Community Education in British Columbia. Vancouver: The Ministry, 1976.

2794 BRITISH COLUMBIA. Royal Commission on Education. *Report.* Victoria: Queen's Printer, 1960.

2795 BUTTRICK, John A. *Educational Problems in Ontario and Some Policy Options.* Toronto: Ontario Economic Council, 1977.

2796 CAMERON, D.M. "Implications of the Smith Report for Education in Ontario." *Canadian School Journal.* 46:3 (April 1968), pp. 6-10.

2797 CREAN, John, FERGUSON, Michael, and SOMERS, Hugh J. *Higher Education in the Atlantic Provinces for the 1970s: A Study.* Halifax: Association of Atlantic Universities, 1969.

2798 FIGUR, Berthold. "Processing Citizens Proposals for Educational Change in a Canadian Province." Ph.D., Stanford University, 1968.

2799 FOGHT, Harold Waldstein. *A Survey of Education in the Province of Saskatchewan: A Report to the Government of the Province of Saskatchewan.* Regina: King's Printer, 1918.

2800 FRECKER, G.A. *Education in the Atlantic Provinces.* Toronto: W.J. Gage, 1957.

2801 GILLIE, B.C. *Survey of Education — North West Territories.* Yellowknife: Department of Education, 1972.

2802 HOLLAND, J.W. "Educational Policy-Making Becomes Public Education: The Work and Times of the Commission on Post-Secondary Education in Ontario." *Journal of International Society of Educational Planners.* 2 (1972), pp. 22-37.

2803 KING, H.B. *School Finance in British Columbia.* Victoria: King's Printer, 1935.

2804 LAMONTAGNE, Charles André. "The Parent Report: An Example of the Use of Comparative Education in Educational Planning." M.A., McGill University, 1968.

2805 McKINNON, Donald T. "An Analysis of the Educational Effort of the Province of Manitoba." M.Ed., University of Manitoba, 1972.

2806 MANITOBA. Educational Commission. *Report.* Winnipeg: King's Printer, 1924.

2807 MANITOBA. Legislative Assembly. Special Select Committee on Education. *Report.* Winnipeg: King's Printer, 1945.

2808 MANITOBA. Royal Commission on Adult Education. *Report.* Winnipeg: King's Printer, 1947.

2809 MANITOBA. Royal Commission on Education. *Report.* Winnipeg: Queen's Printer, 1959.

2810 MANITOBA. Study of the Education of Handicapped Children in Manitoba. *Report on the Education and Training of Handicapped Children.* July 1965. Winnipeg: Legislative Assembly, 1965.

2811 NEW BRUNSWICK. Commission on Education. *Report.* Fredericton: King's Printer, 1932.

2812 NEW BRUNSWICK. Department of Education. Ministers' Committee on Educational Planning. *Education Tomorrow: Report.* Fredericton: Department of Education, 1973.

2813 NEW BRUNSWICK. Royal Commission on the Financing of Schools in New Brunswick. *Report.* Fredericton: Department of Education, 1955.

2814 NEW BRUNSWICK. Royal Commission on Higher Education. *Report.* Fredericton: Queen's Printer, 1962.

2815 NEWFOUNDLAND AND LABRADOR. Royal Commission on Education and Youth. *Report.* St. John's: Province of Newfoundland and Labrador, 1967-68.

2816 NOVA SCOTIA. *Atlantic Provinces Report of the Special Education Committee to the Ministers of Education.* Halifax: Communication Centre, 1973.

2817 NOVA SCOTIA. Royal Commission on Education, Public Services and Provincial-Municipal Relations. *Report.* Halifax: Queen's Printer, 1974.

2818 NOVA SCOTIA. Royal Commission on Provincial Development and Rehabilitation. *Report.* Part 5. *Education.* Halifax: King's Printer, 1944.

2819 ONTARIO. Commission on Post-Secondary Education. *The Learning Society*. Report of the Commission on Post Secondary Education in Ontario. Toronto: Ministry of Government Services, 1972.

2820 ONTARIO. Committee on the Costs of Education. *Interim Reports*. No.1. *Report on the Education of Elementary and Secondary Teachers in Ontario: Facilities, Organization, Administration*; No.2. *School Building Programs*; No.3. *Pupil Transportation*; No.4. *Planning*; No.5. *Educational Agencies and Programme*; No.6. *Compensation in Elementary and Secondary Education*. Toronto: Queen's Printer, 1972-77.

2821 ONTARIO. Department of Education. *Industrial, Technical and Art Education: Synopsis of the Industrial Education Act and the Adolescent School Attendance Act; Recommendations and Amended Regulations for the Establishment, Organization and Maintenance of Day and Evening Schools; the Record of 1912 in Industrial, Technical and Art Education*. Toronto: King's Printer, 1913.

2822 ———. *Report of the Minister of Education on the Subject of Technical Education*. Toronto: Warwick & Sons, 1889.

2823 ONTARIO. Ministry of Colleges and Universities. Manpower Training Branch. Task Force on Industrial Training. *Training for Ontario's Future; Report*. Toronto: Queen's Printer, 1973.

2824 ONTARIO. Ministry of Education. *Report*. Commission on the Organization and Financing of Public and Secondary School Systems in Metro Toronto. Toronto: Queen's Printer, 1974.

2825 ———. *Report*. Task Force on Organization Structure for Education Administration. Toronto: Ministry of Education, 1973.

2826 ONTARIO. Provincial Committee on Aims and Objectives of Education in the Schools of Ontario. *Living and Learning*. Report of Committee (Hall-Dennis Report). Toronto: Newton Publishing Company, 1968.

2827 ONTARIO. Royal Commission on Education in Ontario. *Report*. Toronto: King's Printer, 1950.

2828 PRINCE EDWARD ISLAND. Commission on Education. *Report*. Charlottetown: King's Printer, 1910.

2829 PRINCE EDWARD ISLAND. *Report of the Commissioner on Educational Finance and Related Problems in Administration*. Charlottetown: Queen's Printer, 1960.

2830 PRINCE EDWARD ISLAND. Royal Commission on Education. *Report*. Charlottetown: King's Printer, 1930.

2831 PRINCE EDWARD ISLAND. Royal Commission on Higher Education. *Report*. Charlottetown: Queen's Printer, 1965.

2832 QUEBEC. Commission royale d'enquête sur l'enseignement. *Rapport*. Quebec: Queen's Printer, 1965-66.

2833 QUEBEC. Ministère de l'éducation. Direction générale de la planification. Groupe économie de l'éducation. *Analyse descriptive de l'évolution du financement d'éducation au Québec, 1964-1974*. Quebec: Editeur officiel du Québec, 1975.

2834 QUEBEC. Ministry of Education. *Primary and Secondary Education in Quebec*. Quebec: Editeur officiel du Québec, 1978.

2835 QUEBEC. "The Royal Commission on Education in the Province of Quebec." *Canadian Education and Research Digest*. 3:4 (1963), pp. 284-88.

2836 ROYAL SOCIETY OF CANADA/ACADEMIE DES LETTRES ET DES SCIENCES HUMAINES. *Le Rapport Parent: dix ans après*. Colloque de la société royale du Canada. Académie des lettres et des sci-

ences humaines en collaboration avec Louis Phillippe Audet *et al.*
Montreal: Bellarmin, 1975.

2837 SEATH, John. *Education for Industrial Purposes: A Report.* Toronto: L.K.
Cameron, 1911.

2838 SELINGER, Alphonse Daniel. "Politics and Education Policy in Alberta." Ed.D., University of Oregon, 1967.

10.2.2.3   Intergovernmental

2839 BYRNE, T.C. "Urban-Provincial Relations in Canadian Education."
Education Canada. 9:1 (March 1969), pp. 35-43.

2840 CANADA. Council for the Ministers of Education. *Review of Educational
Policies in Canada.* Ottawa: Queen's Printer, 1975.

2841 _____. *Review of Educational Policies in Canada: Western Region
Report.* Submission of the Ministers of Education for the Provinces of
British Columbia, Alberta, Saskatchewan, and Manitoba. Ottawa: The
Council, 1975.

2842 CANADIAN TEACHERS' FEDERATION. *Policies and Viewpoints on
Matters of Federal Jurisdiction/ Politiques et points de vue sur des questions
relatives à la juridiction fédérale.* Ottawa: The Federation, 1974.

2843 _____. *A Summary of Federal Direct and Indirect Involvement in Canadian Education.* Ottawa: The Federation, 1973.

2844 CHEAL, John E., MELSNESS, Harold C., and REEVES, Arthur W.
Educational Administration. The Role of the Teacher. Toronto: Macmillan, 1962.

2845 DOWNEY, Lorne W. *Financing Post-Secondary Education in Canada.*
Report Commissioned by the Council of the Ministers of Education
of Canada. Edmonton: Human Resources Council of Alberta, 1971.

2846 GRAHAM, John F., and CAMERON, John R. *Financing Post-Secondary
Education in Canada.* Report Commissioned by the Council for the
Ministers of Education of Canada. Halifax: Dalhousie University,
1971.

2847 HODGSON, Ernest Daniel. *Federal Intervention in Public Education.*
Toronto: Canadian Education Association, 1976.

2848 MacKENZIE, N.A.M., and ROWAT, D.C. "The Federal Government
and Higher Education in Canada." *Canadian Journal of Economics and
Political Science.* 16:3 (August 1950), pp. 353-70.

2849 PEITCHINIS, Stephen G. *Financing Post-Secondary Education in Canada.*
Report commissioned by the Council for the Ministers of Education
in Canada. Calgary: University of Calgary, 1971.

2850 STAGER, David A., and COOK, Gail C.A. *Financing Post-Secondary Education: An Examination of the Draft Report of the Commission on Post-Secondary Education in Ontario.* Toronto: University of Toronto Pres,
1972.

2851 _____, and FLUXGOLD, Howard. *Financing Post-Secondary Education
in Canada.* Report commissioned by the Council of Ministers of Education of Canada. Toronto: University of Toronto Press, 1971.

2852 _____, and GERO, John. *Provincial Income Transfers through Government Involvement in the Financing of Post-Secondary Education.* Toronto:
Council for the Ministers of Education of Canada, 1971.

2853 STANBURY, R. "Federal Role in Education (Canada)." *Queen's
Quarterly.* 74:3 (Autumn 1967), pp. 363-79.

2854 TOOMBS, Morley Preston. "Provincial Aid and Local Responsibility in
Education." *Canadian Education.* 10:2 (March 1955), pp. 17-32.

2855 WOODCOCK, L. "Federal Involvement in Education Described." *University Affairs/Affaires universitaires.* 16:13 (December 1975), p. 13.

10.2.3 Special Issues

10.2.3.1 Early Childhood Education

2856 BRYCE, R., *et al.* "Early Childhood Services: Background." *Challenge in Educational Administration.* 13:3 (1975), pp. 4-6.

2857 CORBETT, Barbara Elizabeth. "The Public School Kindergarten in Ontario 1883-1967." Ed.D., Ontario Institute for Studies in Education, 1969.

2858 DOWNEY, L.W. *Opportunities for Infants: Towards a Policy on Early Childhood Development.* Prepared for the Government of Alberta. Edmonton: L.W. Downey Research Associates, 1972.

2859 GRAHAM, Margaret, *et al. Early Childhood Education.* Toronto: Federation of Women Teachers' Associations of Ontario, 1978.

2860 INGLE, R.A., and SAKLOFSKE, D.H. "Recent Trends in Early Childhood Education." *Early Childhood Education.* 6:2 (Spring 1972), pp. 6-14.

2861 PALMER, J. "Preschool Education — Pros and Cons." *Canadian Education and Research Digest.* 6:3 (1966), pp. 174-87.

2862 TSALIKIS, George. *Pre-school Education in Manitoba: The Public Sector.* Winnipeg: Queen's Printer, 1971.

2863 WORTH, Walter H. *Before Six: A Report on the Alberta Early Childhood Education Study.* Edmonton: Alberta School Trustees Association, 1966.

10.2.3.2 Higher Education

2864 ALEXANDER, S. "Canadian Higher Education: A Review of the Graham Royal Commission." *Dalhousie Review.* 55:3 (Autumn 1975), pp. 491-504.

2865 ANGUS, H.F. "Economic Theory of a State-Supported University." *Queen's Quarterly.* 39:2 (May 1932), pp. 261-71.

2866 COLE, R. Taylor. "The Universities and Governments under Canadian Federalism." *Journal of Politics.* 34:2 (May 1972), pp. 524-53.

2867 COMMISSION ON THE RELATIONS BETWEEN UNIVERSITIES AND GOVERNMENTS. *The University, Society and Government; The Report of the Commission.* Ottawa: University of Ottawa Press, 1970.

2868 COOPER, H.M., *et al. Governments and the University.* Toronto: Macmillan, 1966.

2869 CORRY, J.A. "Higher Education in Federal-Provincial Relations." *University Affairs/Affaires universitaires.* 8:2 (December 1966), pp. 1-4.

2870 ———. "Universities, Governments and the Public." *Queen's Quarterly.* 75:3 (Autumn 1968), pp. 424-31.

2871 DAOUST, Gaetan, and BELANGER, Paul. *L'université dans une société éducative: de l'éducation des adultes à l'éducation permanente.* Montreal: Les Presses de l'université de Montréal, 1974.

2872 DAY, Thomas Charles. "Administration-Faculty Conflict over the Distribution of Control in Policy Formulation in Alberta Colleges." Ph.D., University of Alberta, 1971.

2873 DOWNEY, L.W. *Toward a System of Post-Secondary and Adult Eduation for North Western Alberta and Northeastern British Columbia: A Report to the Governments of Alberta and British Columbia.* Edmonton: L.W. Downey Research Associates, 1974.

2874 HARRIS, Robin Sutton. *A History of Higher Education in Canada: 1663-1960*. Toronto: University of Toronto Press, 1976.

2875 HETTICH, Walter. *Expenditures, Output and Productivity in Canadian University Education*. Special Study No. 14. Ottawa: Economic Council of Canada, 1971.

2876 LENNARDS, Jos. L., and HARVEY, Edward. *The Changing Nature of Post-Secondary Education: Attitudes, Costs, Benefits; A Report to the Commission on Post-Secondary Education in Ontario*. [n.p.], 1970.

2877 MURRAY, W.C. "State Support and Control of Universities in Canada." *Proceedings and Transactions of the Royal Society of Canada.* Series 3, 19:2 (1925), pp. 19-32.

2878 NATIONAL CONFERENCE ON CANADIAN UNIVERSITIES. *Report of Post-War Problems*. Toronto: University of Toronto Press, 1944.

2879 OSTRY, Sylvia, ed. *Canadian Higher Education in the Seventies*. Ottawa: Economic Council of Canada, 1974.

2880 STEWART, E.E. "The Role of the Provincial Government in the Development of the Universities of Ontario, 1791-1964." Ph.D., University of Toronto, 1970.

2881 WAINES, W.J. *Federal Support of Universities and Colleges of Canada*. Ottawa: Association of Universities and Colleges of Canada, 1970.

2882 WOODSIDE, Willson. *The University Question: Who Should Go? Who Should Pay?* Toronto: Ryerson, 1958.

10.2.3.3 Technical Training

2883 ALI, Ameer H. "Federal Aid to Education in New Brunswick: The Effects of Federal Aid on the Development of Technical and Vocational Education in New Brunswick." M.Ed., University of New Brunswick, 1966.

2884 BREWIN, Margaret J. "The Establishment of an Industrial Education System in Ontario." M.A., University of Toronto, 1967.

2885 CANADA. Royal Commission on Industrial Training and Technical Education. *Report*. Ottawa: King's Printer, 1913.

2886 CAP, Orest. "Selected Major Historical Events in the Evolution of Vocational-Technical Education." *Canadian Vocational Journal.* 12:2 (April 1976), pp. 38-44.

2887 DENNISON, Donald Gordon. "The Development of Vocational Education in Canada: A Study of Intergovernmental Relations and Their Consitutional Implications." M.A., Carleton University, 1970.

2888 DICKSON, D. "Technical and Vocational Training in Canada." *Education Record.* 8 (January/March 1965), pp. 29-40.

2889 GLENDENNING, Donald Ernest Malcolm. *A Review of Federal Legislation Relating to Technical and Vocational Education in Canada*. Ottawa: Department of Manpower and Immigration, 1968.

2890 GOARD, D.H. *Report of the Commission on Vocational, Technical and Trade Training in British Columbia*. Burnaby, B.C.: Ministry of Education, 1977.

2891 _____. "The Effect of Federal Aid to Technical and Vocational Education on the Total Educational Service." *Journal of Education British Columbia.* 10 (April 1964), pp. 84-99.

2892 MORRISON, T.R. "Reform as Social Tracking: The Case of Industrial Education in Ontario 1870-1900." *Journal of Educational Thought.* 8:2 (August 1974), pp. 87-100.

2893 PAGE, G.T. "Canada's Manpower Training and Education: Federal Policy and Programs." *Canadian Education and Research Digest.* 7:4 (December 1967), pp. 283-98.

2894 PETERSON, Bob. "Federal Government's Role in Training." *Canadian Training Methods.* Part 1, 9:2 (August 1976), pp. 17-18; Part 2, 9:3 (October 1976), pp. 18-21.

2895 SISCO, N.A. "Canada's Manpower Training and Education: A View from Ontario." *Canadian Education and Research Digest.* 7:4 (December 1967), p. 299-304.

2896 ST.JOHN, C. *Ontario Study of Vocational-Technical Training: A Preliminary Report.* Toronto: Department of Educational Planning, Ontario Institute for Studies in Education, 1967.

2897 STAMP, R.M. "The Campaign for Technical Education in Ontario, 1876-1919." Ph.D., University of Western Ontario, 1970.

2898 _____. "Technical Education, the National Policy and Federal-Provincial Relations in Canadian Education, 1899-1919." *Canadian Historical Review.* 52:4 (1971), pp. 404-23.

2899 TREW, P.L. "Federal Contribution to Vocational Training." *Canadian Vocational Journal.* 7:3 (September 1971), pp. 14-16.

2900 WATSON, L., and KERRIDGE, E.L. *An Assessment of the Technical and Vocational Training Act.* Toronto: Department of Educational Planning, Ontario Institute for Studies in Education, 1967.

2901 WHITELAW, J.H. "Quebec — Quiet Revolution in Technical Education." *Canadian University.* 3:4 (June 1968), pp. 18-21.

10.2.3.4   Teachers and Teacher Training

2902 ALTHOUSE, John G. *The Ontario Teacher; A Historical Account of Progress 1800-1910.* Toronto: Ontario Teachers' Federation, 1967.

2903 BAILEY, Alan W. "The Professional Preparation of Teachers for the Schools of the Province of New Brunswick, 1784-1964." Part I: 1784-1900, *Ontario Journal of Education Research.* 7:1 (Autumn 1964), pp. 1-10; Part II: 1900-64; 7:3 (Spring 1965), pp. 231-41.

2904 _____. "The Professional Preparation of Teachers for the Schools of the Province of New Brunswick 1784-1964." Ph.D., University of Toronto, 1964.

2905 BASSETT, G.W. "Teacher Education in Canada as Seen by an Australian Observer." *Canadian Education and Research Digest.* 6:3 (September 1966), pp. 163-73.

2906 BREHAUT, Willard. *Teacher Education in Prince Edward Island.* Toronto: Ontario Institute for Studies in Education, 1972.

2907 BRITISH COLUMBIA. University Commission on the Future of the Faculty of Education. *The COFFE Report.* Vancouver, 1969.

2908 BROWN, C.K., and ENNS, F. "Development of Teacher Tenure Legislation in Alberta." *Alberta Journal of Educational Research.* 12 (March 1966), pp. 41-53.

2909 CAMERON, Donald R. *Teacher Certification in Canada.* Ottawa: Canadian Teachers' Federation, 1960.

2910 CANADIAN Teachers' Federation. *Foundations for the Future: A New Look at Teacher Education and Certification in Canada: Proceedings of a Seminar of teacher Education, Ottawa, May 1966.* Ottawa: Canadian Teachers' Federation, 1967.

2911 DALZIEL, Graham G. "Training Teachers for the North, the Early Development of Teacher Training in North Bay, Ontario, 1905-1920." M.A., University of Toronto, 1976.

2912 GRAHAM, Elizabeth. "Schoolmarms and Early Teaching in Ontario." In *Women at Work 1850-1930*, edited by Janice Acton, Bonnie Shepard, and Penny Goldsmith. Toronto: Canadian Women's Educational Press, 1974, pp. 165-211.

2913 KARR, W.J. *The Training of Teachers in Ontario*. Ottawa: R.J. Taylor, Printer, 1916.

2914 LAZERTE, M.E. *Teacher Education in Canada*. Toronto: W.J. Gage, 1951.

2915 McCURDY, Sherbourne G. *The Legal Status of the Canadian Teacher*. Toronto: Macmillan, 1968.

2916 MYERS, D., and REID, F., ed. *Educating Teachers: Critiques and Proposals*. Toronto: Ontario Institute for Studies in Education, 1974.

2917 NEWCOMBE, Ervin Ernest. "The Development of Elementary School Teacher Education in Ontario since 1900." *Ontario Journal of Education Research*. 8:1 (Autumn 1965), pp. 59-72.

2918 NEWNHAM, W.T., and NEASE, A.S. *The Professional Teacher in Ontario*. Toronto: Ryerson Press, 1965.

2919 PATON, J.M. *The Role of Teachers' Organizations in Canadian Education*. Toronto: W.J. Gage, 1962.

2920 RIEGER, T.F., comp. *Teacher Education and Certification Committees and Policies of the Teachers' Associations in Canada*. Ottawa: Canadian Teachers' Federation, 1966.

2921 ROGERS, John S. "The Organization, Control and Administration of the Teacher Training System of the Province of Ontario, 1900-1920." Ph.D., University of Ottawa, 1972.

2922 SEN, Jayasree. *The Tip of the Iceburg: A Study of the Demand for and Supply of Educational Specialists Requiring Post-Graduate Training*. Toronto: Department of Educational Planning, Ontario Institute for Studies in Education, 1976.

2923 SINGLETON, Isaac Douglas. "Teacher Training and Certification in the Northwest Territories from 1885-1905 and in Saskatchewan from 1905-1935." M.Ed., University of Saskatchewan, 1949.

2924 STEWART, Freeman K. *Interprovincial Co-operation in Education: The Story of the Canadian Education Association*. Toronto: W.J. Gage, 1957.

10.2.3.5   Continuing Education

2925 BOSETTI, R.A. *The Alberta System of Post-Secondary Non-University Education*. Edmonton: Alberta Colleges Commission, 1972.

2926 CANADIAN ASSOCIATION FOR ADULT EDUCATION. *A White Paper on the Education of Adults in Canada*. Toronto: The Association, 1964.

2927 GUNN, C.P. "The Role of Atlantic Provincial Governments in Adult Education." Ed.D., University of Toronto, 1967.

2928 HENSON, Guy. "Adult Education in Nova Scotia." *Canadian Education*. 4:3 (June 1949), pp. 39-58.

2929 INSTITUT Canadien d'éducation des adultes. *Eléments d'une politique: éducation des adultes, 1970*. Montreal: The Institute, 1971.

2930 _____. *Pour une politique de l'éducation des adultes au niveau post-secondaire*. Mémoire au Ministère de l'éducation du Québec. Montreal: The Institute, 1967.

2931 KIDD, J.R., ed. *Adult Education in Canada*. Toronto: Canadian Association of Adult Education, 1950.

2932 _____. *Learning and Society*. Toronto: Canadian Association of Adult Education, 1963.

2933 ROUILLARD, Harriet, ed. *Pioneers in Adult Education in Canada.* Toronto: Canadian Association of Adult Education, 1952.

2934 SMITH, C.H. "Federal Contributions to Education for Adults and to Certain Agencies of Cultural Diffusion: An Analytical Survey of Developments in Canada from 1920-1960." M.A., University of British Columbia, 1960.

2935 VERNON, Foster. "The Development of Adult Education in Ontario, 1790-1900." Ph.D., University of Toronto, 1969.

2936 WANIEWICZ, Ignacy. *Demand for Part-time Learning in Ontario.* Toronto: Ontario Institute for Studies in Education, 1976.

10.2.3.6   Special Education

2937 BAKER, Laura Doris. "The Development of Special Educational Provisions for Exceptional Children in the City of Winnipeg." Ed.D., University of Toronto, 1967.

2938 BALLANCE, Karoline E., and KENDALL, David C. *Report on Legislation and Services for Exceptional Children in Canada.* Toronto: Council for Exceptional Children, 1969.

2939 BEATTIE, H.R. "Special Education — Responsibilities and Provisions." *Canadian Education and Research Digest.* 1:4 (December 1961), pp. 47-60.

2940 CANADIAN COUNCIL ON CHILD WELFARE. *Special Training for School Age Children in Need of Special Care.* Ottawa: The Council, 1927.

2941 LAYCOCK, S.R. *Special Education in Canada.* Toronto: W.J. Gage, 1963.

2942 ———. "Educating the Emotionally Disturbed." *B.C. School Trustees.* 25 (Fall 1969), pp. 16-17.

2943 MORRISON, Brent G. "Exceptional Children: Integration Versus Segregation." M.A., University of Toronto, 1975.

2944 ONTARIO. Council for Exceptional Children. *Policies for the Education of Exceptional Children in Ontario.* Toronto: The Council, 1972.

2945 RITCHIE, Hugh. "Special Services for Children with Learning Disabilities." *Education Canada.* 9:1 (March 1969), pp. 52-3.

2946 SINCLAIR, Samuel B. *Special Training for School-Age Children in Need of Special Care: Ontario's Auxiliary Classes.* Ottawa: Canadian Council on Child Welfare, 1925.

10.2.3.7   Minority Education

2947 ASHWORTH, M. *Immigrant Children and Canadian Schools.* Toronto: McClelland and Stewart, 1975.

2948 BARBER, Marilyn. "The Ontario Bilingual Schools Issue: Sources of Conflict." *Canadian Historical Review.* 47:3 (1966), pp. 227-48.

2949 BERCUSON, Leonard. "Education in the Bloc Settlements of Western Canada." M.A., McGill University, 1941.

2950 BROWN, Craig, ed. *Minorities, Schools and Politics: Canadian Historical Readings.* Toronto: University of Toronto Press, 1969.

2951 DAHLIE, Jorgen. "The Japanese in British Columbia: Lost Opportunity? Some Aspects of the Educaton of Minorities." *B.C. Studies.* 8 (Winter 1970-71), pp. 3-16.

2952 JOHNSTONE, P.A. "Education and Black Social Development in Nova Scotia: An Ethnic Services Approach." *Moccasin Telegraph.* 18:4 (Summer 1976), pp. 11-18.

2953 KUPLOWSKY, Olga. "French-Canadian Bilingual Education for Ethnic Minorities." M.A., University of Toronto, 1971.

2954 McLEOD, Norman R. *Need, Culture and Curriculum, Educating Immigrants and Ethnic Minorities.* Toronto: Board of Education, 1968.

2955 PLANTE, Albert. "Aide fédérale à l'éducation et minorités." *Relations.* 157 (January 1954), pp. 4-6.

2956 PRANG, Margaret. "Clerics, Politicians and the Bilingual Schools Issue in Ontario, 1910, 1917." *Canadian Historical Review.* 41:4 (1960), pp. 281-307.

2957 TORONTO BOARD OF EDUCATION. Research Department. *Immigrants and Their Education.* Toronto: The Board, 1965.

2958 TROPER, Harold. "Alternative Approaches to the Education of Minorities in Canada." *Manitoba Journal of Education.* 10:2 (June 1975), pp. 14-17.

10.2.3.8 Native Education

2959 ARCTIC INSTITUTE OF NORTH AMERICA. Man in the North Project. *Technical Reports: Education in the Canadian North; Three Reports.* Montreal: The Institute, 1973.

2960 CALDWELL, George. *Indian Residential Schools: A Research Study of the Child Care Programs of Nine Residential Schools in Saskatchewan.* Ottawa: Canadian Welfare Council, 1967.

2961 CHALMERS, John W. "Federal, Provincial and Territorial Strategies for Canadian Native Education, 1960-1970." *Journal of Canadian Studies.* 11:3 (August 1976), pp.37-49.

2962 CLEMENT, J. "Education of Indian Children in Canada." *Special Education.* 24 (June 1968), pp. 9-18.

2963 DANIELS, E. "The Legal Context of Indian Education in Canada." Ph.D., University of Alberta, 1973.

2964 DAVEY, R.F. "The Education of Indians in Canada." *Canadian Education.* 10.3 (June 1955), pp. 25-38.

2965 "Education in Northern Canada." *Canadian Education and Research Digest.* 3:2 (June 1963), pp. 85-91.

2966 FOSTER, Douglas Ray. "The Canadian Indian: A Study of the Education of a Minority Group and Its Social Problems." M.Sc., University of Wisconsin, 1963.

2967 HOBART, Charles. "Eskimo Education in the Canadian Arctic." *Canadian Review of Sociology and Anthropology.* 7:1 (February 1970), pp. 49-69.

2968 "Indian and Northern Affairs Education Program." *Northian.* 12:2 (Summer 1976), pp. 20-26.

2969 JAMIESON, Elmer. "Indian Education in Canada." M.A., McMaster University, 1922.

2970 JOBLIN, Elgie. *The Education of the Indians of Western Ontario.* Toronto: Department of Education Research, Ontario College of Education, 1947.

2971 LARONDE, Louis. "The Education of the Indian in Canada." M.A., University of Manitoba, 1912.

2972 LOVEKIN, J.P. "A Focus on Indian Education." *Reporter* (Ontario Teachers' Federation). 15 (October 1969), pp. 5-8.

2973 MacLEOD, John Malcolm. "Indian Education in Canada: A Study of Indian Education with Special Reference to the Briefs Presented to the Joint Committee of the Senate and the House of Commons on Indian Affairs, 1959-1961." M.Ed., University of New Brunswick, 1964.

2974 MacPHERSON, N.J. *Toward a Multicultural, Multi-lingual Education System in N.W.T.* Saskatoon: Indian and Northern Education Program, College of Education, University of Saskatchewan, 1975.

2975 MICKELSON, N.A., and GALLOWAY, C.G. "Education of Indian Children." *Principals.* 10 (November 1969), pp. 35-39.

2976 MOODY, H. "The Education of Indians in Canada." Great Britain Board of Education, *Special Reports on Educational Subjects, 14.* London: Her Majesty's Stationery Office, 1905. pp.363-71.

2977 NATIONAL INDIAN BROTHERHOOD OF CANADA. *Indian Control of Indian Education.* Policy Paper Presented to the Minister of Indian Affairs and Northern Development. Ottawa: The Brotherhood, 1972.

2978 STERLING, Robert. "Native Indian Education in British Columbia." *Bulletin* (Canadian Association in Support of Native People.) 16:2 (July 1975), pp. 12-14.

2979 VALLERY, H.J. "A History of Indian Education in Canada." M.A., Queen's University, 1942.

2980 VERMA, D. "Changing Patterns in Indian Education." *Journal of Education Nova Scotia.* 17 (December 1967), pp. 22-26.

2981 WILLSON, J. Donald. "No Blanket to Be Worn in School: The Education of Indians in Early 19th Century Ontario." *Histoire sociale/Social History.* 7:14 (November 1974), pp. 293-305.

2982 WOODSWORTH, J. "Problems of Indian Education in Canada." pp. 265-74. *The North America Indian Today,* edited by Charles T. Loran and Thomas F. McIlwraith. Toronto: University of Toronto Press, 1943.

10.2.4   Financing

2983 AMUNDRUD, Clarence A. *The Financing of Publically Supported Schools in Saskatchewan.* Regina: Saskatchewan School Trustees Association, 1976.

2984 ARGUE, Kenneth Farnum. *Financing Education in the Canadian Provinces.* Ottawa: Canadian Teachers' Federation, 1942.

2985 _____. *Wealth, Children and Education in Canada: A Report on the Financing of Education in Canada.* Calgary: University of Alberta Press, 1945.

2986 ARMSTRONG, Alex; LAWTON, Stephen; RIDEOUT, E. Brock. *Ontario Elementary Education Expenditure Patterns 1970-1973: Staff Study.* Toronto: Ontario Institute for Studies in Education, 1973.

2987 ASSOCIATION OF UNIVERSITIES AND COLLEGES OF CANADA. Commission on the Financing of Higher Education. *Le financement de l'enseignement supérieur au Canada; rapport d'une Commission à l'association des universités et collèges du Canada.* Quebec: les presses de l'université Laval, 1965; *Financing Higher Education in Canada.* Toronto: University of Toronto Press, 1965.

2988 ATHERTON, P.J. "Financing Post-Secondary Education in Alberta." *Alberta Journal of Education Research.* 16 (September 1970), pp. 137-48.

2989 _____, HANSON, E.J., and BERLANDO, J.F. *Quality Education: What Price?* Edmonton: Alberta Teachers' Association, 1969.

2990 BALLANTYNE, Morna. *Federal Financing of Post Secondary Education in Canada.* Ottawa: National Union of Students, 1978.

2991 BENSON, Ralph. "Determinants of Expenditures for Public Secondary Education in the Province of Ontario." Ph.D., University of Toronto, 1975.

2992 BIRD, Richard M. *Financing Education in Ontario*. Ontario: Commission on Declining School Enrolment in Ontario, 1978.

2993 BOUGHEN, Robert A. "A Study of Educational Finance in Alberta 1958-1971." M.Ed., University of Manitoba, 1974.

2994 BRITISH COLUMBIA TEACHERS' FEDERATION. *The Cost of Education: Who Should Pay and Why*. Vancouver: The Federation, 1967.

2995 _____. Economic Welfare Division. *Education Finance in British Columbia 1969*. Vancouver: The Federation, 1969.

2996 BROWN, G.A. "The Financing and Administration of Some Aspects of Education Shared by the Dominion and the Provinces." M.A., Carleton University, 1961.

2997 BROWN, Wilfred J. *The Impact of Federal Financial Support on Elementary and Secondary Education in Canada*. Ottawa: Canadian Teachers' Federation, 1974.

2998 _____. *New Goals, New Paths. The Search for a Rationale for the Financing of Education in Canada*. (Part I) "Changing Philosophies and their Implications." (Part II) "Restructuring the Financing of Education to Meet Emerging Needs." Ottawa: Canadian Teachers' Federation, 1973.

2999 _____. "Redistributive Implications of Federal Provincial Fiscal Arrangements for Elementary and Secondary Education in Canada." Ph.D., University of Toronto, 1974.

3000 _____, GORDON, Robert, and RIDEOUT, E. Brock. *A Study of Education Finance in Manitoba*. Winnipeg: Manitoba Teachers' Society, 1970.

3001 CAMERON, David Murray. *Schools for Ontario: Policy-Making, Administration and Finance in the 1960s*. Toronto: University of Toronto Press, 1972.

3002 _____. "The Politics of Education in Ontario with Special Reference to the Financing Structure." Ph.D., University of Toronto, 1969.

3003 CAMERON, M.A. *The Financing of Education in Ontario*. Toronto: Department of Educational Research, University of Toronto, 1936.

3004 _____. *Property Taxation and School Finance in Canada*. Toronto: Canadian Education Association, 1945.

3005 CANADIAN TEACHERS' FEDERATION. "Problems and Prospects in Education Finance." *Proceedings*. Seminar on Education Finance, Ottawa, 4-5 1977. Ottawa: The Federation, 1977.

3006 _____. Research Division. *Education Finance in Canada, 1946-1956*. Ottawa: The Federation, 1958.

3007 _____. *Financing Education in Canada*. Ottawa: The Federation, 1965.

3008 CANADIAN UNIVERSITIES FOUNDATION. *Financing Higher Education in Canada/ Le financement de l'enseignement supérieur au Canada*. Ottawa: Research and Information Service, 1960.

3009 CARTER, George E. "Financing Post-Secondary Education under the Federal-Provincial Fiscal Arrangements Act: An Appraisal." *Canadian Tax Journal*. 24:5 (September/October 1976), pp. 505-22.

3010 CRAWFORD, Kenneth Grant. *Provincial Grants to Canadian Schools, 1941-1961*. Toronto: Canadian Tax Foundation, 1962.

3011 DEISEACH, Donald. "Fiscal Equalization of School System Revenues under the Alberta School Foundation Program 1961-1971." Ph.D., University of Alberta, 1974.

3012 "The Financing of Education in British Columbia." *Canadian Education*. 1:3 (April/May/June 1946), pp. 142-48.

3013 FLUXGOLD, Howard. *Federal Financial Support for Secondary Education and Its Effect on Ontario, 1900-1972.* Toronto and Ottawa: Ontario Teachers' Federation; Canadian Teachers' Federation, 1972.

3014 HANSON, Eric J. *Federal-Provincial Fiscal Relationship in Education in Canada.* Edmonton: Alberta Teachers' Association, 1969.

3015 ———. *Financing Education in Alberta.* Edmonton: Alberta Teachers' Association, 1972.

3016 ———. *Provincial-Municipal Finance in Ontario and the Four Western Provinces with Special Emphasis on Education: A Comparative Study.* Edmonton: Alberta Teachers' Federation, 1971.

3017 HARTLE, D.G. "Financing Education: The Major Alternatives." *School Board.* (Winter 1969), pp. 29-40.

3018 HEMPHILL, H.D. "Trends in Educational Finance and the Public Sector, 1946-1960." *Canadian Education and Research Digest.* 7:4 (December 1967), pp. 334-48.

3019 HETTICH, Walter, LACOMBE, Barry, and von Zur-MUEHLEN, Max. *Basic Goals and the Financing of Education.* Ottawa: Canadian Teachers' Federation, 1972.

3020 LAZERTE, M.E. *School Finance in Canada.* Edmonton: Canadian School Trustees Association, 1955.

3021 McCORDIC, William J. "Financing Education in Canada." *Canadian Banker.* 69:1 (Spring 1962), pp. 74-95; 69:2 (Summer 1962), pp. 95-112; 69:3 (Autumn 1962), pp. 90-100.

3022 MANITOBA TEACHERS' SOCIETY. *A Study of Education Finance in Manitoba.* Winnipeg: The Society, 1975.

3023 MOFFATT, H.P. *Educational Finance in Canada.* Toronto: W.J. Gage, 1957.

3024 MOFFATT, H.P., and BROWN, Wilfred J. *New Goals, New Paths: The Search for a Rationale for the Financing of Education in Canada.* 2 vols. Ottawa: Canadian Teachers' Federation, 1973.

3025 MOORE, A.M.; GUTTMAN, A.I.; WHITE, P.H. *Financing Education in British Columbia.* Vancouver: British Columbia Trustees Association, 1966.

3026 ONTARIO SECONDARY SCHOOL TEACHERS' FEDERATION. *At What Cost? A Study of the Role of the Secondary School in Ontario.* Toronto: Ontario Secondary School Teachers' Federation, 1976.

3027 PATERSON, I.W. "Determinants of Expenditures for Education." *Canadian Education and Research Digest.* 7:2 (June 1967), pp. 155-69.

3028 RIDEOUT, E.B. "Financial Support of Education." *Canadian Education and Research Digest.* 8:2 (June 1968), pp. 85-103.

3029 ———, et al. *Meeting the Problems of Declining Enrolment. Education, Social and Financial Implications to School Boards of Declining Enrolments.* Toronto: Ontario Ministry of Education, 1975.

3030 ———, BEZEAU, Laurence M., and WRIGHT, David. *Educational Goals and the Forms of Primary School Finance in the Province of Ontario.* Toronto: Ontario Institute for Studies in Education, 1977.

3031 ROBBINS, J.E. "Financing Canadian Schools." *Journal of the Canadian Bankers' Association.* 39:4 (July 1932), pp. 496-99.

3032 ROBINSON, A.J. "Public Finance in Canadian Universities." *Canadian Tax Journal.* 21:4 (July/August 1973), pp. 351-58.

3033 RUSSELL, Frazer. "Financing Education in Newfoundland 1960-1961 to 1970-1971." M.Ed., Memorial University, 1973.

3034 SHARPLES, Brian. "An Analysis of the Responsiveness of Public Education Financial Support of Economic Growth in the Provinces of
Canada, 1930-1966, and the Implications for the Financing of Education in the Decade 1971-1981." Ph.D., University of Alberta, 1971.

3035 _____. "Provincial Disparities in Educational Expenditures." *Canadian Tax Journal.* 23:4 (July/August 1975), pp. 383-93.

3036 SHELDON, Mary Elizabeth. "Administration and Finance of Education
in Canada with Specific Reference to Ontario." M.A., McMaster University, 1940.

3037 STAGER, D.A. "Some Policy Problems in the Financing of Colleges
Across Canada." *Canadian University.* 6:4 (August 1971), pp. 34-6.

3038 TOOMBS, Morley Preston. "An Analysis of Parliamentary Debates on
Federal Financial Participation in Education in Canada, 1867-1960."
Ph.D., University of Alberta, 1966.

3039 WARREN, Philip J. "Financing Education in Newfoundland." Ph.D.,
University of Alberta, 1962.

10.2.5   Administration

10.2.5.1   General

3040 ANDERSON, Robert Newton. "The Role of Government in Canadian
Education: An Analysis of Bureaucratic Structures." Ph.D., University of Minnesota, 1963.

3041 FOX, James Harold. "The Centralized Control of Secondary Education
in the Province of Ontario." Ed.D., Harvard University, 1937.

3042 GIDNEY, Robert D. "Centralization and Education: The Origins of an
Ontario Tradition." *Journal of Canadian Studies.* 7:4 (November
1972), pp. 33-48.

3043 GILES, Thomas E. *Educational Administration in Canada.* Calgary: Detse-
lig Enterprises, 1974.

3044 HODGSON, E., BERGEN, J., and BRYCE, R., eds. *Organization and Administration of Education in Canada.* Edmonton: University of Alberta,
1976.

3045 MANZER, Ronald A. "The National Organization of Canadian Education." *Canadian Public Administration.* 11:4 (Winter 1968), pp. 494-508.

3046 MUNROE, David. *The Organization and Administration of Education in
Canada.* Ottawa: Information Canada, 1974.

3047 NEATBY, Hilda. *So Little For The Mind.* Toronto: Clarke Irwin, 1953.

3048 PERRY, G.N. "Political Economy of Education." In *Exploiting our
Economic Potential: Public Policy and the British Columbia Economy,*
edited by Ronald A. Shearer. pp. 79-113. Toronto: Holt, Rinehart and
Winston, 1968.

3049 TOOMBS, Morley Preston. "Control and Responsibility in Public Education in Canada." *Canadian Education.* 10:3 (September 1955), pp.
38-49.

3050 TUCKER, Otto George. "The Administration of Publically-supported
Schools in the Northwest Territories of Canada since 1905." Ed.D.,
University of Toronto, 1972.

10.2.5.2   Local Organization

3051 COLLINS, C.P. "Local School District Organization in Canada." *Canadian Education and Research Digest.* 1:2 (1961), pp. 5-24.

3052 ENNS, Frederick. *The Legal Status of Canadian School Boards.* Toronto:
Macmillan, 1963.

3053 FLOWER, G.E. "Local Government and Education." *Journal of Education Nova Scotia.* 17 (December 1967), pp. 6-11.

3054 GOLDHAMMER, K. "Community Politics and Education." *Canadian School Association Bulletin.* 7 (December 1967), pp. 4-23.

3055 LAMB, Robert L. *The Canadian School Trustee in and at Law.* Ottawa: Canadian Teachers' Federation, 1966.

3056 MacKINNON, Frank. *The Politics of Education: A Study of the Political Administration of Public Schools.* Toronto: University of Toronto Press, 1960.

3057 RIDEOUT, Eric Brock. *Statutory Basis for Participation by Municipal Councils and Other Local Government Agencies in the Organization, Administration and Financing of Education in the Province of Saskatchewan.* Toronto: Ontario College of Education, University of Toronto, 1952.

3058 STEWART, Bruce H. *School Board Bargaining Structure and Policy Development.* Toronto: Ontario School Trustees Council, 1977.

10.3   Health Care Policy

10.3.1   Historical Development

10.3.1.1   General

3059 ABBOTT, M.E. *History of Medicine in the Province of Quebec.* Toronto: Macmillan, 1931.

3060 AGNEW, George Harvey. *Canadian Hospitals, 1920 to 1970: A Dramatic Half-Century.* Toronto: University of Toronto Press, 1974.

3061 ARCHER, A.E. *The Development of Health Insurance in Canada.* Toronto: Canadian Medical Association. 1944.

3062 BILSON, Geoffrey. "Canadian Doctors and the Cholera." *Historical Papers.* Canadian Historical Association, 1977. pp. 105-17.

3063 BLACK, Wesley Drewett. *An Analysis of the Political Decision-Making Process; The Emergence of Medicare in British Columbia, 1952-1972: A Report.* Victoria, 1976.

3064 BOTHWELL, R.S., and ENGLISH, J.R. "Pragmatic Physicians: Canadian Medicine and Health Care Insurance, 1910-1945." *University of Western Ontario Medical Journal.* 47:3 (March 1976), pp. 14-17.

3065 BOUVIER, Emile. "L'avant projet de loi d'assurance-santé." *Relations.* 47 (November 1944), pp. 286-90.

3066 BRYCE, P.H. "Evolution of Local Public Health: County Officers." *Public Health Journal.* 2:3 (March 1911), pp. 103-105.

3067 _____. "History of Public Health in Canada." *Canadian Therapeutist and Sanitary Engineer.* 1:6 (June 1910), pp. 287-91.

3068 BULL, William Perkins. *From Medicine Man to Medical Man.* Perkins Bull Foundation. Toronto: G.J. McLeod, 1934.

3069 CANADIAN MENTAL HEALTH ASSOCIATION. *Milestones in Mental Health: A Record of Achievements, 1918-1958.* Toronto: The Association, 1960.

3070 CANADIAN PUBLIC HEALTH ASSOCIATION. *The Development of Public Health in Canada; A Review of the History and Organization of Public Health in the Provinces of Canada.* Toronto: Canadian Public Health Association, 1940.

3071 COLLINS, P.V. "The Public Health Policies of the United Farmers of Alberta Government, 1921-1935." M.A., Western Ontario, 1969.

3072 DESBIENS, Jacques. "Panorama sur l'augmentation des dépenses en soins de santé personnels au Canada de 1946 à 1970." M.A., Laval University, 1977.
3073 FEASBY, W.R. *Official History of the Canadian Medical Services, 1939-1945.* Ottawa: Queen's Printer, 1956.
3074 FERGUSON, John. *A History of the Ontario Medical Association 1890-1920.* Toronto: Murray Printing, 1939.
3075 FOULKES, R.C. "British Columbia Mental Health Services: Historical Perspectives to 1961." *Canadian Medical Association Journal.* 85:11 (September 1961), pp. 649-55.
3076 GELBER, Sylva M. "The Path to Health Insurance." *Canadian Public Administration.* 9:2 (June 1966), pp. 211-20.
3077 GIBBON, J.M. *Three Centuries of Canadian Nursing.* Toronto: Macmillan, 1947.
3078 _____. *The Victorian Order of Nurses for Canada, 1897-1947.* Montreal: Southam Press, 1947.
3079 GOFFMAN, I.J. "The Political History of National Hospital Insurance in Canada." *Journal of Commonwealth Political Studies.* 3:2 (1965), pp. 136-47.
3080 GRAHAM, Donald C. "The Canadian Medical Association: Its Genesis and Development." *Medical Journal of Australia.* (19 May 1962), pp. 772-77.
3081 GRAY, K.G. "Mental Hospitals Act, 1935 (Ontario)." *University of Toronto Law Journal.* 2:1 (1937), pp. 103-13.
3082 HEAGERTY, John J. *Four Centuries of Medical History in Canada: And a Sketch of the Medical History of Newfoundland.* Toronto: Macmillan, 1928.
3083 HOSPITALS DIVISION OF THE DEPARTMENT OF HEALTH, ONTARIO. *The Hospitals of Ontario: A Short History.* Toronto: Herbert H. Ball, 1934.
3084 JACQUES, André. *Les 325 Ans de l'Hôtel-Dieu de Québec, 1639-1964.* Quebec: L'Hôtel-Dieu de Québec, 1964.
3085 JAMIESON, Herber Carss. *Early Medicine in Alberta: The First Twenty-Five Years.* Edmonton: Canadian Medical Association, 1947.
3086 LAFRENIERE, T. "Evolution des lois provinciales d'hygiène." *Revue trimestrielle canadienne.* 1:1 (May 1915), pp. 67-74.
3087 LAVELL, Alfred E. "The Beginning of Ontario Mental Hospitals." *Queen's Quarterly.* 49:1 (Spring 1942), pp. 59-67.
3088 LAYCOCK, J.E. "A Blueprint for Health Services in Canada: An Essay Review." *Social Service Review.* 39:1 (March 1965), pp. 72-82.
3089 MacDERMOT, H.E. *History of the Canadian Medical Association.* 2 vols. Toronto: Murray Printing, 1958.
3090 _____. *One Hundred Years of Medicine in Canada, 1867-1967.* Toronto: McClelland and Stewart, 1967.
3091 _____. "A Short History of Health Insurance in Canada." *Canadian Medical Association Journal.* 50:5 (May 1944), pp. 447-54.
3092 MacTAGGART, Ken. *The First Decade: The Story of the Birth of Canadian Medicare in Saskatchewan and It's Development during the Following Ten Years.* Ottawa: Canadian Medical Association, 1973.
3093 MARSHALL, J.T. "The Development of Public Health in British Columbia." *Canadian Public Health Journal.* 25:8 (August 1934), pp. 359-69.

3094 MATTERS, D.L. "A Report on Health Insurance, 1919." *British Columbia Studies*. 21 (Spring 1974), pp. 28-33.
3095 MAUNDRELL, C.R. "Indian Health, 1867-1940." M.A., Queen's University, 1942.
3096 MEILICKE, Carl Alexander. "The Saskatchewan Medical Care Dispute of 1962: An Analytic Social History." Ph.D., University of Minnesota, 1967.
3097 MITCHELL, Ross. "The Development of Public Health in Manitoba." *Canadian Public Health Journal*. 26:2 (February 1935), pp. 62-70.
3098 PERLIN, A.B. "Medicine in Newfoundland — the Preconfederation Era." *Newfoundland Medical Association Newsletter*. (15 June 1974), pp. 16-18.
3099 PLANTE, André. "Que pense l'ouvrier d'un régime national d'assurance-santé." *Relations*. 220 (April 1959), pp. 93-95.
3100 POULIN, G. "Les problèmes du bien-être et de la santé dans la province de Québec, 1921-1951." *Mémoire*. La commission royale d'enquête sur les problèmes constitutionnels de la province de Québec, Quebec: Imprimeur de la reine, 1954.
3101 _____. "Les problèmes du bien-être et de la santé dans la province de Québec de 1921 à 1954." *Service social*. 13:2, 3, (July/December 1964), pp. 119-72.
3102 POWER, C.G. "Progress in Public Health in Canada." *Canadian Public Health Journal*. 27:8 (August 1936), pp. 380-84.
3103 RICHTER, L. "Improving Canada's Health." *Public Affairs*. 5:3 (Spring 1947), pp. 200-205.
3104 RISK, Margaret. "The Origins and Development of Public Health Nursing in Toronto from 1890-1918." M.Sc.H., University of Toronto, 1973.
3105 RIVARD, Jean-Yves, *et al*. *L'évolution des services de santés et des modes de distribution des soins au Québec*. Annexe 2. Quebec: Commission d'enquête sur la santé et le bien-être, 1973.
3106 ROSE, Theodore F. *From Shaman to Modern Medicine; A Century of the Healing Arts in British Columbia*. Vancouver: Mitchell Press, 1972.
3107 ROSENFELD, Leonard S. "Province-wide Hospitalization in Saskatchewan." *Public Affairs*. 10:3 (June 1947), pp. 157-63.
3108 "The Saskatchewan Story: A Review and Retrospect." *American Journal of Public Health*. 5 (1963), pp. 717-35.
3109 SHEPHERD, F.J. "The First Medical School in Canada: Its History and Founders, with Personal Reminiscences." *Canadian Medical Association Journal*. 15:4 (April 1925), pp. 418-25.
3110 SHILLINGTON, C. Howard. *The Road to Medicare in Canada*. Toronto: DEL Graphics Publishing Department, 1972.
3111 SUTHERLAND, Neil. "To Create a Strong and Healthy Race: School Children in the Public Health Movement, 1880-1914." *History of Education Quarterly*. 12:3 (Fall 1972), pp. 303-333.
3112 SWARTZ, Donald. "The Politics of Reform: Conflict and Accommodation in Canadian Health Policy." In *The Canadian State: Political Economy and Political Power*, edited by Leo Panitch. pp. 311-44. Toronto: University of Toronto Press, 1977.
3113 WARWICK, William. "The Development of Public Health in New Brunswick." *Canadian Public Health Journal*. 26:4 (April 1935), pp. 168-75.
3114 WILSON, Wallace A. "Health Insurance — A Flash-back." *British Columbia Medical Journal*. 2:12 (December 1960), pp. 795-808.

10.3.1.2   Reviews of Policy

3115 ANGUS, H.F. "Health Insurance in British Columbia." *Canadian Forum*. 17:195 (April 1937), pp. 12-14.

3116 BILSON, Geoffrey. "Cholera in Upper Canada, 1832." *Ontario History*. 67:1 (March 1975), pp. 15-30.

3117 BLAKENEY, A.E. "Press Coverage of the Medicare Dispute in Saskatchewan:1." *Queen's Quarterly*. 70:3 (Autumn 1963), pp. 352-61.

3118 BOUVIER, Emile. "Assurance-maladie obligatoire." *Relations*. 10 (October 1941), pp. 257-60.

3119 BRYCE, P.H. "Measures for the Maintenance and Improvement of the Public Health." *Report of the First Annual Meeting of the Commission of Conservation*. Ottawa; 1910, pp. 114-35.

3120 "Canadian Labour Congress, Brief to Health Commissioner." *Canadian Labour*. 7:6 (June 1962), p. 15.

3121 CANADIAN MEDICAL ASSOCIATION. *Report*. Committee on Economics of the Canadian Medical Association. Presented at the Annual Meeting, Calgary, 18-22 June, 1934.

3122 CURRIE, J.Z. "Application of the Public Health Act in New Brunswick." *Journal of the Legislative Assembly of New Brunswick*. Fredericton, 1894.

3123 DAVIDSON, George F. "Canada Considers National Health Plan." *Canadian Welfare*. 19:1 (April 1943), pp. 7-11.

3124 _____. "Proposals for Health Insurance." In *Canada and the World Tomorrow*, edited by Violet Anderson. pp. 116-30. Toronto: Ryerson Press, 1944.

3125 _____. "Revised Health Insurance Plans." *Canadian Welfare*. 20:1 (April 1944), pp. 16-17.

3126 DEFRIES, Robert Davies, ed. *The Federal and Provincial Health Services in Canada*. Toronto: Canadian Public Health Association, 1962.

3127 EVANS, R.G. "Health Services in Nova Scotia — the View from the Graham Report." *Canadian Public Policy*. 6:3 (Summer 1975), pp. 355-66.

3128 GRAUER, A.E. *Public Health*. A study prepared for the Royal Commission on Dominion-Provincial Relations. Ottawa: King's Printer, 1939.

3129 HASTINGS, J.E.F. "Canada's Health Programs." *Current History*. 44:262 (June 1963), pp. 326-32.

3130 HEALTH STUDY BUREAU. *Review of Canada's Health Needs and Health Insurance Proposals*. Toronto: The Bureau, 1945.

3131 HODGETTS, C.A. "The Importance of Public Health: From a National Standpoint." *Public Health Journal*. 1:9 (September 1910), pp. 427-34.

3132 HOLLOBON, Joan. "Bungle, Truce and Trouble: Medicare in Saskatchewan." (Reprinted from a series of articles in the *Globe and Mail*, December 1962). Toronto: *Globe and Mail*, 1963.

3133 HUTCHISON, J.A. "Public Health Legislation in the Province of Quebec." *Public Health Journal*. 4:9 (September 1913), pp. 502-504.

3134 KELLY, A.D. "The Swift Current Experiment." *Canadian Medical Association Journal*. 58:5 (May 1948), pp. 506-11.

3135 LLOYD, Premier W.S. "Address to the Saskatchewan College of Physicians and Surgeons." Regina: Queen's Printer, 1962.

3136 McCULLOUGH, J.W.S. "Public Health in Ontario." *Conservation of Life*. 3:2 (March 1917), pp. 313-20.

3137 McINTOSH, J.W. "The State Health Insurance Movement in British Columbia." *Canadian Public Health Journal*. 21:12 (December 1930), pp. 584-89.

3138 MOTT, F.D. "Prepaid Medical Care under Government Auspices in Saskatchewan." *Canadian Journal of Public Health*. 41:10 (October 1950), pp. 403-10.
3139 ONTARIO. Legislative Assembly. Select Committee on Public Health. *Report*. Toronto, 1878.
3140 QUEBEC MEDICAL ASSOCIATION. *Report of the Committee for the Study of Social Insurance*. Quebec: The Association, 1932.
3141 ROSE, Albert. "Some Major Issues in Developing a Program of Health Services for Canadians." *Social Worker*. 21:5 (July/August 1953), pp. 1-9.
3142 SASKATCHEWAN. Memorandum of Agreement. Government of Saskatchewan and the College of Physicians and Surgeons of Saskatchewan, 23 July 1962.
3143 SHEPS, Mindel C. "Health Reform in Saskatchewan." *Public Affairs*. 9:2 (Winter 1946), pp. 79-83.
3144 STIVER, W.B. "Prepaid Medical-Care Programs in Ontario." *Canadian Journal of Public Health*. 41:10 (October 1950), pp. 411-15.
3145 TAYLOR, Malcolm. "Canada Introduces Hospital Insurance — Plans and Prospects." *Queen's Quarterly*. 64:2 (Summer 1957), pp. 170-77.
3146 _____. "Quebec Medicare: Policy Formulation in Conflict and Crisis." *Canadian Public Administration*. 15:2 (Summer 1972), pp. 211-50.
3147 THOMPSON, Walter Palmer. *Medical Care: Programs and Issues*. Toronto: Clarke Irwin, 1964.
3148 THOMSON, William. "Press Coverage of the Medicare Dispute in Saskatchewan:2." *Queen's Quarterly*. 70:3 (Autumn 1963), pp. 362-71.
3149 TOLLEFSON, E.A. *Bitter Medicine; The Saskatchewan Medicare Feud*. Saskatoon: Modern Press, 1964.
3150 _____. "The Medicare Dispute." In *Politics in Saskatchewan*. edited by N. Ward and D. Stafford. pp. 238-79. Don Mills: Longmans, 1968.
3151 WADE, Mark S. *Notes on Medical Legislation in British Columbia*. Victoria, 1890.
3152 WHERRETT, G.J. "Arctic Survey 1. Survey of Health Conditions and Medical and Hospital Services in North West Territories." *Canadian Journal of Economics and Political Science*. 11:1 (February 1945), pp. 49-60.

10.3.2   Government Policy and Documentation

10.3.2.1   Federal

3153 ADAM, N. Duane. *An Organizational and Management Study of Preventive Services*. Saskatchewan: Department of Public Health, 1966.
3154 ASSOCIATION CANADIENNE POUR LA SANTE MENTALE. Division du Québec. *Mémoire sur l'ampleur du problème de la maladie mentale au Québec*. Montreal: Commission d'enquête sur la santé et le bien-être social, 1967. (memoire 4)
3155 BERRY, Charles Horace. *Voluntary Medical Insurance and Pre-payment*. Special Study Prepared for the Royal Commission on Health Services. Ottawa: Queen's Printer, 1965.
3156 CANADA. Advisory Committee on Health Insurance. *Report of the Advisory Committee on Health Insurance*. Ottawa: King's Printer, 1942.
3157 CANADA. The Community Health Centre Project. *Community Health in Canada; Report of the Project to the Conference of Health Ministers*. Ottawa: Information Canada, 1972-73.

3158 CANADA. Department of National Health and Welfare. *Legislation, Organization and Administration of Rehabilitation Services for the Disabled in Canada, 1970: A Report to the United Nations, International Labour Organization and World Health Organization.* Ottawa: Queen's Printer, 1971.

3159 _____. Research Division. *Hospital and Medical Care for Public Assistance Recipients in Canada.* Ottawa: The Department, 1950.

3160 _____. *Study of Health Services for Canadian Indians.* Ottawa: The Department, 1969.

3161 _____. *Task Force Reports on the Cost of Health Services in Canada.* 3 vols. 1. *Summary*; 2. *Hospital Services*; 3. *Health Services.* Ottawa: The Department, 1971.

3162 CANADA. Department of National Health and Welfare. Health Manpower Research Division. *Health Manpower Studies, 1970.* Ottawa: The Department, 1970.

3163 _____. Long Range Planning Branch. *Regionalization of Health Services in Canada: A Survey of Developments.* Ottawa: The Department, 1974.

3164 _____. Mental Health Division. *Mental Retardation Developments in Canada, 1964-1970.* Ottawa: The Department, 1971.

3165 _____. Mental Health Division. *Services for the Care and Training of Mentally Defective Persons in Canada.* Ottawa: The Department, 1953.

3166 _____. Research Division. *Hospital and Medical Care for Public Assistance Recipients in Canada.* Ottawa: The Department, 1950.

3167 _____. Research and Statistics Division. *The Administration of Public Health in Canada.* Ottawa: The Department, 1958.

3168 _____. Research and Statistics Division. *Mental Health Legislation in Canada.* Ottawa: The Department, 1960.

3169 CANADA. Department of Supply and Services. *Report of the Committee on the Operation of the Abortion Law.* Ottawa: The Department, 1977.

3170 CANADA. Royal Commission on Government Organization. *Report 15: Health Services.* Ottawa: Queen's Printer, 1962.

3171 CANADA. Royal Commission on Health Services. *Emerging Patterns of Health Care.* Ottawa: Queen's Printer, 1965.

3172 _____. *Medical Manpower in Canada.* Ottawa: Queen's Printer, 1964.

3173 _____. *Organized Community Health Service.* Ottawa: Queen's Printer, 1966.

3174 _____. *The Public Financial Aspects of Health Services in Canada.* Ottawa: Queen's Printer, 1963.

3175 _____. *Report.* Ottawa: Queen's Printer, 1965.

3176 _____. *Les services de santé communautaires organisés.* Ottawa: Imprimeur de la Reine, 1967.

3177 _____. *Submission to the Government of Province of Alberta.* Edmonton: 1962.

3178 _____. *Voluntary Medical Insurance and Prepayment.* Ottawa: Queen's Printer, 1965.

3179 GOVAN, Elizabeth. *Voluntary Health Organizations in Canada.* Study Prepared for Royal Commission on Health Services. Ottawa: Queen's Printer, 1966.

3180 KOHN, Robert. *Emerging Patterns in Health Care.* Special Study prepared for the Royal Commission on Health Services. Ottawa: Queen's Printer, 1966.

3181 _____. *The Health of the Canadian People.* Special Study prepared for the Royal Commission on Health Services. Ottawa: Queen's Printer, 1967.

3182 McKERRACHER, Donald G. *Trends in Psychiatric Care*. Special Study prepared for the Royal Commission on Health Services. Ottawa: Queen's Printer, 1966.
3183 MOORE, Percy E. "Health for Indians and Eskimos." *Canadian Geographical Journal*. 48:6 (June 1954).

10.3.2.2   Provincial

3184 ALBERTA. Executive Council. *Mental Health in Alberta: A Report on the Alberta Mental Health Study, 1968*. Edmonton, 1969.
3185 _____. Special Legislative and Lay Committee Inquiring into Preventive Health Services in the Province of Alberta. *Report*. Edmonton: The Committee, 1965.
3186 BRITISH COLUMBIA. Department of Health Services and Hospital Insurance. Mental Health Branch. *A Summary of the Growth and Development of Mental Health Facilities and Services in British Columbia, 1850-1970*. Victoria: The Department, 1972.
3187 _____. Health Security Programme Project. *Health Security for British Columbians*. Victoria: Queen's Printer, 1973.
3188 _____. Royal Commission Appointed to Inquire into Health and Accident Insurance Associations Operating in the Province of British Columbia. *Report*. Victoria: King's Printer, [n.d.]
3189 _____. Royal Commission on Mental Hygiene. *Final Report*. Victoria: King's Printer, 1927.
3190 _____. Royal Commission on State Health Insurance and Maternity Benefits. *Final Report*. Victoria: King's Printer, 1932.
3191 CLARKE, C.K. "Ontario's Government Clinic of Nervous and Mental Diseases." *Ontario Sessional Papers*. 43, Part 6, No. 21, 1911, pp. 101-102. 101-102.
3192 DOUGLAS, T.C. *Saskatchewan Plans for Health*. Regina: Department of Health, 1946.
3193 HANLY, Charles M.T. *Mental Health in Ontario*. Toronto: Queen's Printer, 1970.
3194 MacNAB, Elizabeth. *A Legal History of Health Professions in Ontario*. Toronto: Queen's Printer, 1970.
3195 MANITOBA. Department of Health and Public Welfare. *Special Select Committee on Health Report*. Winnipeg: King's Printer, 1947.
3196 _____. Department of Health and Public Welfare. The Cabinet Committee on Health, Education and Social Policy. *White Paper on Health Policy*. Winnipeg: The Committee, 1972.
3197 _____. Royal Commission on Costs of Hospitalization. *Report*. Winnipeg: The Commission, 1949.
3198 NEWFOUNDLAND. Royal Commission on Health. *Report*. St. John's: The Commission, 1966.
3199 NOVA SCOTIA. Council of Health. *Health Care in Nova Scotia — A New Direction for the Seventies*. Halifax: The Council, 1972.
3200 ONTARIO. Committee on the Healing Arts. *Report*. Toronto: Queen's Printer, 1970.
3201 PRINCE EDWARD ISLAND. *Report*. Premier's Task Force on Extended Care and Alcoholic Treatment Facilities in Prince Edward Island. Charlottetown: The Task Force, 1969.
3202 _____. Department of Health. *Discussion Paper on Health Policy for Prince Edward Island*. Charlottetown: The Department, 1977.
3203 QUEBEC. Commission d'enquête sur l'assurance-hospitalisation. *Rapport*. Quebec: Editeur officiel du Québec, 1960.

3204 _____. Commission d'enquête sur la santé et le bien-être social. *Rapport*. Quebec: Editeur officiel du Québec, 1970.
3205 _____. *Premier rapport du comité de recherches sur l'assurance-santé*. Quebec: Imprimeur de la Reine, 1966.
3206 SASKATCHEWAN. Advisory Committee on Medical Care. *Report to the Government of Saskatchewan. Interim Report 1961, and Final Report 1962*. Regina: Queen's Printer, 1961, 1962.
3207 SASKATCHEWAN. Department of Public Health. *History of the Swift Current Health Region Medical Care Plan, 1946-1966*. Regina: 1969.
3208 _____. *Indian Hospital Care in Saskatchewan*. Regina: Queen's Printer, 1966.
3209 _____. Department of Public Health. Aged and Long-Term Illness Survey Committee. *Report and Recommendations*. Regina: The Department, 1963.
3210 _____. Legislature. Select Special Committee on Social Security and Health Services. *First Report.*, 1943; *Final Report.*, 1944. Regina: King's Printer, 1943-44.
3211 _____. Medical Care Insurance Commission. *Information about the Saskatchewan Medical Care Insurance Plan (and) Hospital Service Plan*. Regina: Queen's Printer, 1972.

10.3.3   Health Insurance

3212 AGNEW, G. Harvey. "Hospital Care Insurance Plans." *Public Affairs*. 4:2 (December 1940), pp. 76-79.
3213 ALBERTA. *Mental Health in Alberta: A Report on the Alberta Mental Health Study, 1968*. Edmonton: Executive Council, Government of Alberta, 1969.
3214 "Assurance-santé." Editorial. *Relations*. 180 (December 1955), pp. 311-13.
3215 BADGLEY, Robin, and WOLFE, Samuel. *Doctor's Strike: Medical Care and Conflict in Saskatchewan*. Toronto: Macmillan, 1967.
3216 BELL, D.K. "Health Insurance in British Columbia." M.A., University of British Columbia, 1939.
3217 BLISHEN, Bernard R. "Social Change and Institutional Resistance: The Case for Medical Care." *Queen's Quarterly*. 72:3 (Autumn 1965), pp. 442-51.
3218 CANADIAN MENTAL HEALTH ASSOCIATION. *Submission to the Royal Commission on Health Services*. Toronto: The Association, 1962.
3219 CASSIDY, H.M. "The British Columbia Plan of Health Insurance." In *Proceedings*. pp. 544-56. National Conference on Social Welfare. Chicago: University of Chicago Press, 1935.
3220 "Les centrales ouvrières et l'assurance-santé." *Relations industrielles*. 13:2 (1958), pp. 175-207.
3221 ELKIN, Larry. "Contentious Aspects of Publicly Controlled Medical Care Insurance Plans." M.A., Carleton University, 1969.
3222 EVANS, R.G., and WALKER, H.D. "Economic Issues in the Provision of Health Services." In *Canadian Economic Problems and Policies*. edited by L.R. Officer and L.B. Smith, pp. 279-302. Toronto: McGraw-Hill, 1970.
3223 _____, and WILLIAMSON, M.G. *Extending Canadian Health Insurance; Options for Pharmacare and Denticare*. Toronto: University of Toronto Press for the Ontario Economic Council, 1978.
3224 GELBER, S.M. "L'assurance-hospitalisation au Canada." *Revue internationale du travail*. 79:3 (March 1959), pp. 265-94.

3225 GENEST, Jacques. "Assurance-hospitalisation." *Relations.* 220 (April 1959), pp. 90-93.
3226 "Health Services and Health Insurance in Canada." *Labour Gazette.* 48:6 (July 1948), pp. 711-15.
3227 KLEM, Margaret C. "Voluntary Health Insurance – Its Growth and Coverage." *Public Affairs.* 9:4 (September 1946), pp. 239-44.
3228 KOHN, Robert. "Some Economic Aspects of Our National Health." *Public Affairs.* 10:2 (March 1947), pp. 88-91.
3229 LANGLOIS, Marcel, "L'hôpital face à l'assurance-hospitalisation." *Relations.* 224 (August 1959), pp. 202-205.
3230 LINDENFIELD, Rita. "Hospital Insurance in Canada: An Example in Federal-Provincial Relations." *Social Service Review.* 33 (June 1959), pp. 148-60.
3231 _____. "The Hospital Insurance and Diagnostic Services Act: Its Federal-Provincial Aspects." Ph.D., University of Chicago, 1963.
3232 MARMOR, Theodore R., *et al.* "National Health Insurance: Some Lessons from the Canadian Experience." *Policy Sciences.* (December 1975), pp. 447-66.
3233 MORIN, C. "L'assurance-santé au Canada." *Service social.* 10:1 (1961), pp. 3-23; 10:2 (1961), pp. 4-21.
3234 RICHTER, L. "The Effect of Health Insurance on the Demand for Health Services." *Canadian Journal of Economics and Political Science.* 10:2 (May 1944), pp. 179-205.
3235 _____. "Health and Health Insurance." *Public Affairs.* 3:3 (March 1940), pp. 141-44.
3236 SAINT-ARNAUD, Georgette, and PARE, Simone. "L'assurance-santé au Québec." *Service social.* 10:1,2,3, (January/December 1967), pp. 164-92.
3237 TAYLOR, M.G. *The Saskatchewan Hospital Services Plan: A Study in Compulsory Health Insurance.* Regina: Health Services Planning Commission, 1949.

10.3.4   Issues in Health Care

10.3.4.1   General

3238 BADGLEY, Robin F., and CHARLES, Catherine A. "Health and Inequality: Unresolved Policy Issues." In *Canadian Social Policy*, edited by Shankar A. Yelaja, pp. 71-87. Waterloo: Wilfrid Laurier University Press, 1978.
3239 BILLETTE, André. "Santé, classes sociales et politiques redistributives." *Sociologie et sociétés.* 9:1 (April 1977), pp. 77-92.
3240 CHARRON, K.C. *Where Are We Now In Health Care in Canada?* Ottawa: Canadian Welfare Council, 1961.
3241 HASTINGS, J.E. "Canada's Health Programs." *Current History.* 44:262 (June 1963), pp. 326-32.
3242 LAFRAMBOISE, H.L. "Health Policy: Breaking the Problem Down into More Manageable Segments." *Canadian Medical Association Journal.* 108:3 (February 1973), pp. 388-93.
3243 MIQUE, Jean-Luc, and BELANGER, Gérard. "Evolution des prix des services de santé: faits et interprétation." *L'Actualité economique.* 48:1 (April-June 1972), pp. 5-37.
3244 ROBERTSON, H. Rocke. *Health Care in Canada: A Commentary.* Ottawa: Information Canada, 1973.
3245 THOMPSON, Walter P. *Medical Care: Programs and Issues.* Toronto: Clark Irwin, 1964.

10.3.4.2 Special Issues

3246 BROWN, Joan. "Occupational Health: The Poor Relation, Part I." *Labour Gazette.* 78:6 (June 1978), pp. 241-45.

3247 _____. "Occupational Health and Safety — The Right to Know." *Labour Gazette.* 78:2,3 (February/March 1978), pp. 71-76.

3248 CHING, D. "Saskatchewan's Occupational Health Act." *Canadian Labour.* 18:4-6 (April-June 1973), pp. 7-9.

3249 DOERN, G.B. "The Political Economy of Regulating Occupational Health: the Ham and Beaudry Reports." *Canadian Public Administration.* 20:1 (Spring 1977), pp. 1-35.

3250 GULDEMOND, Conny. *Citizens in Action: Public Participation in the Planning of Health Care in British Columbia.* Vancouver: Social Planning and Review Council of British Columbia, 1977.

3251 HODGETTS, C.A. "The Divided Responsibility in Regard to Public Health." *Canadian Engineer.* 17:6 (August 1909), pp. 146-49.

3252 LEBLOND, W. "La sécurité du travail, la médecine et l'hygiène industrielles (avec délibérations)." Congrès des relations industrielles de Laval. pp. 133-56. Quebec, 1948.

3253 McGILL, Lynda. *Home Care: A Report to the Nova Scotia Council on Health.* Halifax: Communications and Information Centre, 1972.

3254 McLEOD, J.L. *Consumer Participation, Professional Regulation and Decentralization of Health Services.* Regina: Department of Health, Government of Saskatchewan, 1973.

3255 _____. *Consumer Participation and Regional Structures for Health Administration in British Columbia.* Victoria: Health Security Project, Government of British Columbia, 1974.

3256 MARTEL, P.G. *A Role for the Federal Government in Mental Health.* Sherbrooke: University of Sherbrooke, June 1973.

3257 REA, K.J. "The Saskatchewan Anti-tuberculosis League: A Study in the Organization of Public Health Activity." M.A., University of Saskatchewan, 1956.

3258 RYAN, William. "Community Care in Historical Perspective." *Canada's Mental Health.* Supplement No. 60. (March/April 1969).

3259 SASS, Robert. "Occupational Health and Safety: Contradictions and Conventional Wisdom." *Labour Gazette.* 77:4 (April 1977), pp. 157-61.

3260 _____. "Occupational Health in Saskatchewan." *Canadian Labour.* 20:4 (December 1975), pp. 14-16.

3261 SCHWENGER, C.W. "Health Care for Aging Canadians." *Canadian Welfare.* 52:6 (January/February 1977), pp. 9-12.

10.3.5 Organization and Administration of Health Care

10.3.5.1 Organization

3262 HASTINGS, J.E.F. *The Organization of Medical Care within the Framework of Social Security in Canada.* Geneva: International Labour Organization, 1968.

3263 KELMAN, Vicki. "Health Care and the State — Community Health Centres in Ontario." M.S.W., Carleton University, 1978.

3264 LAZARUS, Morden. *Socialized Health Services. A Plan for Canada.* Toronto: Woodsworth Memorial Foundation, 1976.

3265 LEWIN & ASSOCIATES. *Government Controls on the Health Care System: The Canadian Experience.* Washington, D.C.: National Technical Information Service, U.S. Department of Commerce, 1976.

3266 ONTARIO. Council of Health. *Physician Manpower.* Toronto: The Council, 1974.

3267 PEEBLES, A. "The State and Medicine." *Canadian Journal of Economics and Political Science.* 2:4 (November 1936), pp. 464-76.

3268 ROCHER, G. "La médecine socialisée." *L'union médicale du Canada.* 94:7 (1965), pp. 907-14.

3269 WILLARD, Joseph W. "National Health Grants and Public Health Services." *Public Affairs.* 12:1 (Spring 1949), pp. 12-19.

10.3.5.2 Administration

3270 COLLEGE OF FAMILY PHYSICIANS OF CANADA. *The Evaluation of the Effectiveness of Programs Designed to Distribute Health Manpower Into Under-Serviced Areas.* A Report Prepared for the Department of National Health and Welfare. Ottawa: The Department, 1973.

3271 LA SALLE, Gérald. "L'administration hospitalière." *Relations.* 152 (August 1953), pp. 212-13.

3272 TAYLOR, M.G. *The Administration of Health Insurance in Canada.* Toronto: Oxford University Press, 1956.

3273 _____. "The Organization and Administration of the Hospital Services Plan." Ph.D., University of California, (Berkley), 1948.

3274 THERIAULT, M., and THIBAULT, R. "Les fonctions et les structures administratives des services sociaux dans les hôpitaux psychiatriques de la province du Québec." M.A. University of Laval, 1969.

10.3.6 Financing Health Care

3275 EVANS, Robert G. *Price Formation in the Market for Physician Services in Canada, 1957-1969.* Ottawa: Information Canada, 1972.

3276 "Financing Provincial Hospital Insurance." *Canadian Tax Journal.* 9:1 (January/February 1961), pp. 38-40.

3277 FRASER, R.D. *Canadian Hospital Costs and Efficiency.* Special Studies, No. 13. Ottawa: Economic Council of Canada, 1971.

3278 _____. *Health and General Systems of Financing Health Care Revisited.* (Discussion Paper, 95). Kingston: Queen's University. Institute for Economic Research, 1972.

3279 HANSON, Eric John. *The Public Finance Aspects of Health Services in Canada.* Ottawa: Queen's Printer, 1965.

3280 TAYLOR, Malcolm Gordon. *Financial Aspects of Health Insurance.* Toronto: Canadian Tax Foundation, 1957.

10.3.7 Health Interest Groups

3281 ARMSTRONG, Keith S. "Canadian Rehabilitation Council for the Disabled." *Canadian Journal of Public Health.* 61:3,4 (March/April 1970), pp. 149-51.

3282 AUCOIN, Peter. "Canadian Health Science Policies and Their Formulation." Ph.D., Queen's University, 1971.

3283 CANADIAN FEDERATION OF AGRICULTURE. *Health on the March: A Pamphlet on National Health Insurance Planning for Canada.* Toronto: The Federation, 1943.

3284 CANADIAN LABOUR CONGRESS. "Organized Labour Looks at Medicare." *Proceedings* of Conference at Sault Ste. Marie. Ottawa: The Congress, 1970.

3285 COLLINS, P.V. "The Public Health Policies of the United Farmers of Alberta Government, 1921-1935." M.A., University of Western Ontario, 1969.

3286 "Doctor's Policy on State Medicine." *Financial Post.* 54 (23 January 1960), p. 54.

3287 LOUGHEED, William *et al. Underwriting Canadian Health; A Economic View of Welfare Programs.* Toronto, William Lougheed Associates, 1957.

3288 MOHAMED, A.M. "Keep Our Doctors Committees in the Saskatchewan Medicare Controversy." M.A., University of Saskatchewan, 1964.

3289 PICKERING, Edward A. *Special Study Regarding the Medical Profession in Ontario: A Report to the Ontario Medical Association.* Toronto, 1973.

3290 TAYLOR, M.G. "The Role of the Medical Profession in the Formulation and Execution of Public Policy." *Canadian Journal of Economics and Political Science.* 26:1 (February 1960), pp. 108-27.

3291 TORONTO AND DISTRICT LABOUR COUNCIL. *Medicare: Labour's Opinion.* Toronto: The Council, 1965.

3292 TUOHY, Carolyn J. "The Political Attitudes of Ontario Physicians: A Skill Group Perspective." Ph.D., Yale University.

10.3.8   Health Personnel and Education

3293 CANADIAN MEDICAL ASSOCIATION. *Medical Care Insurance and Medical Manpower.* Conference Manuscripts of the Centenary Meeting of the Association. Montreal: The Association, 1967.

3294 CLUTE, Kenneth F. *The General Practitioner: A Study of Medical Education and Practice in Ontario and Nova Scotia.* Toronto: University of Toronto Press, 1963.

3295 NEW BRUNSWICK. Study Committee on Nursing Education. *Report.* Fredericton: The Committee, 1971.

3296 NEWFOUNDLAND. Royal Commission on Nursing Education. *Report.* St. John's: The Commission, 1974.

3297 NOVA SCOTIA. Hospital Insurance Commission. *Report.* Advisory Committee on Nursing Education. Halifax: The Commission, 1969.

3298 WILLARD, Joseph W. "Has Canada Enough Doctors?" *Public Affairs.* 11:1 (December 1947), pp. 26-30.

3299 WOLFSON, Alan D. "Supply of Physicians' Services in Ontario." Ph.D., Harvard University, 1975.

APPENDICES

Appendix I
Primary Source Material in the
Public Archives of Canada

In Canada provincial governments, universities, corporations, churches, and other private organizations hold archival materials of varying quantity and quality. The *Union List of Manuscripts* gives a researcher a brief description of all known sources of archival material. As the Public Archives of Canada (P.A.C.) has the largest and most significant holdings of archival material in Canada, we decided to concentrate on the preparation of a listing of relevant archival references from materials available at the P.A.C.

A preliminary review of all inventories produced by the P.A.C. revealed an enormous amount of material of potential significance to researchers in the formation, development, and administration of social welfare policy in Canada. For reasons of economy and efficiency, we decided to examine primarily the records of those federal government departments, crown corporations, task forces, commissions, committees, etc., involved in the making of social welfare policy in the twentieth century. For example, Record Group 29 — the papers of the Department of National Health and Welfare — and Record Group 27 — the papers of the Department of Labour — were particularly useful sources. In addition, we reviewed the more detailed file lists of thirty-eight departmental record groups available in the Public Records Division, from which we selected items of particular relevance. These items are given a separate listing in this Appendix.

We also examined private individuals' manuscripts, corporate records, and non-federal public records held in the P.A.C. Manuscript Division. The file lists revealed the papers of many prominent politicians, social reformers, and non-government organizations concerned with the development of social welfare policies in Canada. The emphasis here, as well, was on listing the most accessible and more recent material directly related to social welfare policy. This we interpreted to mean primarily the listing of papers related to social welfare policy in the era of industrial capitalism in Canada. Consequently, a systematic search of the records of New France, British North America, and of the fur trading companies (in which references to social welfare are scattered and more difficult to uncover) was not undertaken.

Wherever possible, references included in this Appendix were checked for their contents, and a brief annotation accompanying the reference was prepared. The abbreviations used in preparing individual references are explained in the following pages.

Wherever possible, a volume number, a file number, and a file title have been specified for each item. However, in cases where it would have been too time consuming to list every file a volume range and a general title has been used instead. In the Manuscript Division in particular, many references are made only to a collection of papers, since it would have been impossible to choose items dealing with social welfare policy from chronological or nominal file lists (for example, lists of letters with only dates and correspondents' names given). The criteria for the inclusion of particular collections lay in the assessment by the researchers of the significance of the contribution of a person or an organization named on a file list, to the formation of social welfare policy.

If the title of a file was such that it was unclear whether the contents were relevant, an effort was made to review the file in detail. This explains why some of the annotations are more detailed than others. However, it became obvious that a file or a volume could include a wide range of material. It was decided therefore to classify archival material only under the ten major headings used for the secondary source material in this *Bibliography*.

Excluded from the *Bibliography* but not insignificant for a researcher, are the Prime Ministers' Papers. The Public Archives of Canada has most of the known surviving papers of all the Prime Ministers since Confederation. The papers include memoranda on all major policy decisions, supporting documents, reports, and correspondence accumulated during their careers. The wealth of material to be found in the Prime Ministers' Papers, has led the Public Archives of Canada to produce computer indexes that will make the papers more accessible to researchers. However, since many of the inventories are still classified nominally and chronologically, a researcher must be very familiar with a policy issue and the people involved before being able to consult the papers of the Prime Minister concerned. The staff at the Public Archives of Canada provides a specialized reference and inquiry service for researchers interested in these large and heavily used collections.

List of Abbreviations

P.A.C.   Public Archives of Canada
RG   Record Group.
          This term is followed by a corresponding number and name.
MG   Manuscript Group.
          This term is also followed by a corresponding number and name.
S.R.E.   Selective Retention Entry.
          The use of this term in a reference means that the material is being
          held by an archivist for processing. Although the material is often un-
          sorted and not yet classified in volumes and files, it can usually be
          made accessible to researchers.
ACC. #   Accession Number.
          This is the first number assigned to material when it is held for Selec-
          tive Retention Entry.
Vol.   Volume
(R)   Restricted.
          Access to volumes and files with this classification is restricted by the
          application of the federal government's thirty-year rule or by the ex-
          pressed wishes of the donor of the papers. Researchers wishing to use
          these papers or records should consult the archivist in charge of the
          collection in order to find out the appropriate procedures which must
          be followed to gain access to the material.
(C)   Closed.
          Some government records and manuscripts have been closed to the
          public. In the case of government records, it may be for reasons of na-
          tional security or individual privacy. Private records may be closed as
          specified by the donor. Researchers should consult the archivist in
          charge in order to find out how to gain access.
(E)   Excluded.
          Some government departments will allow researchers to use material
          restricted under the thirty-year rule. However, some of the material
          from a volume may still be excluded and be retained by the
          department.
(10.2') or (3cm)
          Such measurements refer to the amount of shelf space the material
          occupies at the P.A.C.
MF   Microfilm.
          Some records and papers have been transferred to microfilm for
          safety and ease of access. Reel numbers have been specified where a
          microfilm reference appears in the *Bibliography*.

1.0   Origins of the Welfare State

P.A.C.   MG 18. E6. *Papers of Jeanne Mance*. Photocopies 1650, 1659, p. 15.
          Papers contain letters on recruiting sisters and raising money for the
          Hotel-Dieu of Montreal, which she founded.
P.A.C.   MG 24. A45. *Papers of Governor Duckworth. A Report for the Society for
          Improving the Condition of the Poor of St. John's Newfoundland.*
          1810-1811, pp. 1669-80. MF:M-3717.
P.A.C.   RG 1. Executive Council 1764-1867. E15A. *Board of Audit: Lower
          Canada*. Commissioner, House of Correction, Quebec. Vol. 270.
          1808-1829. Commissioner, House of Correction, Trois Rivières. Vol.

270. 1816-1826. Commissioner, House of Correction, Montreal. Vols. 272-276. 1802-1827. Commission for the Relief of the Insane and Support of Foundlings Vols. 292-297. 1801-1828. These reports are concerned mainly with the construction costs but could include information on how these institutions were run.

P.A.C. MG 9. A. Provincial, Local and Territorial Records. *New Brunswick, Health and Welfare.* Vols. 115-118. 1823-1867. MF:M-1667 to M-1668. Records relate to almshouses, public infirmaries, boards of health, disabled seamen, lunatic asylums, medical licensing, public health, and quarantine regulations, especially in regard to scarlet fever and smallpox.

P.A.C. MG 17. A20. *St. Vincent de Paul Society.* Originals. 1860-1922. (3″). Records include reports of visiting committees and reports of relief expenditures for the poor.

P.A.C. MG 32. B11. *Papers of Hon. E. Davie Fulton.* Originals. 1943-1968. (R) (43′8″). Papers contain scattered material on social welfare accumulated while he was Minister of Justice and Acting Minister of Citizenship and Immigration.

P.A.C. MG 32. B12. *Papers of Paul Martin.* Originals. 1905-1968. (200′7″). (R). Papers include correspondence, memoranda, speeches, articles, and clippings on social welfare policies made while he was Minister of National Health and Welfare. (1946-1957).

P.A.C. MG 30. A94. *Papers of J.L. Cohen.* Originals, n.d., 1923-1951. (R) (10.3 cm). These papers relate to his work as a labour lawyer and active campaigner for progressive social and labour legislation, particularly unemployment insurance and state medicine.

P.A.C. MG 32. C12. *Papers of Grace McInnis.* Originals. 1910, 1918, 1928-1951, 1967-1977. (4.6 m). Papers include correspondence, clippings, and speeches on many areas of social welfare policy e.g. abortion laws, child care, rights of the handicapped, guaranteed income, pensions, maternity leave, and mothers' allowances.

P.A.C. MG 28. IV.3. *Papers of Liberal Party of Canada.* Originals. 1878-1976. (99.4 m). MF:1948-1971: M-2178.

P.A.C. MG 28. IV.1. *Papers of Co-operative Commonwealth Federation and the New Democratic Party of Canada.* Originals, 1918-1976. (72.36 m) (R). MF:28 reels; C-4476 to C-4478, C-9264 to C-9272, C-9272 to C-9290. Papers include research, correspondence, convention proceedings, provincial files, policies, and activities of youth and womens' groups.

P.A.C. MG 28. IV.2. *Papers of Progressive Conservative Party.* Originals. (12″). MF:48 reels; 1878, 1921-1958, 1968. (R).

P.A.C. MG 28. IV.7. *Papers of Social Credit Association of Canada.* Originals. 1933-1972. (1 m).

P.A.C. MG 27. I.B5. *Papers of John Campbell Hamilton Gordon, 7th Earl of Aberdeen.* Vol. 13. 1893-1927. The papers of the Governor General include papers of his wife, Ishbell, who founded the Victorian Order of Nurses in Canada and who was the first president of the National Council of Women. This volume contains her notes, briefs, speeches, and printed material on immigration and labour.

P.A.C. MG 27. III. C4. *Papers of Agnes Campbell MacPhail.* Originals, 1921-1945. (3′5″). Papers include correspondence and briefs on penal reform, rural education, public health, co-operatives and women's affairs.

P.A.C.   MG 27. III.D6. *Papers of Louise Lucas*. Originals, 1928-1948. (1').
Papers record her activities in the United Farmers of Canada and the
C.C.F. in the 1930s in Saskatchewan. Files include briefs, position
papers, and correspondence with the C.C.F. and U.F.C. on issues
such as health insurance, unemployed youth, education, and
women's rights.

P.A.C.   MG 27.III.C7. *Papers of James Shaver Woodsworth*. Originals,
1891-1976. (3.05 m). Papers include correspondence, diaries, note-
books, lectures and speeches, printed material, personal papers, and
subject files on a wide range of topics such as divorce, immigration,
crime, and socialism and reports of the Bureau for Social Research
(1917). Although material covers a long time period, it is scattered,
as he destroyed many files.

P.A.C.   RG 29. Department of Health and Welfare. *Labour Youth Federation
of Canada*. Vol. 774, File 22. 1942-1944. File contains the report of
their National Constituent Convention (September 1942), a memorandum on health and briefs to the Prime Minister on physical fitness,
minimum wage laws, and child labour laws.

P.A.C.   MG 28.I10. *Papers of Canadian Council on Social Development. Quebec
Commission on Social Insurance*. Vol. 43. File 406. 1931.

P.A.C.   MG 28.I10. *Papers of Canadian Council on Social Development. Community Organization Division*. Vol. 157. 1935-1959. Papers include information on financial campaigns, community chests, and proceedings
of provincial and national committees.

P.A.C.   MG 27.III.D4. *Papers of Irene Parlby*. MF: 1 reel M-587.n.d., 1953,
1958. Photocopies, n.d., 1959 (9 pages). Microfilm reel includes an
M.A. Thesis, "The Honourable Irene Parlby" by Clare McKinlay,
1953, and material on education, public health, and women's rights.

P.A.C.   MG 31. D63. *Papers of Florence B. Bird*. (Anne Francis) Vol.5. *Royal
Commission on the Status of Women*. 1967-1971. (10 cm). Papers include her notes, clippings, and correspondence collected while she
was chairperson of the Royal Commission.

P.A.C.   MG 28.I.10. *Papers of Canadian Council on Social Development. Community Organization Division*. Vol. 157. 1935-1959. Papers include information on financial campaigns, community chests, and proceedings
of provincial and national committees.

P.A.C.   MG 28.III.26. *Bronson Family Papers*. Vols. 693-764. 1833-1952. (20΄).
These volumes relate to the family's activities in public welfare.
There are letterbooks, correspondence, and legal papers on maternal
and child welfare, relief in the 1930s, tuberculosis epidemics, sanito-
ria, and treatment.

P.A.C.   MG 27.I.D15. *Papers of Samuel Leonard Tilley*. Originals. 1802-1902.
(11'). Papers include correspondence on hospitals, penitentiaries,
promotion of emigration to New Brunswick, almshouses and poor
laws, lunatic asylums' reports, education, and the Fund for Sick and
Disabled Seamen.

2.0   Organizations and Political Pressure Groups and Social Wel-
fare Policy

P.A.C.   RG 29. Department of National Health and Welfare. *National Committee for Mental Hygiene*. Vol. 97. File 156-2-4. 1922-1946. Contains
annual reports, financial statements, and correspondence relating to
grants made by the federal government to the N.C.M.H. to promote
its work.

P.A.C.   MG 31. E17. *Papers of Margaret E. MacLellan.* Originals, 1936-1972. (7'4"). Papers relate to her activities in several women's organizations promoting a variety of changes in policies directed at women. Vol. 6 contains briefs and reports on women offenders, and correspondence with the Canadian Corrections Association and the Elizabeth Fry Society 1945-1972.

P.A.C.   MG 28. I.103. *Papers of Canadian Labour Congress.* Originals. n.d., 1883, 1893, 1908-1970. (53.11 m) MF: 1918-1928, 1956-1970: 24 reels, M-2028 to M-2049, M-2214, M-3244. (R & C). Papers relate mainly to records of the TLC, ACCL & CCL before CLC was formed in 1956. Only a small portion of the early TLC records have survived.

P.A.C.   RG 44. Department of National War Services. *War Charities Files.* Vol. 38-43. 1939-1954. *Registration of War Charities Organizations.* Vols. 66-72. 1939-1954. Correspondence files relating to applications from various organizations for registration under the War Charities Act, and reports of their work activities in Canada. The registers contain brief administrative outlines of various war service organizations registered under the War Charities Act.

3.0   The Welfare State in Canada

P.A.C.   RG 14. Canada. Committees, House of Commons. D.4.11. *Select Committee to Examine and Report Upon a National Plan of Social Insurance.* Vol. 1846. 1943. (.05 m).

P.A.C.   RG 33/89. Royal Commission on the Status of Women. *Papers and Research Articles.* Vols. 26, 28. 1967-1971. MF: reels C-6798 to 6799, C-6800 to 6801. Papers include: N. Darrell, "Negative Income Tax — Will it Work?" p. 22. H. Richard, "The Guaranteed Income." p. 27.

P.A.C.   RG 29. Department of National Health and Welfare. *Canadian Welfare Council.* Vol. 97. File 156-2-2, 1921-1949. Contains annual reports, financial statements, and correspondence from the Canadian Welfare Council to the federal government mainly on the grants it received and the work it performed.

P.A.C.   RG 116. Company of Young Canadians. *C.Y.C. Files.* Vols. 1-186. 1965-1976. (60 m). Files contain information on the internal organizational structure, administration, public relations, field project reports, files on citizen and social welfare groups in Canada, and a few consultants reports.

P.A.C.   MG 32.B5. *Papers of Brooke Claxton.* Originals. 1898-1960. (R) (25.25 m). Photocopies 1918-1919. (R) (1 cm). Papers contain scattered material on social welfare policy relating to issues in the early 1940s when he became Minister of Health and Welfare.

P.A.C.   MG 27.III.B9. *Papers of Henry Herbert Stevens.* Originals. 1911-1975. (25.70 m). Transcripts 1958, 1966. (20 cm). (R). Papers include material he collected on unemployment, relief, and immigration during the 1930s while he was Minister of Trade and Commerce and Chairman of the Royal Commission on Price Spreads and Mass Buying.

P.A.C.   MG 27.II.D13. *Papers of Newton Wesley Rowell.* Originals, 1824-1942. (4.66 m); Photocopies 1950 (6 pages); Transcripts 1917-1920 (17 pages). Papers relate to his activities as Minister of Health (1919-1920), Chief Justice of Ontario (1936-1938), and Chairman of Royal Commission on Dominion Provincial Relations (1937-1938).

P.A.C.   RG 29. Department of National Health and Welfare. Interdepartmental Committee on Social Security (Confidential). Vol. 1682. File 20-J-9A. 1961-1963. (R).

P.A.C.   RG 47. Dominion-Provincial Conferences. *Dominion-Provincial Conference, 1935.* Series 3, 6 volumes, 1935-1936. (3'8"). Volume 2 contains several confidential documents: 1. *Confidential Record of Proceedings of Conference and Sub-Conferences.* Ottawa, 9-13 December 1935, p. 250 (est.) especially the record of Subcommittee on Constitutional Questions and the Subcommittee on Unemployment and Relief Questions; 2. Canada, Department of Labour. *Memoranda on Unemployment and Relief.* p. 108 (est.); 3. Canada, Department of Labour. *Memoranda of Information in Relation to Various Social Services in Canada.* p. 32; 4. Dominion-Provincial Conference, 1935. *Constitutional Documents for Submission to Continuing Committee on Constitutional Questions.* Ottawa. 1936, p. 25 (est).

P.A.C.   RG 47. Dominion-Provincial Conferences. *Dominion-Provincial Conference, 1934.* Series 5. 1934. (2"). Records include the resolutions of the 1933 conference, a synopsis of the interim report of the Department of Labour on Dominion unemployment relief, and memoranda on unemployment and relief 1934.

P.A.C.   RG 47. Dominion-Provincial Conferences. *Dominion-Provincial Conference on Reconstruction, 1946.* Vols. 73-75, 1946. (20 cm). Records include list of submissions and proposals presented, statements made by provincial premiers on the Tax Agreement of 1946, statistics on relief expenditure, public debts, and people classified as unemployables.

P.A.C.   RG 19. Department of Finance. *Dominion-Provincial Taxation Agreements.* Vol. 3709. 1945-1948. These records contain copies of the agreements, statistics for each province, and the proposals of the Government of Canada discussed at Dominion-Provincial Conference on Reconstruction, 1945.

P.A.C.   RG 19. Department of Finance. *Tax Policy Series.* Vols. 3919-3940, 4236-4268, 4394-4410. 1932-1969. (R).

4.0   The Organization and Administration of Social Welfare Policy

P.A.C.   RG 29. Department of National Health and Welfare. Parliamentary Material. Vols. 1695-1712. 1945-1974. (R). (3.7 m) Records contain cabinet decisions (1962-1965); proposed legislation (1954-1968); minutes of cabinet meetings (1945-1963); material tabled for Parliament (1957-1974); and questions asked in the House of Commons on health and welfare (1957-1972).

P.A.C.   RG 29. Department of National Health and Welfare. *Social Security Group.* Vol. 51. File 40-6-1. 1947-1948. This group of civil servants and outside advisors met with the Minister of National Health and Welfare in secret to discuss how to implement the Green Book Proposals on Social Security, which were put forward at the Dominion-Provincial Conference in 1945. Included are the minutes of these meetings and drafts made for the Minister's speech to the House of Commons on social security.

P.A.C.   RG 44. Department of National War Services. *Voluntary War Relief Files.* Vols. 44-65. 1939-1954. Correspondence files relating to applications and reports from voluntary war relief organizations to send money, clothing, or foodstuff overseas.

6.0   Social Welfare Policies for People Out of Work

P.A.C.   RG 27. Department of Labour. *Unemployment Relief Branch.* Vols. 38, 52-54. 1931-1936. (1¼"). Records include financial statements on the administration and control of relief and the records of the Commissioner of Unemployment Relief.

P.A.C.   RG 27. Department of Labour. *Unemployment Assistance and Relief Measures.* Vols. 613-614. 1931-1953. Records contain dominion/provincial agreements, memoranda, information on grants, and Orders-in-Council.

P.A.C.   RG 27. Department of Labour. *Relief Measures.* Vols. 2020-2271. 1930-1942. (230'). Files deal with most aspects of the relief measures undertaken by the federal government during that time.

P.A.C.   RG 27. Department of Labour. *National Employment Commission.* Vols. 3346-3388. 1934-1945. (48'). Records contain the final report of the Commission and transcripts of the submissions from private groups and individuals concerned with employment and the administration of relief during the Depression.

P.A.C.   RG 27. Department of Labour. *Unemployment Insurance Files.* Vols. 3454-3459, 1940-1965. (4'). (R). Files include correspondence with various groups of workers and with workers who were in excluded categories of employment such as lumbering, agriculture, government, hospitals, charitable institutions, and education.

P.A.C.   RG 27. Department of Labour. *Unemployment Insurance Commission.* Vol. 3534. File 3-26-42-1; Vol. 3537. File 3-26-42-4. 1952-1965. (R). Files contain correspondence from unions, companies, workers, and individuals on the administration of U.I.C. along with proposals to change the regulations.

P.A.C.   RG 27. Department of Labour. *Unemployment.* Vol. 3530-3531. File 3-26-36. 1950-1963. (R). File contains suggestions and representations made by various interest groups on how to deal with unemployment insurance and benefits.

P.A.C.   RG 29. Department of National Health and Welfare. *Unemployment Assistance.* Vols. 918-921. 1949-1966. (R). Records include reports of various federal-provincial conference committees, cabinet committees, and interdepartmental committees and memoranda on cost sharing, legislation revision, and discussion with the provinces.

P.A.C.   RG 10. Department of Indian Affairs. *Unemployment Insurance.* Vol. 7990-7991. File 1/19-5 to 774/19-5. 1941-1963. (R).

P.A.C.   RG 50. Unemployment Insurance. *Organization, Application, Function and Procedures of the Unemployment Insurance Commission.* Vols 24-31. 1935-1965. (R). Records include earlier draft bills and acts; interpretation and analysis of the 1940 Act; amendments and regulations; and union action concerning the Unemployment Insurance Commission.

P.A.C.   RG 33/48. Royal Commissions. *Committee of Inquiry Into Unemployment Insurance Act. 1961-1962.* Records relate to the administration of the committee, its relations with government departments, private organizations, and individuals.

P.A.C.   RG 24. Department of National Defence. C9. *Unemployment Relief Scheme.* Vols. 85, 156-158, 2953-3188. 1932-1937. (89'). Records include headquarters and district files as well as reference files on policies; departmental reports; information on housing, medical services, riots, strikers, parliamentary inquiries, and news clippings on the camps set up in 1932 for single homeless men.

P.A.C.   RG 40. Department of Insurance. Series 3. *Records relating to the Preparation of the Unemployment Insurance Act, 1934-1941.* Vols. 24-27. 1934-1955. Also includes records of the Advisory Committee on the Unemployment Insurance Act.

P.A.C.   MG 30. E133. *Papers of Andrew G.L. McNaughton.* Vols. 17-99. 1932-1936. (8.5 m). These volumes contain correspondence, memoranda, clippings, policy statements, and reports on unemployment relief in the 1930s.

P.A.C.   MG 28. I103. *Papers of the Canadian Labour Congress.* Memorandum to government re unemployment insurance. Vol. 168. n.d.

P.A.C.   RG 27. Department of Labour. *Surveys — Maternity Leave.* Vol. 1903. File 38-11-3-4. 1971. File contains correspondence, questionnaires, statistics and submissions from interest groups; also contains the I.L.O. convention regulations on maternity leave.

P.A.C.   RG 27. Department of Labour. *Social Security — Unemployment Assistance in Canada — General.* Vol. 3584. File 11-9-5-1. Pt. 1. 1950. File contains unemployment statistics gathered by Department of Labour. These are compared to those from the Canadian Welfare Council.

P.A.C.   RG 27. Department of Labour. *Commission of Inquiry on the Unemployment Insurance Act.* Vols. 3390-3391. File 8-4-18. 1961-1965. File contains submissions to the inquiry from interest groups, summaries of the Gill Commission report, and internal memoranda discussing the implications of the Commission's recommendations.

P.A.C.   MG 28.I.10. Canadian Council on Social Development. *Unemployment Relief and Public Assistance.* Vols. 13-17, 42, 44, 50, 63-65, 68, 78, 99-100, 119-128. 1929-1964. Papers include proceedings of C.C.S.D. committees and conferences, statistics and reports on relief in the 1930s, other briefs, and correspondence.

P.A.C.   RG 27. Department of Labour, Women's Bureau. *Research, Statistics and Surveys on Maternity Protection.* Vol. 1904. File 38-11-6-3. 1966-1968. File contains a review of civil service regulations, bills and acts and the Canada Safety Code as well as two studies produced for the Department of Labour on maternity protection: 1) E. Enfrin, "Maternity Leave Provisions in Selected Collective Agreements," December 1967, pp. 1-4 and 4 pages of tables; 2) Documentation of a study on maternity protection for women done by Sheila Woodsworth under contract to the Women's Bureau, 1966, p. 63.

P.A.C.   RG 33/89. Royal Commission on the Status of Women. *Papers and Research Articles.* Vol. 30. 1967-1971. MF: reels C-6801 to 6802. Papers include: M. Spencer, "Maternity Leave Provisions in Canada and Other Countries," p. 19.

7.0 Social Welfare Policies For People Who Cannot Work

P.A.C.   RG 27. Department of Labour. *Pensions for Veterans and Veterans' Dependents.* Vol. 3529. Box #14. File 3-26-29. 1947-1965. (R). File contains suggestions and representations from various veterans' and widows' groups and the correspondence and memoranda of the Minister concerning more benefits for veterans and veterans' dependents especially those who served in World War I.

P.A.C.   RG 27. Department of Labour. *Old Age Pension.* Vol. 3529. File 3-26-27. 1947-1965 (R). File contains suggestions and representations from unions, manufacturers, insurance companies, and various individuals on changes in the Old Age Pension scheme.

P.A.C.   RG 27. Department of Labour. *Government Employees Compensation Branch.* Vols. 43-45. 1949-1955. (8″). (R). Records concern Provincial Workmens' Compensation Boards and federal government reimbursement for its employees.

P.A.C.   RG 27. Department of Labour. *Accident Prevention and Compensation Group*. Vols. 3443-3453. c. 1919-1964. (7'). (R). Records refer to provincial compensation legislation as well as organizations concerned with accident prevention and compensation for government employees.

P.A.C.   RG 91. Yukon Territorial Records. *Welfare*. Vols. 72-73. File 36. Parts I-II, 1918-1937.

P.A.C.   RG 29. Department of National Health and Welfare. *Old Age Pensions*. Vols. 125-159, 1927-1954. (R). Records give an outline of the administration of the Old Age Pension Act along with financial and statistical summaries.

P.A.C.   RG 10. Department of Indian Affairs. *Workmen's Compensation Act*. Vols. 6806-6808. Files 460-1 to 460-10. 1920-1948.

P.A.C.   RG 10. Department of Indian Affairs. *Allowances to Aged Indians*. Vols. 8388-8393. Files 1/29-5 to 673/29-5. 1948-1970 (R).

P.A.C.   RG 10. Department of Indian Affairs. *Blind Indians*. Vols. 8196-8197. File 29-11. 1948-1965. (R).

P.A.C.   RG 10. Department of Indian Affairs. *Deaf Indians*. Vol. 8206. File 29-18. 1946-1965. (R).

P.A.C.   RG 10. Department of Indian Affairs. *Care of Handicapped Indians*. Vols. 8202-8206. File 29-17. 1947-1965. (R).

P.A.C.   RG 10. Department of Indian Affairs. *Workmen's Compensation*. Vol. 7991. File 1/19-6. 1948-1965. (R).

P.A.C.   RG 35. Department of Veterans Affairs. *Care of the Aging Veteran*. Vol. 280. 1962. Report prepared by D.V.A. for the World Veterans Federation, p. 52.

P.A.C.   RG 33/74. Royal Commissions. *Canada, Commission on the Administration of the Pension Act*. Vols. 1-4. 1932-1933. (1'4"). Records include minutes, submissions, memoranda, and a copy of the report submitted on the administration of veterans' pensions.

P.A.C.   MG 17. F2. *Federated War Service Commission of the Churches of Canada*. Originals. 1918-1926. (10 cm). Records include information on their work amongst demobilized soldiers, hospitalized wounded, dependents of soldiers, widows and orphans.

P.A.C.   MG 30. C103. *Papers of Edwin A. Baker*. Originals. c. 1965. 936 pages. Papers are the typed transcripts of an oral history project by Marjorie Wilkins Campbell with E.A. Baker who helped to establish the Canadian National Institute for the Blind and in 1920 became its managing director.

P.A.C.   MG 28. I.103. *Papers of the Canadian Labour Congress*. House of Commons Joint Committee on Old Age Security. Vol. 169. 1950.

P.A.C.   MG 28.I.233. *Papers of Canadian Institute for the Blind*. MF: 1906-1950, 2 reels, M-3795, M-3796. Papers relate to the Institute's work promoting services for the blind and better allowances.

P.A.C.   MG 28.I.5. *Papers of Canadian Patriotic Fund Association*. Originals. 1900-1922. (30 cm). Papers relate to funds raised and distributed for Canadians wounded or disabled in the South African War, and their widows and dependents.

P.A.C.   RG 85. Northern Administration. *Ordinances — Northwest Territories including Insane Persons Allowances*. Vol. 1321. File 530-540. Pts. 1 & 2. 1938-1960.

P.A.C.   RG 38. Veteran Affairs. *Subject Files*. Vols. 137-246. 1914-1945. (42'). These files relate to various subjects e.g. blinded veterans, the Halifax explosion, British war guests, hospitals, parliamentary committees

and inquiries, employment, pensions, prosthetic services, rehabilitation, treatment services, and veteran's organizations.

P.A.C.   RG 35. Interdepartmental Committees. *Canada. Interdepartmental
Committee on Veterans Affairs*. Series 6. 1945-1946. (3″). Records
include four files consisting of memoranda and drafts of bills relating to
veterans benefits; files of the Deputy Minister of Veterans Affairs; a
copy of the final report of the committee; notes, speeches, short histories on such topics as rehabilitation and pension legislation.

P.A.C.   RG 19. Department of Finance. *Militia Pensions*. Vols. 2472-2475.
1827-1871.

P.A.C.   RG 29. Department of National Health and Welfare. *Old Age Assistance, Blind Persons and Disabled Persons Assistance Acts*. Vol. 163-174.
1945-1958. (R). Volumes include acts and regulations for each province, transfers made between the federal and provincial governments, and policies dealing with special groups e.g. mental patients,
Japanese evacuees, and veterans.

P.A.C.   RG 29. Department of National Health and Welfare. *Blind Persons' Allowances*. Vol. 159A 163. 1936-1951. (R). Volumes deal with provincial legislation and administration, statistics, and general
correspondence.

P.A.C.   RG 29. Department of National Health and Welfare. *Old Age Pensions*.
Vol. 1278. File 30-6-3. 1905-1969. (R). File includes resolutions and
briefs of Old Age Pensioner associations.

P.A.C.   RG 29. Department of National Health and Welfare. *Blindness Control
Division*. Vol. 912. 1917-1958. (R). This volume includes material on
policies and procedures adopted, national health grants, surveys,
treatment facilities, and correspondence with interest groups.

P.A.C.   RG 33/89. Royal Commission on the Status of Women. *Papers and
Research Articles*. Vol. 27. 1967-1971. MF: reels C-6799 to 6800.
Papers include: M. Gaudette, "The Canada Pension Plan and Married
Women," p. 16.

8.0   Social Welfare Policies for "Marginal" People

P.A.C.   RG 76. Immigration Branch. *Canadian Citizenship Act and Regulations*.
Vol. 518-519. File 801544. Parts 6-10. 1936-1952. MF: C-10-614,
C-10-615.

P.A.C.   RG 76. Immigration Branch. *Deportation of Insane Persons from
Canada: Policy and Instructions*. Vol. 597. File 865252. 1913-1939. MF:
C-10, 666 to C-10, 667.

P.A.C.   RG 76. Immigration Branch. *Chinese Immigration Act and Amendments*.
Vol. 587-589. File 827821. Pts. 1-3. 1892-1948. MF: C-10, 659 to
C-10, 661.

P.A.C.   RG 27. Department of Labour. *Immigration and Labour Files*. Vols.
275-292. Originals. 1943-1965. (13′). (R). Files deal particularly with the
Employment Service and the Special Services Branches of the
Department of Labour on the relationship between the labour market
and immigrants e.g. the effect of immigrants on the labour market;
cost of their training, medical care, education, and social services.

P.A.C.   RG 73. Solicitor General's Department. *Manuscript on Prison Theory
and Practice by C.W. Topping*. Vol. 14. File 1-11-8. 1924-1943.

P.A.C.   RG 73. Solicitor General's Department. *Commission Appointed to Investigate Penitentiary Administration*. Vol. 35-36. File 10. 1913.

P.A.C.   RG 73. Solicitor General's Department. *Commission Appointed in 1936
to Investigate the Penal System of Canada, Dorchester*. Vols. 41-42. File
1-20-11. Parts 1-8. 1931-1957.

P.A.C.   RG 73. Solicitor General's Department. *Commission to Investigate the Management of Penitentiaries, St. Vincent de Paul.* Vol. 43. File 3-20-10. 1897-1899.

P.A.C.   RG 73. Solicitor General's Department. *Commission Appointed in 1936 to Investigate the Penal System of Canada.* Vol. 43-44. Files 4-20-11, 5-20-11, 6-20-14, 7-20-14, 8-20-14. (Various individual penitentiaries.) 1936-1937.

P.A.C.   MG 11. Colonial Office, London. C.O. 384 *Emigration, Original Correspondence.* 1817-1857; 1872-1896. MF: B-876 to B-888; B-943 to B-962; B-1735 to B-1749; B-1984 to B-1989; B-2065 to B-2069. (59 reels). These records relate to the emigration of British people to British colonies. Amongst official correspondence between governments is the correspondence of private emigration societies, Crown Agents, and others. Recurring topics include the emigration to Canada of deaf mutes, pauper children, women, Chinese, and the Irish.

P.A.C.   MG 11. Colonial Office, London. C.O. 384/127 Emigration/1880/Dispatches: Eastern Australia and Miscellaneous. *Landing of Pauper Immigrants in Halifax, N.S.* — copy of the Report with Proclamation issued, prohibiting the landing of pauper or destitute immigrants in the port of Halifax. 19 January 1880. MF: B-2065.

P.A.C.   MG 24.I156. *Norwich Emigration Records.* 1835-1852. 51 pages. Records contain emigration circulars issued by the Poor Law Commissioners for England to govern the sponsoring of emigration by the poor with copies of related correspondence resolutions, and lists.

P.A.C.   MG 24.J14. *Papers of Rev. William King.* Originals. 1836-1895. MF: 1849-1895. C-1462, C-2223. Papers contain information and news clippings on slavery and settlement of fugitive slaves in Canada.

P.A.C.   MG 19.F26. *Newhouse Seth (Da-yo-de-ka-ne) Papers.* 1885. 312 pages. Newhouse was an Onandaga Indian, who in 1880 began codifying the culture and history of his people, particularly the institutions and problems of government affecting Indians. His views were disputed by other chiefs and their version was published by the Royal Society of Canada in the Proceedings for 1911 under the title, *Traditional History of the Confederacy of the Six Nations*, with Duncan Campbell Scott credited as author.

P.A.C.   MG 24.B1. Neilson Collection. *Neilson-Mondelet Penitentiary Commission.* Vol. 13. 1834.

P.A.C.   MG 24.K22. *Mary Ann Shadd Cary Papers.* Originals. 1852-1889. 19 pages. Transcripts n.d. 7 pages. Photocopies 1852-1871. 34 pages. Papers relate to her work with anit-slavery societies and the abolition movement.

P.A.C.   RG 4. Civil and Provincial Secretaries' Office, Canada East 1760-1867. B.63. *Immigration.* 1853. (3″). Records contain general reports on immigrants with comparisons to previous years; decisions regarding cholera and quarantine and copies of the Act to Amend and Consolidate Laws Relative to Emigrants and Quarantine.

P.A.C.   RG 5. Civil and Provincial Secretaries' Office, Canada West, 1788-1867. B.21. *Immigration Records Relating to the Encouragement of,* Vols. 1-3. 1840-1844. (8 cm). Records include information on prices, wages, and prospects for employment and land settlement in various districts.

P.A.C.   RG 5. Civil and Provincial Secretaries' Office, Canada West, 1788-1867. B.27. *Prison Returns.* Vols. 1-7. 1823-1861. (25 cm). Gaol calendars and returns of prisoners by district with correspondence, statistical records, and medical certificates.

P.A.C.   MG 17.D1. *Moravian Brethren.* Originals. 1827-1955 (8 cm). Transcripts, 1752, 1770-1779. (20 cm). MF: 1749-1944: A548-572, M-484-535. (77 reels). Index Reel: A572. Records relate their missionary work amongst the Inuit, which was financed by the Society for the Propagation of the Gospel.

P.A.C.   MG 32.B1. *Papers of Hon. Richard Albert Bell. Ministerial Files, Department of Citizenship and Immigration.* Vols. 71-100. 1955-1963. (R). (21'3"). These files include policy and case files on citizenship, immigration, and Indian Affairs.

P.A.C.   MG 30.C72. *Papers of W.J. Bossy.* Originals. Vols. 1-30. 1920-1973. (R). (3.61m). Papers relate to his activities as a teacher of new Canadians and as a Ukrainian community organizer. He established the New Canadian Service Bureau in Montreal.

P.A.C.   MG 30.C119. *Papers of Louis Rosenberg.* Originals. n.d., 1829-1975. (R) (6.7 m). Papers relate to his work as a sociologist and demographer of Jewish people in Canada, and his position as Western Canadian Director of the Jewish Colonization Association, 1919-1940.

P.A.C.   MG 29.C16. *Papers of James Mavor.* Originals. 1922, 9 pages. Transcripts 1898-1899. 98 pages. Papers relate only to his work in immigration and include material used for several government reports he wrote on Doukhobor immigration to Canada.

P.A.C.   MG 28.I.173. *Papers of Ontario Labour Committee for Human Rights.* Originals. 1945-1972. (26'). (R). Papers relate to the Committee's efforts to provide public education and to monitor and intervene in cases of ethnic, religious, and racial discrimination in Toronto in the 1940s and later throughout Ontario.

P.A.C.   MG 29.C98. *Papers of Baron Maurice Hirsch Auf Gereuth.* Photocopies 1891-1964, n.d. 190 pages. Some of the material relates to Baron de Hirsch's activities in sponsoring Jewish immigration to Canada and provisions made in Montreal for their settlement.

P.A.C.   MG 28.V.86. *Papers of Baron de Hirsch Institute and Hebrew Benevolent Society.* Originals. 1863-1950. (5 m). MF: 2 reels, M-3787 to M-3788. Papers relate to the care of the Jewish poor in Montreal and the settlement of Jewish immigrants in Canada.

P.A.C.   MG 29.E18. *Papers of John Lowe.* Originals. 1815-1911. (11'9"). Papers relate mainly to immigration, pauperism, public health, and Indian scrip speculation, which were gathered while he was Deputy Minister of Agriculture, 1888-1895.

P.A.C.   RG 36. Boards, Offices, Commissions (non continuing). Series 24. Canada. *Canadian Committee on Corrections.* Vols. 1-34. 1965-1969. (11'4"). (R). Records consist of correspondence, briefs from interest groups, studies, drafts of the report, memoranda, and recommendations made in the broad field of corrections.

P.A.C.   RG 36. Boards, Offices, Commissions (non continuing). Series 27. Canada. *British Columbia Security Commission.* Vols. 1-44. 1942-1948. (R). (16'4"). Records consist of correspondence, memoranda, reports, and clippings on the evacuation and settlement of Japanese people from coastal British Columbia during World War II.

P.A.C. RG 36. Boards, Offices, Commissions (non continuing). Series 33.
        Canada. Committee on Juvenile Delinquency. Vols. 1-2. 1961-1963. (R).
        (16″). Records consist of reports, recommendations, briefs, submissions, memoranda, and correspondence on the nature and extent of
        juvenile delinquency in Canada.

P.A.C. RG 36. Boards, Offices, Commissions (non continuing). Series 34.
        Canada. Correctional Planning Committee. Vols. 1-13. 1958-1960. (R).
        (9′). Records consist of surveys of programmes in Canada and elsewhere, surveys of selected institutions and specific problems such as
        drug addiction, staff selection, as well as correspondence with interest
        groups, provincial governments, and other countries.

        Canadian Penitentiary Service Museum, Correctional Staff College,
        Kingston, Ontario. *Records of the Kingston Penitentiary.* 1805-1968.
        (R). Records deal with every aspect of prison administration and contain reports and policy directives from the Minister of Justice to the
        wardens. A complete list of these records can be consulted at the
        Records Division of the Public Archives of Canada.

        Canada, Solicitor-General's Department, Canadian Penitentiary Service, Regional Office, Vancouver, British Columbia. Records deal
        with every aspect of prison administration as well as containing
        reports by commissioners, and inspectors. A complete list of these
        records can be consulted at the Records Division of the Public Archives of Canada.

P.A.C. MG 28.I85. *Canadian Citizenship Council Papers.* Originals. Vols.
        1-108. 1941-1969. (36′). Papers show the link between the Council activities and research on immigrants and the federal and provincial
        governments. Copies of pamphlets produced and a brief history of the
        Council are included.

P.A.C. RG 85. Northern Administration C. Northern Administration and
        Lands Branch. 1 (a) *Central Registry Files.* Vols. 1-248, 251-353,
        360-539, 549-562, 627-653, 688-722, 729-731, 740-743, 1044-1045,
        1053-1515, 1662-1666, 1675-1683, 1866-1884, 1890-1903, 1909-1910,
        1915-1929, 1962. 1892-1971. This major series covers all aspects of
        Northern Administration Branch activities, including the development of social policy for the Inuit and the provision of public health
        facilities, schools, and the maintenance of law and order in the North.
        A computer index, a card index, and various file lists are available at
        the P.A.C. for researchers.

P.A.C. RG 17. Department of Agriculture. *Immigration Branch.* Vols.
        2392-2414, 2690. 1842-1893. Records include departmental correspondence on all aspects of immigration plus subject files, records,
        and registers which relate to quarantine, cholera, private emigration
        societies, shipping companies, and services for immigrants.

P.A.C. RG 17. Department of Agriculture. *Records of the Minister, Deputy
        Minister, and Secretary.* Vols. 1-1487. 1852-1925. Records include all
        their correspondence on several topics, including immigration and especially the arrangements made between the federal government and
        various shipping companies and their agents posted overseas, which
        are found in the secret and confidential letterbooks and correspondence. (Vols. 1631-1662).

P.A.C.   RG 27. Department of Labour. *Japanese Division*. Vols. 640-662.
1940-1965 (7'). (R). Records contain information on the policy and on
the administration of the evacuation of the Japanese from the coastal
areas of British Columbia and the administration of their placement,
housing, segregation, repatriation, naturalization and on mail cen-
sorship during and after World War II.

P.A.C.   RG 73. Solicitor General's Department. *Special Reports on Penitentiaries to the Minister*. Vol. 66. File 1-12-3. Pt. 1. 1919-1929. Records contain memoranda sent to the Deputy Minister by the Superintendent
of Penitentiaries. Subjects dealt with include the separation of young
prisoners and non-violent prisoners, and the kind of work, education,
and religious instruction given to prisoners. Also included are annual
reports on the penitentiaries and a brief from the Canadian Council
on Agriculture.

P.A.C.   RG 73. Solicitor General's Department. A2. *Penitentiary Branch —
Correspondence*. Vols. 1-43, 47-161, 163-171. 1874-1967. (42'). (R). Files
relate to policy and procedure in federal penitentiaries. Included
are annual reports, reports of wardens, conferences, inspections, and
study groups, special inquiries into penal practices, and individual
case files.

P.A.C.   RG 10. Department of Indian Affairs. *Miscellaneous Assistance*. Vols.
8197-8199. 1946-1966. (R) (E). Records consist mainly of case files
and policy directives dealing with general welfare assistance to Indians
for a variety of situations e.g. house rental, cost of medical examina-
tions, travelling expenses to appear in court, destitution after release
from prison or hospital, prosthetics, etc. Correspondence between
Indian agents and the federal government deals with policy on responsibility for disabled, blind, and destitute Indians who were ineligi-
ble for provincial assistance.

P.A.C.   RG 10. Department of Indian Affairs. *Welfare: general*. Vols.
6923-6937. Files 1/29-1 to 987/29-3. 1921-1965 (R).

P.A.C.   RG 10. Department of Indian Affairs. *Relief Food Assistance*. Vols.
7094-7097. Files 1/10-3 to 777/10-3. 1888-1965. (R).

P.A.C.   RG 10. Department of Indian Affairs. *Welfare Equipment and Supplies*.
Vol. 7093. File 142/10-1. 1908-1967.

P.A.C.   RG 10. Department of Indian Affairs. *Taxation of Indians*. Vols. 8870,
7978. File 1/18-21 to 1/18-21-1. 1918-1966. (R).

P.A.C.   RG 10. Department of Indian Affairs. *Reports*. Vols. 8437-8474. File
1/23-1-2 to 501/23-35. 1909-1968. (R). These are monthly and semi-
annual reports of school inspectors, social workers, housing and fur
supervisors, and welfare teachers. Also included are various reports
of the House of Commons.

P.A.C.   RG 13. Department of Justice. *Remissions Branch*. Vols. 1128-1367,
1888-1962 (17.5 m). MF: reels, M-1776 to M-1895. Registers give
examples of how the remission service functioned, the nature of the
crime, and punishment given. Correspondence is included between
the Minister of Justice and the Governor General.

P.A.C.   RG 18. Royal Canadian Mounted Police. *Records of the R.C.M.P.*
Vols. 1-3193. 1868-1965. (Vols. 2321-2375, 3194-3221 are restricted).
These records are arranged in 6 sections. a) Comptroller's Office
(1874-1920). b) Commissioner's Office (1868-1954). c) Division and
Detachment Records (1874-1965). d) Yukon Records (1897-1951).
e) Dominion Police Records (1872-1919). f) Headquarters Series

(1902-1925). They contain official correspondence, accounts, office records, orders and regulations, crime reports, detachment records, and daily journals.

P.A.C.   RG 26. Department of Citizenship and Immigration. *Records of the Department of Citizenship and Immigration.* Vols. 1-179. 1880-1979. Records include early statistical ledgers re immigrants; correspondence of the Deputy Minister's office and material relating to ethnic groups and immigrant services funded by federal grants.

P.A.C.   RG 76. Immigration Branch. *Chinese Division.* Vols. 694-703. Pts. 1-10. 1885-1902. (.9 m). MC:C-9510 to C-9513. Records consist of general registers kept by the immigration agencies on Chinese immigrants.

P.A.C.   RG 76. Immigration Branch. *Registration of Chinese in Canada under Section 18 of the Chinese Immigration Act of 1923.* Vol. 223. File III414. 1942-1943, 1958. MF: C-7372.

P.A.C.   RG 76. Immigration Branch. *Scheme between Britain and Canada Governments: Settlement of British Families on Land. (The 3000 British Families Settlement Scheme of the Empire Settlement Act).* Vol. 248-249. File 179046. Pts. 1-9. 1925-1935. MF: C-7397-7398. File contains photos, lists, pamphlets, reports, and posters.

P.A.C.   RG 76. Immigration Branch. *Proposed emergency fund for Empire Settlement Immigrants during the first year in Canada.* (Empire Settlement Act) Vol. 346. File 371860. 1928-1932. MF: C-10,253.

P.A.C.   RG 76. Immigration Branch. *II. Immigration Agency Records.* Vols. 677, 678, 693. 1887-1908. (.325 m). MF: reels, C-10, 678 to C-10, 680, C-9510. Records consist of 1) letterbooks kept by John Hoolahan, Dominion Immigration Agent in Montreal, 1893-1916, which show correspondence with government, individuals, and prospective immigrants. 2) Statistics on immigrants and deportees, 1897-1905. 3) Reports and Head Tax Registers of the New Westminister Agency on the control of Chinese immigration, 1887-1898; 1907-1908.

P.A.C.   RG 76. Immigration Branch. *Central Registry Series.* Vols. 1-677, 679-682, 712. 1873-1970. (458'8"); MF: 328 reels. Index to series on MF: reels, M-1983 to M-1990. These records contain material on the administration of immigration. These include case records; immigration acts; reports; actions of labour; government negotiations with societies, shipping and railway companies; special groups, and deportation.

P.A.C.   RG 76. Immigration Branch. *Criticisms and Suggested Changes of Policy on Immigration.* Vols. 243-245. File 165172. Pts. 9-16. 1938-1952. MF: C-7392 to C-7393. These criticisms and suggested changes come from a wide cross-section of Canadians and various interest groups, often promoting the immigration of one racial group over another or protesting policy because of the unemployment of Canadians.

P.A.C.   RG 76. Immigration Branch. *Proposed emergency fund for Empire Settlement Immigrants during the first year in Canada.* (Empire Settlement Act) Vol. 346. File 371860. 1928-1932. MF: C-10,253.

P.A.C.   RG 76. Immigration Branch. *Chinese Immigration.* Vol. 121. File 23625. MF: C-4784. 1908-1911. This file contains a report on Chinese immigration by W.L. Mackenzie King.

P.A.C.   RG 76. Immigration Branch. *Help for Destitute Immigrants.* Vol. 133. File 32437 MF: C-4797. 1898-1927.

P.A.C. MG 28.I10. *Papers of Canadian Council on Social Development. Juvenile Immigration.* Vols. 6, 12, 25-26, 35-36. 1923-1934. Papers include surveys, correspondence with the Department of Immigration, and interest groups such as the I.O.D.E. and immigration societies.

P.A.C. MG 28.I10. *Papers of Canadian Council on Social Development. Juvenile Justice.* Vols. 13, 31, 50, 56-57, 88-91, 97-99, 102. 1923-1973. Papers include juvenile and family court legislation, reports by the Council Committee, and other studies and statistics on delinquency.

P.A.C. MG 28.I10. *Papers of Canadian Council on Social Development. Gaols and Reformatories.* Vols. 7, 97-99. 1926-1973. Papers include a study on the cost of crime by the Canadian Criminology and Corrections Association, conference reports, briefs and a Senate study on parole, and correspondence with the government and other interest groups.

P.A.C. MG 29.E16. *Papers of William Purvis Rochfort Street.* Originals. 1885-1900. (3"). Papers include letters sent by and to him when he was Chairman of the Half Breed Commission in 1885.

P.A.C. MG 27.B6. *Papers of Henry Charles Keith Petty — Fitzmaurice, 5th Marquess of Lansdowne.* MF: reels, A.623-627. 1883-1889. These papers include correspondence while he was Governor General, on the alleged distress of state-aided emigrants, the Half Breed Bill of Rights, Indian education, and the immigration of Chinese and crofters to Canada.

P.A.C. MG 27.IC4. *Papers of Edgar Dewdney.* Originals. 1877-1899. (1'2"). MF: 3 reels, M-2815 to M-2817. 1861-1926. Papers collected are mainly Indian Affairs departmental files concerning all aspects of government policy towards Indians and the Northwest Rebellion while he was Superintendent of Indian Affairs, 1888-1892.

P.A.C. MG 27.II.D15. *Papers of Clifford Sifton.* Originals. 1889-1957. (99´). Transcripts, 1891-1955. (4"). MF: C-449 to C-600, C-401 to C-445, C-2171 to C-2179. Eighty percent of these papers relate to the period 1896-1905 when Sifton was Minister of the Interior and had responsibility for immigrant land settlement and Indian Affairs. Some other material is included on penitentiaries and education in the West.

P.A.C. MG 29.E15. *Papers of Edmund Allen Meredith. Asylums and Prisons.* Vol. 5-6. 1860-1880. Records include memoranda, notes, and correspondence on prison reform legislation and asylums; the minute book of the Saint John Penitentiary (1868-1880) and reports of investigations of that penitentiary (1875-1877).

P.A.C. RG 33/89. Royal Commission on the Status of Women. *Papers and Research Articles.* Vols. 25-27, 29. 1967-1971. MF: reels: C-6798-6800, 6801-6802. Papers include: Dr. M.A. Bertrand, *et al,* "Brief on Female Crime," p. 175; E. Ferguson, "Immigrant Women in Canada," p. 68; F. Hawkins, "Women Immigrants in Canada," p. 40.

P.A.C. RG 76. Immigration Branch. *White Slave Traffic (Prostitution) Reports.* Vol. 569-570. File 813739. Pts. 1-6. 1909-1933. MF: C-10,648 to C-10,649.

P.A.C. MG 11. Colonial Office, London. C.O. 384/154. Emigration/1885/-Dispatches: Eastern Australia and Miscellaneous. Lansdowne, *Report on Emigrant Pauper Children.* 11 March 1885. MF: B-2066.

P.A.C. RG 76. Immigration Branch. *G. Bogue Smart, Chief Inspector of British Immigrant Children and Receiving Homes.* Vol. 170. File 54087. 1921-1948 MF: C-7327. Vol. 200. File 83981. 1899-1933 MF: C-7354. Vol. 266. File 222479. 1902-1904 MF: C-7814-5. Vol. 343. File

364372. 1906-1907 MF: C-10,251 to C-10,252. Vol. 363. file 465378. 1906-1907 MF: C-10,264. Vol. 592. File 838075. 1912-1926 MF: C-10,663. Records include reports of his visits to U.K. to inspect juvenile immigrants; correspondence between the government and receiving homes; annual reports on juvenile immigration to Canada.

P.A.C.   MG 29.C58. *Papers of Charlotte A. Alexander*. Originals. 1885-1893. (10″). Records contain correspondence relating to children she assisted in emigrating to Canada from England, and summaries of various cases in an indexed register.

9.0   Social Welfare Policies for Women, Children and the Family

P.A.C.   RG 27. Department of Labour. *Employment of Children*. Vol. 3529. File 3-26-28. 1941-1945. File contains letters from interest groups concerning the registration of children under 16 for National Selective Service during World War II, and a departmental memorandum on the Proposal for Uniform Child Labour Legislation in the Canadian Provinces, which summarizes the I.L.O. conventions, 1919-1937 and the varying legislation in the provinces in 1941.

P.A.C.   RG 29. Department of National Health and Welfare. *Child and Maternal Health Division*. Vols. 989-993. 1920-1970. Statistics, surveys, special projects, correspondence with interest groups e.g. Canadian Council on Child Welfare and their reports.

P.A.C.   RG 29. Department of National Health and Welfare. *Vanier Institute of the Family*. Vols. 892-893, 895. 1964-1967. Reports and correspondence.

P.A.C.   RG 29. Department of National Health and Welfare. *Welfare Federation of Montreal*. Vol. 893. File 20-W-23. 1945-1955. Correspondence and reports.

P.A.C.   RG 27. Department of Labour. *Day Nurseries*. Vol. 3538. File 3-26-45. 1942-1946. File contains the letters and petitions of working women; women's groups, unions, social service agencies, churches, and daycare centres protesting the lack of commitment by the federal government to daycare after World War II.

P.A.C.   RG 27. Department of Labour. *Wartime Daycare of Children*. Vols. 609-611. 1942-1951. Records include correspondence received and sent by the Department, plans, and negotiations with the provinces.

P.A.C.   RG 35. Interdepartmental Committees. *8. Working Papers of the Committee on Daycare*. Vol. 6. 1971-1972. (R). Records contain background studies, cost estimates, conference reports, and reports from the Department of Labour and the Department of Manpower and Immigration, and some internal correspondence with the Committee.

P.A.C.   RG 35. Interdepartmental Committees. Department of Labour. *7. Wartime History of the Employment of Women and Daycare of Children*. Vol. 20. n.d. Records contain 1) Confidential comments on the wartime programme: employment of women. 2) Department of Labour Report, I: "Employment of Women," n.d. p. 86. 3) Department of Labour Report, II: "Daycare of Children," n.d. p. 18. 4) Appendices for Pts. I & II outlining acts and agreement with provinces.

P.A.C.   RG 27. Department of Labour. *Research, Statistics, Surveys on Daycare for Children*. Vol. 1904. File 38-11-6-42. 1966-1967. The file contains the research, design, statistics, and background material used for a study of daycare for the Department of Labour.

P.A.C.   RG 27. Department of Labour. D.A. Millichamp, Department of Labour. *Survey of the Dominion-Provincial Wartime Day Nursery Programme in Ontario.* Submitted to Mr. B. Beaumont, Director of Child Welfare, Department of Public Welfare, Ontario. (29 October 1945), Vol. 611. Files, 6-52-1, Vol. 3, 1946.

P.A.C.   RG 33/89. Royal Commission on the Status of Women. *Papers and Research Articles.* Vols. 25, 30. 1967-1971. MF: C-6798, 6802 to 6803. Papers include: G. Blais, "A Study of Daycare in Canada," p. 62. Canadian Welfare Council. "A Study of Family Desertion in Canada," p. 261. H. Clifford, "Daycare — An Investment in People," p. 59. M. Gaudette, "La législation des provinces canadiennes en matière d'obligation alimentaire et de garde des enfants."

P.A.C.   RG 91. Yukon Territorial Records. *Health and Child Welfare.* Vol. 53. File 32274. MF: M-2864. 1920-1926.

P.A.C.   RG 91. Yukon Territorial Records. *Maintenance of Illegitimate Children.* Vol. 65. File 518. MF: M-2873. 1942-1946.

P.A.C.   RG 76. Immigration Branch. *Investigation of Pauper Children.* Vol. 94. File 10216. MF: C-4759. 1893-1901.

P.A.C.   RG 10. Department of Indian Affairs. *War Funds, Pensions, Enlistments, Estates, Dependents' Allowances.* Vols. 6762-6806. Files 452-1 to 452-963. 1916-1957. (R).

P.A.C.   RG 10. Department of Indian Affairs. *Care of Children.* Vols. 6937-6942. 8387-8388. Files 1/29-4 to 987/29-4. 1936-1966. (R).

P.A.C.   RG 10. Department of Indian Affairs. *Needy Mothers' Allowances.* Vol. 8194-8195. File 29-7. 1945-1964. (R).

P.A.C.   RG 10. Department of Indian Affairs. *Children's Aid Services.* Vol. 8199. File 29-14. 1954-1963. (R).

P.A.C.   RG 10. Department of Indian Affairs. *Agreement with Children's Aid Societies, Ontario.* Vol. 8199. File 1/29-16-1. Pt. 1. 1954-1957. (R). (E). File outlines the agreement and responsibilities to be undertaken by Children's Aid Societies to extend child welfare services in Ontario to Indian Reserves.

P.A.C.   RG 10. Department of Indian Affairs. *Juvenile Delinquency.* Vol. 7979. File 373/18-28 to 479/18-28-1. 1955-1963.

P.A.C.   RG 76. Immigration Branch. *Empire Settlement Houseworker Problems.* (Empire Settlement Act) Vol. 361. File 434173. 1923-1936. MF: C-19263.

P.A.C.   RG 35. Interdepartmental Committees. *Co-ordinator, Status of Women.* Series 8. Vols. 1-12. 1966-1975. (8'). (R). Records consist of the papers of five working parties of an interdepartmental committee set up to examine recommendations of the Royal Commission on the Status of Women. These five working parties were concerned with 1) economic participation of women; 2) women in public life; 3) education and training of Canadian women; 4) family life and community service; 5) disadvantaged women. Also included are minutes of meetings, reports, and research studies.

P.A.C.   MG 9. Provincial, Local and Territorial Records. B. Nova Scotia. 11. *Cape Breton Legislative Council.* Originals. 1790-1803. 27 pages. Included are copies of ordinances on the expenditure of public revenue for the support and maintenance of bastard children, 1803.

P.A.C.   MG 32.C25. *Papers of Thérèse Casgrain.* Originals. 1818-1975. (202 cm). Papers relate to her work on women's rights in Quebec and as Vice President of the National Council of the C.C.F.

P.A.C.   MG 30.C27. *Papers of W.L. Scott.* Originals. 1872-1944. (2.3 m).
         Papers concern his work as a lawyer active in drafting and promoting
         child welfare legislation and wife desertion legislation.

P.A.C.   MG 30.C97. *Papers of John J. Kelso.* Originals. n.d., 1880-1935. (R)
         (4.2 m). Papers relate mainly to his child welfare activities and to the
         promotion of child protection legislation in 1888 and 1893 in Ontario.

P.A.C.   MG 30.E256. *Papers of Charlotte E. Whitton.* Originals. c. 1914-1975.
         (R) (36.25 m). Papers relate to her work in child and social welfare in
         the 1920s and 1930s as the Executive Director of the Canadian Wel-
         fare Council. They include some independent studies she carried out
         and her involvement in municipal politics in Ottawa in the 1950s and
         1960s.

P.A.C.   MG 28.I25. *Papers of National Council of Women.* Originals.
         1893-1963, 1967. (7.9 m). Papers include records, briefs, minutes,
         correspondence, and reference material documenting the Council's
         efforts to improve the welfare of women.

P.A.C.   MG 28.I198. *Papers of Y.W.C.A. of Canada.* Originals. 1870-1973.
         (9.9 cm). Papers include the Association briefs on women's health,
         Indian women, divorce legislation, and studies connected with the
         Association's services.

P.A.C.   MG 28.I164. *Papers of Montreal Council of Women.* Originals. n.d.,
         1893-1973. (2.44 m). Papers include minutes, annual reports, project
         reports, publications, petitions, and briefs on reforms affecting
         women, e.g. prisons, public health, migration and settlement, voca-
         tional training, and legal status and franchise for women in Quebec.

P.A.C.   MG 28.I231. *La fédération des femmes canadiennes-françaises.* Origi-
         nals. 1918-1975. (1.25 m). Papers include information on charitable
         societies, social welfare, divorce, and charitable works.

P.A.C.   MG 28.I129. *Papers of the Montreal Society for the Protection of Women
         and Children.* Vols. 1-11. 1882-1970. (8'4"). Papers include minutes of
         board meetings, committee reports, and copies of collected annual
         reports of several social agencies, published as *Welfare Work in Mont-
         real 1922-1930*, 1936, and the Director's notes and speeches on legal
         aid and personal social services.

P.A.C.   MG 28.I10. *Papers of Canadian Council on Social Development: Child
         Welfare.* Vols. 1, 3-4, 6-10, 18-19, 24-30, 35, 37-41, 44-45, 48-50,
         59-61, 66-67, 77, 80-84, 110-111. 1923-1968. Files on child welfare
         cover a wide range of topics such as adoption, protection laws, mainte-
         nance costs, programmes for dependent children, and studies carried
         out by the C.C.S.D.

P.A.C.   MG 28.I10. *Papers of Canadian Council on Social Development. Family
         Welfare.* Vols. 22-23, 28, 40, 42-44, 51, 61-62, 70, 76. 1925-1971.
         Papers include correspondence and studies on family desertion, un-
         married parents, surveys by the Council in specific cities, and methods
         of raising private funds for private family welfare agencies.

P.A.C.   MG 28.I10. *Papers of Canadian Council on Social Development. Family
         Allowances.* Vols. 41, 57-58. 1930-1965. Papers include views for and
         against, and correspondence with government and private family wel-
         fare agencies.

P.A.C.   MG 28.I10. *Papers of Canadian Council on Social Development. Mothers'
         Allowances.* Vols. 10, 43, 57-58, 63. 1924-1965. Papers include copies
         of some surveys by C.C.S.D.; summaries of provincial legislation at
         particular times during that forty-year period, and general correspon-
         dence with interest groups and governments involved.

P.A.C.   MG 28.I10. *Papers of Canadian Council on Social Development. Maternal Welfare.* Vols. 39, 41, 53, 57-58, 74. 1929-1965. Papers include proceedings and reports of the Maternal and Child Hygiene Division, information gathered on maternity leave, desertion, legal separations, and the white slave traffic, as well as correspondence.

10.0   Social Welfare Policies for Maintaining the Labour Force

10.1   Housing Policy

P.A.C.   RG 85. Northern Administration. *Welfare Housing and Housing for Destitute Eskimos and Indigents.* Vol. 1291. File 310-9-1. 1961-1962. File contains correspondence, memoranda and a policy paper on housing for northern residents, with comments by departmental personnel.

P.A.C.   RG 19. Department of Finance. *Interdepartmental Committee on Housing.* Vol. 4017-4018. 1945-1946. Records deal with the work of the Interdepartmental Committee on the problem of postwar housing. There are many background studies as well as correspondence, minutes of meetings, publicity material, and speeches by the Executive Secretary, M. Sharp and Minister of Finance, J.L. Isley.

P.A.C.   RG 10. Department of Indian Affairs. *Indian Houses (General).* Vols. 6835-6857. Files 191/29-2 to 991/29-2. 1906-1965. (R); Vols. 8190-8193. File 29-2. 1931-1967. (R).

P.A.C.   RG 35. Interdepartmental Committees. *Canada. Interdepartmental Housing Committee.* Series 4, vols. 1 & 2. 1942-1946. (8´). Records consist of material relating to housing policy, 1942-1946 with correspondence on education and taxation problems, various residential construction surveys, and statistics gathered during this period and presented to the Committee.

P.A.C.   MG 30.B93. *Papers of Horace L. Seymour.* Originals. 1921-1940. (6'8"). Papers concern his work in private and public town planning and the Commission of Conservation.

P.A.C.   MG 30.C105. *Papers of Noulan Cauchon.* Originals. n.d., 1899-1931. (2.52 m). Papers relate to his activities as a prominent town planner in Ottawa and also include reports on housing, urban renewal, and public health.

P.A.C.   MG 30.C110. *Papers of John M. Kitchen.* Originals. n.d., 1922-1939. (10 cm). Papers include correspondence, reports, and reference material on town planning and slum clearance in Montreal, 1929-1935.

P.A.C.   RG 38. Department of Veterans' Affairs. *Veterans' Land Administration.* Vols. 247-260, 356, 360, 368. 1917-1972. (6'10"). (R). Records contain applications for benefits under the Soldier Settlement Act (1919) and the Veterans' Land Act (1942); land title appraisal documents; histories of the settlers' establishment and transfer of titles. Various reports and studies by students on the operation of the Veterans' Land Act are included.

10.2   Education Policy

P.A.C.   RG 19. Department of Finance. *Grammar School Fund, Canada West.* Vol. 2470. 1840-1867.

P.A.C.   RG 10. Department of Indian Affairs. *Indian Education — General.* Vols. 7180-7194. Files 1/25-1 to 511/25-1-024. 1896-1966; Vols. 8753-8810. Files 511/25-1-027 to 1/25-21. 1890-1966. (R).

P.A.C.   MG 18.E28. *Incarnation, Marie Guyart dite Marie de Transcripts*. XVII century, 417 pages. Her letters constitute a valuable source of information on the education of young Indian and French girls for the period 1645-1672.

P.A.C.   RG 4. Civil and Provincial Secretaries' Office, Canada East. 1760-1867. B.30. *Education Records*. 1767-1856. (21'). Records include pay lists, petitions, correspondence, and a few reports on the system of education. (Vol. 14).

P.A.C.   MG 9. Provincial, Local and Territorial Records. A. *New Brunswick. Education*. Vols. 110-113. 1803-1858. MF: M-1665 to M-1667. Records include reports, letters, petitions, and returns from superintendents, inspectors, and trustees.

P.A.C.   RG 5. Civil and Provincial Secretaries' Office, Canada West. 1788-1867. B.11. *Reports on Common and Grammar Schools*. Vol. 7. 1843, 1850.

P.A.C.   MG 17.B1. *Church of England. Society for the Propogation of the Gospel in Foreign Parts*. Transcripts 1700-1881 (3.15 m). MF: 101 reels: A-28, A-152-250. 1630-1889. Records relate mainly to education and missions in the Maritimes, Ontario, and British Columbia.

P.A.C.   MG 17.E1. *Church of Scotland: Colonial Committee*. 1836-1887. MF: A-655-660. Papers relate to the financing and provision of ministers, schoolmasters, and schools in the colonies.

P.A.C.   MG 28.I83. *Papers of Association of Universities and Colleges of Canada*. Originals. 1963-1968. (18'). (R). Papers include briefs, correspondence, research, and draft reports of Bladen Commission on the Financing of Higher Education in Canada, 1963-1967, and the Snider Commission Report: "Who Doesn't get to University and Why!" 1970.

P.A.C.   MG 28.I68. *Papers of National Farm Radio Forum*. Originals. 1940-1965. (39'6"). Papers include references to all social policies introduced during the period which were discussed on radio as part of this adult education project.

P.A.C.   MG 28.I102. *Papers of Canadian Teachers' Federation*. Originals. Vols. 1-106, 1920-1977. (26.7 m). Papers include reports, briefs, replies from members of Parliament, copies of provincial associations' activities on bargaining positions held by teachers, especially on the Prairies.

P.A.C.   MG 28.I122. *Papers of the Commission on Relations Between Universities and Governments*. Originals. 1959-1969. (10'). Papers include correspondence, memoranda, proceedings, submissions, related papers, clippings, and draft of the final report.

P.A.C.   MG 28.I124. *Papers of Frontier College*. Originals. 1874-1975. (59.92 m). Papers include correspondence with instructors, government, railways, newspapers, the Principal's files; draft of E.W. Bradwin's book, *The Bunkhouse Man*; correspondence with the Department of National Defence and Relief Camp Superintendents; and a survey of conditions in relief camps in the 1930s. (Vol. 198).

10.3   Health Care Policy

P.A.C.   RG 91. Yukon Territorial Records. *Public Health*. Vol. 67. Files 5, 7, 8. 1900-1919. Records deal with epidemics of smallpox and influenza, and with general public health services.

P.A.C.   RG 10. Department of Indian Affairs. *Rehabilitation*. Vols. 8206-8211. File 29-20. 1952-1966. (R).

P.A.C.   RG 29. Department of National Health and Welfare. *Public Health Services: Medical Service for Indigents.* Vol. 182. File 302-1-7. 1933-1948. File contains correspondence between the Federal Department and the Provincial Departments of Health on the responsibility for the medical care of indigents and transients.

P.A.C.   RG 29. Department of National Health and Welfare. *Health Insurance.* Vols. 1058-1144. 1928-1973. (57´). (R). Records contain all relevant material collected by the Directorate of Health Insurance Studies. This includes bills, acts, regulations, reports, reference material, statistics, and correspondence with interest groups, e.g. College of Physicians and Surgeons (Ontario), V.O.N., Canadian Dental Association. There are minutes and reports of the Advisory Committee on Health Insurance (1942-1963); the subcommittee on Health Insurance Finance (1943-1960); the special Committee on Social Security (1943-1945), and various other departmental and interdepartmental committees set up to examine aspects of health insurance in Canada and elsewhere.

P.A.C.   RG 29. Department of National Health and Welfare. *Public Health Services — General.* Vol. 180. File 300-1-2. 1940. File contains a transcript of the interview held between the Deputy Minister of Health, Dr. Wodehouse, and the Rowell-Sirois Commission on the federal government's jurisdiciton over health matters; submissions and that part of the Royal Commission report on health services.

P.A.C.   RG 29. Department of National Health and Welfare. *Control and Treatment of Communicable Diseases.* Vols. 1-18. 1815-1968. (6´). Earliest records deal with lepers in New Brunswick. Most of the material relates to smallpox, tuberculosis, bubonic plague, and cholera in all provinces around 1900-1920.

P.A.C.   RG 17. Department of Agriculture. *Smallpox Epidemic, B.C.* Vol. 2736. File 93498. 1892-1894, 1896. File includes correspondence on the vaccination of Chinese and Japanese immigrants and a printed report of the Royal Commission into the smallpox epidemic in B.C. 1892.

P.A.C.   RG 38. Department of Veterans' Affairs. *Treatment Services.* Vols. 205-222. 1916-1947. File list includes various subjects under this heading e.g. pay and allowances while undergoing treatment, provisions for psychiatric care, tuberculosis, venereal disease, occupational therapy, and the National Committee for Mental Hygiene.

P.A.C.   MG 40.F1. Royal Army Medical College. *Sir James McGrigor, #1. Annual Returns and Reports of the Sick. #2. Annual Sanitary Reports,* 1819-1891. MF: A-875 to A-880. #1 includes detailed reports and case histories of diseases, health inspections, hospital accommodation, and treatment and #2 includes reports on public health, prisons, and hospitals.

P.A.C.   RG 4. Civil and Provincial Secretaries' Office, Canada East. 1760-1867. B.65. *Canada East: Lunatic Asylums.* 1844-1867. (1´2″). Records include correspondence, returns, admission papers, petitions on the establishment of asylums, and a report by Dr. Rees on the Toronto Lunatic Asylum.

P.A.C.   RG 4. Civil and Provincial Secretaries' Office, Canada East. 1760-1867. B.66. *Cholera Records, Canada East.* 1854. (2″). Records include correspondence, returns, memoranda, and other papers on cholera in the Lunatic Asylum; appointment of a Board of Health and their quarantine regulations.

P.A.C.   MG 30.B56. *Papers of George Brock Chisholm.* Originals. 1917, 1934-1971. (90 cm). Papers relate to his work while Director General of Medical Services during World War II, and his position as Deputy Minister of the Department of National Health and Welfare, 1944-1948.

P.A.C.   MG 31.E11. *Papers of Emmett M. Hall.* Originals. 1918-1972. (4'8"). Papers consist of correspondence, memoranda, reports, and pamphlets dealing with the Royal Commission on Health Services 1961, and the work done for the Hall-Dennis report on the Aims and Objectives of Education in Ontario, 1965-1968.

P.A.C.   MG 28.I75. *Papers of Canadian Lung Association.* Originals. 1901-1977. (8 m). MF: 14 reels, C-4480 to C-4493. 1900-1964. Papers document early epidemiology, campaigns to arrest the spread of tuberculosis, and various cures the Association promoted.

P.A.C.   MG 28.I63. *Papers of Dominion Council of Health.* Originals. 1919-1962. (70 cm). MF: 4 reels, C-9814 to C-9817. 1919-1958. Records include minutes of meetings of this advisory council and reference papers on all aspects of health care in Canada.

P.A.C.   MG 29.E66. *Papers of Augustus Jukes.* MF: M-1614, n.d. 1878-1889. Papers include information on disease among Indians in the Northwest Territories and the Metis, and a paper he prepared to the Annual Meeting of the Canadian Medical Association, Banff 1889, entitled "The Endemic Fever of the Northwest Territories," (p. 16) which discusses the effect of white settlement on Indian health.

P.A.C.   MG 28.I165. *Canadian Psychiatric Association Collection.* Originals. 1835-1973. (3.3 m). MF: 1 reel, M-4600. 1854-1862, 1905-1916. Among the papers of the Association are reports, theses, and books collected on the history of psychiatry: Vols. 7-17, 1835-1973. (2 m).

P.A.C.   MG 28.I171. *Papers of Victorian Order of Nurses.* Originals. n.d., 1897-1972. (1.67 m). Papers include minutes, general correspondence, reports, briefs, historical pamphlets, and clippings on V.O.N. activities.

P.A.C.   RG 29. Department of National Health and Welfare. *Industrial Health.* Vols. 615-618. 1919-1953. (R). Files include minutes of the Technical Advisory Committee on Industrial Hygiene, conference papers and proceedings, interdepartmental correspondence, and correspondence with interest groups such as the Canadian Medical Association and insurance companies, as well as copies of bills and acts under consideration during World War II.

P.A.C.   RG 29. Department of National Health and Welfare. *Dominion Council of Health.* Vol. 255. File 339-6-8. Pts. 1-3. 1933-1953. (R). File contains minutes of meetings, correspondence between the federal government, council members, and provincial departments of health.

P.A.C.   RG 29. Department of National Health and Welfare. *Victorian Order of Nurses.* Vol. 891-892. 1945-1967. Correspondence and reports.

P.A.C.   RG 29. Department of National Health and Welfare. *Dental Health.* Vols. 906-907. 1939-1959. Records contain correspondence with interest groups, legislation, reports, conferences.

P.A.C.   RG 29. Department of National Health and Welfare. *Medical Rehabilitation.* Vols. 907-912. 1949-1966. Records deal with administration, disability allowances in provinces; correspondence with interest groups; advisory and interdepartmental committees and subcommittees.

P.A.C.   RG 29. Department of National Health and Welfare. *Government and Non-Government Health Organizations*. Vols. 852-885. 1947-1967. Records contain correspondence and conference discussions of various health issues.

P.A.C.   RG 29. Department of National Health and Welfare. *Epidemiology Division: Venereal Disease*. Vols. 491-505. 1920-1954. Records include correspondence between the Federal Department of Health and various interest groups such as the Social Hygiene Council of Canada.

P.A.C.   RG 17. Department of Agriculture. *Quarantine and Public Health Branch*. Vols. 2430-2472. 1854-1912. Records include early minute books of the conference on cholera in 1866, correspondence of Central Board of Health, 1854 and the correspondence of Director General of Public Health, Dr. F. Montizambert (1899-1912), mainly on quarantine service and epidemics.

P.A.C.   RG 29. Department of National Health and Welfare. *Dominion-Provincial Health Conferences*. Vol. 23. 1927-1946. This volume traces the history of the Department of Health and the widening of its functions during that period to include pensions, health, and unemployment insurance, and federal grants to provinces.

P.A.C.   RG 29. Department of National Health and Welfare. *Dominion Council of Health*. Vol. 255. File 339-6-8. Pts. 1-3. 1933-1953. (R). This file includes the minutes of meetings in which information on developments in public health was debated, and correspondence to its members from the federal government.

P.A.C.   RG 29. Department of National Health and Welfare. *National Health Grants*. Vols. 346-426. 1919-1950. Most of the records relate to post World War II grants by the federal government to the provinces for hospital construction, professional training, tuberculosis control, public health, cancer control, rehabilitation etc. The early records are mainly concerned with venereal disease control.

P.A.C.   RG 29. Department of National Health and Welfare. *Epidemiology Division*. Vols. 1145-1277. 1899-1975. (39.6 m) (R). Records contain information on 86 communicable diseases and their incidence in Canada; research and prevention; correspondence with interest groups.

P.A.C.   RG 85. Department of National Health and Welfare. Northern Administration. *Report on Disease and Death in Canada's North*. (prepared by Dr. J.S. Willis, Northern Health Service, Department N.H.W. Ottawa, June 1962. p. 16). Vol. 1956. File A-1003-20. Pt. 1. 1960-1963. Report gives a statistical summary and an outline of health services provided by the federal government in the North.

P.A.C.   RG 29. Department of National Health and Welfare. *Mental Health Division*. Vols. 307-314. 1946-1959. (R). Records include correspondence with private interest groups e.g. Canadian Medical Association, Canadian Welfare Council.

P.A.C.   RG 29. Department of National Health and Welfare. *Mental Health*. Vols. 302-303. 1946-1958; Vols. 901-906. 1931-1967. (R). These records include general correspondence with interest groups, information on legislation, research, epidemiology, and rehabilitation.

P.A.C.   MG 27.III.D6. *Papers of Louise Lucas. State Health Plans*. Vol. 3. 1935-1941. This file contains reference material, news clippings, statements by the United Farmers of Canada and the Canadian Medical Association on health insurance and state medicine, and compares these to schemes in Europe, Britain, U.S.A., and Commonwealth countries.

P.A.C.   RG 29. Department of National Health and Welfare. *Dominion Council of Health*. S.R.E. Acc #75-6/35. 1919-1973. Records include copies of the minutes of meetings #1-82. Microfilm copies of the minutes of meetings #1-74, 1919-1958 are on reels C-9814 to C-9817. (Originals are held in P.A.C. MG 28.I63).

P.A.C.   RG 29. Department of National Health and Welfare. *Occupational Health*. Vols. 506-517, 619-621. 1938-1959. (R). Records include several reports of provincial field surveys of working conditions; correspondence with interest groups such as the Canadian Nurses Association, on health and safety plans and the placement of nurses.

P.A.C.   RG 29. Department of National Health and Welfare. *Hospitals Insurance Studies*. Health Insurance and Resources Branch. Vols. 1364-1382. 1948-1972. (R) (3.3 m). Records include studies of hospital insurance in other countries; correspondence with the provinces; and an examination of their hospital insurance programmes.

P.A.C.   MG 27.III.F7. *Papers of Kate Massiah*. Originals. 1901-1936. (1″). Records relate to correspondence received from prominent political figures regarding the establishment of a Department of Health.

Appendix II   Libraries

Assemblée nationale du Québec, Québec.

Canada Mortgage and Housing Corporation, Government of Canada, Ottawa.

Canadian Council on Social Development, Ottawa.

Canadian Tax Foundation, Toronto.

Canadian Teachers' Federation, Ottawa.

Centre for Criminology, University of Toronto, Toronto.

Centre for Newfoundland Studies, Memorial University, St. John's.

Department of Health, Government of Saskatchewan, Regina.

Department of Health and Social Development, Government of Manitoba, Winnipeg.

Department of Human Resources, Government of British Columbia, Victoria.

Department of Social Services and Community Health, Government of Alberta, Edmonton.

Department of Social Services, Government of Saskatchewan, Regina.

Faculty of Social Work, University of Toronto, Toronto.

Health and Welfare Canada, Government of Canada, Ottawa.

Helen Mann Library, School of Social Work, University of Manitoba, Winnipeg.

John P. Robarts Library, University of Toronto, Toronto.

Legislative Library, Government of Alberta, Edmonton.

Legislative Library, Government of British Columbia, Victoria.

Legislative Library, Government of Manitoba, Winnipeg.

Legislative Library, Government of New Brunswick, Fredericton.

Legislative Library, Government of Nova Scotia, Halifax.

Legislative Library, Government of Saskatchewan, Regina.
Library of Parliament, Government of Canada, Ottawa.
MacOdrum Library, Carleton University, Ottawa.
Maritime School of Social Work, Dalhousie University, Halifax.
Ministry of Community and Social Services, Government of Ontario, Toronto.
National Library of Canada, Ottawa.
Ontario Institute for Studies in Education, Toronto.
Plains Research Centre, University of Saskatchewan, Regina.
Public Archives of Canada, Ottawa.
School of Social Work, University of British Columbia, Vancouver.
Thomas Fisher Rare Books Library, University of Toronto, Toronto.
Université Laval bibliothèque, Québec.
University of British Columbia, Vancouver.
Victoria College Archives, University of Toronto, Toronto.

Appendix III   Periodicals

This Appendix lists all those periodicals searched to obtain references to materials relating to Canadian social welfare policy. We have included the date of commencement of publication and the years (inclusive) of publication of volumes (or issues) of each periodical which was comprehensively examined.

In addition, a thorough check was made of the Canadian Periodical Index (C.P.I.). This index, which commenced publication in 1938, is a subject compilation of citations of journal and magazine articles. (Some citations appearing in the *Bibliography* were obtained directly from the C.P.I.). The periodicals have been divided into eight groupings according to orientation.

Name of Periodical	Date of Publication of First Volumes	Years Examined for Bibliography	
Academic Periodicals			
Acadiensis	1971	1971	1977
Archiviaria	1975	1975	1978
Canadian Annual Review	1901	1901	1977
Canadian Historical Association Papers	1922	1922	1977
Canadian Historical Review	1920	1920	1978
Canadian Journal of Economics	1968	1968	1977
Canadian Journal of Economics and Political Science (superseded by Canadian Journal of Economics and Canadian Journal of Political Science)	1935	1935	1977
Canadian Journal of Political Science	1968	1968	1977
Canadian Public Administration	1958	1958	1977

Canadian Public Policy	1975	1975	1977
Canadian Review of Sociology and Anthropology	1964	1964	1977
Canadian Tax Journal	1953	1953	1978
Histoire sociale/Social History	1968	1968	1977
Journal of Canadian Studies	1966	1966	1978
Journal of Political Economy	1892	1892	1977
Journal of Social History	1967	1967	1978
L'Actualité Économique	1925	1925	1977
Public Affairs	1937/38	1937/38	1978
Quarterly of Canadian Studies	1971	1971	1976
Ontario History (Historical Papers began publication in 1899)	1949	1889	1977
Queen's Quarterly	1893	1938	1977
Recherche sociographique	1960	1960	1977
Relations	1941	1941	1978
Review of Historical Publications Relating to Canada (superseded by Canadian Historical Review	1896	1896	1917/18
Revue d'histoire de l'Amerique française	1947	1947	1977
Saskatchewan History	1948	1948	1977
Social Science Index	1974	1974	1978
University of Toronto Quarterly	1931	1931	1977
Urban History Review/Revue d'histoire urbaine	1972	1972	1977
Legal Journals			
Bulletin of Canadian Welfare Law	1972	1972	1978
Canadian Law Journal	1885	1885	1922
Canadian Bar Review	1923	1923	1978
Canadian Business Law Journal	1975/76	1975/76	1978
Canadian Journal of Family Law	1978	1978	
Canadian Legal Aid Bulletin	1977	1977	1978
Dalhousie Law Journal	1973	1973	1978
Index to Canadian Legal Periodical Literature	1961	1961	1978
Index to Foreign Legal Periodicals	1960	1960	1978
Manitoba Law Journal	1884	1884	1977
McGill Law Journal	1952	1952	1977
Osgoode Hall Law Journal	1958/59	1958/59	1977
Ottawa Law Review	1966	1966	1978
Queen's Law Journal	1971	1971	1977
Saskatchewan Law Review	1935	1935	1978
University of Toronto Law Review	1935/36	1935/36	1978
Journals Relating to Labour			
Bulletin des relations industrielles	1945	1945	1951
Canadian Labour	1956	1956	1977
Relations industrielles (supersedes Bulletin des relations industrielles)	1951	1951	1978
Labour/Le travailleur	1976	1976	1978
Labour Gazette	1900	1900	1977
Business Periodicals			
Canadian Banker	1893	1893	1971
Canadian Banker and I.C.B. Review	1971	1971	1978
Canadian Business	1938	1938	1977
Industrial Canada	1900	1900	1973
Social Welfare Periodicals			
Abstracts For Social Workers	1965	1965	1978
Canadian Journal of Corrections	1958	1958	1970

Canadian Journal of Corrections			
and Criminology	1971	1971	1977
Canadian Welfare	1924/25	1924/25	1977/78
Intervention	1971	1971	1977
Perception (amalgamation of			
Canadian Welfare and			
Digeste Social	1977/78	1977	1978
Service sociale	1951	1951	1977
Social Welfare History Group			
Newsletter	1956	1956	1977
Social Worker, The	1932	1932	1978
Popular Journals			
Bystander, The	1880	1880	1883
Canadian Dimension	1963	1963	1977
Canadian Forum	1920	1920	1977
Cité libre	1950	1950	1969
L'action nationale	1933	1933	1977
Last Post	1970	1970	1977
Week, The	1883	1883	1896
Periodicals Relating to Specific Issues			
(Ethnicity, Education, Health, Housing, Community Planning, etc.)			
Canadian Education Index	1965	1965	1977
Canadian Ethnic Studies	1969	1969	1978
City Magazine	1974	1974	1977
Education Canada	1961	1961	1978
Habitat	1958	1958	1977
Housing and People	1970	1970	1977
Native People	1969	1969	1978
Plan Canada	1959	1959	1978

Appendix IV
Bibliography of Bibliographies

We have used the major headings and subheadings of the *Bibliography* to classify the subject bibliographies listed here.

1.0-4.0

ADVISORY COMMITTEE ON RECONSTRUCTION. *Guides for Post-War Reconstruction Studies.* Ottawa: Canadian Library Council, National Research Council Library, 1944.

CANADIAN TAX FOUNDATION. *Index of Canadian Tax Foundation Publications, 1945-1971.* Toronto: Canadian Tax Foundation, 1976.

CHERWINSKI, W.J.C. "Bibliographical Note: the Left in Canadian History, 1911-1969." *Journal of Canadian Studies.* 4:4 (November 1969), pp. 51-60.

ISBESTER, A. Fraser. *Industrial and Labour Relations in Canada: A Selected Bibliography.* Kingston: Industrial Relations Centre, Queen's University, 1965.

KEALEY, Gregory S., HANN, Russell G., KEALEY, Linda, WARRIAN, Peter. *Primary Sources in Canadian Working Class History 1860-1930.* Kitchener: Dumont Press, 1973.

KENNEDY, W.P.M. "Select Bibliography of Social and Industrial Conditions in Canada." *Annals of the American Academy of Political and Social Sciences.* 107 (May 1923), pp. 303-307.

LeBLANC, André G., and THWAITES, James D. *Le monde ouvrier du Québec; bibliographie retrospective.* Québec: Les Presses de L'Université du Québec, 1973.

MONTY, Vivienne. *Bibliography of Canadian Tax Reform.* Toronto: York University, Law Library, 1973.

MURRAY, Elsie McLeod. "Post War Planning for Canada." *Ontario Library Review.* 28:4 (November 1944), pp. 459-73.

ONTARIO HISTORICAL SOCIETY. *Index to the Publications of the Ontario Historical Society 1899-1972.* Toronto: Ontario Historical Society, 1974.

ONTARIO. Ministry of Colleges and Universities. *Ontario Since 1867; a Bibliography.* Ontario Historical Studies Series. Toronto: Queen's Printer, 1973.

PALTIEL, Freda L. *Poverty: An Annotated Bibliography and References.* Ottawa: Canadian Council on Social Development, 1966.

RIOUX, Bernard. *Travail syndicalisme: bibliographie.* 2 vols. Montreal: Conseil de développement social du Montréal métropolitan, 1972.

SCHLESINGER, Benjamin. *Poverty in Canada and in the United States; An Annotated Bibliography.* Toronto: University of Toronto Press, 1966.

SOUTHAM, P. *Bibliographie des bibliographies sur l'économie, la société et la culture du Québec 1940-1971.* Québec: Université Laval, 1972.

THIBAULT, Claude. *Bibliographia Canadiana.* Toronto: Longman, 1973.

TREMBLAY, Louis-Marie. *Bibliographie des relations du travail au Canada, 1940-1967.* Montreal: Presses de l'Université de Montréal, 1969.

TRUAX, Keitha Lynne. "Income and Poverty in Canada." *Ontario Library Review.* 56:4 (December 1972), pp. 217-29.

WOODWARD, Agnes. *Poverty/Pauvreté.* Ottawa: Canadian Council on Social Development, 1967.

5.0 Comparative Social Welfare Policy: Canada and Other Countries

INTERNATIONAL LABOUR OFFICE. *Bibliography on Social Security.* (Bibliographical Contributions No. 20). Geneva: International Labour Office Library, 1963.

World Bibliography of Social Security. Vol. 1-16. Geneva: International Social Security Association, 1963-1978.

6.0 Social Welfare Policies for People Out of Work

6.2 Unemployment Insurance

CANADA. Unemployment Insurance Canada. *A Selected Bibliography on Unemployment Insurance in Canada, Great Britain and the United States.* Ottawa: June 1972.

7.0 Social Welfare Policies for People Who Cannot Work

8.0 Social Welfare Policy for "Marginal" People

8.1 The Justice and Correctional Systems

CANADA. Solicitor General Canada. *Canadian Criminology: Annotated Bibliography; Crime and the Administration of Criminal Justice in Canada/ Criminologie canadienne; bibliographie commentée: la criminalité et l'administration de la justice criminelle au Canada.* Ottawa: Queen's Printer, 1976.

CANADIAN CRIMINOLOGY AND CORRECTIONS ASSOCIATION. *Correctional Literature published in Canada.* Ottawa: Canadian Council on Social Development, 1971.

8.2   Immigration Policy

CANADA. Department of Citizenship and Immigration. Economic and Social Research Division. *Citizen, Immigration and Ethnic Groups in Canada, a Bibliography of Research.* Vol. 1, 1920-1958. Ottawa: Queen's Printer, 1960; Vol. 2, 1959-1961. Ottawa: Queen's Printer, 1962; Vol. 3, 1962-1964. Ottawa: Queen's Printer, 1964; Vol. 4, 1964-1968. Ottawa: Queen's Printer, 1969.

_____. *Canadian Immigration and Emigration 1946-1957, a Bibliography.* Ottawa: Departmental Library, Department of Citizenship and Immigration, 1958.

RICHMOND, Anthony H. *Immigrants and Ethnic Groups in Metropolitan Toronto.* (Ethnic Research Programme, Research Report E1). Toronto: Institute for Behavioural Research, York University, 1967.

SWANICK, Eric L. *Canadian Immigration Studies in the 1960s and in the 1970s: an Introductory Bibliography.* Exchange Bibliography No. 1179. Monticello Illinois: Council of Planning Librarians.

8.3   Intergroup Relations and Policy

ABLER, Tom, SANDERS, Douglas, WEAVER, Sally. *A Canadian Indian Bibliography 1960-1970.* Toronto: University of Toronto Press, 1974.

CANADA. Bilingualism Development Programme. Research and Planning Branch. *Selected Bibliography on Francophone Minorities in Canada.* 2 vols. Ottawa: Secretary of State, 1972.

DWORACZEK, Marian J. *Minority Groups in Metropolitan Toronto, a Bibliography.* Toronto: Research Branch Library, Ontario Ministry of Labour, 1973.

GREGOROVITCH, Andrew. *Canadian Ethnic Groups: A Selected Bibliography of Ethno-cultural Groups in Canada and in the Province of Ontario.* Toronto: Queen's Printer, 1972.

TREMBLAY, Marc Adelard. "Bibliographie sur l'administration des indiens du Canada et des Etats-Unis. 1970. (Unpublished paper available from Bibliothèque nationale du Québec).

9.0   Social Welfare Policies for Women, Children and the Family

BAKAN, David, EISNER, Margaret, NEEDHAM, Harry G. *Child Abuse; a Bibliography.* Toronto: Canadian Council on Child and Youth, 1976.

CANADIAN WELFARE COUNCIL. *The Day Care of Children; an Annotated Bibliography.* Ottawa: Canadian Welfare Council, 1969.

"Changing Canadian Society." *Ontario Library Review.* 59:3 (September 1975), pp. 171-81.

DUSSAULT, C. "Bibliographie du service sociale canadien-français." *Service social.* 10:3 (October 1961), pp. 122-41.

QUEBEC. Commission d'enquête sur la santé et le bien-être social. *Bibliographie sur les services sociales* (par) la commission. Annexe 23. Quebec: Editeur officiel du Québec, 1971.

SCHLESINGER, Benjamin. *The Multi-Problem Family; a Review and Annotated Bibliography.* Toronto: University of Toronto Press, 1970.

SHEPPARD, Judy. *Social Work Reference Aids in the University of Toronto Libraries.* (Reference Series No. 18). Toronto: John P. Robarts Library, University of Toronto, 1973.

VANIER INSTITUTE OF THE FAMILY. *Canadian Resources on the Family; Catalogue.* Ottawa: The Institute, 1972.

10.0 Social Welfare Policies for Maintaining the Labour Force

10.1 Housing Policy

ARMSTRONG, F.H. "Urban History in Canada: Present State and Future Prospects." *Urban History Review/Revue d'histoire urbaine.* 1. (1972), pp. 11-14.

ARTIBISE, Alan F.J. "Canadian Urban Studies." *Communique: Canadian Studies.* 3:3 (April 1977), pp. 1-130.

BOURNE, L.S., and BIERNACKI, C.M. *Urban Housing Markets, Housing Supply and the Special Structure of Residential Change: A Working Bibliography.* Toronto: Centre, 1977.

CANADA. Advisory Committee on Reconstruction. *Housing and Community Planning; Final Report of the Subcommittee; Bibliography.* Ottawa: King's Printer, 1946.

CANADA. Department of Regional Economic Expansion. *Bibliography on Canadian Land Market Mechanisms and Land Systems Information.* Rosalind Lambert and Laval Lavalée, eds. Urban paper A 76.2. Ottawa: The Department, 1976.

CARDINAL, Michel. *Urbanisme et logement: bibliographie.* Montreal: Conseil de développement social du Montréal métropolitain, 1972.

CENTRAL MORTGAGE AND HOUSING CORPORATION. *Housing for the Aged: Bibliography.* Ottawa: The Corporation, 1968.

————. *Housing: History Bibliography.* Ottawa: The Corporation, 1977.

————. *The Seventh Age: A Bibliography of Canadian Sources in Gerontology and Geriatrics 1964-1972.* Ottawa: Environics Research Group Ltd., 1972.

CHAMBERLAIN, S.B., and CROWLEY, D.F. *Decision-Making and Change in Urban Residential Space: Selected and Annotated References.* (Bibliographic Series Report No. 2). Toronto: Centre for Urban and Community Studies, University of Toronto, 1970.

COMMUNITY PLANNING ASSOCIATION OF CANADA. *Canadian Housing Resource Catalogue.* Ottawa: The Association, 1975.

COOPER, I., and HULCHANSKI, J.D. *Canadian Town Planning 1900-1930; A Historical Bibliography: Volume I: Planning.* (Bibliographic Series No. 7). Toronto: Centre for Urban and Community Studies, University of Toronto, 1978.

————. *Canadian Town Planning 1900-1930: A Historical Bibliography Volume II: Housing.* (Bibliographic Series No. 8). Toronto: Centre for Urban and Community Studies, University of Toronto, 1978.

DILL, John, MACRI, Paul, COBLENTZ, H.S. *Current References Relating to Housing and Land Issues in Canada.* (Exchange Bibliography No. 842). Monticello, Illionis: Council of Planning Librarians, 1975.

HULCHANSKI, John D. *Thomas Adams. A Biographical and Bibliographic Guide.* (Papers on Planning and Design No. 15). Toronto: Department of Urban and Regional Planning, University of Toronto, 1978.

ONIBOKUM, Ade. *Study of Housing Need and Bibliography.* Waterloo: Department of Geography and Planning, University of Waterloo, 1968.

ONTARIO. Department of Economics and Development. Regional Development Division. *A Bibliography for Regional Development.* Toronto: Queen's Printer, 1966.

ONTARIO WELFARE COUNCIL. *A Study of Housing Policies in Ontario: Bibliography.* Toronto: The Council, 1973.

SILZER, V.J. *Housing Rehabilitation and Neighbourhood Change: Britain, Canada and U.S.A.; An Annotated Bibliography.* Toronto: Centre for Urban and Community Studies, University of Toronto, 1975.

SOUTHAM, Peter. *Le logement au Québec 1935-1972.* Quebec: Institut supérieur des sciences humaines, Université Laval, 1973.

STELTER, Gil. *Canadian Urban History: A Selected Bibliography.* Sudbury: Laurentian University, 1972.

SWANICK, Eric L. *Land Use in Canada During the Seventies: An Introductory Bibliography.* (Exchange Bibliography No. 1180). Monticello, Illinois: Council of Planning Librarians, 1976.

VELIKOV, Velitchko. *Provincial and Federal Use and Land Ownership Policies and Their Potential Impact on Political Economic and Social Conditions in Canada.* (Exchange Bibliography No. 993). Monticello, Illinois: Council of Planning Librarians, 1976.

WHITNEY, Joan. *Habitat Bibliography: A Selected Bibliography of Canadian References on Human Settlements.* (Exchange Bibliography No. 1137-1138). Monticello, Illinois: Council of Planning Librarians, 1976.

10.2   Education Policy and Administration

CANADIAN TEACHERS' FEDERATION. *Early Childhood Education.* (Bibliographies in Education No. 28). Ottawa: The Federation, May 1972.

————. *Education Finance in Canada.* (Bibliographies in Education No. 11, August 1970; No. 47, October 1974; No. 62, January 1978).

————. *Pre-Service Teacher Education in Canada.* (Bibliographies in Education No. 1). Ottawa: The Federation, 1969.

CHILD, Alan H. "The History of Canadian Education: A Bibliographic Note." *Social History/Histoire sociale.* 8 (November 1971), pp. 105-17.

COCKBURN, Ilze. Reference and Information Services. *Elementary Teacher Education Certification.* OISE (Current Bibliographies No. 9). Toronto: Ontario Institute for Studies in Education, 1974.

FINLEY, Eric Gault. *Sources à consulter en vue d'une compilation bibliographique sur l'évolution de l'education au Canada français.* Montreal: Centre d'études canadienne-françaises, McGill University, 1966.

HARRIS, Robin Sutton, and TREMBLAY, Arthur, comps. *A Bibliography of Higher Education in Canada.* (Studies in the History of Higher Education in Canada, No. 1). Supplement 1965. Toronto: University of Toronto Press, and Presses Universitaires Laval, 1960.

IRONSIDE, Diana, compiler. *The Literature of Adult Education; a Selected List of Holdings from the Research Library in Adult Education of the Canadian Association for Adult Education.* Toronto: Canadian Association for Adult Education, 1961.

KENDALL, D.C., BALLANCE, K.E., SAYWELL, P. "Legislation for Exceptional Children in Canada: Supplementary Report." *Special Education.* 47 (November 1972), pp. 19-32.

REYNOLDS, Roy. *A Guide to Published Government Documents Relating to Education in Ontario.* (OISE Department of History and Philosophy Archives Series 2). Toronto: Ontario Institute for Studies in Education, 1972.

STEVENSON, H.A., and HAMILTON, W.B. *Canadian Education and the Future: A Selected Annotated Bibliography 1967-1971.* London: University of Western Ontario, 1972.

THOM, Douglas J., and HICKCOX, E.S. *A Selected Bibliography of Educational Administration: A Canadian Orientation.* Toronto: Canadian Education Association, 1973.

THOMSON, Murray M., and IRONSIDE, Diana. *A Bibliography of Canadian Writings in Adult Education.* Toronto: Canadian Association for Adult Education, 1956.

THWAITES, J.D. *The Quebec Teacher 1939-1971: A Study of Secondary Sources and a Bibliographic Guide to Primary Material.* Quebec: Laval University, 1972.

TRACZ, George S. *Annotated Bibliography on Determination of Teachers' Salaries and Effective Utilization of Teacher Manpower.* (Educational Planning Occasional Papers No. 10/71). Toronto: Ontario Institute for Studies in Education, 1971.

10.3   Health Care Policy

CANADA. Department of Labour. Accident Prevention Division, Library. *Occupational Safety and Health: Selected Holdings of the Technical Library/ Bibliographie: securité et hygiène professionnelles: choix de volumes de la bibliothèque technique.* Ottawa: Information Canada, 1974.

COOPER, I., and HULCHANSKI, J.D. *Canadian Town Planning 1900-1930: A Historical Bibliography: Volume III: Public Health.* (Bibliographic Series No. 9). Toronto: Centre for Urban and Community Studies, University of Toronto, 1978.

DUSSAULT, Gilles. *Le monde de la santé 1940-1975. Bibliographie.* Quebec: Institut supérieur des sciences humaines, Université Laval, 1975.

MEAGHER, Heather. *The Medicare Crisis in Saskatchewan: A Bibliography prepared by the Legislative Library.* Regina: Saskatchewan Legislative Library, 1963.

MIHALYKO, Jane. *Bibliography on the Saskatchewan Health System.* Regina: Research and Planning Branch, Saskatchewan Department of Public Health, 1973.

MILLER, Genevieve, ed. *Bibliography of the History of Medicine in the United States and Canada 1939-1960.* Baltimore: John Hopkins Press, 1964.

NADEAU, Pierre. *Santé: bibliographie.* Montreal: Conseil de dévéloppement social du Montréal métropolitain, 1972.

Appendix V   Chronology of Social Welfare Legislation

The purpose of this Chronology is to assist the user of the *Bibliography* by putting many of the issues covered there into time perspective. What follows is an outline of significant social welfare legislation primarily at the Dominion/Federal level of government, with reference made to the more significant historical developments at the provincial level.

Since the provinces were constitutionally interpreted to have jurisdiction in social welfare, virtually all social welfare policy that did exist before World War I was provincial. In the early periods 1840-1870,

1871-1895, 1896-1915, the Chronology lists important developments, many of which occurred in Ontario.

The interwar period had been one of transition, in which new powers were assumed by the central government, while the period after World War II has been one of expansion and consolidation, a period in which the federal government has attained the dominant role. These developments are also reflected in the Chronology.

Lastly, it should be stressed that the Chronology is meant to be indicative rather than exhaustive. It is a first attempt to record briefly the main events in the advance toward the welfare state since 1840.

The following abbreviations have been used:

Alta	Alberta
B C	British Columbia
Dom	Dominion (1867-1947)
Fed	Federal (1948-)
L C	Lower Canada
Man	Manitoba
N B	New Brunswick
Nfld	Newfoundland
N S	Nova Scotia
Ont	Ontario
P E I	Prince Edward Island
Que	Quebec
Sask	Saskatchewan
U C	Upper Canada
U P C	United Province of Canada (1841-1867)

References consulted in preparing the Chronology included:

ANGERS, F.-A. *La sécurité sociale et les problèmes constitutionnels*. Vols. I, II. Commission royale d'enquête sur les problèmes constitutionnels. Quebec: Imprimeur de la Reine, 1955.

CANADA. Health and Welfare Canada. Policy and Program Development and Coordination Branch. *A Chronology of Social Welfare and Related Legislation 1908-1974. Selected Federal Statutes*. Ottawa: The Branch, Health and Welfare Canada, February 1975.

_____. *Chronology of Selected Federal Social Welfare Legislation By Program 1876-1976*. Ottawa: The Branch, Health and Welfare Canada, 1976.

CORRY, J.A. *The Growth of Government Activities Since Confederation*. Background Study for the Royal Commission on Dominion-Provincial Relations. Ottawa: King's Printer, 1939.

GRAUER, A.E. *Housing*. A Study Prepared for the Royal Commission on Dominion-Provincial Relations. Ottawa: King's Printer, 1939.

_____. *Labour Legislation*. A Study Prepared for the Royal Commission on Dominion-Provincial Relations. Ottawa: King's Printer, 1939.

_____. *Public Assistance and Social Insurance*. A Study Prepared for the Royal Commission on Dominion-Provincial Relations. Ottawa: King's Printer, 1939.

_____. *Public Health*. Background Study for the Royal Commission on Dominion-Provincial Relations. Ottawa: King's Printer, 1939.

MELICHERCIK, John. *The Development of Social Welfare Programmes in Canada. Chronology of Significant Events at the National and Ontario Levels.* Faculty of Social Work, Wilfrid Laurier University, 1975.

MINVILLE, E. *Labour Legislation and Social Services in the Province of Quebec.* A Study Prepared for the Royal Commission on Dominion-Provincial Relations. Ottawa: King's Printer, 1939.

ONTARIO. Department of Public Welfare. *An Historical Review of Ontario Legislation on Child Welfare.* Prepared by C. Owen Spettigue. Toronto: The Department, 1957.

POULIN, Gonzalve. L'assistance sociale dans la province de Québec. Annexe 2 au Rapport de la commission royale d'enquête sur les problèmes constitutionnels. Quebec: Imprimeur de la Reine, 1955.

SPLANE, R.B. *Social Welfare in Ontario 1791-1893.* Toronto: University of Toronto Press, 1965.

WALLACE, E. "The Changing Canadian State; A Study of the Changing Conception of the State as Revealed in Canadian Social Legislation 1867-1948." Ph.D., Columbia University, 1950.

DEVELOPMENT OF SOCIAL WELFARE POLICY 1840 – 1870

People Out of Work	People Who Cannot Work	"Marginal" People	Women, Children and the Family	Maintaining the Labour Force
Act of Union (UPC) 1840. District Councils Act (UC) 1841. Township councils given limited powers in relief of the poor. Municipal Corporations Act (UC) 1849. Gave municipalities the powers to establish houses of refuge and gaols. Amendment to Municipal Corporations Act (UPC) 1858. Authority to grant outdoor relief. Board of Inspectors of Prisons, Asylums, and Public Charities (UPC) 1859. Municipal Institutions Act (UC) 1866. Mandate to establish houses of industry and refuge in counties of over 20,000 population. Smaller counties had to amalgamate for this purpose. B.N.A. Act (Dom) 1867. Matters in regard to charitable institutions lodged with provinces. Amendment to Municipal Institutions Act (UC) 1867-68. Removed mandatory provision.	Act of Union (UPC) 1840. Mentally ill, retarded taken into gaols, hospitals and other public institutions, (Ont, Que, NS, NB) 1840-1870. First asylums for mentally ill, Saint John, N.B. 1836; Toronto 1841. Royal Commission on Kingston Penitentiary (UPC) 1849. Prison Inspection Act (UPC) 1857. authorized establishment of prisons for criminal lunatics. B.N.A. Act (Dom) 1867. Superannuation Act (Dom) 1870. Pensions for public servants.	Act of Union (UPC) 1840. Kingston Prison becomes the institution for long-term prisoners in (UPC) 1840. Royal Commission on Gaols (UPC) 1848-49. Act for the Better Management of the Provincial Penitentiary (UPC) 1851. Prison Inspection Act (UPC) 1857. Board of Inspectors for Prisons, Asylums, and Public Charities (UPC) established Dec. 1859 under Prison Inspection Act. B.N.A. Act (Dom) 1867. Offences Against the Person Act (Dom) 1867. Immigration Act (Dom) 1869. Canada's first immigration Act. Limited entry of diseased, lunatics, etc.	Toronto House of Industry Act (UC) 1840. Infants Real Estate Act (UC) 1849. Laws on Rape, Abortion, Abduction (UC) 1851. Apprentices and Minors Act (UC) 1851. Prison Inspection Act (UPC) 1857. First juvenile offenders legislation (UC) 1857. Prisons for Young Offenders Act (UC) 1859. Act to Secure to Married Women Certain Separate Rights of Property (UC) 1859. B.N.A. Act (Dom) 1867.	District Health Councils (UC) 1840. Queens College founded (UC) 1842. Normal schools founded (UC) 1847. Public Health Act (UC) 1849. Building Societies Act (UPC) 1849. Grammar School Acts (UC) 1853, 1855. Board of Inspectors for Prisons, Asylums, and Public Charities (UPC) 1859. B.N.A. Act (Dom) 1867.

DEVELOPMENT OF SOCIAL WELFARE POLICY 1871 – 1895

People Out of Work

Code municipal (Que) 1871.
Charity Aid Act (Ont) 1874.
Royal Commission on the Treatment of the Poor in the County of Digby, NS, 1886.
Houses of Refuge Act (Ont) 1890.
Appointment of City Welfare Officer, Toronto, 1893.

People Who Cannot Work

First institution for the deaf, Belleville, (Ont) 1870.
First institution for the mentally retarded, London (Ont) 1870.
First institution for the blind, Brantford (Ont) 1872.
Charity Aid Act (Ont) 1874. First Act providing grants-in-aid.
Compensation to families for accidental death (Dom) 1874.
Railway Accidents Act (Dom) 1881.
Pension Fund Societies Act (Dom) 1887.
Training School for Mentally Retarded Children, Orillia (Ont) 1888.
Workmen's Compensation for Injuries Act (Ont) 1888.
Houses of Refuge Act (Ont) 1890. First legislative mention of powers to assist the aged.

"Marginal" People

Prison and Asylums Act (Ont) 1868.
J.W. Langmuir appointed Inspector of Prisons (Ont) 1868-82.
Dominion Lands Act (to encourage immigration) (Dom) 1872.
The Indian Act (Dom) 1876. Authorized that moneys from sale of Indian lands, property or timber, be invested, and form of payment or assistance to Indians. Authorized band chiefs to frame rules and regulations of public health.
The Indian Act (Dom) 1880. Established Department of Indian Affairs.
Mercer Reformatory for Females (Ont) 1878.
Summary Convictions Act (Dom) 1886.

Women, Children and the Family

Extension of the Rights of Married Women (Ont) 1872.
Charity Aid Act (Ont) 1874.
Humane Society (Ont) founded 1877.
Married Women's Property Act (Ont) 1886.
Trial and Punishment of Juvenile Offenders Act (Dom) 1886.
Infants Act (Ont) 1887.
Protection of Neglected Children's Act (Ont) 1888.
Commitment of Persons of Tender Years Act (Ont) 1888.
Royal Commission on the Prison and Reformatory System of Ontario 1890.
Prohibition against abortion and sale of contraceptives added to Criminal Code (Dom) 1892.
Children's Protection Act (Ont) 1893.
Act Respecting the Arrest, Trial and Imprisonment of Youthful Offenders (Dom) 1894.

Maintaining the Labour Force

Quarantine and Health Act (Ont) 1867.
First provincial agricultural college (Ont) 1874.
Industrial Schools Act (Ont) 1874.
Department of Education (Ont) 1876.
Landlord and Tenant Act (Ont) 1877.
Reformatories and Industrial School Act (NB) 1877.
Compulsory School Attendance (Ont) 1881.
Free libraries (Ont) 1882.
Adulteration Act (Dom) 1884.
First full time secretary of Health Councils (Ont) 1884.
Public Health Act (Ont) 1884.
Public Health Act (Que) 1886.
Night School for Minors (NS) 1888.
Truancy Act (Ont) 1891.
Certification of teachers (Ont) 1895.

DEVELOPMENT OF SOCIAL WELFARE POLICY 1896 – 1915

People Out of Work	People Who Cannot Work	"Marginal" People	Women, Children and the Family	Maintaining the Labour Force
Founding of Settlement Houses 1890-1915.	Public support of mental hospitals (BC) 1897. Lunatic Asylums and the Custody of Insane Persons (Ont) 1897. Mavor Report (Ont) 1900 on Workmen's compensation. Helen MacMurchy appointed Commissioner of Feeble Minded (Ont) 1906. Government Annuities Act (Dom) 1908. Census of Feeble Minded (Ont) 1908. Act Respecting Industrial Accidents (Que) 1909. Royal Commission on Workman's Compensation (Ont) 1910. Workman's Compensation Act (Ont) 1914; (NS) 1915. Act Respecting Reception Hospitals for the Insane (Ont) 1914.	Founding of settlement houses 1890-1915. Closing of Ontario Reformatory for Boys 1904. Juvenile Delinquents Act (Dom) 1908. First Juvenile Court, Winnipeg 1909. Immigration Act amendments (Dom) 1910. Indian Act amendments (Dom) 1914, concerning health of Indians.	Spread of Children's Aid Societies in the various cities and provinces 1895-1915. Regulation into Ontario of Certain Classes of Children Act (Ont) 1897. Children's Protection Act (BC) 1901. Children's Protection Act (Alta) 1909. Neglected Children's Act (P.E.I.) 1910. Children's Protection Act (NS) 1910. Juvenile Delinquents Act (Dom) 1908. Child Welfare Act (Ont) 1908. Illegitimate Childrens Act (Ont) 1911.	Public Works (Health) Act (Dom) 1899. First Director General of Public Health (Dom) 1899. Board of Education Act (Ont) 1903. Royal Commission on University of Toronto (Ont) 1905. Provincial control over technical education (NS) 1907. Meat and Canned Foods Act (Dom) 1907. Expansion of Normal Schools (Ont) 1908. Patent Medicine Act (Dom) 1908. Industrial Education Act (Ont) 1911. Appointment of Municipal Medical health offices made compulsory (Ont) 1911. Accommodation Act (Ont) 1913. First provincial housing legislation. Thomas Adams, Town Planner appointed to Commission on Conservation 1914. Act to Assist the Construction of Dwellings in Towns and Villages (Que) 1914-1919.

DEVELOPMENT OF SOCIAL WELFARE POLICY 1916 – 1940

People Out of Work

Commission on Unemployment (Ont) 1916.
Mathers Commission (Dom) 1918.
Dominion Grants for Relief 1920-21.
Royal Commission on Seasonal Unemployment (Man) 1928.
The Unemployment Relief Act (Dom) 1930 (Renewed each year 1931-39.)
Relief camps (Dom) 1932.
Civic Relief Commission, Montreal, 1933.
Poor Law Relief ends in NB, NS 1933.
Public Works Construction Act (Dom) 1934.
Unemployment and Social Insurance Act (Dom) 1935.
Purvis Report (Dom) 1936-37.
National Employment Commission (Dom) 1936-37.
National Employment Commission (Dom) 1937.
Privy Council decision on unemployment insurance 1939.
Unemployment Insurance Act (Dom) 1940.

People Who Cannot Work

Royal Commission on Feeble Minded (NS) 1916.
Workman's Compensation Act (BC) 1916; (Alta) (NB) 1918; (Man) 1920; (Que) 1926; (Sask) 1929.
The War Charities Act (Dom) 1917.
Order in Council (Dom) 1917; Board of Pension Commissioners.
Soldiers Civil Re-establishment Act (Dom) 1918.
Royal Commission on Mental Defectives (Ont) 1919.
The Pension Act (Dom) 1919.
Royal Commission on Mental Hygiene (BC) 1925.
Act Respecting Psychiatric Hospitals (Ont) 1926.
The Old Age Pension Act (Dom) 1927.
The War Veterans Allowance Act (Dom) 1930.
Mental Hospitals Act (Ont) 1935.
Quebec opts into Pension Act 1936.
Pension Act amendment to extend pensions to blind persons aged 40+ (Dom) 1937.

"Marginal" People

Indian Act amendments (Dom) 1924; Superintendent General of Indian Affairs given responsibility of Eskimo Affairs.
Immigration Act (Dom) 1927; further exclusions in the Revised Immigration Act.
Juvenile Delinquent Act (Dom) 1929; amendments.
Family Court (Ont) 1929.
Royal Commission on Immigration and Settlement (Sask) 1930.
Archambault Commission (Dom) 1938; examination of the prison system.
Supreme Court Report (Fed) 1929. Gave Federal Government jurisdiction over Inuit.

Women, Children and the Family

Mothers Allowances (Man) 1916; (Sask) 1917; (Alta) 1919; (Ont) 1920. Report on Mothers Pensions (BC) 1920; Royal Commission on Mothers Allowances (NB) 1924; (NS) 1930.
Adoption Act (Ont) 1921; (Que) 1924.
Children of Unmarried Parents Act (Ont) 1921.
Legitimation Act (Ont) 1921.
Public Charities Act (Que) 1921.
Foundling Act (Que) 1921.
Child Welfare Act (Man) 1924.
Royal Commission on the Administration of the Child Welfare Division (Man) 1929.
First House of Commons Report on Family Allowances 1929.
Ross Commission (Ont) 1930.
Quebec Social Insurance Commission 1930.
Department of Public Welfare established (Ont) 1930.
Child Maintenance Act (Ont) 1931.
Toronto Department of Public Welfare Founded 1931.
Report on Family Allowance (Que) 1932.
Social Allowances Commission (Que) 1936.
Social Welfare Courts Established (Que) 1937.
First Société d'adoption et de protection de l'enfance (Que) 1937.
Mothers Allowance (Que) 1938.

Maintaining the Labour Force

Rent Control (Dom) 1915-18.
Town Planning Act (Man) 1916; (PEI) 1918; (BC) 1925; (Sask) 1928; (NB) 1936.
Soldier Resettlement Act (Dom) 1917.
Grants in aid to finance housing construction (Dom) 1919.
Technical Education Act (Dom) 1919.
Compulsory education to age 16 (Ont) 1919.
Royal Commission on Health Insurance (BC) 1919, 1932.
Department of Health/Dominion Council of Health (Dom) 1919.
Agricultural schools established (Que) 1922.
Sanitary Units Act (Que) 1928.
Apprenticeship Act (Ont) 1928.
Department of Pensions and National Health (Dom) 1928.
Royal Commission on Health and Public Charities (Nfld) 1930.
Saskatchewan Cancer Commission 1930.
Public Health Act (Que) 1932.
Royal Commission on Education (NB) 1932.
Bruce Report on Toronto Housing (Ont) 1934.
Housing Act (NS) 1932; (NB) 1935.
Dominion Housing Act 1935.
Medical Relief Scheme (Ont) 1935.
City of Toronto Comprehensive Bylaw 1936.
Home Improvement Loans Act 1937.
National Housing Act (Dom) 1938.
The Youth Training Act (Dom) 1939.

DEVELOPMENT OF SOCIAL WELFARE POLICY
1941 – 1962

People Out of Work

Revision to Unemployment Insurance Act (Fed) 1946, 48, 50-59.
National Employment Service (Dom) 1941.
Unemployment Assistance Act (Fed) 1956.

People Who Cannot Work

Increase in blind persons pension (Fed) 1943, 44, 47, 49, 57, 62.
The War Service Grants Act (Fed) 1944.
The Department of Veterans Affairs Act (Fed) 1944.
The Veterans Rehabilitation Act (Fed) 1945.
The War Veterans Allowance Act (Fed) 1946.
Old Age Pensions Act Amendment Extended; blind persons pensions to those 21+ (Fed) 1947; 18+ 1957.
Federal-Provincial Mental Health Grant 1947.
The Pension Act amendments (Fed) 1948.
Order in Council (Fed) 1951; National Advisory Committee on Rehabilitation.
Major Revision of Pension Act (Fed) 1951.
The Blind Persons Act (Fed) 1951.
The Old Age Assistance Act (Fed) 1951/52. Means tested pensions to persons 65 to 69.
Order in Council (Fed) 1953; grants for rehabilitation of disabled.
Mental Health Act (Ont) 1954.
The Disabled Persons Act (Fed) 1955.
Increase in Disabled Allowances (Fed) 1957, 62.
Clark Report on Economic Security for the Aged in The United States (Fed) 1959.
Vocational Rehabilitation of Disabled Persons Act (Fed) 1961.
Public Health Act (Ont) 1962.

"Marginal" People

Dickson Report (NB) 1946.
Laycock Report (Sask) 1946.
Commission of Inquiry on the Penitentiary System (Fed) 1947.
King policy on immigration for national development without distorting present balance 1947.
Department of Justice Committee on Revisions (Fauteaux Report) (Fed) 1956.
Canadian Bill of Rights (Fed) 1960.

Women, Children and the Family

Federal day care subsidies 1942.
Day Nurseries Act (Ont) 1942.
Marsh Report (Fed) 1943.
Royal Commission on Provincial Development and Rehabilitation (Davidson Commission) (NS) 1944.
Department of Social Welfare (Que) 1944.
Committee to Investigate Child Welfare (Alta) 1944.
McTague Report (Fed) 1945.
Family Allowance Dept of National Health & Welfare (Fed) 1945.
Consolidation of Child Welfare Acts under Public Welfare Act (Ont) 1954.
Quebec Royal Commission on the Constitution 1955.
Unemployment Relief Act (Fed) 1956.
First Municipal Social Welfare Service in Quebec, Montreal 1957.
General Welfare Assistance Act (Ont) 1960.
Schooling Allowances (Que) 1961.

Maintaining the Labour Force

Rent Control, Wartime Housing Limited (Fed) 1941.
Veterans Land Act (Fed) 1942.
The Vocational Training Coordination Act (Dom) 1942.
Heagerty Report (Health Insurance) (Fed) 1943.
Central Mortgage and Housing Corporation abandonment of Wartime Housing Limited 1946.
Alberta Free Hospital for Maternity 1947.
Saskatchewan Prepaid Hospitalization Plan 1947.
Royal Commission on Adult Education (Man) 1947.
Hospital Grants (Fed) 1948.
Public housing in Toronto 1948.
Joint loans for public housing (Fed) 1949.
National Housing Act amendments eliminate joint loans (Fed) 1954.
Hospital Insurance & Diagnostic Services Act (Fed) 1957.
Cameron Report on Education (Alta) 1959.
Royal Commission on Education (Man) 1959.
Royal Commission on Education (BC) 1960.
Development of Community College system (Ont) 1960s.
Technical and Vocational Training Assistance Act (Fed) 1960.
Hospital Insurance Act (Que) 1961.
Medicare (Sask) 1962.
Royal Commission on Higher Education (NB) 1962.

DEVELOPMENT OF SOCIAL WELFARE POLICY
1963 – 1978

People Out of Work

Revisions to Unemployment Insurance Act (Fed) 1968.
Revision to Unemployment Insurance Act (Fed) 1971: increased labour force coverage, benefits, period of coverage; reduced eligibility; indexation of benefits; added maternity benefits.
Revisions to the Unemployment Insurance Act (Fed) 1975.
Revisions to the Unemployment Insurance Act (Fed) 1978: increased eligibility requirements.

People Who Cannot Work

Boucher Report (Social Assistance) (Que) 1963.
The Established Programmes (Interim Arrangements) Act (Fed) 1964/65.
Canada Pension Plan Act (Fed) 1965.
Senate Committee on Aging (Fed) 1966.
Senate Committee on Poverty (Fed) 1966.
Canada Assistance Plan Act (Fed) 1966.
The Pension Benefits Standards Act (Fed) 1966/67.
Old Age Security Act Amendment (Fed) 1966. Established guaranteed income supplement; 1972 indexation; 1975 spouses allowance established, and repealed; Old Age Assistance Act.
Mental Health Act (Ont) 1967.
Canada Manpower and Immigration Council Act (Fed) 1967. Replaced National Advisory Council on Rehabilitation.
The Federal-Provincial Fiscal Arrangements Act (Fed) 1972.
Canada Pension Plan Act Amendments (Fed) 1974.
The Family Allowances Act (Fed) 1974.
The Established Programmes Financing and Fiscal Arrangements Act (Fed) 1977.

"Marginal" People

Sedgewick Report (Fed) 1964.
Dept of Justice Committee on Juvenile Delinquency 1965.
White Paper on Immigration 1966.
Point system introduced for immigration 1967.
Royal Commission on Bilingualism and Biculturalism (Fed) 1967.
New regulations relating immigration to labour market (Fed) 1974.
Green Paper on Immigration (Fed) 1975.

Women, Children and the Family

Boucher Report (Social Assistance) (Que) 1963.
Welfare grants administration established (Fed) 1963.
The Youth Allowances Act (Fed) 1964.
Canada Assistance Plan (Fed) 1965.
Day Nurseries Act (Ont) 1966.
The Divorce Act (Fed) 1968.
Abortion and sale of contraceptive devices made legal (Fed) 1969.
Royal Commission on the Status of Women (Fed) 1970.
Unemployment Insurance Act (Fed) 1971. Maternity benefits extended by amendment 1975.
Family Relations Act (BC) 1972.
Social security review (Fed) 1973-77.
The Family Allowances Act (Fed) 1974. Indexation of Family Allowances.
Royal Commission on Family and Children's Law (BC) 1975/76.
Matrimonial Property Act (Alta) 1977.
Social Security Act (Fed) 1978.
Family Law Reform Act (Ont) 1978.

Maintaining the Labour Force

Royal Commission on Health Services (Fed) 1963.
National Housing Act Amendments in public housing, non-profit housing (Fed) 1964.
The Training Allowances Act (Fed) 1966.
The Medical Care Act (Fed) 1966/67.
The Health Resources Fund Act (Fed) 1966/67.
Parent Report (Education) (Que) 1966.
Royal Commission on Educational Youth (Nfld) 1967/68.
The Adult Occupational Training Act 1967.
Bank Act changes (Fed) 1967.
Urban renewal abandoned (Fed) 1969.
Committee on the Healing Arts (Ont) 1970.
Hastings Report (Ont) 1971.
Castonguay-Nepveu Report (Health) (Que) 1971.
Rent review boards established in several provinces 1973-76.
National Housing Act Amendments in Assisted Home Ownership Program (AHOP) Coops 1973.
Royal Commission on Education, Public Services and Provincial-Municipal Relations (NS) 1974.

INDEXES

Subject Index (Part One)

Liste des sujets (Part One)

Index of Authors